MW00610925

Making the
MexiRican
City

LATINOS IN CHICAGO AND THE MIDWEST

Series Editors
Omar Valerio-Jiménez, University of Texas at San Antonio
Sujey Vega, Arizona State University

Founding Editor
Frances R. Aparicio

A list of books in the series appears at the end of this book.

Making the MexiRican City

MIGRATION, PLACEMAKING, AND ACTIVISM IN GRAND RAPIDS, MICHIGAN

Delia Fernández-Jones

**UNIVERSITY OF
ILLINOIS PRESS**
Urbana, Chicago, and Springfield

© 2023 by the Board of Trustees
of the University of Illinois
All rights reserved
1 2 3 4 5 C P 5 4 3 2 1
♾ This book is printed on acid-free paper.

Library of Congress Cataloging-in-Publication Data
Names: Fernández, Delia M., author.
Title: Making the MexiRican city : migration, placemaking, and
     activism in Grand Rapids, Michigan / Delia Fernández-Jones.
Description: Urbana : University of Illinois Press, 2023. | Series:
     Latinos in Chicago and the Midwest | Includes bibliographical
     references and index.
Identifiers: LCCN 2022032889 (print) | LCCN 2022032890 (ebook) | ISBN
     9780252044847 (cloth) | ISBN 9780252086946 (paperback) | ISBN
     9780252053993 (ebook)
Subjects: LCSH: Hispanic Americans—Michigan—Grand Rapids—
     History. | Hispanic Americans—Michigan—Grand Rapids—
     Politics and government. | Mexican Americans—Michigan—Grand
     Rapids—Social conditions. | Puerto Ricans—Michigan—Grand
     Rapids—Social conditions. | Immigrants—Michigan—Grand
     Rapids—Social conditions. | Grand Rapids (Mich.)—Ethnic
     relations. | Grand Rapids (Mich.)—Race relations. | BISAC: SOCIAL
     SCIENCE / Ethnic Studies / American / Hispanic American Studies
     | HISTORY / United States / State & Local / Midwest (IA, IL, IN, KS,
     MI, MN, MO, ND, NE, OH, SD, WI)
Classification: LCC F574.G7 F37 2023 (PRINT) | LCC F574.G7 (EBOOK) |
     DDC 305.868/073077456—dc23/eng/20220815
LC record available at https://lccn.loc.gov/2022032889
LC ebook record available at https://lccn.loc.gov/2022032890

For J&L
Para mi familia y la suya, también

Contents

Acknowledgments

This book comes from spending time with my close-knit extended family. I treasured the detailed narratives of how my family members migrated to Grand Rapids—from Puerto Rico, Texas, and Mexico. Parallel stories of migration and settlement constituted a regular part of my upbringing. While growing up, I benefitted from endless tales that my parents and grandparents told me about their journeys and their lives in Grand Rapids.

For my maternal grandparents, maintaining a sense of their ethnic Mexican identity presented a formidable challenge as white Grand Rapidians stressed English as the only acceptable language and whiteness as the norm. Nevertheless, my maternal grandfather maintained his connection to his identity as a mariachi singer and guitar player. He also emerged as an active member of the Mexican Patriotic Committee and served on the board of directors for the Latin American Council. Meanwhile, working as a hairdresser increased my grandmother's social network, and her salon soon emerged as an important landmark in Grand Rapids' burgeoning Latino community.

Spending time with the Puerto Rican side of my family taught me about how my paternal grandparents located housing in Grand Rapids, established friendships, and supported community activism efforts—although their participation in these activities remained limited due to their demanding work schedules. They passed to their children a genuine commitment towards improving Latino community life, and some of their children soon became active in the Latin American Council, much like my maternal grandfather. The Fernández Bar, the fruit of my grandfather and his children's labor, became a lively center of community life in Grand Rapids.

Occasionally, the stories my Mexican and Puerto Rican family members told overlapped. For instance, my Puerto Rican aunts described how the area's Latina youths often donned the same hairstyle, primarily because my grandmother Juanita's familiarity with the latest American hairstyles was limited to the ubiquitous beehive, which my Mexican aunts also wore. They also recalled how, during the 1970s, the Latin American Council served as a hangout spot for both Mexican and Puerto Rican teenagers. They told me how Mexican and Puerto Rican residents of Grand Rapids formed close bonds and no one could remember a time when they did not reside in the same neighborhoods. Thus, the underlying moral in most of these stories was simple: Grand Rapids may not have always welcomed Latinos, but the interethnic community we formed made it home. For their help in raising me to know the stories included in this book and the ones that have yet to be documented, I dedicate *Making the MexiRican City* to *mi familia*—the Murillo and Fernández families and all our extended kin.

I especially want to thank the oral history participants I interviewed for this book. I am honored that they entrusted to me their painful and joyful memories of making Grand Rapids home. I am thankful to Gordon Olson and the various students who assisted him in recording oral histories with the Latino community's earliest pioneers, including my grandmother, a decade before I conceived this project. I am extremely thankful for my uncle, Rafael Hernández, who always answered my questions about his parents and growing up MexiRican at any time of the day, whenever I asked. I am also grateful for the conversations I have had with people who have passed on since I started this project. Thank you to Carmen Berríos, Juan Báez, Marilyn Vega, and their families for my requests for interviews and several follow up conversations. I am particularly thankful for the interviews I did with my family members who are not here to celebrate this accomplishment but whose stories live on in this book: Luisa Fernández, Cirilo Fernández, Rosalía Espíndola, Rosa Pérez, Juanita Murillo, and Juanita Vásquez, *presente!*

In addition to my very supportive extended family, I have had an excellent team of publishing professionals who have helped bring this work to fruition. Dawn Durante demystified the publishing process for me. Thank you for advocating for this project. Dom Moore and Ellie Hinton stepped in during a pandemic and answered all my questions with grace and patience. Tikia Hamilton served as a thorough, generous developmental editor. Rich Mares ensured that I chose just the right words to convey my message throughout the book. The blind reviewers for this book mentored me throughout this process with thoughtful feedback and critical suggestions. I am thankful for their commitment to me as a scholar and to this project. This book is so much better because of these colleagues.

I have been fortunate to receive a wealth of encouragement at Michigan State University. This book received institutional support from the Humanities and Arts Research Program as well as the Diversity Research Network under Deborah

Johnson. My colleagues have been incredibly supportive. Both Walter Hawthorne and Lisa Fine have been excellent chairs of the history department during my journey. Emily Conroy-Krutz, Helen Veit, Noah Kaye, Elyse Hansen, Sidney Liu, Ed Murphy, Mickey Stamm, Naoko Wake, Nakia Parker, and Steve Smith have been amazing colleagues and friends to me during this process. I appreciate the steadfast support and mentorship I continuously receive from LaShawn Harris, Pero Dagbovie, and Glenn Chambers. Thanks to Jasmin Howard and Dani Willcut who served as research assistants. I am especially grateful for the keen insights that my brilliant graduate advisee, Ethan Veenhuis, offered on this project.

In addition to the history department, the Chicanx/Latinx Studies program at Michigan State University (MSU) has been an integral part of this journey. Thank you to directors Eric González Juenke and Isabel Ayala for their intellectual and material support while I was writing this book. From research assistants to course buyouts, both Isabel and Eric have been invested in my tenure journey since I arrived on campus. I am incredibly grateful to learn about leadership from you both. Thanks to Stephany Bravo and Vanessa Aguilar for their help as research assistants. I also acknowledge all the CLS graduate and undergraduate students I interacted with and those students who took the History of Mexican Americans in the United States course with me while I was writing this book. It is an honor to work with you all and share space with you. Our discussions are reflected in these pages. I am especially grateful to James Radick, an exceptionally sharp undergraduate student who read the manuscript, making suggestions to ensure undergraduate readers could access and understand it.

Time spent with patient archivists and having conversations about history with other historians has made this book a reality. Bill Cunningham was instrumental during its earliest iterations. His more than thirty years of experience at the Grand Rapids City Archives and Records Center helped me to find creative ways to document Latino life in Grand Rapids. Anthony Wright and Matthew Ellis, Bill's successors, have done an excellent job in making archives accessible. Tim Gleisner and Julie Tabberer have been helping me since the first day I stepped on to the fourth floor of the Grand Rapids Public Library. I am thankful to both for our riveting conversations about history and Grand Rapids. Tim and Julie's staff have also graciously helped me over the years, earning my gratitude: Colleen Alles, Jennifer Andrew, Benjamin Boss, Rachel Burns, M. Christine Byron, Drew Damron, Heather Edwards, Melissa Fox, Tim Gloege, Colleen Marquis, Will Miner, Jennifer Morrison, Karolee Tobey, and Ruth Van Stee. Father Dennis Morrow and Angela Yondo enthusiastically helped me access the Diocese of Grand Rapids' archives. I am lucky to have met Diana Rivera, who has been instrumental to collecting and archiving Michigan's Latino history within MSU's special collections. Lastly, I am thankful to my colleagues on the Kutsche Office of Local History's advisory council and the Michigan Historical Commission, especially Sandra Clark, for their ideas and conversations on how to make Michigan history more accurate and inclusive.

Several colleagues from institutions across the country have read, commented, and had conversations about this book and its importance. I am grateful to be a part of such an amazing network of scholars: Sergio González, Felipe Hinojosa, Theresa Delgadillo, Claire Fox, Ramón Rivera-Servera, Gerardo Cadava, Ariana Ruiz, Karen Mary Dávalos, Emiliano Aguilar, Laura Fernández, Marie Lerma, Yuridia Ramírez, Anne Martínez, Larry La Fountain-Stokes, Llana Barber, Cecilia Márquez, Emma Amador, Mirelsie Velásquez, Kim McKee, Danielle Olden, Tyran Steward, Leticia Wiggins, and Clay Howard. I especially thank Alyssa Ribiero for being unfailingly available to help me work out issues both big and small with this book via text, e-mail, and phone call.

I have been fortunate to receive compassionate, genuine mentorship from various scholars. Thanks to David Stark (and Gladysin Huerta-Stark), who introduced me to academia and who believed that I could become a professor. Matthew Daley and I have always had the best conversations about local history and Michigan. So much of this book is rooted in my experiences during graduate school at Ohio State while I was under the guidance of attentive mentors, including Lilia Fernández, Kevin Boyle, Judy Wu, and Stephanie Smith. Thanks to all of you for investing in me and preparing me for this stage of my career. Many thanks also to Randal Jelks, who has advocated for me and mentored me throughout my journey in academia—I am so fortunate to have him in my corner. I am also especially grateful for Theresa Delgadillo, who often thinks of me for amazing opportunities and gently guides me whenever I ask.

I took a one-semester pre-tenure leave to write my book and live in Chicago. The Newberry Library became my home for writing and intellectual discussion while I was there. I am grateful for the space to discuss my ideas with colleagues, especially Ben Johnson and Adam Goodman, who read and commented on various chapters. I am also deeply grateful for Hilda Vásquez, Tikia Hamilton, Sakeena Everett, Soulit Chacko, and Claudia Castillo, who wrote alongside me at various coffeeshops across Chicago. Those weekly and even daily meet-ups helped me finish this book. Thanks also to Ramzie Casiano, Elvia Malagón, and especially Mariana Saucedo for making Chicago feel like home.

Numerous friends and scholars have made Lansing welcoming and full of joy. I am especially grateful for those who were here for a short amount of time but who made my life so rich: Jessica M. Johnson, Vanessa Holden, Mariama Lockington, Sir Henry, Sara Fingal, Dustin Barr, Chezare Warren, Maribel Santiago and Melo, Xhercis Méndez, Nikolay Karkov, Aleia Brown, Amy Lewis and Quinn Jiles, and Celcius Magbitang and Lin-Chi Wang.

Jonathan, Jonny, and I have a village of people both in Lansing and outside of it who support us every day. I am so thankful for every single act of support and kindness you all have shown us. Thank you to cousin-colleague Yomaira Figueroa-Vásquez, Tacuma Peters, Maceo, Troy, and Chuleta; Tamara Butler; Gilianne Narcisse; Tiffany Bourgeois and family; Yalidy Matos-Dailey and family; Mariana Saucedo; Maddie Aguillón and Carmen Rose; Andrea Gómez-Cervantes and family; Kelsey Calpito and family; Brittany Fernández and Legend; Maggie, Emilio, Ariana, and Michael Rojas; Francisco and Brady Velasquez and Zoë Cruz; Omaira, Tony, and Antonella Ruiz; Delois Campbell; Gimely Reyes; Leslie Gonzáles and family; the Fortman family; Breannah, Clay, Simon, and Alba Oppenhuizen; Terry Flennaugh and Joy Hannibal as well as Elijah and Faith; Angélica DeJesús, Santos Ramos, and Kira; Rashida Harrison and Khamari; the Fowlks family; my *primo*, Alejo "Papito" Sepúlveda; Glenn, Terah, and Langston Chambers; and Estrella, Dylan, Mexica, and Reina Torrez-Miner. Kristin Mahoney, Kaveh Askari, and the Azhoney Café came into my life right when I needed them the most. I would like to acknowledge Tacuma Peters, my cousin-friend-colleague who has showed up to write with me outside in the cold, on Zoom, and in person during a pandemic. I could not have done this without our accountability partnership.

I owe more thank-yous than I can write to my family. To the Jones, Peterson, and Strayhorn families, thank you for welcoming me and always supporting Jonathan, Jonny, Jordyn, and me. Thanks to my siblings. They and their families are my built-in best friends, proofreaders, brainstormers, and group chat entertainers. Lucy, Anbrocio, Anbrocio III, Chantel, Anbrocio IV, Acelia, Meia, Alyssa, Emilio, Diego, Mateo; Juan, Carrie, Luis, and Lorenzo; and Nico, Amy, and Lena make my heart so full. I love you all.

Since graduate school, my parents have been my best research assistants. There are no words to accurately describe how thankful I am for them. They took every opportunity to tell people about their daughter—the history professor—and about this book. Returning from local football games, the store, or a funeral, they brought phone numbers, e-mail addresses, and names to look up on Facebook of people who wanted to be interviewed. At the drop of a hat they would rattle off stories and answer my questions about 1970s Grand Rapids. They identified people in uncaptioned photos from the archive and encouraged me to look again for sources I was sure did not exist. I was wrong; they were right. I could have written a book without them, but not this book. For that reason and so many others, I dedicate *Making the MexiRican City* to them.

My life is so much more fun with Jordyn and Jonny in it. Jordyn's insistence that we treat ourselves and take time for self-care has made this process fulfilling and manageable. Much of the joy I have in my life stems from watching Jonny grow and experience the world. His passion, determination, and love of life are models for me every day. Thank you, *mijo*, for reminding me of what is truly important.

Thank you to my generous, inquisitive, and hilarious partner, Jonathan, for his steadfast belief that I would finish this book and be awarded tenure. His pep talks, teamwork, ideas for efficiency, and insistence that I take much-needed breaks got me over the finish line.

Last, I thank the numerous community members who saw me at church with my parents or at community events and asked how the book was going. Their repeated words of encouragement to keep going, and their insistence that this was important to them and for our community, comforted me when I felt isolated, motivated me when I was discouraged, and continue to serve as a daily inspiration. *Este es para la familia suya, también.*

A Note on Terminology

A variety of terms are needed to describe the principal actors in this history with accuracy. I use "Mexican national" to refer to someone holding Mexican citizenship. I use "Mexican American" to refer to someone who enjoys Mexican descent but also possesses U.S. citizenship. I also use "Mexican" to refer to ethnic Mexicans who can be either Mexican nationals or Mexican Americans. Note that many of the historical actors were a part of mixed-status families. For example, some people in a family were Mexican nationals and others were Mexican Americans. This has encouraged me to refer to many of them as "Mexican."

Throughout the twentieth century, Mexican Americans and Puerto Ricans have referred to themselves collectively as "Spanish-speaking," "Spanish," "Latin," "Latin American," and "Latino." For that reason, I use these collective identifiers interchangeably. I opted not to use the term "Latinx" because it was not in use during the period I examine. This does not imply that nonbinary Latinx people did not exist at the time—indeed, they did. However, by using only the terms in use at the time, I endeavor to avoid anachronistic and ahistorical portrayals of the community, given the limited personal archives that are extant on this population.

Historically, Mexican Americans have referred to themselves as "Mexican" and "Chicano," whereas Puerto Ricans have referred to themselves primarily as "Puerto Ricans" and, on some occasions, as "Boricuas." When using the terms "Chicano" and "Boricua" in this book, however, I am referring to the politicized terms these groups used during the 1960s and 1970s social movements.

I also use the terms "African American" and "Black" interchangeably. To be sure, while Latinos can be Black, in the context of these discussions, I use "Black" to mean African American, "Afro-Latino" to mean Latinos of African descent, and "Latino" to include Latinos of all racial backgrounds.

Making the
MexiRican
City

Introduction

During the late 1960s, my paternal grandmother, Luisa Fernández, often returned home from the hair salon with red cheeks. Likely, her rosy complexion stemmed from sharing one or several glasses of wine with my maternal grandmother, Juanita Murillo, one of the few Spanish-speaking hair stylists in Grand Rapids, Michigan. These occasional visits to Juanita's salon offered a respite from caring for ten children. Although Luisa rarely confessed to drinking, the two women needed and enjoyed the opportunity to imbibe in the salon, where they could speak freely and simply be themselves. Even more, in a majority-white, Midwestern city, there were few welcoming public spaces for Latinas to relax and speak to each other in Spanish.

Of Mexican American heritage, Juanita Murillo was one of a handful of bilingual hairdressers working in Grand Rapids during the 1960s and added to the small but growing number of Latino-owned businesses in the area. From a family of Mexican farmworkers who relocated to Texas and then migrated to Michigan in the 1920s, Juanita was born in 1934 in Saginaw, Michigan, where her family tended the fields. Though she left school in the eighth grade to work, she spoke both English and Spanish. At sixteen she married Porfirio Murillo, a Mexican national who migrated to Saginaw in 1947 for agricultural work. As a young girl, Juanita often dreamed about returning to the land of her parentage; marrying Porfirio offered the chance of escaping the majority-white, rural culture of Saginaw, where a young Mexican American woman found little to entice her or her growing family. But in 1954, instead of relocating to Mexico, Porfirio moved Juanita and their three children to the city of Grand Rapids—less than 130 miles from Saginaw—in search of a manufacturing job. Compared to Saginaw, Grand Rapids boasted more economic opportunities for Mexicans, as more and more Latinos began to call the city home.

Luisa Fernández did not speak much English, relying instead on the Spanish she learned in her Puerto Rican home. Born in 1926 in Cagüitas, a barrio between Aguas Buenas and Caguas, Puerto Rico, Luisa met and fell in love with Pío, whom she subsequently married in 1951. Pío, who was from Caguas, decided to join his father-in-law and uncles-in-law in Michigan as farmworkers. They labored in a rural area not far from where the Murillos lived in Saginaw. Following a similar trajectory as Porfirio Murillo, Pío soon looked for a job away from the fields. He secured employment in a bakery in Grand Rapids and brought his wife and their four children from Puerto Rico in 1955. At that time, a community of a handful of Puerto Ricans as well as some welcoming Mexican Americans in the area helped them settle.

Together, Mexicans and Puerto Ricans started to transform the area around them. When these two groups arrived en masse in the 1940s and 1950s, Grand Rapids had few places where these migrants could interact with one another and escape the harsh sounds of English that surrounded them. This eventually led to MexiRican families, including my own, as members of these groups intermarried. However, within fifteen years of the arrival of the Murillos and Fernándezes, Latinos had succeeded in generating a few venues and spaces in Grand Rapids where they could gather, speak Spanish freely, and form lasting relationships. This transformation included the founding of Juanita's salon, where Luisa and many other Latinas found rest, hospitality, and open arms as they made Grand Rapids into a home.

These separate but interrelated journeys that my grandparents pursued, along with those of their *compadres* and *comadres*, are what fill the following pages. As a historian, my formal training intersects with an oral storytelling tradition to connect the experiences of Latinos in Grand Rapids to the social, economic, and political forces that have produced and inhibited social mobility for Latinos in the United States. While my work is part family history, my aim is more expansive. *Making the MexiRican City* incorporates interviews with nearly thirty members of the Grand Rapids Latino community—some are associated with my family, but most are not. This book also relies extensively on research amassed from archives in Puerto Rico, Mexico, Texas, Washington, D.C., and Michigan, as well as other archives around the country. This book represents experiences that extend beyond my family's parallel migration stories to recapture how Latinos made a place for themselves in Grand Rapids and to fill a gap in existing studies on Latinos.

*   *   *

Making the MexiRican City examines the placemaking practices that Mexicans and Puerto Ricans used to make a home for Latinos in Grand Rapids throughout the twentieth century. I reveal how Latinos calculated their strategies in resisting racism and discrimination in Grand Rapids—a smaller city nestled in a region that remained pro-business, religiously conservative, and overwhelmingly white. Outside of their places of origin and areas with larger concentrations of other Latinos, this community exemplifies how a numerical minority with limited resources can transform an indifferent, at times hostile, locale into a setting that meets their material and cultural needs. I argue that the interethnic relationships that Latinos formed and sustained were key to this process. Mexican nationals, Mexican Americans from Texas, and Puerto Ricans pursued parallel and, at times, interdependent and intersecting journeys to Michigan from the 1920s to the 1970s. Once they arrived, structural forces and their personal agency compelled them to interact as they searched for housing and jobs and re-created cultural practices in Grand Rapids. As such, they also fashioned a pan-Latino solidarity that crossed ethnic boundaries among themselves—and later with a small population of Cubans who joined the community in the 1970s—to develop a form of institutional activism that emphasized working within the system to advocate for social change. Latinos used this to challenge inequality in antipoverty funding, policing, and education. As this strategy evolved, it exposed and exploited the cracks in both overt and structural racism that bred Latino marginalization, though white and Black allies also contributed to this success. This book thus simultaneously reveals the intricate process of pan-Latino placemaking by amending Latino geographies via drawing attention to the Midwest and to smaller cities, detailing solidarity formation, and illuminating Latino responses to conservative environments using institutional activism and allies.

It is important to understand the varied landscape of urban America, while also recognizing the various priorities of Latino immigrants and migrants in those areas. The scholarly and media attention given to the nation's metropolises can erase the reality that in every place Latinos settled they faced an exclusionary environment to some degree. Facing a multitude of challenges—xenophobia, immigration issues, economic exploitation, housing segregation, English-only policies, educational marginalization, police abuse, and general exclusion from belonging—Latinos across the country, in areas urban and rural, both small and large, have had to organize to ameliorate their conditions. Thus, in every place in which a substantial number of Latinos settle, they do the work to make that place viable. While this book begins with an examination of immigration and migration, attention to placemaking and activism is essential. Without it, long-term settlement would be impossible. *Making the MexiRican City* shows us what was necessary for a Latino community, and also other communities of demographic minorities, to be established. This helps us to better understand our recent past, not just in Grand Rapids, but in communities across the country.

GRAND RAPIDS:
A LENS FOR UNDERSTANDING RACISM, RELIGION, AND RESISTANCE

Grand Rapids is an ideal place to study how marginalized people make a way for themselves with limited resources because, while demographically similar to many urban places, it retains the cultural mores of smaller towns. With a population of 175,000, the city in the early to mid-1900s boasted the demographic diversity seen in Chicago or Detroit, the region's two largest cities. Before Mexicans and Puerto Ricans arrived in the 1940s and 1950s, a small, often marginalized Anishinaabe community—whose Anishinaabe ancestors laid claim to this area for centuries—resided in Grand Rapids. Additionally, an expanded Black population also contributed to the city's evolving racial demographics as African Americans fled the South's racial violence and limited opportunities. Otherwise, "native whites," or the descendants of Europeans, represented the majority population in Grand Rapids. Not surprisingly, they also dominated local political and business hierarchies.

In other ways, Grand Rapids shared many social values with an archetypal American small town. White businessmen and politicians who held power in Grand Rapids joined religious communities that practiced social conservatism. Even more, the plethora of churches that dotted city blocks created the impression of a smaller rural or suburban community. Their presence was an omnipresent reminder of the role religious devotion played in this community. However, these conservative mores and powerful business interests existed in a multiracial, class-diverse urban area, not a small town.

Various forces combined to create a particular brand of religio-economic conservatism in Grand Rapids before Latinos and African Americans arrived en masse. Some of the most pious members of the area's many reformed Protestant churches, especially Dutch Calvinists, aspired to be honest, hard-working, thrifty, and generally cautious of engaging too readily in the secular world—outside of civic engagement—and hoped God would reward them for adhering to those principles.[1] Though the members of this community comprised about 12 percent of the population by the mid-twentieth century, they successfully combined their commitment to religious piety with civic engagement. This blend garnered a solid base of support for their political and economic efforts.[2] Their attitude toward work meshed well with the goals of the single-business owners, many in the furniture industry, who stressed self-reliance among their workers. In addition, moral reformers stressed efficiency in "good government" that preferred that they and like-minded business professionals lead the city rather than working-class people.[3]

Events in 1911 led to the solidification of this tripart conservative environment. When Dutch and Polish immigrant furniture workers revolted against furniture manufacturers for better wages and shorter workdays in 1911, all three of these forces—business owners, religious institutions, and moral reformers—joined to squash this working-class rebellion. As historian Jeffrey Kleiman found, furniture factory owners stalled negotiations. The union representing the workers was in disarray and not in a financial position to support them.[4] Moreover, Reformed Protestant pastors told their mostly Dutch immigrant workers that their union "and the Reformed Church were incompatible due to the fact that the union was 'not based on the brotherhood of man, but is for material purposes only.... [Its] principles based 'merely ... on humanity and earthly welfare without recognizing God in any respect.'"[5] Seeking better wages was part of a quest for materialism that went against their religious virtues. All of this weakened the union's ability to represent the workers. For its part, the Roman Catholic diocese did not openly support Polish strikers, a sign it had adopted the more conservative values of its Protestant counterparts.

Moral reformers, many of them bankers and furniture manufacturers, had the most long-lasting effects on the city's conservatism. They instituted a charter revision in 1916 that stripped power from the mayor's office, likely motivated by the mayor's support of workers in 1911. They also moved to the at-large election of commissioners, severely limiting the power of immigrant ethnic communities to elect their own representatives. Lastly, the committee instituted a city manager who held much of the decision-making power and was elected by the commissioners. In making these changes, the 1916 Charter Revision Committee ensured that "voters of the city would have no direct say in the formal leadership of their community."[6] This charter, parts of which remain in place today, made it hard for cross-class, cross-ethnic, and cross-racial alliances to form, limiting voters' ability to wield power over policymaking in Grand Rapids.

These dynamics in the state's second-largest urban area allow for an examination of how religious and business conservatism intersected with resistance to racial progress in the mid-twentieth century. Reformed Protestants were the dominant religious group in Grand Rapids, and the Protestant ethos and notions of middle-class respectability—common in many midwestern locales—seeped beyond the setting of religious spaces. These ideas shaped social relations in the city from neighborhood dynamics to business dealings, as historian Randal Jelks argues.[7] As Jelks discovered, with limited mobility and the specter of racism guiding their every move, Black Grand Rapidians often felt compelled to replicate that same respectability to enjoy some semblance of equality. Latinos migrating to the area found that they were expected to adopt similar social norms. By the 1960s, after two waves of Black migrants from the U.S. South and a large migration of Mexicans and Puerto Ricans, this religio-economic system combined with broader ideas on race to limit social mobility for the Black and Latino communities as well as for working-class peoples.

In Grand Rapids the ideas of white racial innocence, meritocracy, and religion coalesced in the 1960s and 1970s as a formidable obstacle to social progress. As Daniel Martínez HoSang asserts, white racial innocence is the notion that whites can "[disavow] any interest or investment in racial inequality" and adopt the "tenets of race neutrality"—an ideology that allowed whites to legitimate segregation in California.[8] In Grand Rapids, this notion of race neutrality also combined with a religious meritocracy. Believing that God rewards people for their hard work, and by distancing themselves from remedying racial injustice, religious conservatives in Grand Rapids ignored the plight of Latinos and African Americans while blaming those groups for any hardships they experienced. After finding that reformed Protestants eagerly signed racial covenants for housing in Grand Rapids, two members of a liberal section of this community charged that the "Christian Reformed people in Grand Rapids . . . bear a heavy responsibility for the degradation and defeat which affect almost every family which we have confined to life in Grand Rapids' inner city ghetto."[9] However, as did white people across the country in the late 1960s, whether they were religious or not, the local churches did not take any large-scale actions to remedy this situation. The few liberal members of the church operated as strong allies for the city's minorities, but white resistance from European immigrants and their descendants to social progress for Black and Latino peoples in Grand Rapids continued throughout the twentieth century.

While religion played an influential role in crafting the outlook on race relations, so too did capitalism and business efforts. Business leaders and local administrators, who were sometimes one and the same, subscribed to the idea that if it was good for business then it was good for Grand Rapids.[10] This placed the responsibility of remedying racial inequality outside of their purview. Moreover, Todd Robinson, a historian of Black Grand Rapids, found that politicians and business leaders, as "liberal" whites, managed the system of racial progress to benefit themselves in what he calls "managerial racism." This system "relied on strict procedures designed to bog down racial change while effectively presuming a position of compliance."[11] Indeed, Latinos fought an uphill battle for access to federal antipoverty relief, jobs, and education against politicians who promised to do more for them but did so at the slowest rate possible and only as long as it did not disrupt the business community.

Just as it was in the 1960s and 1970s, Grand Rapids' racial politics can be seen as a microcosm for a dynamic playing out on the national stage. Donald Trump rose to prominence and the presidency on similar forces by welcoming open racial hostility, doubling down on "white racial innocence" and pandering to religious ideologies of deservedness and entitlement. On the other hand, Democratic politicians—as the opposing party—have long promised racial change that will not alienate the other party. Organizing to subvert this dynamic has long played out in Grand Rapids as well as around the country.

RELATIONAL HISTORIES:
LATINO MIGRATION, PLACEMAKING, AND ACTIVISM

Understanding how Latinos persisted in Grand Rapids even with limited resources from the 1920s to the 1970s is instructive for marginalized people's survival in the present. I take into account the work of previous scholars of the Latino Midwest who have since the 1990s painstakingly unearthed histories of Mexican and Puerto Rican migrations, labor, settlements, cultural contributions, and resistance, rescuing these narratives from certain erasure. I apply Natalia Molina's concept of "relational" history of racial formation that identifies this phenomenon as a "mutually constitutive process" to that of Mexicans and Puerto Ricans.[12] I view their individual and pan-ethnic Latino identities and experiences in migrating, forming communities, and fighting for their rights as developing interdependently. Examining the intricacies of their interethnic relationships down to their quotidian acts reveals how relational histories are not just studies of similar phenomenon, but they uncover the parallel, intersecting, and overlapping existences of marginalized people. In excavating these relational histories, I consider three themes to understand Latinos in Grand Rapids in the twentieth century: migration, placemaking, and activism.

MIGRATION

While recent immigrants and migrants comprise a fair share of the Latino population in the Midwest, scholars have revealed that other Latinos have roots dating back at least a century. A diverse group of Latinos populated the Midwest prior to many other areas of the country. Dionicio Valdés's classic *Al Norte* argues that these demographic shifts occurred due in part to Mexican and Puerto Rican willingness to fill labor shortages, as white business leaders and politicians often looked to Latinos to perform work that few others would. Eileen Findlay documents how these groups attempted to stymie their own exploitation.[13] Their decisions to relocate continued to be prompted by the various and evolving needs of the region's white majority, but Latinos have also spearheaded placemaking efforts to transform the Midwest to be culturally, socially, and financially responsive to their needs.[14] Thus, studies that characterize Latinos as "new" to the Midwest often overlook their nearly century-long contributions to labor and culture in the region.

Latino migration experiences to Grand Rapids are comparable to the rest of the region in that they were grounded in labor migration. As they did elsewhere in the country, Mexican nationals labored on railroads in Grand Rapids during the 1920s, and they patronized these same rail lines en route *al norte*.[15] From Milwaukee to Chicago to Detroit and other midwestern cities, Latinos comprised the bulk of the laborers performing the most arduous, dirty, and dangerous work on the nation's rail system.[16] Additionally, white farmers and planters' associations frequently recruited workers from Texas, facilitating the emergence of the "Tejano diaspora," as historian Marc Rodríguez has named the phenomenon, across the country, but especially in the Midwest.[17] Michigan employers disseminated announcements among Tejanos, promising free transportation and guaranteed employment if they relocated to cities large and small, such as the densely populated Saginaw or the sparsely populated Caro, Michigan. Well into the 1960s, farmers continued to depend on Mexican Americans as agricultural workers, though with no intention that they stay in Michigan. Mexican Americans were regarded as "temporary" workers whose residency many whites discouraged. During World War II, however, as some Mexican Americans secured jobs in the war industry, Mexican nationals replaced them as part of the nationwide implementation of the Bracero Program, a bilateral agreement between the United States and Mexico to contract Mexican laborers to work on U.S. fields during the war. The United States also recruited Puerto Ricans, who hoped to overcome economic hardship in the wake of the Great Depression, to do similar work. This brought Mexican nationals, Mexican Americans, and Puerto Ricans around the United States, including the Midwest.[18] The latter group filled farm jobs and other forms of labor in Michigan, as they also did in the Northeast and California, many obtaining their positions under state-sponsored programs.[19] Just as the Bracero Program encouraged the migration of both Mexican Americans and Mexican nationals, state-sponsored migration experiments devised originally to promote Puerto Rican temporary relocation to the mainland combined to facilitate a socially engineered Latino diaspora to the Midwest.

In subsequent years, family members and friends joined Mexicans and Puerto Ricans in the Midwest, where they pursued economic opportunities and established communities, transforming various locales. Chicago flourished as the epicenter of Latino life in the Midwest.[20] During the first half of the twentieth century, the Windy City welcomed the largest number of Latino immigrants and migrants of any other midwestern enclave. Though many eventually relocated to the Chicago suburbs, northwest Indiana, and Michigan, many Mexicans and Puerto Ricans selected Chicago as their first destination. Despite the plethora of industrial jobs, as in the case of many other migrants—including African Americans arriving during the Great Migration—Latino migrants and immigrants soon discovered that Chicago was no "promised land."[21] Repelled by the massive urban landscape and frequently excluded from the local economy, these migrants and immigrants pursued economic opportunity in nearby areas. Other Mexicans and Puerto Ricans tried their luck in the fields and factories of large cities, such as Milwaukee, Wisconsin, and small towns like Lorain, Ohio, and Goshen, Indiana.[22]

Grand Rapids became a destination for Mexicans and Puerto Ricans as early as the middle of the twentieth century.

Socioeconomic class, almost a direct result of migration, played a key role in the various forms of placemaking and activism that took place in Grand Rapids. Some Latinos, specifically those who arrived in the 1940s and 1950s, had access to higher-paying jobs than their counterparts who came ten and twenty years later. This influenced their ability to help support their family members and friends as they relocated to Michigan. It also affected their perspectives on the issues Latinos faced in the 1960s and 1970s and how best to address them. Though this was both an ethnically and class-diverse community of Mexicans and Puerto Ricans, they often worked together in transforming the area into one that would meet their needs.

PLACEMAKING

As Latinos did elsewhere in the Midwest, Latinos in Grand Rapids experienced marginalization and exclusion, which often hindered their ability to belong. But their willingness to make spaces where they could feel welcome transformed Grand Rapids' cultural, social, and political landscape. Here I draw on the concept of Latino placemaking advanced by two groundbreaking scholarly contributions: *The Latina/o Midwest Reader* (2017) and *Latinx Placemaking in the Midwest: Building Sustainable Worlds* (2022).[23] These books survey nondevelopment forms of Latino placemaking, including festivals, zines, community centers, migrations, and social movements, among many other examples, through a wide range of disciplinary and interdisciplinary methods. I utilize Latino placemaking to emphasize how empowering this process can be for Latinos in areas where their lived experiences and desires for self-determination were relegated to the margins. Social scientists Katia Balassiano and Marta Maria Maldonado argue that placemaking is when "place is used in pursuit of shared socially and culturally specific goals," for "improved livability." They also acknowledge that with attachment to place comes "control over one's spatialized environment and the ability to make or influence decisions for one's betterment."[24] Within this framework, I take this notion further to examine the empowerment that stems from transforming a place to fit a community's needs. I historicize the processes through which Latinos, as a numerical minority with limited resources, found avenues to meet their cultural, religious, economic, political, and educational needs.

When Mexicans and Puerto Ricans first settled in Grand Rapids from the 1920s to the 1950s, placemaking occurred in intimate spaces. As a smaller population, they forged connections in their living rooms, their workplaces, and church pews. These communal spaces helped Mexicans and Puerto Ricans form friendships and romantic relationships that would constitute the first Mexican–Puerto Rican marriages in the city. This process is reminiscent of what feminist scholar bell hooks recognizes as "homemaking"—the process in which "Black women resisted by making homes where all black people could strive to be subjects, not objects, where we could be affirmed in our minds and hearts despite poverty, hardship, and deprivation, where we could restore to ourselves the dignity denied us on the outside in the public world."[25] Mexicans and Puerto Ricans strived for the same dignity as did African Americans—and made places for themselves to obtain it. In the 1950s and 1960s, Latinos formed recreational and religious spaces to express their cultural identities and to retain them in the face of the pressure to assimilate. In forming these bonds, Mexicans and Puerto Ricans realized they shared the same grievances about inaccessible social services, treatment from the police, and an inequitable school system that marginalized their children. Coalitions formed, and they took their placemaking efforts to the public sphere, transforming their immediate surroundings and the institutions that oppressed them.

In seeking change, Latinos in Grand Rapids faced different challenges than their counterparts in larger cities. Previous scholars of placemaking have focused on Chicago's La Villita, Pilsen, and Humboldt Park neighborhoods—as well as the Mission District in San Francisco and Spanish Harlem in New York City—in order to foreground how Mexicans and Puerto Ricans have reinvigorated spaces by pooling resources to transform an area.[26] While La Villita and the Mission District are mostly the home of Mexican Americans, Grand Rapids' small Latino population included both Mexican and Puerto Rican residents, and placemaking required different considerations. Mexicans, Puerto Ricans, and other Latinos first had to negotiate their relationships across ethnic and racial barriers to form the base of a community. Moreover, they lacked access to social and financial capital, so they leaned on Black and white allies and accessed available municipal resources: to create a community center, the Latin American Council; to challenge discrimination in municipal hiring, particularly the police department; and to form a school that catered to Latino youths' needs. Whether they endeavored to "make place" in their living rooms, churches, community centers, public plazas, antipoverty organizations, city departments, or the local school system, Latinos emerged as critical change agents in Grand Rapids from the 1920s to the 1970s and laid the foundation for generations of Latino migration to come.

Women played, and continue to play, an integral role in safeguarding communities' survival via placemaking. While many studies concentrate on men's leadership roles within their respective communities, this book adds to work that recognizes that women perform many of the unseen, albeit critical, tasks associated with placemaking.[27] Latinas in Grand Rapids, more so than the men, preserved and re-created their cultural traditions with limited resources. They also spearheaded various campaigns to increase federal antipoverty funding, which they hoped would give their communities access to social services as well as educational and cultural resources. Meanwhile, guided by a spirit of community uplift, women often functioned as community ambassadors. From the Mexican American women in the 1940s and 1950s who fed, clothed, and housed migrant families as they trickled in from nearby rural farms to the Puerto Rican women who ensured that their kinfolk had access to food and other resources that were vital to cultural retention, women helped transform Grand Rapids into a more inclusive and welcoming environment for Latinos. In many cases, the friendships Mexicans and Puerto Ricans established during their visits to hair salons, churches, or other people's homes formed the basis of pan-Latino solidarity in Grand Rapids. Lastly, while battling machismo and traditional notions of leadership in their communities, especially regarding the distribution of federal antipoverty grants in the 1960s and 1970s, women stepped into these critical roles and often helped smooth over internal political rifts. They prioritized the broader concerns of the community over ego and visibility.

ACTIVISM

In transforming oppressive institutions, Mexicans and Puerto Ricans engaged in resistance that ranged from quotidian acts of defiance to precise, calculated institutional activism. The *convivencia diaria*—everyday actions—of Latinos is key to understanding resistance. As many scholars have revealed, even the seemingly most mundane actions can operate as forms of resistance.[28] Latinos' refusal to allow their life chances to be circumscribed by Grand Rapids' racially exclusive climate was political. Determined to form their own spaces and maintain their own traditions, these resisters sought to remake Grand Rapids into a more culturally inclusive city. Some residents weighed the benefits of abandoning parts of their identities to accelerate social acceptance, but ultimately most demanded that they be incorporated into the broader social fabric—not as assimilationists, but *as Latinos*.

While radical demands and strategies dominate the bulk of the scholarship on Latino activism in the 1960s and 1970s, Latinos' institutional organizing for more reformist goals in Grand Rapids was also part of a common approach to activism at this time. From the Chicano moratorium in Los Angeles, the Lincoln Hospital takeover in New York City, and numerous school walkouts across the country, these more revolutionary acts of resistance are synonymous with Latino political organizing in scholarship and public memory.[29] For Mexicans and Puerto Ricans in Grand Rapids who sought self-determination, factors such as their relatively limited population and the city's deeply conservative landscape combined to discourage the large public protests seen elsewhere. Moreover, many of their goals were not revolutionary but rather reformist in nature. They wanted inclusion in the city's political, municipal, and educational infrastructure, making them more akin to Latino communities in other secondary cities (e.g., San Francisco, Milwaukee, and Lawrence, Massachusetts) and to more reformist organizers in larger cities (e.g., San Antonio or New York) who wanted to force their local governments and institutions to respond to their needs.[30] In achieving that, Latinos in Grand Rapids selectively used the rhetoric of cultural nationalist movements to make their points and to energize the Latino community while prudently employing smaller-scale protest strategies. They also opted for more institutional approaches, such as forming alliances with white and Black organizers, working with the federal government via the war on poverty, taking up lawsuits, and ensuring that federal and state antidiscrimination policies were enforced. Their organizing style and their goals bore the most similarities to their Latino midwestern counterparts living in smaller cities, including those in South Bend, Indiana, who operated the Midwest Council of La Raza with funds from the University of Notre Dame, and Black organizers in Indianapolis who made allies out of white residents and worked within the system.[31] Activism in Grand Rapids and elsewhere has taken a variety of approaches to fit the context of a particular struggle. Examining this type of organizing in resistance movements demonstrates how the fight for civil and human rights is part of a multipronged process among activists who pursued varying and oftentimes competing strategies to achieve tangible results.[32]

Successful organizing among Mexicans and Puerto Ricans in Grand Rapids, no matter how moderate or gradual, rested on pan-Latino solidarity. As social scientists have shown, forming relationships and a shared community among Mexicans and Puerto Ricans allowed people to see themselves as part of one social group. Though it was not seamless, Mexicans and Puerto Ricans embraced their commonalities when they chose to date one another or form friendships.[33] These same relationships were also the basis of political organizing. While scholarship on Latino solidarity during the 1960s and 1970s often looks at this interethnic unity as solely part of a political moment, when Mexicans and Puerto Ricans organized for political reasons, they were in fact doing so alongside their friends, in-laws, and neighbors.[34] Scholarship on San Francisco confirms that having a prior relationship before organizing for civil rights helps to strengthen pan-Latino solidarity, as seen among Latinos from various ethnic groups who participated in unionism before taking their organizing outside of the shop floor.[35] In Grand Rapids, where Latinos organized as a part of a political fight in the 1960s and 1970s, their shared Latino solidarity was almost two decades old by the time their struggle with the state rose to the surface.

Even with a strong relationship base, mobilizing against the City of Grand Rapids for equal treatment threatened Latino solidarity due to tension based on race, ethnicity, class, gender, and ego. When a Mexican American male organizer once stressed an inability of Mexicans and Puerto Ricans "to get along" to explain why Latinos had not succeeded in garnering further civil rights in Grand Rapids, and not structural inequalities in city governance, Puerto Rican and Mexican women rebuffed the claim.[36] They relied on the same personal connections that forged the original communal bonds to help them rally other Latinos to continue the pursuit of equality, regardless of the tensions among some members. The process of pan-Latino solidarity formation is complex, but the work of the activists who proceeded to organize would create opportunities for Latinos in a city that afforded them none.

Examining activism at the hyperlocal level provides an example of when inter-ethnic solidarity and organizing is the most effective strategy. In Grand Rapids, where Mexicans and Puerto Ricans together made up 5 percent of the population and had a connection that preceded pursuits of political activism, and where both white and Black Grand Rapidians did not recognize them as belonging, the formation of one, pan-Latino core of solidarity was the necessary strategy. But pan-Latino solidarity is not the answer for every instance of discrimination or activism. This conceptualization of solidarity invites multiple critiques, both historically and contemporaneously. Focusing on a collective Latino identity has the power to homogenize Latinos across ethnic lines, which often elevates white Latinos at the expense of Afro-Latinos and Indigenous Latinos.[37] Solidarity as a strategy works when it emerges from the local context where relationships among community members and between communities can build trust in the intentions of each group joining the movement. With Mexican and Puerto Rican pursuits for equality in the mid-twentieth century, pan-Latino solidarity united Latinos and engendered the possibility of transformative change.

Relationships among African Americans and Latinos also shaped the history of Latino activism in Grand Rapids. Latinos' fight for better treatment corresponded with the civil rights struggle of African Americans, the city's larger minority group.[38] Some Black and Latino activists turned to interracial organizing in the 1960s and 1970s. As with interethnic solidarity, interracial coalitions proved well-suited for some endeavors, but not all. Frederick Douglass Opie's work on Black-Latino coalitions in New York in the 1970s identifies the ideal conditions for this type of organizing: "when [both groups] shared a language, a political goal, an employer, or class status as well as when they operated within the same spaces."[39] Interracial coalitions in Grand Rapids support this framework. In the 1970s, when Black and Latino organizers challenged discriminatory hiring in municipal jobs that excluded both groups, they formed a "minority" coalition to challenge the City of Grand Rapids. Similar tactics emerged in Philadelphia, where Black and Puerto Rican organizers challenged Mayor Frank Rizzo's corrupt administration.[40] In contrast, when federal anti-poverty funding was needed to address the issues of language discrimination and xenophobia that many Latinos faced and the anti-Black racism endured by African Americans—and by Afro-Latinos, for that matter—they would pursue separate paths to remedies, with Latinos stressing their differences from African Americans. I frame Latinos' actions in claiming dissimilarity from African Americans as part of the "politics of recognition." As scholars José E. Cruz, Sonia Song-Ha Lee, and Lorrin Thomas note, Puerto Ricans in New York used this strategy, though problematic, to garner recognition as an aggrieved minority group in need of resources in an environment that recognized only white and Black.[41] The conservative environment in Grand Rapids and the limited funds available through federal programs influenced these decisions. Regardless, examining both the cooperation and conflict in Latino and Black coalitional activism unearths lessons for current and future organizers.

READING AGAINST THE GRAIN: RECONSTRUCTING A HISTORY OF LATINOS IN GRAND RAPIDS

Locating Latino voices within a history that emphasizes the contributions and experiences of white residents was not an easy task. Adopting the methodologies of social historians, especially those whose central focus is historically marginalized groups, I learned to read against the grain of the documents I found. Few archives I visited maintained records for Latino community life. For this reason, I focused on sources that conveyed the history of Grand Rapids and of the United States more broadly, and I then attempted to locate Latinos' seemingly hidden voices.[42] I soon discovered that, when read against the grain, many records reveal demographic information about the first Mexican and Puerto Rican immigrants and migrants and placemaking. In re-creating this relational history, I also used these sources to clarify the connections between the paths and experiences of Mexicans and Puerto Ricans in Michigan. I also engaged with primary sources on African Americans. Paying close attention to the moments of intersecting and overlapping experiences among Mexicans, Puerto Ricans, and African Americans helped to reveal how Latinos, as a group, fit into this majority white city.

While repositories in Grand Rapids contain voluminous collections on the city's white population, Latinos do not enjoy similar levels of municipal, state, and private record keeping. Some institutions boast a few small collections that pertain to Latinos, but most of my work reconstructing this history was done document by document. In archives throughout Grand Rapids, I looked at any available material that might detail the lived experiences of Latinos, including local jail records, city assessor files, and unprocessed local documents from federal antipoverty programs. In small offices in various Catholic churches, I pored over baptism, confirmation, and marriage records, with anxious church personnel looking on. They feared that, within a xenophobic political climate, investigations would negatively impact the immigrants and migrants residing in their communities. Around Michigan, I regularly visited small libraries that housed historical society records and larger collections at various universities, eager for evidence of more than just a fleeting presence of Latinos. Eventually, I located yearbooks, local newspapers, organizational records, and personal collections of ephemera that revealed the lasting contributions of the Latino community. Federal records and presidential libraries and their archives provided the necessary sources to reconstruct how national policies affected Latinos' lived experiences in Michigan. Piece by piece, the documents began to illuminate a more comprehensive portrait of life in Grand Rapids for Latinos.

Reports from the City of Grand Rapids and other municipal organizations that rarely mentioned Latinos failed to offer a comprehensive portrait of community life—their day-to-day activities and the relationships they formed across ethnic and racial lines. Given the deafening silences in city archives, oral histories spoke the loudest. Interviewing Latinos and documenting their firsthand accounts of life in Grand Rapids illuminated Latinos' burgeoning solidarity during the early years of settlement along with the ways they worked to form a community in an otherwise segregated city. Oral histories also laid bare the extent to which written documents were misleading or downright biased. While the local press frequently focused attention on the interethnic conflict, my interviews with community members confirmed that the problems that arose in the Latino communities were typically individual and did not damage the spirit of solidarity and collective organizing. Additionally, traditional sources failed to capture the gendered dynamics of migration, settlement, and political activism. My interviews with Latinas underscored their integral roles in community building and achieving civil rights even as I had to read against the grain of their gendered notions of leadership, which often had them refusing to take direct credit for their efforts.[43]

Though this is the first nonfiction work to chronicle Latino community development in Grand Rapids, the definitive story of Latinos in this city remains to be told. I highlight the experiences of Mexicans, Puerto Ricans, and, to a much lesser extent, Cubans, since these groups represented the largest Latino populations in Grand Rapids from 1920 to 1978, and the largest source base to consult.[44] This is not to suggest that other Latino cultures were absent from Grand Rapids. Some residents of the city had origins in Peru and the Dominican Republic, but these

Latino ethnic groups comprised a smaller percentage of the community during this period. Thus, they do not figure into this monograph in a substantial way.

The population and dynamics of the Latino community in Grand Rapids shifted in 1978, providing a natural endpoint for this study. Primarily, the Latin American Council (LAC), the main community service organization and basis of several chapters of this book, began dissolving in 1978, signaling a shift in the landscape of organizing and activism. In addition, in the early 1980s, U.S. foreign policy toward Central America and Cuba changed dramatically, leading to fluctuating immigration patterns from those regions. With the establishment of the North American Free Trade Agreement (NAFTA), U.S. foreign and economic policies also changed toward Mexico. NAFTA created a new wave of Mexican immigration to the United States in the 1990s.[45] The influx of new immigrants and migrants changed the city's Latino population so dramatically that the post-1980 period deserves its own study. At the same time, Latino activists who worked as pioneers in the earliest grassroots civil rights campaigns retired from politics, and a new generation of activists emerged. The new and diverse Latino ethnic groups that arrived after 1980 helped to transform the urban landscape in Grand Rapids, offering ample terrain for future scholars to extend studies of Latino community life in the Midwest, especially given resulting shifts in intergroup dynamics and the increasing availability of source material.

OVERVIEW

This book begins by examining Latino migration journeys from the 1920s to 1960s, then considers Latinos' placemaking efforts from the 1940s to the 1970s, and closes by analyzing the beginnings of formal organizing from the 1960s to 1978. The final three chapters of the book thematically chronicle concurrent events: Latino engagements with institutional activism via the formation of a grassroots community center, challenges to the police department, and a fight for equal education between 1968 and 1978.

Chapter 1, "Trained and Tractable Labor," details the parallel and intertwined migration and immigration journeys of Mexicans, Mexican Americans, and Puerto Ricans who relocated to the Grand Rapids area from the 1920s to the 1960s, with some consideration of the broader patterns of Latino migration to Michigan and the Midwest. The forces of exploitation, imperialism, and racism brought these disparate immigrant and migrant groups onto a converging path. This time period marks the first occasion that Latinos in Grand Rapids and Michigan could consider their similar journeys. Chapter 2 then illustrates how familial networks helped Mexicans and Puerto Ricans settle in Grand Rapids from the 1940s to the 1960s, marking the beginning of the process of pan-Latino community formation. I also examine how Mexicans and Puerto Ricans considered their place within the racial binary in Grand Rapids, with special attention to the area's first generation of Latino children and teenagers.

Chapter 3 examines placemaking via the creation of shared religious and recreational spaces during the 1940s to the 1970s. Overlapping and shared experiences in migration and settlement helped Mexicans and Puerto Ricans see what they had in common. Moreover, their exclusion from all white recreational venues and the desire to have places of their own led them to create pan-Latino spaces. As a numerical minority, Latinos learned to borrow spaces and use all available financial and human resources to provide venues—from dances to churches to festivals—for Latinos to gather and enjoy each other's company. This period initiated their attempts to mitigate the discriminatory treatment they faced in Grand Rapids. During the tumultuous 1960s and 1970s, some Latinos used their public gatherings, specifically festivals, to convey an apolitical stance. They intended to also attract white Grand Rapidians, with the hope that white residents would view them as nonthreatening and spend money at their events.

Chapter 4 demonstrates the remedies Latinos attempted to deploy against discriminatory treatment and to address the poor material conditions they experienced. Spanning the late 1960s to the early 1970s, this chapter recounts how Mexicans and Puerto Ricans used their pan-Latino solidarity to engage in a type of political placemaking to gain recognition as an overlooked and aggrieved minority group in Grand Rapids. As a recently formed grassroots organization, the LAC provided a base for Latinos to engage with the "politics of recognition." The LAC lobbied the City of Grand Rapids to distribute federal antipoverty funds from the Community Action Program and the Model Cities Program to the Latino community, just as those groups had given funds to African American organizations. This fight, along with the introduction of new community leaders, brought into relief tensions in the community based on ethnicity, race, gender, and personalities that would threaten the pan-Latino solidarity of this community.

As chapter 5 shows, the successful fight to receive federal antipoverty money delivered the LAC much needed, albeit limited, resources to provide for the community during the early 1970s. By the time the LAC received federal funding, the Nixon administration was delivering diminishing amounts to antipoverty initiatives. Through an analysis of the council's social service offerings and cultural programming, chapter 5 argues that the LAC used its available resources for Latino community members, relationships with non-Latinos, and antipoverty funds to create a social safety net for Latinos and a physical and intellectual site of belonging for Latinos in Grand Rapids. Latinos in this Midwest setting used the LAC to bolster their pan-Latino solidarity during a period of nationalist social movements such as the Chicano movement and the Puerto Rican nationalist movement.

Chapters 6 and 7 address the greatest challenges Latinos faced in Grand Rapids in the 1970s: inequality in policing and education. Chapter 6 discusses how a coalition of Black and Latino organizers used institutional methods of activism and interracial unity to protest police brutality and object to the city's resistance to hiring Black and Latino police officers. Through engaging with federal policies and eventually suing the City of Grand Rapids, this coalition aimed for inclusion in the police department as a means to stem police abuse. The chapter describes white resistance to social progress, including demographic changes to the police department, and how LAC organizers helped to combat this rhetoric. Chapter 7 chronicles the fight Latinos engaged in for bilingual and bicultural education for their children. Including the broader experiences of Latinos in Michigan and not just in Grand Rapids, I reveal how Latinos expended every resource available to them, including African American education administrators, to go outside of the local school system and create a culturally competent educational experience for Latino students through a state-level grant. Led by the LAC, the community provided grassroots solutions to educational challenges when local schools fell short. Showcasing the talents of Latina educators, this chapter elucidates how women in the 1970s safeguarded the educational future for the community.

The epilogue captures the state of continued Latino migration, placemaking, activism, and education in Grand Rapids since 1978, after which time the community expanded not only in size but in diversity. Labor migration, familial connections, and perceived safety continued to draw Latinos then, and the same remains true today. I highlight the continued fight to safeguard placemaking from encroaching gentrification and the ways that community leaders have fought back against larger institutional forces, like powerful local and national non-profits. The epilogue shows that there has been almost a hundred years of painstaking work to create and protect Latino placemaking that has made Grand Rapids home for Latinos.

– 1 –

Trained and Tractable Labor

As secretary for Michigan Field Crops (MFC), a Saginaw-based growers' association that represented close to forty companies throughout the state, Max Henderson was worried. He feared that the local sugar beet industry would never witness another time when "large pools of willing, trained and tractable labor [would] work at the wages which farmers can afford to pay." Thus, while attending a Farmers and Manufacturers Beet Sugar Association (FMBSA) meeting in 1948, Henderson cast about for ways to save the sugar crop that year. He recruited some Mexican Americans—Michigan's long-standing agricultural workforce—to return to the fields, but he still lacked the number of workers he needed. A great many others shared Henderson's concerns. During the FMBSA meeting, one member wondered aloud whether there was "no great pool of workers from foreign countries or from over-populated agricultural sections" to replace Mexican Americans.[1] They had once used Mexican braceros, Mexican nationals recruited to work in the United States on six-month contracts through a bilateral agreement between the United States and Mexico, but Michigan did not receive enough of these temporary workers to prop up the MFC farmers. Next, they turned to Puerto Ricans to help fill the labor gap. Reading these descriptions against the grain, the FMBSA's low regard for Mexican Americans and other migrant workers becomes strikingly clear—planters preferred to employ people so economically vulnerable that they would accept the poor working conditions and low pay that the Michiganders offered.

Michigan farmers' interest in Mexican and Puerto Rican workers was a result of a long history between the United States, Mexico, and Puerto Rico. U.S. military forays into both places in the 1800s put Mexico and Puerto Rico—informally and formally—under the purview of the United States. U.S. imperial ambitions in the Mexican-American War succeeded in 1848 when Mexico ceded vast tracts of land to its northern neighbor after the war. Thereafter, Mexicans living in the ceded territories lost land under a changing societal hierarchy, which ranked them near the bottom with limited access to the resources they once owned. The Spanish-American War in 1898 had similar consequences for Puerto Ricans. Despite U.S. claims of their intent to liberate Spain's colonies, the United States colonized Puerto Rico as part of a broader effort to expand its influence and economic control in Latin America. Under this regime, Puerto Ricans were subject to U.S. colonial control, with U.S. administrators in charge of the economic fate of the island.

Michigan planters regularly conflated the identities of Mexicans, Mexican Americans, and Puerto Rican laborers, although each group exhibited its own distinct identities and histories. For example, their emphasis on employing "foreign" workers while still recruiting mainly from Puerto Rico and Texas exposes the planters' attitudes: Latinos did not belong in Michigan or the Midwest, no matter their citizenship status. They regarded this workforce merely as, at best, temporary residents. Excluding them from U.S. categories of belonging allowed farmers to exploit the workers' vulnerability and discourage protest.[2] The FMBSA viewed these laborers and prospective workers as "tractable" people from "overpopulated agricultural sectors" who would work at the low wages farmers paid.[3] These statements indicated that exploitability was chief among their desired characteristics for potential workers. And they succeeded in recruiting laborers from Puerto Rico, Texas, and Mexico who were, in fact, desperate for a means of survival.

Recruiters did not intend to transform Michigan into a destination for Mexican and Puerto Rican long-term settlement, but that is what occurred. Between the 1920s and the 1960s, labor migration shifted the demographics of the greater Midwest. The region's sparse population of Mexicans and Puerto Ricans grew into a permanent presence. While recruiters and farmers merely sought to fill temporary labor shortages, Mexicans and Puerto Ricans—working in agriculture, on the railroad, and in various other industries—eventually settled in Michigan, to the dismay of the predominantly white residents. These temporary workers carried a strong attachment to their individual cultures, which at times intersected, helping them to later form pan-Latino solidarity. Their placemaking efforts ensured that more Latinos could and would have a home and a claim to belonging in Michigan. Labor recruiters unwittingly set in motion demographic shifts that would transform the political and cultural landscape across Michigan and the greater Midwest.

The exploitation of Mexican nationals, Mexican Americans, and Puerto Ricans resulted from the twin legacies of imperialism and racism, which had rendered these groups vulnerable to predatory labor recruitment. As scholars have shown, Mexican nationals, Mexican Americans, and Puerto Ricans took advantage of the chance to contract with labor recruiters from the United States, who promised an alternative to the harsh living conditions they endured elsewhere.[4] Michigan companies hired some of the most aggressive recruiters, starting at the turn of the twentieth century. Through state-sponsored programs that emerged as by-products of the uneven power dynamic between Mexico and the United States as well as the colonial relationship between Puerto Rico and the United States, U.S. officials encouraged and facilitated migration among otherwise destitute workers.

This chapter draws attention to the root causes of displacement that resulted in immigration and migration, reminiscent of similar phenomena in other Latin American countries and other places that experienced the United States' impe-rialist interventions throughout the twentieth century. It also calls attention to the ways these imperialist actions and labor recruitment combined to change the demographic makeup of the United States. Specifically, it helps us to understand how Mexicans and Puerto Ricans were put on parallel and interdependent jour-neys to the Midwest. Last, it details how people came to Michigan and then to Grand Rapids, where they hoped to build new lives.

EMIGRATION AND THE CONDITIONS
IN MEXICO, PUERTO RICO, AND TEXAS

From the mid-1800s to the early 1900s, U.S. imperialist actions in Mexico, Puerto Rico, and Texas led some of the most impacted people to seek refuge elsewhere. The Mexican-American War of 1848 and the Spanish-American War in 1898 impacted the distribution of land, capital, and other resources in the aforementioned areas. Elite Mexicans, Puerto Ricans, and Tejanos—Mexican Americans from Texas—aided white U.S. business owners. Government admin-istrators profited from this process of displacement and loss. White Americans then situated themselves atop the local racial and power hierarchies, dislodging the elites and toppling those beneath them on the social ladder. This manifested in three different phenomena: economic dislocation and civil war in Mexico; land theft and dispossession in Texas; and colonial exploitation and later neo-liberalism in Puerto Rico. While it is important not to conflate these three issues, the root causes, and more importantly, the effects that these situations had on everyday people are interrelated and, at times, overlapping. Mexicans, Puerto Ricans, and Tejanos left reeling in the new societal order experienced violence, racism, and systemic inequalities, which inspired many of them to migrate and immigrate for survival.

The Mexican-American War resulted in a balance of power that favored the United States, wherein Mexicans were subjected to the political will and domination of Anglo Americans. This arrangement culminated in a long-standing desire of U.S. political leaders to acquire the land and resources located beyond their southern border. "It is impossible not to look forward to distant times, when our rapid multiplication will expand itself beyond those limits, and cover the whole Northern if not the Southern continent," President Thomas Jefferson opined in an 1801 letter to James Monroe, then governor of Virginia.[5] After a contrived border dispute in 1845, the United States entered into war with Mexico, a nation still recovering from its war of independence from Spain.

The three-year conflict resulted in massive land transfers to the United States, large expenditures of resources, and many casualties on both sides, though Mexico and Mexicans bore the brunt of the losses. The Treaty of Guadalupe Hidalgo, which ended the war, guaranteed the rights of the tens of thousands of Mexicans living in newly ceded U.S. territories to claim U.S. citizenship.[6] However, the new citizens' protections under the law remained limited as white Americans treated them as categorically nonwhite.[7] Many of them lost land and were forced to migrate as a means of survival.[8] There were other dangerous ramifications. For example, in 1882, a Mexican man was lynched for attempting to take a white man to court, illustrating the precarity for Mexicans exercising their equal rights.[9] U.S. laws and policies—enforced through violence—permitted Anglo settlers in the Southwest to wrangle power, resources, and status away from Mexican Americans, consigning them to what amounted to second-class citizenship.

In the wake of the Spanish-American War, U.S. and British companies, with the help of Mexico's president and dictator Porfirio Díaz, also profited immensely by exploiting Mexican resources. Díaz hoped to make Mexico a competitor in the growing global economy through modernization campaigns. However, bringing the industrial revolution to Mexico also meant inviting foreign investors to participate in and, ultimately, undermine the local economy. U.S. and British financiers purchased large, fertile land plots for their respective agricultural and oil industries to ransack. The country's poorest people suffered most under this arrangement. The industrialization project started by Díaz, which led to the free rein of foreign interests, limited the self-sufficiency of peasant farmers who lost their land. This led to a widespread revolt—the Mexican Revolution, which ended in 1920 after a decade of fighting and 1.5 million deaths.[10]

The war wreaked havoc on the Mexican economy, contributing to lasting political and economic instability. For instance, though the revolution officially ended in 1920, parts of Mexico remained defiant with leaders like Pancho Villa, who continued to fight until his death in 1923. Mexico underwent several irregular transitions of power well into the twentieth century. Mexicans had immigrated to the United States in large numbers during and after the revolution to flee the violence. Over the next several decades, economic and social conditions in Mexico continued to deteriorate. The Great Depression exacerbated the situation because, while afflicting nations worldwide, it particularly devastated countries struggling with modern development.[11] By the time World War II began, the economic state of Mexico motivated many Mexicans to search for work in the United States, hoping to provide for their families. U.S. recruitment efforts via the Bracero Program furthered this aim.

Similar imperial impulses fueled the United States to gain control over Puerto Rico. During the "splendid little war" with Spain in 1898, the Spanish ceded control of Cuba, Guam, the Philippines, and Puerto Rico to the United States. After varying degrees of bloodshed in which hundreds of thousands of people lost their lives—with U.S. soldiers making up the minority and Filipino civilians constituting the majority due to disease and famine—Cuba and the Philippines eventually achieved independence.[12] Puerto Rico then became situated in the legal limbo of a "commonwealth" in which it is neither a sovereign nation nor a state. In reality, the island functions as the longest-standing colony of the United States.[13] Beginning in 1898, the United States enacted a series of laws and policies in Puerto Rico to benefit U.S. businesses. For example, by devaluing the Spanish peso and replacing it with the U.S. dollar, U.S. administrators guaranteed that U.S. sugar companies could purchase large land holdings in Puerto Rico for a pittance of what they were worth. Economic exploitation occurred alongside political subjugation, as American economic interests controlled the island's government. Puerto Rico's first civilian governor, Charles Allen, served for less than two years between 1900 and 1901. However, soon after his appointment, U.S. companies controlled the majority of the sugar production on the island, though absentee landholders assumed authority over many local farmlands.[14] After leaving his formal post, in 1907 Allen formed the American Sugar Refining Company, one of the largest sugar trusts at the time, with interests in Puerto Rico and throughout the Caribbean.[15] Allen and U.S. growers purposefully molded the island's economy into a commercial monocrop system that favored sugar, deprioritizing the island's other cash crops, tobacco and coffee—actions that devastated the local economy and caused smaller landholders and subsistence farmers to turn to wage labor.[16]

Two important pieces of legislation sanctioned this perpetual cycle of dependency between Puerto Rico and the United States. The Foraker Act of 1902 prohibited Puerto Rico from initiating its own trade agreements and barred the island from setting tariffs, prohibiting Puerto Ricans from having sovereignty over their economic affairs.[17] The Jones Act of 1917 imposed U.S. citizenship on Puerto Ricans but allowed only Puerto Ricans living on the mainland to vote in federal elections. Combined, the two acts reduced Puerto Rico to a colony, shredding any presumed sense of independence. Unable to benefit from import taxes, the United States became Puerto Rico's only trade partner. Reluctant to transport their refinery equipment, administrators insisted that sugar refinement be shifted to the U.S. mainland.[18] This decision ensured that any profits derived from the refinery process bypassed Puerto Rican residents. The disparity between Puerto Ricans and U.S. business owners only deepened over time.

The Great Depression amplified Puerto Rico's economic quandary. As with many regions of the U.S. mainland, a quarter of the population on the island was unemployed at the height of the Depression. Those fortunate enough to locate work barely earned enough to support themselves and their families. A twelve-hour workday in Puerto Rico at the time yielded only 50 cents in wages. The average weekly wage amounted to about $3.34, and daily survival often necessitated that families spend at least 94 percent of this amount on basic items such as food.[19] As a result, many Puerto Ricans had to prioritize their most pressing needs, leaving some needs unmet. For example, prior to arriving in Michigan in 1955, my paternal grandmother, Luisa Fernández, resided in Cagüitas, where she witnessed Depression-era suffering as an eight-year-old child. After her mother grew ill and could not work, her father realized his wages could not support a family of five. Her father decided to send Luisa to live with and work for a family that was faring better during the Depression.[20] Even if Luisa's mother had been able to work, her low wages would have barely supplemented her husband's pay. Job opportunities for women on the island were largely limited to domestic work and needlework production, the latter of which paid about 2 cents an hour or less.[21] Yet, despite the dire situation facing many Puerto Rican families, sugar company owners maintained high profits throughout the Depression years.[22] This in turn heightened labor tensions within the agricultural industry, and government planners searched for ways to bring more manufacturing opportunities to the island.[23]

Local officials also addressed these economic struggles by devising state-sponsored migration programs. Starting around World War II and continuing until the late 1960s, the island engaged in what was called Operation Bootstrap. Luís Muñoz Marín, president of the Puerto Rican senate, and Teodoro Moscoso, a policymaker with a history in public service, led this pursuit of modernization programs in the 1940s. Policymakers' trials with industrialization included using companies owned by the Puerto Rican government and, eventually, free-market experimentation. The island's administration tried to lure mainland businesses with tax exemptions, loose environmental regulations, and low wages. Five years after the start of Operation Bootstrap, Puerto Rico gained almost fifty new industries manufacturing a range of goods, including pearl buttons, pharmaceuticals, radios, and handbags.[24] They also bolstered the tourism industry, and the Caribe Hilton opened in 1949. Other hotel chains soon followed suit. Some Puerto Ricans, however, worried that relying on too many mainland businesses would hurt the island in the long run.

These critics were correct—Operation Bootstrap undermined Puerto Rico's attempts to gain economic self-sufficiency. The program never addressed the usurious relationship between the United States and Puerto Rico, nor did the proponents of Operation Bootstrap acknowledge that the island's financial instability resulted from earlier U.S. policies such as the Foraker and Jones Acts. Instead, the program that administrators touted as a success had adversely affected the island. The new Operation Bootstrap companies created factories in the island's urban centers, causing a demographic shift from rural to urban areas. With fewer rural farmworkers, the island suffered a food shortage. U.S. employers also preferred to hire women, whom they could pay lower wages. When men did obtain jobs at the factories, they reported that they were underemployed. The remedies created to solve economic dilemmas caused by U.S. imperial policies only encouraged more Puerto Ricans to leave in search of new opportunities.[25]

For Tejanos and Mexican nationals living in Texas, the limited labor opportunities and segregation in Texas provided the impetus to relocate northward. Many employers in Texas discriminated against Mexican Americans and kept them out of desirable jobs in foundries. White employees also received higher wages for the same work.[26] Across the Southwest, Mexicans worked in railroads, irrigation systems, and tended livestock, but in Texas, agricultural production and processing remained the main source of income for many working-class Mexicans. These jobs paid low wages and guaranteed arduous working conditions, little to no prospects for advancement, and the constant specter of obsolescence from mechanization.[27] Tejanos often suffered attendant forms of structural racism in Texas in addition to the limited employment opportunities. Many resided in segregated barrios and attended all-Mexican schools, a situation that worsened as the twentieth century progressed due to white flight, with white residents fleeing to the suburbs in the hopes of staving off integration.[28] These conditions pushed many laborers in Texas to seek out better conditions elsewhere.

In the decades following the Mexican Revolution and World War I, racial violence also compelled Mexicans to move north. The prevalence of anti-Black violence during the years leading up to the civil rights movement is well known, and indeed Black migrants endured the greater share of white racial violence. But scholars estimate white vigilantes and white mobs lynched six hundred Mexicans and Mexican Americans who resided in the Southwest between the 1850s and the 1920s. Many of these acts occurred in Texas, the state with the longest border with Mexico. As with African Americans, many Mexican victims of lynching were arbitrarily accused of crimes that ranged from murder to cheating at cards.[29] This form of extralegal violence denied the accused due process, which perhaps shows the intent behind these acts. Racial violence and intimidation toward Mexicans—and African Americans for that matter—represented the attempts of white Americans to maintain political, social, and economic dominance as demographics changed nationwide from the late 1800s to the 1920s.[30] Many Mexicans and Tejanos soon realized that residency in Texas could mean increasing marginalization and financial insecurity and it could also cost them their lives.

As is the case of so many migrants in the United States and throughout the world, leaving and seeking work elsewhere developed into a viable form of resistance as well. Oral histories have shown how migrants recognized their agency in these situations. When interviewed in 1997, Guadalupe Vargas recalled that when she first proposed relocation from Texas, she thought of her son's future. Originally from Mexico, Guadalupe's family moved in 1921 to Texas, where she and her parents sought work as farmworkers. Guadalupe married but soon lost her husband and one of her children to a devastating illness. Magdaleno, her surviving child, eventually joined Guadalupe in the fields. Together with Guadalupe's parents, they migrated within Texas, where Guadalupe met her second husband, Daniel Vargas, who had relocated to Texas after the Mexican Revolution.

Daniel's hard work, excellent English-language skills, and ambition while working on fields in Texas led to his promotion to a crew leader. Still, he and Guadalupe desired a great deal more for Magdaleno than toiling in the fields. "I wanted my son to have an education because when you work in the fields, you stay one day and then it's over," Guadalupe remarked.[31] She recognized that, if Magdaleno remained a farmworker, his schooling would revolve around the harvest schedule, making him fall behind, decreasing the quality of his education, and increasing the chances he would leave school before graduating. With Magdaleno's future at stake, the couple contemplated leaving Texas and abandoning farmwork altogether. They followed through on the decision in the early 1940s and moved to give their family, especially Magdaleno, more opportunities.

"THEY STARTED WALKING TO TRY TO GET TO MICHIGAN": THE DEMAND FOR MEXICAN LABOR IN MICHIGAN

The need for Latino labor in the Midwest emerged at the turn of the twentieth century and greatly increased during and after World War II. Many regional and local industries, namely railroads and agriculture, came to depend on Mexican, and later Puerto Rican, labor. In the 1910s, European immigrants started swapping farmwork for industrial work with the economic changes that occurred during World War I. This left agricultural labor shortages, which Mexican nationals swiftly filled. After the war, agribusiness remained dependent on the labor that Mexican nationals and Mexican Americans could provide. The Great Depression, however, caused the forced repatriation of many Mexican nationals from the Midwest as local and federal administrators attempted to save U.S. jobs for "real Americans."[32] The outbreak of the Second World War made the region's recruitment of Mexican nationals necessary again. At first, Michigan companies relied on Mexican Americans who had settled nearby, and further recruitment to Michigan stalled until the 1940s. The flow of labor started again with the use of state-sponsored recruitment programs that employed Mexican nationals in the 1940s and included Puerto Ricans in the early 1950s. Almost fifty years of Latino recruitment had a lasting impact on Michigan and the Midwest.

In the late 1800s and early 1900s, the pernicious effects of racism and imperialism nearly guaranteed ongoing hardship for those who remained in Mexico and Texas. Mexicans soon landed upon immigration and migration to seek out a fresh start. Since the 1900s, Mexican nationals and Mexican Americans from Texas had worked along rail lines and agricultural circuits, which carried them to the Midwest and Michigan. Mexican workers also pursued opportunities with U.S.-based steel and automotive industries during World War II, as they hoped to fill industrial employment shortages resulting from the war. To survive, Mexicans frequently combined work within multiple industries, never quite abandoning one position for another. They encountered various forms of discrimination in Michigan, but the slightly improved pay, working conditions, and other nearby job opportunities in the Midwest helped to reward their decisions to migrate.

Railroad lines facilitated the labor migration of Mexican and Tejano laborers across the United States and to the Midwest. After the 1882 Chinese Exclusion Act, which greatly reduced the number of Chinese migrants working within the railroad industry, railway work essentially morphed into "Mexican work." Responding to the travel demands of major railway hubs in El Paso, Laredo, San Antonio, and other places, railway companies eagerly recruited Mexican workers. Yet, as patrons, Mexicans also took advantage of the expanding rails as families began to explore opportunities beyond the Southwest. By 1920, about 54,000 Mexicans had already traveled to the Midwest, Northwest, and Northeast.[33] Railroad geography brought Mexicans to the Midwest because lines in Central Texas connected with Kansas City, which then connected to Chicago, and then to Michigan, providing a path for those migrating to follow.

As one of Grand Rapids' first Mexican settlers, Daniel Vásquez landed in West Michigan via a similar route. Migrating from San Luís Potosí to El Paso during the late 1920s, he subsequently mounted the rails in the direction of Chicago and then Detroit, before eventually settling in Grand Rapids around 1929.[34] Like Vásquez, many Mexican men who ended up in Michigan reported working at some point along their journey on the very lines that carried them to the Midwest. Some worked on the Chesapeake and Ohio Railway, the Michigan Central Railroad, and the Baltimore and Ohio Railroad, which provided access to West Virginia, Kentucky, Illinois, and New York.[35] Those who arrived in Michigan availed themselves of the opportunities in growing cities like Detroit, Grand Rapids, Lansing, and Kalamazoo. The availability of railroad jobs in Michigan became well-known among Mexican Americans. In 1950, eighteen-year-old Santos Rincones and his brother, two migrant farm-working Tejanos, heard of the jobs in Michigan from a friend. Along with their father, they detoured from their migrant farm-working route to stop in Grand Rapids and inquire about the jobs. When they arrived, their father "did not want them to stay there," Santos recalled. He gathered his sons and returned to the migrant trail. Undeterred, Santos and his brother "started walking to try to get to Michigan." Somebody told their father they were leaving that night—he caught them and reluctantly offered to take the family to Grand Rapids instead of having his sons make the long journey alone.[36] Railroads served a dual function for Mexicans in the early twentieth century by providing an alternative to migrant farm working and opening new destinations to settle outside the Southwest.

Within the Midwest and Michigan, some Mexicans had access to additional labor opportunities, which included industrial manufacturing. Many Mexicans and Mexican Americans learned of these openings and traveled to the nation's great industrial centers, including Chicago and Gary, Indiana, where they secured work in the meatpacking and steel industries. In the 1920s, the Detroit-based Ford Motor Company recruited elite Mexican workers directly from Mexico while hiring a host of others who had first worked farms in Michigan.[37] Chevrolet, based in Saginaw, also provided many Mexican migrants with part-time and full-time employment.[38] Rather than return to Texas or Mexico, where industrial work remained scarce and where racism and violence threatened their survival, Mexicans and Mexican American migrants in this era assumed multiple positions in a variety of industries.

In the Midwest and Michigan, agricultural work emerged as another major labor opportunity for Mexicans and Mexican Americans, who have served as the bedrock of the state's commercial agricultural workforce since the early 1920s. Labor migrants could travel to states across the Midwest and find eager employers in need of workers to pick and harvest crops that included blueberries, apples, cherries, onions, celery, and sugar beets. Saginaw Valley sugar companies dominated Michigan's agricultural sector, as well as in the recruitment of Mexican Americans. Those hired by Michigan sugar companies worked temporarily in Michigan, but others decided to permanently relocate there.

Michigan growers would advertise job opportunities in San Antonio, as well as other large Texas cities and border locales.[39] Tejanos who had worked in the fields for years often became recruiters themselves, and they served as go-betweens for future Tejano workers and Michigan growers.[40] For example, the Beet Growers' Employment Committee of Saginaw paid $100 to Frank Cortez's company, the Cortez Employment Agency of San Antonio, to contract workers for Michigan fields. While he owned one of the largest agencies that Michigan growers used, he was only one of several agents helping to recruit workers.[41] During the early 1920s, my maternal great-grandparents, Eugenio and Marihilda Muñoz, learned of farmwork in Saginaw, likely from these types of recruiters, and left Texas with their daughter Juanita, hoping to find more economic opportunities.

Other Mexicans, demonstrating their high degree of geographical mobility, worked on a migratory circuit that funneled them to various parts of the country, including Michigan, to work in the fields and in various industries. Settling in Grand Rapids in 1928, the Cerda family stands as an example. Luciano and Juanita Cerda left Mexico around 1922 and arrived in Oklahoma, where their son Octavio was born four years later. In 1928, they carried Octavio to Grand Rapids, where they soon celebrated the births of their daughters Socorro and Josefina.[42] The places where Juanita gave birth to their children reveals the route the family traveled to Michigan. Additionally, since the Cerda family likely engaged in farmwork, the fact that the whole family traveled together indicates how, at one point or another, they may have all worked the fields together to help provide for their expanding family. As the Depression set in, however, repatriation campaigns began across Michigan, especially in Detroit, leading to a lull in the migration. It was not until after the Depression that Mexican Americans began arriving in Michigan in larger numbers again.

World War II provided the catalyst for increased labor recruitment and migration to the Midwest from Mexico, Texas, and Puerto Rico. Though the United States attempted several federal programs to end the Great Depression, it was not until the nation reentered wartime production and infused the economy with massive amounts of government spending that the Depression subsided. With so many men away at war and every industry needed to power the "arsenal of democracy," labor shortages abounded. From manufacturing to railroads to agriculture, the United States required an influx of workers to help aid the war effort, including large groups of women and African Americans who were previously shut out of most industrial sectors.[43]

The availability of jobs helped precipitate the Second Great Migration among African Americans, with families relocating from the South to urban areas in the North and West. Mexican Americans already in the Midwest transitioned into industrial jobs. Tejanos still living in Texas and Puerto Ricans on the island looked to the urban North as a solution for their economic and social issues as well, triggering a large northward exodus among Latinos. On returning from war, the nation's Latino and African American veterans along with their families demanded a new social order that respected their wartime contributions and promised them equal opportunities for prosperity. After a brief lull, the nation underwent an economic boom as peacetime production of everything from cars to refrigerators kept production high and Americans employed. With persistent labor shortages, Michigan employers in both industry and agriculture tried to meet consumer demand by recruiting Mexican Americans from Texas.

However, Mexican Americans alone could not support the entire commercial farming industry in Michigan during and after World War II. Though farmers attracted over nine thousand Mexican Americans from Texas in 1943, they still relied on a small number of Japanese American internment camp workers; "Okies" from Oklahoma, Missouri, and Arkansas; and African Americans as well. Across Michigan, Mexican Americans comprised 40 percent of the agricultural labor force, but a noticeable decline in the migrant workforce caused growers to become concerned about impending labor shortages.[44] In anticipation, they turned to state-sponsored programs that sparked the migration of Mexican nationals and Puerto Ricans to Michigan.

Mexican nationals likely recognized the irony in U.S. agricultural companies calling for laborers in the 1940s. Just a few years earlier, repatriation campaigns led to the forcible exodus of Mexican nationals and their U.S.-born children, despite the fact that the latter were U.S. citizens. By 1942, the nation's desperate need of agricultural workers led to the passage of the Emergency Farm Labor Act, which enabled the Bracero Program. This bilateral agreement between the United States and a reluctant Mexico dictated that only Mexican men between the ages of eighteen and thirty-five could travel to the United States under six-month, renewable contracts. The program stipulated that workers would receive the standard prevailing wage for their work, access to housing, clean water, and cooking privileges or prepared meals, though there was little oversight to ensure these promises. Those necessities rarely, if ever, materialized.[45] The two countries envisioned the Bracero Program as a temporary measure to fix the labor shortage caused by the war. Growers became accustomed to paying low wages to farmworkers, and the program was continually renewed under different legislation until 1964. Mechanization efforts, a growing public outrage at the braceros' working conditions, and a looming free-trade zone near the Mexican-U.S. border combined to make the program less appealing.

That the Bracero Program impacted Michigan was an unintentional consequence. Compared to other states, Michigan had somewhat limited participation in the program. Braceros only made up about 14 percent of Michigan's seasonal farmworkers in the 1950s.[46] In comparison, they made up 27 percent of California's workforce, 37 percent of Arizona's, and 69 percent of New Mexico's.[47] The program's greatest impact on Michigan was likely in how it displaced Tejano farmworkers across the country, leading more Tejanos to seek work in Michigan. Initially, the Mexican government banned braceros from going to Texas due to the poor treatment they experienced there. Once that ban was lifted, Mexican braceros began to compete with Mexican Americans for jobs. Using the "standard prevailing wage" clause of Bracero Program contracts, employers paid Mexican workers less than Tejanos, a practice that undermined any sense of bargaining power among the latter group. The competition from braceros encouraged many Tejanos to migrate to meet their economic needs during World War II and in the postwar period. Displacement by braceros led many Tejanos to Michigan. Even with braceros and Tejanos in the fields in Michigan, growers worried they would still lack the workers needed to maintain the agricultural industry. They turned to Puerto Ricans to fill this gap.

"DESCRIBEN HORRORES EN CAMPOS DE MICHIGAN": PUERTO RICANS PATH TO MICHIGAN AND THEIR EXPERIENCES IN THE FIELDS

During World War II and the immediate postwar period, about 151,000 Puerto Ricans left the island in hopes of finding jobs on the mainland.[48] The War Manpower Commission (WMC), responsible for addressing the ongoing labor shortages, placed some of those Puerto Ricans in jobs stateside. Just as the Bracero Program ignited the migration of thousands of Mexicans to the United States, Operation Bootstrap and the WMC fueled the relocation of two thousand Puerto Ricans seeking industrial jobs across the United States, mainly on the East Coast.[49] The WMC sent Puerto Ricans to work for railroad companies, manufacturing plants, and food-packing companies like the Campbell Soup Company.[50] The direct industrial recruitment of Puerto Ricans to the mainland during World War II was minimal when compared to the migration that occurred after World War II. Between 1950 and 1960, out-migration of Puerto Ricans increased threefold from the decade prior, to 470,000 people.[51] Governmental agencies and agricultural recruiters collaborated to bring Puerto Ricans to fields throughout the northeastern and midwestern United States. While the ones who arrived in Michigan found horrifying labor conditions, their citizenship allowed them to seek other opportunities across the region and state, including Grand Rapids.

To manage the growing number of Puerto Ricans arriving on the mainland, in 1947 the Puerto Rican Bureau of Employment and Migration set up offices on the mainland that facilitated the growth of the Puerto Rican diaspora in the United

States. In response to the thousands of people leaving, those offices became the Migration Division, which helped Puerto Rican transplants settle. According to historian Virginia Sánchez-Korrol, the Migration Division's "primary responsibilities . . . [were the] organization and monitoring of the general migratory stream from Puerto Rico, including seasonal agricultural migration."[52] The Migration Division also worked with the U.S. Employment Services and the Puerto Rican government to match potential workers with industries suffering from labor shortages. Less than a year after the New York offices opened, the Puerto Rican government opened the Migration Division in Chicago. During the 1950s, more cities followed suit with branches of the division in Cleveland, Ohio; Hartford, Connecticut; Philadelphia; and Rochester, New York. Over the course of sixteen years, the Migration Division made, on average, over twenty thousand placements each year.[53]

Puerto Rican administrators on the island and on the mainland purposefully encouraged people to spread across the country. A rise in backlash against the number of Puerto Ricans who arrived in New York City prompted the administrators and the division to urge Puerto Ricans to go elsewhere.[54] "Nueva York no es la única ciudad" (New York is not the only city), stated one subheading in a brochure designed for migrants, informing its readers that Michigan, Illinois, Ohio, and California also boasted large Puerto Rican communities.[55] When migrants arrived at the Chicago Migration Division office, the administrators sent them to small towns and cities throughout Michigan, like Romeo and Zeeland, while the Farmworker Placement Program chose locations like Saginaw, Bay City, Caro, Bad Axe, and Dexter.[56] The majority of workers hoped to find jobs in manufacturing, but most were placed in agricultural jobs alongside Mexican Americans and other bracero workers during the late 1940s and 1950s.

Michigan companies recruited Puerto Ricans precisely because of a shortage of ethnic Mexican workers. By the spring of 1950, an urgent need emerged for the large-scale recruitment of workers in Michigan. Sugar beet growers' associations in Michigan worried about that year's crops, especially because a noticeable contingency of Mexican American workers had transitioned to industrial jobs. Max Henderson, secretary for Michigan Field Crops, worked with then Puerto Rican governor Luís Muñoz Marín to save Michigan's crops during the summer of 1950. Through a program the local press dubbed Operation Airlift, they contracted over five thousand Puerto Rican workers to fill the ongoing labor shortage in the sugar beet industry. Most of these laborers were men who forwarded their wages to their families in Puerto Rico. Within months of announcing Operation Airlift, Henderson and Muñoz Marín had succeeded in crafting a plan to harvest that year's sugar beet crop, with the unintended result that it had placed thousands of Puerto Ricans and Mexican Americans into contact with one another. Despite its early success, the program to recruit larger numbers of Puerto Ricans failed utterly within three months.

In June 1950, a plane crash served as a bad omen for what became a tumultuous summer for Puerto Rican workers in Michigan. Though labor migrants had been arriving since March, in June growers required more workers to block and thin the crops. In response, Michigan Field Crops contracted Eastern Airways to fly sixty-five Puerto Rican workers from San Juan, Puerto Rico, to Saginaw, Michigan, on a CW Commando—an aircraft previously used for military engagements, not commercial travel.[57] The plane went down over the Atlantic, killing twenty-eight of the sixty-five Puerto Rican passengers on board. Three survivors returned to Puerto Rico following the traumatic accident, but the remaining men traveled to Michigan via bus, illustrating how desperate for economic opportunity they were.[58] After an investigation into this incident, U.S. authorities installed more guidelines governing the flights from Puerto Rico to Michigan, including a requirement for mandatory stops midway through.[59] Puerto Ricans would continue to come to Michigan that summer, and the journey was only one of the challenges they would encounter.

As Mexicans had discovered through their participation in the Bracero Program, Puerto Ricans taking part in Operation Airlift encountered job instability, irregular compensation schedules, and generally inferior conditions. One Puerto Rican worker, Santos Cintrón, calculated his earnings for one paycheck at over $47, but discovered on payday that he owed the Michigan Sugar Company $9.69, purportedly for travel expenses and food.[60] Others reported similar deductions.[61] Reminiscent of complaints from Mexican braceros and Mexican American workers, Puerto Ricans insisted that employers exaggerated the travel and food advances.[62] The travel costs were exorbitant, the food was of poor quality, and the housing was subpar. *El Imparcial*, one of Puerto Rico's daily newspapers, ran a picture of Puerto Rican farm hands in Michigan with the headline, "Describen Horrores en Campos de Michigan" (They describe horrors in Michigan fields). The journalist likened the horrible conditions on Saginaw fields to "esclavitud en pleno siglo viente y bajo de la bandera norteamericana" (slavery in the middle of the twentieth century under the U.S. flag).[63] This comparison not only called attention to Michigan farmers' gross abuses of Puerto Ricans, but also the island and its residents' particular condition as colonial subjects of the United States.

Unbeknownst to the workers, planters tried to exploit Puerto Rican labor in other ways, usually by undercutting their hourly wages or by paying them on irregular schedules. The farmers calculated pay at a per-acre rate and often arranged to compensate the workers at the end of the season—practices that mirrored their exploitation of Mexican Americans, who worked in family units and were paid per acre. Using every member of their families ensured their collective survival. Many Puerto Rican workers described toiling in the fields for between ten and eleven hours each day, and calculated their projected earnings accordingly.[64] However, they soon realized that working as individuals, as opposed to working as part of a family unit like most Mexican Americans, meant they could only cover a small acreage, despite their long hours. For many, this arrangement failed to compensate for the sacrifice of migration.

But many workers refused to cower under the exploitative conditions set by the farmers and responded to the work contract in several ways. Some workers, like Lorenzo Ramírez, who had relocated to Grand Rapids after working in Saginaw, asked Governor Muñoz Marín to intercede on their behalf.[65] The governor sent Eulalio Torres to Saginaw to assist workers and farmers in amending the abusive work agreements. Other workers established alliances with Mexican Americans who had worked in the Saginaw fields for decades. For additional assistance, they looked to nearby Detroit, where they hoped the Catholic Church would help them address their labor issues.

Many of the Puerto Rican farmhands simply walked off their jobs since their U.S. citizenship allowed them easier access to alternative sources of employment than braceros or other foreign workers. At the end of the 1950 growing season, 80 percent of the contracted workers left Michigan.[66] Some tried to return to Puerto Rico, but the great majority looked for jobs elsewhere on the mainland. Like Mexican Americans, they pursued opportunities in Chicago, Cleveland, and other industrial cities. Others pursued farmwork in California, Colorado, New York, Ohio, and Illinois, while some even followed Tejanos back to Texas. Some of the men who stayed in Michigan relocated to Detroit or traveled across the state performing farmwork in small towns before eventually arriving in Grand Rapids in search of more prosperous job opportunities.[67]

"AT FIRST THEY WERE FARMWORKERS": FIFTY YEARS OF MEXICAN AND PUERTO RICAN MIGRATION TO GRAND RAPIDS, 1920–1970

Even though some Latino migrants came to Grand Rapids via rail lines and for manufacturing jobs, agricultural work connected Mexicans, Tejanos, and Puerto Ricans. The abundance of farms surrounding Grand Rapids drew many Mexicans and Puerto Ricans to the area. They engaged in a step migration pattern that included several temporary stops before arriving at a final destination. After leaving the east side of the state or from other migrant routes that traversed western and northern Michigan, the various, intersecting, and overlapping paths that Latinos forged brought them to Grand Rapids. They hoped to leave arduous fieldwork behind in exchange for higher-paying industrial labor.

Some of the earliest ethnic Mexicans to arrive in Saginaw quickly discovered that, just 130 miles away, Grand Rapids offered far greater prospects. Such was the case for Pedro López, whose arrest record when read against the grain reveals the migration route he undertook. Social service agencies in Grand Rapids that documented demographic information in the city in the early 1920s did not survey the small number of Mexicans in the area at the time. Thus, arrest records provide the most details about Grand Rapids' first Mexican settlers. The police first arrested López in San Antonio, Texas, for fighting, and then again in Saginaw two years later for larceny from a store. After he migrated to Grand Rapids that same year, police arrested him again for felonious assault.[68] While police departments created these records to document arrests, they reveal a common path migrants took to western Michigan—from Texas to Saginaw to Grand Rapids. The city's wide range of jobs attracted migrants searching for a better life.

Kent County, where Grand Rapids is situated, had many agricultural opportunities. Farms comprised about 63 percent of the land in the county. In the 1940s, about 190 small family farms dotted the rural landscape near Michigan's second largest city.[69] Unlike the east side of the state, where over ten thousand laborers worked on commercial farms, during the early 1940s, West Michigan received about three thousand Mexican American workers a year.[70] Many of those migrants in West Michigan would decide to settle there permanently.

This was the case of the Aguilar family, who regularly traveled to Michigan from Laredo, Texas. This Tejano family worked annually for a family farm in Hudsonville, Michigan, located about thirty miles outside of Grand Rapids. In 1948, the family matriarch, Juana Aguilar, refused to return to Texas in the open-air cab of a pick-up truck, as they had done every previous year. Instead, the family settled in Hudsonville and later in nearby Grand Rapids.[71] For Mexican Americans, Grand Rapids provided access to both industrial and agricultural jobs in the area. Staying there was often preferable to returning and working in their hometowns, where they might directly encounter the intertwined effects of both imperialism and racism.

Puerto Ricans also worked in various agricultural towns before finding higher-paying jobs in Grand Rapids. Juan and Rafael Pérez, who first arrived in Saginaw from Puerto Rico in the late 1940s, serve as an example. Unlike Puerto Ricans who migrated via the Farmworker Placement Program, the two men did not travel with a contract, though Operation Airlift likely inspired their decision to relocate to Michigan. After arriving in Saginaw, their friend Juan Báez, an Afro–Puerto Rican man from Río Grande, a municipality on the island's northern coast, joined their caravan through several Michigan agricultural towns one summer.[72] After leaving Saginaw, the Pérez brothers and Báez settled in Lake Odessa, Michigan, a town thirty-five miles east of Grand Rapids.

Although Latinos were poorly received in other Michigan cities, Lake Odessa offered relatively fair treatment as well as steady employment.[73] In the late 1940s and early 1950s, Puerto Ricans were just the latest group to work on Lake Odessa's fields and at their canning company. In World War II, large groups of Mexican Americans worked in the area along with Japanese prisoners of war, Jamaicans, and African American migrants from the South.[74] Juan Báez and the Pérez brothers formed a community with other Puerto Ricans, including distant relatives of the Pérez brothers; my grandfather Pío Fernández; and my great-uncle Marcial Hernández. To earn extra money while in Lake Odessa, the Pérez brothers started an informal restaurant in their shared kitchen to feed their friends and fellow farmworkers.[75] But the area could not provide the type of income these migrants desired to support their families.

Many of the men in West Michigan wanted to earn enough money to finance their family's relocation from Puerto Rico. My grandfather Pío, for example, had four children and a wife, Luisa, who remained behind in Aguas Buenas, Puerto Rico. To increase his earnings, he and Marcial relocated to Grand Rapids, where industrial jobs proved more plentiful than in Lake Odessa. Paco Sánchez was another Puerto Rican who moved from a rural area to find a higher-paying job. The Migration Division in New York sent him to the farming towns outside of Grand Rapids to pick cherries, onions, and apples in 1950. At one point, he was temporarily assigned to cook for other Puerto Rican field workers.[76] Like many Puerto Ricans and the Mexicans who came before them, Sánchez found that "at first they [Mexicans and Puerto Ricans] were farmworkers" before moving into other industries.[77] After toiling in the fields, he secured a position working on the railroads and later in a bakery, finally earning enough money to bring his family from Puerto Rico. His wife, Santa Sánchez; his sister-in law, Guadalupe Figueroa; and his brother-in-law, Leopoldo Figueroa—who joined him at the bakery—all moved to Grand Rapids in 1951.[78] Like Figueroa, other Puerto Ricans who came to Michigan after the 1950s bypassed the fields and went straight to cities like Grand Rapids to work in higher-paying, nonagricultural jobs based on the recommendations of friends and family.

"I DIDN'T WANT TO GO BACK TO TEXAS": A LATINO TRANSFORMATION OF MICHIGAN AND THE MIDWEST

Though the Farmworker Placement Program was a catastrophe on many accounts, Puerto Ricans consistently migrated to Michigan throughout the 1960s, though in significantly smaller numbers than came in the 1950s and than went to other places. The negative reputation of farmwork in Michigan and limited economic opportunities for Puerto Ricans likely deterred large numbers of Puerto Ricans from continuing to come en masse. The Farmworker Placement Program, how-ever, continued into the 1960s, sending large numbers of Puerto Ricans to places throughout the Northeast and a small number to Michigan. Despite Michigan's poor reputation as a place for Puerto Rican farmworkers, the desperate condi-tions on the island still led some to take their chances.

Subsequent generations of Mexicans and Mexican Americans continued to transform Michigan's demographic landscape. After World War II, some pur-sued industrial opportunities, but many Mexican Americans hoped that farm-work would provide secure and sustainable employment. The Arizola family, for instance, annually journeyed from Texas to Michigan well into the 1950s. Bernardino and Lucía Arizola, along with their eight children, became familiar with the yearly migration. As their children grew and married, they too joined the migrant circuit, though many of them eventually settled in Grand Rapids. By the 1970s, long-established migrant families had exited the fields, providing a window of opportunity for the next generation of Mexican and Mexican Ameri-can migrants intending to re-create a home in Michigan.

At present, farmers still rely on Latino labor, which helps to account for why farmwork has become increasingly associated with Latino immigrants and mi-grants. Mexican Americans have had a continuous presence in Michigan fields. Since the late 1980s, Mexican nationals have also come in increasing numbers to work in the state's agricultural industry. One Kent County administrator estimated that, in the mid-1980s, 50 percent of the area's Mexican workers were undocu-mented.[79] From the 1990s to the present, farmers have increasingly employed Central Americans. Michigan employers continue to recruit Puerto Ricans to this day. They remain subject to exploitation due to the ongoing colonial relationship between the United States and Puerto Rico. This allowed Oceana County farmers to recruit displaced Puerto Ricans in the wake of Hurricane María's devastation of the island in 2017.[80]

When Max Henderson and the growers he represented searched for workers to man their fields in 1948, they might not have imagined the profound ramifica-tions their recruitment would have on Michigan. Yet, the presence of Mexicans and Puerto Ricans in Michigan at mid-century and in the present is not mere happenstance. Instead, it was decades—even a century—in the making. U.S. imperial desires for land and resources also pulled people into its influence. The legacies of imperialism and racism then made it difficult for people to remain in Mexico, Texas, and Puerto Rico, though many did. Those who left hoped Michigan would offer them a respite from the unstable conditions at home. The recruitment campaigns aimed at Mexicans and Puerto Ricans placed them on a parallel and interdependent path toward Michigan and Grand Rapids. Their journeys not only brought them in direct contact with one another, but their migrations also showed them how similarly they were situated in the racial and ethnic hierarchies in the United States. Their shared experiences would serve as a basis for the pan-Latino solidarity that emerged soon after.

These movements drastically changed the demographic landscape of the Midwest. The need for workers and the dire economic conditions of the Depression spurred four major waves of immigration and migration during World War II and in the postwar period in the United States: African Americans from the South to the North; Mexican Americans engaged in the Tejano diaspora to the Midwest; Mexican nationals through a state-sponsored labor migration program; and Puerto Ricans who also participated in state-sponsored migration initiatives as well as those who traveled on their own.

Many migrants who came to Michigan hoped to make enough money to return home and live comfortably. But these migrants likely realized that returning home and remaining there was not a viable option. They then looked for ways to make Michigan their home. Others sought out West Michigan not just for its better economic opportunities but also for its improved social conditions. For instance, Guadalupe Vargas and her husband, Daniel, among the first Mexicans to settle in Grand Rapids, relocated to Michigan so their son, Magdaleno, would have a chance at a decent education once they settled off the migrant circuit. As many migrants soon realized, settling was not an easy process, but as Guadalupe said, "I didn't want to go back to Texas."[81] They met resistance in West Michigan, but they confronted it as part of a growing community, endeavoring to build better lives in the Midwest and to make Grand Rapids a livable space. Mexicans and Puerto Ricans leaned on their networks of family and each other, as chapter 2 illustrates.

– 2 –

Families Helped Each Other

In 1948, Eligio Castro and his wife, Elvira Flores, probably had to sneak into their home on Curve Street. At the time, the road, only a few blocks long, was all-white and occupied primarily by Dutch families. African Americans were excluded from this southwest neighborhood, but Castro and Flores—both Mexican Americans—reported Curve Street as their address when they baptized their son at the Cathedral of St. Andrew. Nevertheless, the Castro-Flores family soon disappeared from the 1948 city directory.[1] Perhaps the Castro-Flores family had only temporarily settled in Grand Rapids. They might have returned to their native Texas or the nearby fields with the approach of the new planting season. Or perhaps their neighbors protested their presence along what they wanted to remain an all-white street.[2]

However, ten years later, Julio and Marilyn Vega felt good about moving into that same house on Curve Street. Neighborhood dynamics had changed in the decade since Flores and Castro moved out. What was once an all-white street with a few Mexican Americans clandestinely living there slowly transformed into a more diverse area by the late 1950s. The Vegas' family friends, Rosa and Rafael Berríos, had already resided in the Curve Street home for two years. This provided assurance to Julio, who arrived from Puerto Rico in the early 1950s, and Marilyn, a Michigan native with both Black and white ancestry. Perhaps they too could make this house a home. Surely, their friendship with the Berríos family helped them to find this house and encouraged their decision to relocate there.[3]

Once Mexicans and Puerto Ricans arrived in Grand Rapids from the 1930s to the 1960s, they found a city that subscribed to a Black-white racial imaginary and the consequent segregation in housing and jobs. During this time, the Latino population in Grand Rapids grew, comprising about 5,000 of the total population of 175,000.[4] At the same time, the Second Great Migration was occurring. Tens of thousands of African Americans came to Grand Rapids, the seat of Kent County, for industrial jobs and to escape violence in the Jim Crow South; this increased the Black population in the county from 3,000 in 1930 to 14,630 by 1960.[5] Segregation in Grand Rapids became commonplace and more rigid in tandem with the growing population of Latinos and African Americans. Federal policies worsened the situation. The Federal Housing Administration (FHA) and the Home Owners Loan Corporation (HOLC) both worked to refinance mortgages and identified the parts of cities that would be labeled "desirable"—and thus eligible for investment.[6] Desirability, however, often used race as a metric, leaving Latinos and African Americans with limited housing options. Exclusively white suburbs formed in this period, and many Grand Rapids manufacturers moved their facilities outside the city limits, further impairing both housing and job opportunities. While Grand Rapids had a diverse economy, the safe, high-paying jobs went to few Latino and Black workers. As many of these new immigrants and migrants found, the process of finding and securing both jobs and housing for African Americans, Mexicans, and Puerto Ricans were intertwined, as so much depended on one's position within the local racial hierarchy.[7]

The process for Mexican and Puerto Rican families to settle in Grand Rapids often rested on women's unseen labor and children's contributions, as well. Though Mexican and Puerto Rican migration was often male-driven, migrants were able to settle because women accompanied them and found creative ways to contribute to the well-being of their families. Women had made progress in securing jobs during World War II, but many employers still regarded them as disposable labor. In Grand Rapids, Latinas accepted their status as temporary laborers, often on agricultural fields or produce packing plants. Over time, they transformed these positions into a viable means to support their families. Additionally, younger Mexicans and Puerto Ricans also began a long process of making space for themselves in Grand Rapids through their experiences in the school system and in helping to bolster the family economy. To make a place for Latinos in a racially segregated Grand Rapids required a broader community of support and contributions from all members of the family.

The first Mexican and Puerto Rican migrants to settle in Grand Rapids worked diligently to negotiate their position within the city's racial and social hierarchy by utilizing familial, ethnic, and interethnic networks and friendships to locate jobs and housing. Like many Latino immigrants and migrants to the Midwest, Mexicans and Puerto Ricans found that their proximity to either whiteness or Blackness determined their ability to access housing and suitable employment.[8] Mexicans and Puerto Ricans came into frequent contact with one another while navigating these racial dynamics in Grand Rapids. This built and reinforced networks and began the process of building pan-Latino solidarity. Thus, the period between the early 1940s and the late 1950s marked the beginning of a transition from the individual, albeit parallel and at times overlapping, journeys that Mexicans and Puerto Ricans pursued to come to Michigan to one of increasing interconnectivity and collaboration as Latino Grand Rapidians. Mexicans and Puerto Ricans faced challenges when encountering the Black-white racial binary in everyday life. However, as Guadalupe Vargas, part of a pioneering Mexican family in Grand Rapids, remarked about this period, "families helped each other."[9]

Grand Rapids' housing dynamics reveal that small urban areas share the same discriminatory trappings as larger cities. However, with fewer housing options available in this smaller city, people innovated to navigate housing segregation and settle in this area via kinship and friendship networks. The smaller population also allows for a thorough examination of racial identity among Latinos, especially as it pertains to the discrimination they faced in housing, revealing a more nuanced understanding of how racism functioned.

"MEDIUM COPPER, DARK CHESTNUT, AND SWARTHY": CONFRONTING A RACIAL DICHOTOMY IN GRAND RAPIDS

By the mid-twentieth century, the Black-white racial dichotomy had solidified around the country, leaving both Mexicans and Puerto Ricans at a disadvantage as a seemingly invisible minority. The presence of more African Americans in Grand Rapids alongside European immigrants and their descendants encouraged the latter group to grasp for ways to distance themselves from Black migrants. The easiest way forward was to claim whiteness, something few Mexicans or Puerto Ricans and even fewer African Americans could do with success. With this came certain privileges in Grand Rapids. For example, racial housing covenants indicated only "Caucasians" could live in particular homes. In adding language to a deed of a house that made stipulations about the sale of the house, covenants often prevented non-whites from purchasing homes in all-white neighborhoods. This allowed Polish, Italian, Dutch, Lithuanian, and a host of other European-descended peoples to claim that they were "Caucasian" or white. While their ethnic heritage could continue to play a positive role in their private lives, the divides between European ethnic groups became less and less prevalent in the public sphere. African Americans made up no more than 10 percent of Grand Rapids, and the State of Michigan had passed nondiscrimination laws in the early 1900s. Still, white Grand Rapidians throughout the first half of the twentieth century chose to enforce segregation with "colored" sections and entrances at local theaters and restaurants. A white admissions officer also barred an African American student from attending a local medical college.[10] When African

Americans launched lawsuits to challenge and overturn these practices in the early 1920s, informal segregation persisted. Though Mexicans and Puerto Ricans had experienced colorism—a system of preferential treatment for lighter skin within their own communities—what they encountered in Grand Rapids was different given the rigidity of the racial dichotomy in the city. Thus, the question arose as to where Mexicans and Puerto Ricans would fit in this Black-white binary. Centuries of colonization in Latin America and the U.S. system of racial hierarchies further obfuscated this complex issue.

Locally and nationally, Mexican Americans presented a unique case for racialization. The 1848 Treaty of Guadalupe Hidalgo rendered them legally "white." The treaty that ended the Mexican-American War stipulated that Mexicans living in the areas ceded to the United States could become U.S. citizens. The 1790 Naturalization Act, however, asserted that only free white people could be citizens of the United States, a law passed to prevent African Americans from becoming citizens. Thus, a law meant to keep freed Black people out of the democratic politic inadvertently made Mexican Americans—whose ancestry included Spanish, Indigenous, and African peoples—white. Mexican Americans' lived experiences revealed the contradiction in what Laura Gómez, scholar of Mexican Americans and race, refers to as being "legally white and socially non-white."[11]

Throughout the nineteenth and twentieth centuries, ethnic Mexicans' treatment under the law when they went to buy homes, find public accommodations, or marry interracially depended on class, gender, phenotype, language ability, the socioeconomic context of their locations, and their citizenship status. The politics around marriage provides an example of this treatment, since laws often forbade African Americans and whites from marrying each other. Mexican Americans complicated the system. Some Mexicans could marry whomever they pleased. Other Mexicans were barred from marrying interracially, depending on the context. The changing dynamics of intermarriage between white men and Mexican women illustrates this point. Before the Mexican-American War in the Southwest, intermarriage was scandalous, but it became more tolerable in the late nineteenth century. Not coincidentally, this practice gained acceptance as white men could gain access to land that Mexican families held through Mexican women.[12] However, in California in the 1950s, a Mexican woman, Andrea Pérez, and an African American man, Sylvester Davis, were blocked from getting a marriage license because Pérez listed her race as "white" and interracial marriage was not allowed.[13] California's contestation of the Pérez-Davis marriage harkened back to earlier attempts by the state to police sexuality and uphold the racial hierarchy by claiming to protect white women's purity against African American men.[14] Unlike California, Michigan repealed its antimiscegenation law in 1883. Thus, it was legal in Grand Rapids for Cecil San Miguel, a middle-class

Mexican man, to marry a white woman, Betty Parish, in 1949.[15] His status as a middle-class, lighter-skinned Mexican also made it socially acceptable for him to marry a white woman. Mexican Americans found that local context determined the fate of their challenges against segregation in both schools and juries.[16] The local racial dynamics, class divisions, skin color, and English-language abilities—among a plethora of other factors—determined when Mexicans were white or nonwhite.

Skin color, hair type, language, class, and gender determined the racial categorization of Mexican Americans in Grand Rapids against the backdrop of a Black-white binary. For example, lighter-skinned Mexican Americans' cultural differences could give them away as nonwhite, but white Grand Rapidians saw darker Mexican Americans with more Indigenous or African features as a clear Other. A lack of English-language skills or even just the presence of a Spanish accent represented a nonwhite cultural marker that also kept Mexicans from whiteness. Even if Mexicans were labeled "not white," white Grand Rapidians remained confused as to how to classify them. Jail records of Mexican Americans reveal the ways local white police officers tried to interpret the implications of Mexicans' status as socially nonwhite but legally white.[17]

The Grand Rapids Police Department's choice in how to categorize the race of Mexican arrestees illustrates how the presence of Mexicans complicated the polarized notion of race in the United States. From the 1920s to 1944, Grand Rapids police records listed both the color and the complexion of an arrested individual on a fingerprint card. "Color" equated to the period's social understandings of race.[18] While white offenders had a "white" color and "white" or "light" complexions, Mexican Americans had various combinations. In the case of Albert Aguirre, for instance, arresting officers described him as "light chocolate" in complexion but listed his color as "white." The fingerprint cards described other offenders as "Mexican" or "white" in color and for complexion they were marked as "Mexican," "medium copper," "light," "dark," "medium dark," "dark chestnut," "swarthy," and "white."[19] The practice of indicating Mexicans' color as "white" likely reflected that Mexicans were racially white in a legal sense, but their skin complexion signified an Otherness not forced on Europeans. Some Mexican men had one race listed on an arrest record from the 1930s and another race listed on documents in the 1940s, showing the difficulty in classifying Latinos under a Black-white dichotomy.[20] These imprecise classifications also reveal the weaknesses of socially constructed racial categories. The Grand Rapids Police were certain of one thing, however: Mexican Americans were not Black. They labeled African Americans as "Black" or "negro" in color and "dark brown," "medium brown" and "light brown" in complexion, indicating the different positions the two groups occupied in Grand Rapids' racial hierarchy.[21]

Mexican exclusion from an all-white fraternal lodge reaffirmed their position in limbo between white and nonwhite. In 1964, Miguel Navarro, a Mexican American migrant from Mercedes, Texas, and local business owner, applied for membership at the Moose Lodge, a local fraternal order, after a member invited him. Upon paying his ten-dollar application fee, Navarro recounted that he was denied admittance because "I was not considered as a Caucasian, [due to] my Mexican heritage." Disheartened, Navarro lamented that in this "All American City, such a thing could happen to me." This same exclusion happened to at least four other Mexican American men.[22] Despite any uncertainty about Mexican American's racial status, their treatment left little doubt: the neighbors, teachers, police officers, and white Grand Rapidians they encountered would view them as a nonwhite, not Black, foreign people and as part of an in-between group that should be denied access to the privileges possessed by white Grand Rapidians.

Similarly, white people in Michigan and around the country excluded from opportunities darker-skinned Puerto Ricans whose African ancestry was read via their physical features as well as those with brown skin tones that pointed toward multiraciality. Puerto Ricans responded by manipulating their understanding of race to carve out a place for themselves in the U.S. racial dichotomy. Puerto Ricans, who perceived race as a spectrum, found their race was determined on the mainland by the "one-drop rule"—wherein any African ancestry classified a person as "negro."[23] Facing employment discrimination during the Depression, Puerto Rican workers in New York felt the need to prove their U.S. citizenship to employers and tried to differentiate themselves from African Americans to avoid even worse treatment. In the 1930s, they began carrying identification cards when they searched for work to achieve these goals. Beyond citizenship information, the cards also listed the cardholder's complexion as determined by a local employment office staffed by elite Puerto Ricans. An examination of these IDs from the 1930s to the 1940s found that, in many instances, the complexion of the same Puerto Ricans became lighter over time. For example, in the 1930s, if someone were identified as "dark" in complexion, they would be listed as "fair" in the post–World War II period.[24] The complexion of these workers obviously did not actually change. Instead, Puerto Ricans used the malleability and constructionist nature of race to distance themselves from the pejorative treatment their African American counterparts faced, regardless of their shared features in some cases. For Puerto Ricans and Mexicans living in Michigan, their skin color and racial identification overlapped with and departed from the ideas of race they brought from their places of origin.

For Puerto Ricans with darker complexions, discrimination in Grand Rapids tended to arise from their skin color. Afro–Puerto Ricans who settled in Grand

Rapids remembered that whites called them the "n word."[25] Rubén Sánchez, the
son of some of the first Puerto Ricans to settle in the area, recalled hearing the slur
as a young boy looking for housing with his family in the 1950s. In the 1960s, Rosa
Collazo, a light-skinned woman with kinky, curly hair, remembered other schoolchildren calling her this in Grand Rapids.[26] The rigid categorizations disoriented
young Puerto Ricans trying to find their place in the city. Another Afro–Puerto
Rican put his experience in the greater context of U.S. race relations. Juan Báez,
one of the earliest Puerto Rican migrants to the area, recalled that the bigotry he
experienced was "not bad" in comparison to what his brother experienced after
migrating to Georgia. He felt his brother more directly experienced egregious
racism.[27] The search for housing, jobs, and youth experiences would demonstrate
where Mexicans and Puerto Ricans stood within the city's racial and social hierarchies. This societal structure also placed them into contact with one another
as they found their options similarly limited.

"IF YOU WERE DARK-SKINNED YOU COULDN'T GET AN APARTMENT": EXPANDING NETWORKS AND THE SEARCH FOR HOUSING

In the face of inequitable federal housing policies and a racially restrictive housing
market in Grand Rapids, Mexican Americans and Puerto Ricans formed coalitions to create and expand their networks. The FHA's and the HOLC's policies
often resulted in federally approved racial segregation in housing. While this
affected African Americans, Mexicans and Puerto Ricans also dealt with uncertainty when trying to shelter their families in Grand Rapids.[28] Unwilling landlords
and limited housing in the post–World War II era constrained their choices. The
challenges of securing homes often appeared insurmountable, but the willingness
of Latinos to collaborate sped up the process of placemaking in Grand Rapids.

Long before the Vega family heard that there might be a house for rent from one
of their connections, a small, industrial neighborhood about a half a mile away
from Curve Street held a diverse cross-section of Grand Rapids' poorest newcomers from Mexico, Texas, Europe, and the U.S. South. Friends and coworkers
probably relayed to fresh arrivals that there was affordable housing there. In the
late 1920s, the neighborhoods near Wealthy Street and Grandville Avenue abut-
ted the Pere Marquette Railroad Depot and industrial manufacturers. While the
Grandville Avenue area would become a hub of Latino life fifty years later, those
new arrivals in 1920s, while living close to their place of employment, likely heard
the constant hum of trains while breathing in fumes from burning coal, similar
to other Mexican migrants across the region.[29] In Grand Rapids' industrial areas,
African Americans who arrived during the First Great Migration from Alabama
or Mississippi lived in some of the city's most dilapidated housing next door to

Eastern Europeans who came in the late 1910s. Mexican nationals, mostly men, joined them in the mid-1920s.[30]

During this period, many bachelors lived as boarders in temporary housing with other Mexican families—or certainly near other Mexicans—and often near their place of work. Some of the first Mexican immigrants who decided to settle in Grand Rapids first found housing near the Cathedral of St. Andrew. For example, in 1936 brothers Louis and Rosendo Fernández reported living with two other men in a boardinghouse across from the cathedral.[31] All four men were railroad workers and lived only a ten-minute walk from their employers. If the men were Catholic, the cathedral would have been a familiar institution.[32] Others lived in homes on streets directly in front of the railroad tracks. Peter Cortez and Benino Tovar were two of those residents. They were listed as living at 315 and 307 King Court Southwest, respectively, and those addresses ended up being home to various Mexican men, women, and families during the 1930s.

Many of the areas Latinos lived in were redlined, or deemed ineligible for investment, and housing covenants did not allow them many alternative options. HOLC surveyors assigned areas a grade to describe the potential for investment and color-coded their investment security maps based on those ratings. They chose green for A ("best"), blue for B ("still desirable"), yellow for C ("definitely declining"), and red for D ("hazardous"). Federal administrators often denied investment to those areas in the failing grade, D, and deemed them an investment risk.[33] King Court, the street that many Mexicans called home, was not even included in the study. Its proximity to industrialized zones perhaps made it obvious that it would not be an area worthy of investment. The areas immediately surrounding the neighborhood scored a D grade for the type of inhabitants—"Negro" and Italian, specifically—and "age and obsolesce" of the areas. King Court shared many of those characteristics. There were few alternative options for quality housing for nonwhite people in this area in the 1930s and 1940s. Most of the areas in grade A in Grand Rapids were protected by racial covenants. "None of the said premises or any part thereof shall be occupied by any person not of the Caucasian race," read one such covenant.[34] There is ample evidence that African Americans in Grand Rapids encountered these covenants, but no records on Latinos challenging covenants. Perhaps the size of their small population did not put them into contact with these legal agreements.[35] However, as more and more Latinos descended on the southwest side in the late 1940s and early 1950s, white neighbors and neighborhoods had to decide where—if anywhere—exactly Latinos would fit.

Xenophobia and anti-Black racism informed the white resistance when Latinos tried to move into certain neighborhoods in Grand Rapids. In the 1950s, some working-class white families on the south side of Grand Rapids had the option of leaving for newly built suburbs. Many of those families were renting homes on the southwest side when mortgages became more affordable due to postwar housing policies.[36] Other families did not have the means or the desire to leave their neighborhoods within the city limits. Instead, white landlords and home-owners in Grand Rapids and around the country deemed their neighborhoods all-white spaces and protected them from any foreign or Black intrusion. Their resistance explicitly rested on the belief that foreigners and Black people dragged down housing values, but these homeowners also expressed their implicit racism. The FHA reaffirmed this mindset via its underwriting manual, which guided lenders throughout the 1930s and 1940s to loan money to potential occupants of a neighborhood only if they were of the same "social and racial classes" of exist-ing residents.[37] Some white people cloaked their refusal to rent or sell to those groups as a way to protect their monetary investments in their neighborhoods. When these methods failed to stop families of color from moving in, white resi-dents would pressure and harass their new neighbors.

Mexican Americans encountered opposition to their presence on the southwest side of Grand Rapids, but they were undeterred from seeking homes in the area. In 1957, Miguel Navarro, the same Mexican American who would be later denied entry into the Moose Lodge, earned enough money to buy his own home. Navarro approached a seller on Tulip Avenue, a couple of streets over from Curve Street, but the owner refused to sell to him. Only when Navarro sought the intercession of his previous employer, who was Dutch like the homeowner, did he agree to sell. Even then, Navarro said, his neighbors tried to create a petition to get him out of the neighborhood. Navarro and his family stayed in their new home, though his neighbors refused to acknowledge him for six or seven months.[38]

Other Mexican Americans reported similar treatment in the area. The Agui-lar family, who traveled from Laredo to Michigan for farmwork, moved into the Grandville Avenue area, about ten blocks away from Curve and Tulip Streets in the 1950s. One of the Aguilar children, Simon, understood that he and his fam-ily were unwelcome. He remembered speaking Spanish to one of his cousins at the grocery store below the Aguilars' home. After they started talking, the young woman cashier wondered aloud to another employee, as if the boys did not know English as well, if the Mexican teenagers were talking about them in Spanish. Aguilar sarcastically responded in English that she should "really not be so vain" and continued shopping.[39]

Afro–Puerto Ricans met more severe discriminatory behavior than the snide comments and discomfort directed at Mexican Americans. For example, Paco and Santa Sánchez were turned away from numerous homes when they first arrived in the early 1950s. Paco and Santa were Afro–Puerto Rican and could easily be taken for African Americans. Their son, Rubén, later recalled going to look for houses only to be told, "we don't rent to n-----s."[40] This was not surprising given that as late as 1967, a survey of whether or not people would rent to "negroes" in Grand Rapids found that only 30 percent would. Some of the landlords contacted told the surveyors a flat-out "no," while others blamed it on their white tenants or suggested that African Americans rent in other neighborhoods where they would be "more comfortable."[41] Limited options meant that Puerto Ricans had to be creative in securing housing.

My paternal grandmother's experience reflected how Puerto Ricans dealt with anti-Black racism when trying to secure housing. Her husband and children's physical appearance reflected a range of Indigenous, Spanish, and African ancestries, so when my grandparents went to look for an apartment, my light-skinned grandmother went with her light-skinned brother instead of her husband—who might have been read as Black—and only her children with lighter skin. During their outings to look for housing, she let her brother, who spoke English, talk with the prospective landlords. Echoing the Sánchez's experience, she remembered that if you were "dark-skinned, you couldn't get an apartment" on Grandville Avenue.[42] Using her ability to pass as white, she spearheaded her family's attempts to secure housing in Grand Rapids. Once they found a home, my grandparents formed a pattern of securing an apartment and sneaking in until they were discovered. They endured this performance for about a year until they eventually purchased a home.[43] For Afro–Puerto Ricans, it was clear: landlords and would-be sellers concluded that these families might not be African American, but they were still Black and foreign under Grand Rapids' Black-white dichotomy. Ultimately, whites viewed them as undesirable neighbors.

With these challenges, Mexicans and Puerto Ricans found ways to help each other find housing and settle in Grand Rapids. For example, the easiest way to know if one's family would be welcomed was to check the houses around the available rental. A few of the first Mexican leaders in the area helped to facilitate this process. Daniel Vásquez and Daniel Vargas, who arrived in the late 1920s and early 1940s, respectively, could be counted on to take new migrants around to find housing. Daniel Vargas's daughter, Virginia, remembered that for some migrants, the first stop in this quest was the home of already-settled Mexican families: "a lot of times they would bring families to the house and feed them" first and let the newcomers stay with them for a couple of days before looking for housing.[44] As for Vásquez, he likely learned these strategies while first helping his family settle. He and his wife, Consuelo, had helped to find her brothers a house to rent. In 1941, the Vásquezes owned a home at 566 Sheldon Avenue. By 1946, the year Consuelo's brothers moved to Grand Rapids, all three of them—Elías, Narciso, and Cecil—lived at 569 Sheldon, a few houses away.[45]

Mexican couples also helped Puerto Ricans when they first arrived, in a show of burgeoning pan-Latino solidarity. Some members of these groups had a history of working with one another on agricultural fields. By the 1950s, some Mexicans and Puerto Ricans had started to intermarry. Mexicans and Puerto Ricans whose journeys to Michigan did not intersect quickly grew accustomed to each other as they worked in the same industries and often came into close contact. Their willingness to help one another and see each other as social equals nurtured the creation of a pan-Latino solidarity.

Anti-Black racism in housing led some of the earliest Mexican settlers to help Puerto Rican migrants. For example, Gregorio and Aurora Chávez, Mexican Americans from Texas, housed Paco and Santa Sánchez after they could not find housing because they were Afro–Puerto Ricans. In the early 1950s, the Chávez family was extremely helpful to the Sánchezes. According to Rubén Sánchez, most of the Chávez children had left the home by the time the Sánchezes arrived in Grand Rapids, which created space for his parents and siblings to sleep in the living room.[46] Mexican American assistance helped Puerto Ricans settle, and it had emerged as an act of solidarity against racist housing restrictions. These acts also helped cultivate pan-Latino solidarity by literally bringing Mexicans and Puerto Ricans under one roof. The first wave of Puerto Ricans then went on to help the next Puerto Ricans secure housing in Grand Rapids.

The help Puerto Ricans offered to one another illustrates the continued role that familial and friendship networks played when surviving in a new city. To afford the rent, these migrants utilized a common strategy of doubling up, popular among a variety of communities in the post–World War II era.[47] For example, Dionisio Berríos and his wife, Carmen, moved into a house in 1954.[48] By 1955, Carmen's sister, Irene Agosto, moved in with them.[49] Just two years later, Irene married Dionisio's brother, Mateo, and the two couples lived together until they could find and afford separate housing. With limited social connections on arriving in the area, doubling up meant that these migrants had the emotional and financial support they needed to rebuild their lives.

Just as the early Mexican community had homes for area bachelors in the 1920s, Puerto Ricans did the same when they arrived some thirty years later. Ringuette Court Southeast provided a home to many roving bachelors who settled in the city before finding their own place. Before moving to Curve Street, Julio Vega lived at 813 Ringuette, a small home in an alleyway near the intersection of Division and Franklin.[50] Later, after Julio married, José Ramos, a distant relative of Julio, continued to live there for a couple of years. When Ramos moved out, other Puerto Ricans took over the home. Other Latinos came to this same neighborhood as well. Just next door, at 809 Ringuette, Pedro "Pete" and Cruzita Gómez, a Puerto

Rican and Mexican couple who came from East Chicago, Indiana, moved in.[51] Eventually, my paternal grandfather also resided there. Pío Fernández's family of six briefly lived at the house on Ringuette, and soon after, his brother-in-law Marcial Hernández moved his family into the home.[52] These stories indicate the housing market's paucity for Puerto Ricans. Migrants sought houses where they could be sure the owner would rent to them, using as evidence the presence of previous Puerto Rican tenants. This treatment reinforced the bonds within the Puerto Rican community because Puerto Rican families had to rely on and support each other to make this constant shuffle between homes work.

This constant mobility also represented a strategy Puerto Ricans used to make ends meet. "[We] moved because the house was too big for me and the bills were high. They were hard to pay," my grandmother, Luisa Fernández, recalled during an interview.[53] She also remembered moving a lot because the landlord was "going to sell [the house]"—indicating the changing neighborhood dynamic. The shifting racial demographics in those neighborhoods and the availability of suburban housing could have encouraged her white landlord to abandon the area. This instability pushed many migrants to attempt to purchase their own homes in the southeast side when they could. Until then, they relied on the community to help find housing that they could obtain.

"I CALLED MY BROTHER AND TOLD HIM HE COULD WORK HERE": FRIENDSHIP, FAMILIAL CONNECTIONS, AND THE QUEST FOR STABLE EMPLOYMENT

Familial connections and friendships helped Mexicans and Puerto Ricans navigate discrimination when searching for jobs in Grand Rapids. For most Grand Rapidians, jobs were in abundance. A study on postwar economies suggests that Grand Rapids fared well during the Depression and during World War II because of its diversified economy as compared to other Rust Belt Midwest cities, which may have had only one or two major employers.[54] The report concluded that "industrial stability was more pronounced, employment was more diversified, and the general level of civic welfare was appreciably higher."[55] Postwar economic demands, Grand Rapids' diverse economy, and the burgeoning suburban economic development allowed business owners to thrive in the city. However, Mexicans and Puerto Ricans learned the availability of certain opportunities depended on one's race, ethnicity, and especially gender. Time of arrival also factored into how successful people were in finding high-paying, secure jobs. The railroad industry, manufacturing factories, bakeries, and commercial nurseries employed most of these newcomers. Some still used agricultural work to supplement their incomes in Grand Rapids as deindustrialization began and temporary layoffs became more regular. Recently settled migrants benefited from the wide variety of different jobs along with familial connections and friend networks.

As chapter 1 details, Santos Rincones started working on railroads after a friend told him about job openings, like many Mexican men who settled in Grand Rapids. Rincones quickly began making more money than he had on agricultural fields. It only took him one day after arriving in Michigan to obtain a position working for the C&O Railroad. He laid spikes with a segregated work crew that separated whites and "coloreds" (African Americans and Mexicans), an action that reified the Black-white racial binary in the city.[56] His increased pay hardly offset the long hours and arduous work. Other Mexican workers reported that unions refused to train them for more technical jobs. This discrimination trapped Mexican railroad workers in the dirtiest, most dangerous, and low-paying jobs. Santos worked there for two years before looking for a manufacturing job that he hoped would pay more and have better working conditions.

Some of the earliest Mexican Americans to arrive in Grand Rapids found that, when one person got into a manufacturing job, it was usually easier to get other people into it. For example, Daniel Vargas, one of the community founders, started working for JC Miller Company, which specialized in making and selling welding equipment, in the late 1930s. He and the owner, J. C. Miller, built such rapport that Miller asked him to recruit others from his hometown of Crystal City.[57] Vargas recalled, "I called my brother and told him he could work here." Vargas ended up recruiting his brother and nineteen other workers for Miller's Grand Rapids operation. In another instance, Santos Rincones's wife, Juanita Rincones, arrived in Grand Rapids in the late 1940s with her family, and within weeks her father, mother, and cousins were working at the Wolverine Metals plant.[58] About three-fourths of Mexican American men worked in some type of manufacturing industry by the mid-1940s. They served as die casters, sanders, machine operators, and general laborers for Kent Castings, American Seating Company, Mueller Furniture Company, Grand Rapids Brass Company, and American Excelsior, among other employers.[59] The jobs once reserved for native whites and European immigrants finally became available to Mexican Americans in the postwar era.

Like Mexican Americans, the first Puerto Ricans to arrive in Grand Rapids netted the best employment prospects when relying upon recommendations from their friends. Dionisio Berríos, from Caguas, Puerto Rico, was one of few Latinos to obtain a job at General Motors. In the early 1930s, General Motors's Fisher Body Stamping Plant opened in Wyoming, a southwestern suburb of Grand Rapids, along with a few other manufacturing plants. These businesses helped the suburb develop rapidly. However, not many Latinos worked at Fisher. In 1955, Berríos's military experience, two years of GI Bill–funded college, and command of English secured him this position. A year later, he helped get his friend Julio Vega into GM as well.[60] However, Berríos and Vega were exceptions. In the 1950s, most Mexican and Puerto Rican men worked in industries other than auto manufacturing in Grand Rapids. Thus, Berríos and Vega held highly desired but not universally available jobs.

While they made up a small workforce of auto manufacturers, a network of Mexicans and Puerto Ricans supported each other when finding jobs in local commercial bakeries. Local wholesalers Michigan Bakery and Peter Wheat Bakery were located within a mile of the neighborhoods where Mexicans and Puerto Ricans lived. Divisions of national companies like Keebler and Sara Lee operated a little farther away from the city's center. In the mid-1940s, about 10 percent of all Spanish-surnamed Grand Rapidians—mostly Mexican Americans at the time—worked for bakeries. In the 1950s, many of the earliest arriving Puerto Rican newcomers also found employment in Michigan bakeries. Juan Báez, one of a group of Puerto Rican men to arrive in Grand Rapids in the late 1940s, immediately procured a job at Michigan Bakery. The presence of Mexican American workers at Michigan Bakery likely signaled to Báez and others that the company would hire Spanish speakers.

As family members traveled from Puerto Rico to reunite with their fathers and brothers who settled in Grand Rapids first, they too helped one another find jobs in this area of the food industry. Brothers, cousins, and friends from back home often worked together at the same bakeries. For example, my paternal grandfather, Pío Fernández, and my grandmother's uncle, Rafael Pérez, both worked at Peter Wheat Bakery.[61] Nicolas Escribano, a Puerto Rican former farmworker and a cousin of Rafael Pérez, also quickly found a position there after leaving the fields in 1965.[62] Bakeries had various skilled positions, training some employees to use the mixing equipment and assigning others to prep ingredients for mixing. They also needed janitorial staff. For Mexican and Puerto Rican employees without the English-language skills needed to perform more technical jobs, employment as a janitor at the bakeries allowed them to work with their friends and relatives.

Because bakeries did not often undergo job market fluctuations from deindustrialization, they often provided people with long careers. Juan Báez provided for his family of five with his bakery job. His stable position turned into a career, finally retiring after forty-two years at Michigan Bakery and its subsidiaries.[63] After finally leaving the railroads, Santos Rincones went to work for Keebler, where he remained for thirty-four years—twenty-four of those years as an assistant mixer. He managed this feat while being illiterate in English and Spanish. Instead, he employed another skill: memorization. He committed to memory all the recipes and lists of ingredients for various cookies. "No one knew he couldn't read except for the boss," his wife remembered.[64] Though bakeries were not a booming industry in the postwar era across the country, they gave people like Báez and Rincones access to stable employment. Through friendships and previous work experiences, Mexican and Puerto Rican men who arrived in the 1940s and 1950s found jobs that helped their families settle in Grand Rapids.

"PORQUE ELLA EMPEZÓ A TRABAJAR, TODOS . . . TRABAJAMOS ALLÍ": SECURING WORK FOR WOMEN IN GRAND RAPIDS

As Latino men carved out a niche for themselves in the economic landscape, women also leaned on their networks to help them secure opportunities. Gender roles for Latinas in the 1950s dictated that their social networks consisted primarily of other women and family members. These relationships proved important to survival. The work women did also fell under gendered expectations. They were employed in industries where they would work alongside other women and were often paid wages that would contribute to household finances but were insufficient to support a family. The women who obtained industrial or high-paying work likely owed it to the familial and fictive kinship networks they maintained.

Most Mexican and Puerto Rican women, including those with formal education, in this era had few job options when they first arrived. Trainings, certifications, and degrees did not ensure that women would find success. Clerical jobs were out of reach to many Mexican and Puerto Rican women before and immediately after the war. For example, Juanita Baltierrez had taken typing and shorthand in Chicago before she moved to Grand Rapids with her father in the 1950s, but Michigan businesses would not hire her.[65] Instead, Latinas often found work as domestics and laundresses, and cared for their children and those of others in their homes. Guadalupe Vargas—whose husband, Daniel, recruited workers from Texas to work at JC Miller—cleaned houses for forty cents a day in the 1940s. She recalled that she "used to wash and iron, clean windows," for that sum, and occasionally her employer paid her bus fare.[66] Latinas were not alone. Black women in Grand Rapids could not use the skills and academic degrees they brought with them to Grand Rapids, either. Laverne Davis, a Black woman whose mother came from Chicago after she married a man originally from Baldwin, Michigan, remembered watching her frustrated mother struggle to find employment as a teacher because of a city's reluctance to hire Black women as teachers in the 1940s.[67] Such labor constraints made it particularly hard for single women in the city, many of whom were relying on support payments from the father of their children. For example, Juanita Bueno was just one of many women who petitioned the courts multiple times for child support from her husband, who was not financially supporting his family.[68] Instead, many women, married or not, had to pool their wages with other members of their household, demonstrating how community networks facilitated the settlement of Latinos in Michigan.

Occasionally, some of the industries that employed Latino men also hired women, but this was usually based on familial connections. After Juanita Baltierrez could not find anyone to hire her for clerical work, she joined her father, Anastasio Rodríguez, at Michigan Bakery. The company had recruited him from his mixing job at Silver Cup Bakery in Chicago. A widower, Rodríguez moved his four children, including Juanita, and two brothers to Grand Rapids with him. Her father's position at Michigan Bakery meant that Juanita could find employment there as a mixer's helper, but not all women had access to these connections through male relatives and friends.

The Berríos and Agosto women show that a few women made their own connections without male support. Irene Agosto, whose extended family had come to Grand Rapids, first found a job at Ajax Aluminum, which produced aluminum storm windows and doors during the early 1950s. The small company was close to her house. After she began there, so too did her sister, Carmen Berríos, and her sister-in-law, Rosa Berríos. As Carmen Berríos later recounted, "porque ella empezó a trabajar, todos los Berríos trabajamos allí" (since she found work there, all the Berríos family worked there).[69] Having started as general laborers, the women within three years had advanced to more technical positions. Carmen's work as a screener involved cutting aluminum and fitting mesh screen to storm doors, and Rosa worked as a glasscutter.[70] While Juanita Baltierrez's father had helped her get a job at a bakery, Carmen actually helped her husband, Dionisio, find a position at Ajax when he was on a temporary layoff at GM.[71] In the 1950s, five of Ajax's thirty employees belonged to the same extended Puerto Rican family. While it was common for Mexican women to work alongside female family members during World War II, the Berríos family shows the importance of familial networks in securing employment in the postwar period.[72] The Berríos and Agosto women exemplify the ways women relied on one another to contribute to their families' economic survival.

By the mid- to late 1950s, women had a much easier time finding employment, signaling a major shift in the economy and the status of women workers. For example, after being widowed with children in 1959, Juanita Baltierrez needed higher-paying work than the bakery could provide. A friend knew someone at Lear Siegler, which made products for airplanes among other industrial materials. Though she was hired as a temporary worker on the assembly line, she parlayed that ninety-day assignment into a twenty-year career.[73] The job Juanita landed was highly coveted, so much so that Lila García, a Mexican American teenager, lied about her age to be hired at a similar factory during the 1950s and early 1960s. Lila made it two weeks before the other women, both Latina and white, discovered the lie and turned her into the boss.[74]

For women like Lila García who were unable to access industrial work, semi-agricultural jobs in commercial nurseries provided opportunities for women to contribute directly to their family economies. Both the retail sale and wholesale of flowers in commercial nurseries supported the gardening and landscaping industries. Neither entirely industrialized nor agricultural, commercial nurseries represented various labor sectors. Latinas employed in this industry worked directly with agricultural produce but did not pick and harvest as they did in the fields. Instead, commercial nurseries hired them to pack flowers, which combined skill sets that many Latinas had gained in other work experiences. Handling fresh flowers necessitated a delicate touch so as not to damage the flowers, just as how agricultural workers handled Honeycrisp apples—one of the most delicate varieties—every fall on local fields. Packaging flowers was also part of a routinized labor system that also would have resembled assembly lines in factories.

Employers might have sought women, in general, for such work to keep wages low and because of gendered assumptions about women's deservedness of wages. To keep profits high, many companies paid women low wages based on the erroneous but convenient wage system concept that women merely contributed to their families but were not the primary breadwinners. Employers' heteronormative assumptions imagined women's wages as available to support those of their husbands, fathers, and brothers.[75] However, many women were looking for work to provide for their children or parents independently, while many others simply wanted, or needed, to provide for themselves. For example, after being fired from her factory job, Lila García moved on to a commercial nursery in search of a way to live on her own. At Molesta Floral, she found gendered and racialized divisions of labor. She recalled that almost exclusively women worked with her at Molesta Floral. This was not uncommon. In agricultural packing plants, employers assumed that women's smaller hands would be nimbler and gentler than their male counterparts, facilitating packing.[76] However, she also stated that, while white women worked in the front of the shop, Latinas and a few Mexican and Puerto Rican men at the shop had few direct interactions with customers. They instead provided labor that was both often invisible to consumers and more strenuous.[77] As elsewhere, labor segmentation based on gender, race, and ethnic identity was abundant in this industry.

Produce packing, another semi-agricultural industry, attracted Latinas primarily because they were familiar with produce and because packinghouses were accessible. While many of the commercial nurseries had facilities within the city limits, packing plants were usually located outside of the city. Nevertheless, Grand Rapids' proximity to productive farms caused this type of industry to flourish and made it possible for Latinas to work there. The construction of highways in the 1950s and the short distance from the city to farms allowed Latinas to commute daily to packing plants in rural areas. Husbands and teenage children would support their mothers by driving them to their jobs, since many newly arriving women did not have licenses. María Zambrana, who previously lived in New York and Florida, recalled how her neighbor—a fellow Puerto Rican and my grandmother Luisa Fernández—helped her get a job packing celery in Borculo, Michigan. Along with a couple of other women, María and Luisa traveled together to their jobs with family members taking turns to pick them up and drop them off. While male networks helped bring Mexicans and Puerto Ricans to Grand Rapids, women established separate connections to access job opportunities.[78]

"WHEN I WAS ELEVEN, I WAS WORKING SEVEN-TO-EIGHTEEN-HOUR DAYS": THE FAMILY ECONOMY—CHILDREN AND MOTHERS MAKING ENDS MEET

Most families faced the harsh reality that they did not make enough money to make ends meet. By the late 1950s, the high-paying jobs in Grand Rapids that drew the earliest Mexican and Puerto Rican migrants were not always available to their relatives and friends who arrived later. Though Grand Rapids' economy continued to grow, many of these companies simply did not open high-paying positions to Latinos or African Americans. Thus, many Mexicans and Puerto Ricans needed to combine work in various industries or require every member of the family to financially contribute if they hoped to stay in Michigan.

Mexicans and Puerto Ricans of all ages took to the fields to earn much-needed money, sometimes years after the family unit had transitioned off the migrant trail and into industrial jobs. When lay-offs occurred, many of these families chose to stay rather than seek other locales with more job options. Some of them had bought homes in the area and enrolled their children in the local schools, and were reluctant to uproot themselves again. Many families that decided to stay found ways for everyone to contribute. The city's proximity to agricultural areas meant that Mexicans and Puerto Ricans could make extra money on farms without having to return to the migrant trail. They could have shared information from the community and regional knowledge to determine which farmers paid the most. Their relationships with local farmers also may have helped them access these contracts as well.

On weekends, school vacations, or during layoffs, men, women, teenagers, and children ventured into Grand Rapids' rural periphery to balance the shortfalls in their budgets. Rafael Hernández, whose parents met in the fields of Lake Odessa, Michigan, after migrating from Texas and Puerto Rico in the early 1950s, remembered how he and his cousins would drive thirty miles outside of Grand Rapids to pick celery, onions, and whatever else needed harvesting before returning home at the end of the day in the 1960s and 1970s.[79] My Puerto Rican aunt,

Rosalía Espíndola, also worked on farms with her siblings. "When I was eleven, I was working seven-to-eighteen-hour days," she explained, to help pay for her Catholic school tuition and uniform. After she had repeated bouts with sun poisoning, a doctor recommended she not return to field work.[80] In another instance, while trying to enjoy his summer breaks, José Flores recalled working alongside his Tejano cousins when the migrant circuit brought them to Michigan.[81] Even when people were long settled, they knew that the fields could provide a backup. Miguel Navarro, who owned a home and eventually a business, used the fields to fill in for his lost wages during a layoff.[82] For many families, these outings made the difference between them having to give up their lives in Michigan, either to return home or join the migrant trail.

While Grand Rapids was close enough to the fields that people could go there and back in a day, sometimes families went a bit farther away and stayed outside the city for weeks at a time. While men worked in the city, it was often their wives who headed up these temporary households in agricultural areas. Moreover, these women without formal educations nevertheless possessed the math skills to manage not only day-to-day expenses but also their family's long-term economic futures. José Flores recalled that his mother was the one who calculated the family's annual budget.[83] From the cost of school clothes and food, his mother knew exactly how many pounds of blueberries her kids had to pick to ensure that their needs would be met for the year. Lila García's mother performed a similar role. Lila, who would go on to work at Molesta Floral, spent her summers as a kid and teenager on the fields in Grant, Michigan, with her mother and siblings. Her mother packed a few household items to make their meager migrant housing more livable for her and her daughters.[84] Women played an integral role in ensuring this summer and weekend work was worth it. Through using all the networks at their disposal, Mexicans and Puerto Ricans found multiple ways to scratch out a living while working alongside one another in Grand Rapids.

"I WAS OTHER": YOUTH EXPERIENCES IN GRAND RAPIDS

Due to the instability in work and existing outside the Black-white racial dichotomy, Mexican and Puerto Rican children in Grand Rapids often felt as if they did not belong. They also grew up with an awareness of their precarious financial situation in Grand Rapids and how different they were from other children. In particular, the requirement that students speak only English in school formed a separation between the first generation of young Latinos in Grand Rapids and their culture. Young people perceived their classmates' judgment and felt ashamed of their ethnic identity, making later placemaking efforts even more important.

Summers and school breaks in the fields had a profound effect on Latino children in Grand Rapids. For example, as children Lila García and José Flores often experienced poverty in two settings: rural migrant housing and blighted neighborhoods in urban Grand Rapids. For Lila, the near-constant dislocation and finding low wages in both locations led to her dropping out of school at sixteen. Her search for high-paying jobs ended in her early twenties when she and her husband were hired in 1965 at General Motors in nearby Lansing. José Flores, on the other hand, channeled his frustration with his economic position into motivation. He finished high school, then college, and eventually completed a doctorate in education. He not only became one of few Latino high school teachers in the area, but he also emerged as one of few Latinos to attain a position of leadership on the Grand Rapids Board of Education. Having neither a completely urban nor rural childhood provided Latino youths with a distinctive life experience.[85]

In addition to shifting between urban and rural spaces, Latino children in the 1940s and 1950s also lived outside of the Black-white binary, much like their parents did. In the early 1950s, nonwhite students constituted only 6 percent of the local school district.[86] Latino youths bore the weight of discrimination on two fronts equally: for their skin color and their language abilities. In Grand Rapids, as elsewhere, public schools in the postwar era fixated on assimilating the children of migrants and immigrants. English immersion—forcing Spanish-speaking students not only to learn but also to use only English—served as the prevailing pedagogical strategy for English-language learners. Educators thought this would accelerate the process of learning a language. In reality, students would miss important content and feel isolated and ostracized. Irma García (later Irma Aguilar), whose Mexican American family migrated from San Antonio to Chicago to Saginaw and finally settled in Grand Rapids in the 1940s, remembered the two years she spent in the third grade, as she mastered what "sounded like gibberish" at Madison Park Elementary School.[87] While she was eventually successful in school, other families recalled the damage that English immersion did to their children's ability to retain Spanish. Juanita Baltierrez, who came from Chicago to Grand Rapids as a teenager, recounted that in "those years, they didn't want you to speak Spanish to your children because they thought when they went to school, they would have problems, so as a result none of our children speak Spanish."[88] Without the ability to speak Spanish, many Latino children became disconnected from their culture and yet still distant from mainstream American culture.

English immersion created isolating experiences. Mexican and Puerto Rican children did not always live near one another and therefore did not attend the same schools. My aunt, Rosalía Espíndola, was eleven when my grandparents moved their family from Caguas, Puerto Rico, to Grand Rapids. Her first memories of the local school system traumatized her. As she recalled, she appeared to be so lonely that her teacher permitted Miguel, her younger brother, who was not yet of school age, to join the class so that she could talk to someone during breaks. What's more, a lack of communication commonly resulted in physical confrontations with classmates.[89] Other migrants recounted similar instances of isolation and confusion as they navigated new social hierarchies. For many students, this was the first time they attended a school with white children, Black children, or both.

Many of these young Mexicans and Puerto Ricans engaged with ideas of being American and of citizenship while trying to understand the connections between race and belonging. Irma García said of her time in Grand Rapids Public Schools: "Life was a struggle, life was hard. I was not white. I was not Black. I was Other . . . and in school, minority was the Other, and even going into [high school] that meant there was only about ten, fifteen friends that you had . . . so it was difficult. There was a lot of parents that would not allow anybody to play with somebody as dark as you."[90] The Other experience truly isolated her and many other Mexicans and Puerto Ricans who were neither light enough to be categorized as white or dark enough to be Black. Puerto Ricans that whites perceived to be African American had different experiences. Rubén Sánchez was about eight when he first came to Grand Rapids with his family. He knew that the housing discrimination his family encountered was related to his skin color, but the harassment in school came from both his language and his Blackness. Whites rejected him because of the darkness of his skin, and African Americans dismissed him because he spoke Spanish rather than English. Irma, Rubén, and other Mexican and Puerto Rican children did not fit into the notion of a "Black and white" Grand Rapids—and they encountered a backlash for confusing the social hierarchy.

Culture, including food, also factored into how young people adjusted to Grand Rapids. Young Latinos often faced challenges when trying to show that they belonged in their neighborhoods and in their schools. Bringing lunches with food that was different from their white and Black classmates' lunches generated feelings of shame or embarrassment. Irma García stated: "Our lunches might have consisted of tortillas with some leftover meat or something and rolled up in a Butternut Bread wrapper . . . then you would get to lunch and put [the tortilla] under the table because tortillas were not known then, so everybody would look at you like 'what are you eating?'"[91] She specifically mentioned Butternut Bread, a national brand with a regional bakery in Grand Rapids. To Michigan-raised Irma, carrying lunch in a Butternut Bread wrapper symbolized that she belonged in her Grand Rapids classroom regardless of the ethnically distinctive food inside. Navigating these feelings of belonging and discrimination made the transition to

Michigan difficult for adults and children—both felt the difference in their daily actions. These feelings of not belonging eventually helped Mexican and Puerto Rican children bond. They and their parents would find ways to make space for themselves in the racial and social fabric of Grand Rapids.

MAKING HOME AND SETTLING IN GRAND RAPIDS

Curve Street had morphed into a Latino street by the end of the 1960s. Grandville Avenue, the major corridor in southwestern Grand Rapids, had grown into a neighborhood shared between Latinos, African Americans, and some white families. While many Black residents were segregated into the southeast side, some Latinos lived alongside them there as well. By the 1970s, increases in immigration and migration reinforced that Latinos—as an ethnic group—were categorically nonwhite in terms of their treatment by civil authorities and other social groups. Regardless of their racial identification, by this period many saw themselves as ethnically Latino, as the next chapter discusses.

What started as a slow process of neighborhood transformation from previously all-white neighborhoods, jobs, and schools, ended in a highly visible Latino population in Grand Rapids built using familial networks and friendships. A wide range of strategies fostered a stable Latino presence in Grand Rapids—from using white intermediaries to doubling up and sneaking into neighborhoods. When they left Texas, Mexico, or Puerto Rico, they may have envisioned Michigan as a place that was devoid of the problems they left behind. Indeed, they found housing, though in decline, of higher quality than the aluminum-roofed homes or drafty migrant housing that some Puerto Ricans and Mexicans had endured elsewhere. The jobs did not pay as much as they hoped, but the diversified economy offered many ways to help them make ends meet. When they fell behind or layoffs hit, they knew exactly how to make up budget shortfalls: they went back to doing the work they knew on the area's surrounding farms. For some people, labor in the fields offered harsh reminders of lives they wanted to evade. For others, the open country reminded them of home. While cities elevated their quality of life, Grand Rapids' proximity to rural areas provided an escape, if they wanted or needed it. They also soon established a community to depend on as well.

New migrants to the region continued to practice the survival strategies that earlier migrants employed. They also came to rely on the hospitality of that pioneer wave of migration. The demographics of the 1940s and 1950s gave way to much larger population shifts among Latinos and the city as a whole. The quiet Latino community of 500 people in the 1940s became 1,000 in the 1950s and 5,000 by the mid-1960s, while in 1960, Grand Rapids' population reached 177,000. The continued migration of extended families and friends spurred the growth of this community. These newcomers relied on their networks to help them settle, just as those before them had. The work earlier migrants completed in finding amicable landlords and bosses who would give their family and friends a chance made it possible for other people to come and stay in Grand Rapids.

Many of the young people who grew up in two different worlds developed into community leaders by the 1970s. They were often uniquely situated to attend to the needs of their parents' generation, to their peers who also grew up in Grand Rapids, and to incoming Latino immigrants and migrants. They also recognized the benefits of forming relationships across ethnic and racial lines. Their white and Black allies were valuable connections in Grand Rapids, but this generation also understood the value in sustaining the relationships among Mexicans and Puerto Ricans to guarantee the success of the community.

These efforts also transformed the relationship among Mexicans and Puerto Ricans. The groups started as newcomers to the area, having traveled parallel and interdependent journeys to end up in constant contact with one another. Given their similar opportunities in housing and labor, they shared many experiences. This small community also began to venture out beyond their jobs and homes to make space for themselves in public recreational and religious venues. As the community grew, so too did these activities in size, scale, and importance, which also begot the long process of maintaining their ethnic identities while negotiating a collective, pan-Latino solidarity via their placemaking efforts.

– 3 –

A Gathering Place

Red, white, and green streamers adorned a 1964 Pontiac Bonneville convertible as it slowly drove from the Cathedral of St. Andrew through downtown Grand Rapids to Calder Plaza, in September 1971 (fig. 1). The route was no more than a mile. The car was acting as a float in the city's Mexican Independence Day parade and festival. The Fernández Bar had sponsored it. My paternal grandfather, Pío Fernández, started the bar in 1970 in the city's southeastern section after years of working at Peter Wheat Bakery. He served a variety of Mexican, Puerto Rican, Black, and white patrons, though Mexicans and Puerto Ricans filled the bar most nights. Meanwhile, the float in the 1971 parade represented some of the identities in the community. Virginia Fernández, my aunt and Pío's daughter, sat on the back seat of the convertible holding a large Puerto Rican flag. Next to her, a Mexican boy dressed in a mariachi suit held a U.S. flag of the same size. Along the route from downtown to the festival, observers witnessed a portrayal of Mexican, Puerto Rican, and U.S. identities along with a very public and proud display of belonging.

By all accounts, Calder Plaza was and still is the heart of Grand Rapids. The municipal buildings of both the City of Grand Rapids and Kent County share the plaza with world-renowned sculptor Alexander Calder's *La Grande Vitesse*. The bright red abstract sculpture is the focal point of the plaza, weighing over forty tons and standing forty-three feet tall. The City of Grand Rapids welcomed this addition to the downtown landscape when it was commissioned in 1969 and funded through the National Endowment of the Arts. Its popularity convinced the city to incorporate the sculpture into its official logo, which still adorns all official documents and the city flag. The plaza and sculpture became synonymous with Grand Rapids. Hosting a Mexican Independence Day festival on Calder Plaza

Figure 1. The Fernández Bar Float, 1971. Courtesy of the Grand Rapids History and Special Collections, Archives, Grand Rapids Public Library, Grand Rapids, Michigan. "Photos of 1971 Parade," folder 10, box 3-5, collection 321.

marked how far Latinos had progressed in making Grand Rapids their home. In the 1970s, during one weekend in the middle of September, Latinos transformed the Calder into a place with meaning to them.

This photograph and its context are emblematic of the Latino placemaking in Grand Rapids that Mexicans and Puerto Ricans undertook from the late 1940s to the early 1970s, during which they grew from a community of five hundred to eleven thousand. In the post–World War II period, Latinos were confined to housing in specific neighborhoods, but their religious devotion, desire for recreation, and entrepreneurship inspired them to claim space for themselves throughout the city. Decades of festivals at St. Andrew's grew in both size and prominence over time until it culminated in holding an annual festival in downtown Grand Rapids. White flight in the 1960s and increased immigration and migration as family and friends sought to reunite in the city combined to increase the visibility of Latino places along the Grandville Avenue corridor in southwestern Grand Rapids in neighborhoods that previously excluded them. Though this neighborhood remained racially mixed—with some whites staying and some African Americans moving into these areas—Mexicans and Puerto Ricans began to transform the area, which made Latinos more noticeable in churches and local businesses. Over the course of three decades, these immigrants, migrants, and their descendants turned Grand Rapids into a place in which they could celebrate their identities and cultures.

Mexicans and Puerto Ricans engaged in placemaking during the onset of the Cold War, an era when many people were experiencing simultaneous prosperity and increased pressure to conform to Americanness.[1] These conditions informed the identities and solidarities Latinos formed in this period. Many Americans with European ancestry shed their ethnic markers and embraced a white racial identity that was becoming synonymous with being American.[2] While Latinos in Grand Rapids faced pressure to assimilate, their skin color and refusal to relinquish their cultural characteristics did not allow for them to be seen as wholly American or white like their European-descended counterparts.[3] Instead, Latinos' adjustment to living in Grand Rapids is best described by Vicki Ruíz's term, "cultural coalescence." She argues that Mexican "immigrants and their children pick, borrow, retain, and create distinctive cultural forms."[4] During a reactionary time in a conservative city where some in the dominant culture frowned on dancing, drinking, and public celebrations in general, Latinos—on some occasions—did alter their cultural celebrations in Grand Rapids. However, they more often celebrated their culture vibrantly with folkloric dancers, men dressed as *chaparros* riding horses, and live music that stretched well past the acceptable norms. Festival planners, aware of their environment, manipulated these events to fit within local expectations. Through imagery and events at the festivals, planners crafted a celebratory image of Latinos that would still attract white attendees. This balance allowed their festivals to earn money while protecting their ability to hold future events. Thus, these negotiations in placemaking were not only necessary to convert Grand Rapids into a home, but they also served as a safeguard against assimilation in the long term.

Pan-Latino relationships formed in shared spaces, though the process of building bonds was not seamless. Sometimes relationships among Mexicans and Puerto Ricans developed unevenly, with shifting levels of trust, respect, and affection. In Grand Rapids, Mexican Americans outnumbered Puerto Ricans almost three to one, so Puerto Ricans had little choice but to avail themselves of the cultural resources that Mexican Americans provided. But perceived racial differences still lingered among Mexican and Puerto Rican residents as they confronted the systemic white supremacy embedded in Grand Rapids institutions.

These tensions, however, existed alongside the most emblematic examples of pan-ethnicity: intra-Latino relationships. Using Latino identity scholar Frances

Aparicio's term, intra-Latino relationships denotes interethnic pairings among Latinos.[5] Mexican and Puerto Rican romantic unions developed as people spent time living, worshiping, and celebrating next to one another in the Midwest. The presence of MexiRican children—those of Mexican and Puerto Rican parentage—deepened the relationships between Mexican and Puerto Rican families and furthered their pan-Latino solidarity. Though at times imperfect, these interethnic relationships would serve as the foundation of the rest of the broader Latino community.

By the 1970s, the relationship between Mexicans and Puerto Ricans transformed from that of parallel and interdependent journeys to communal and intersecting experiences in settling. Through the process of placemaking, Mexicans and Puerto Ricans forged pan-Latino identities—while maintaining separate ethnic identities—and simultaneously produced an image of Latinos that would draw in the greater Grand Rapids community and incentivize spending money on Latino business endeavors. When Mexicans and Puerto Ricans realized their new homes lacked the cultural resources they enjoyed in their places of origin, they improvised, with many women performing the work to facilitate such innovation. Latinos created spaces and borrowed ones from their white and Black neighbors. They built religious institutions, created recreational experiences for themselves that ranged from dances to baseball leagues, and, through festivals, they crafted an acceptable image of the Latino community in Grand Rapids, allowing them to maintain their public celebrations.

While the 1940s to the 1970s are often seen through the lens of assimilation for many European groups, Mexican and Puerto Rican experiences reveal a nuanced narrative of this period. People who could not access whiteness in this era, as well as those who did not wish to, retained their ethnic identities during a period of conformity and assimilation. Placemaking played an essential role in identity retention and the formation of a new, pan-Latino identity that helped Mexicans and Puerto Ricans survive in Grand Rapids.

FROM THE MEXICAN APOSTOLATE TO ST. JOSEPH THE WORKER: THE RELIGIOUS FOUNDATIONS OF PAN-LATINO PLACEMAKING

Mexicans in Michigan first adopted the Catholic Church as a place of their own, reflecting the centrality of the church for Latinos throughout the twentieth century. Located in downtown Grand Rapids, new migrants regularly sought out the Cathedral of St. Andrew. As chapter 2 mentions, some early Mexican migrants even lived across the street from the cathedral. Most of the community settled into neighborhoods in the southwestern and southeastern areas as early as the

1930s, only a short walk or commute to the cathedral. As the permanent population grew, pioneering families like the Vargases and Vásquezes worked to receive recognition for Mexicans from the local Catholic diocese. While Protestant Mexicans and later Puerto Ricans also moved to Grand Rapids, the overwhelming majority of this Latino community was Catholic, and many of the early and most impactful placemaking efforts originated in the Catholic Church.[6] Their first endeavor was the Mexican Apostolate, the official branch of outreach to the Mexican community.[7] Part of the apostolate's mission was to give Mexicans in the 1940s and early 1950s a distinct space to worship as well as a priest for their parish—both of which it finally delivered in the 1950s.

Without a permanent priest, the community seemed to wait until a Spanish-speaking, Mexican priest came to Grand Rapids to perform important sacraments. For example, marriage records reveal that Father Olivario García performed the nuptials for seven couples on one day: April 19, 1949.[8] García was there temporarily and did not appear again in the records. He may have stopped in Grand Rapids during a break from ministering to Mexican migrant farmworkers in western and northern Michigan. Attending to migratory workers outside of Grand Rapids was a habitual form of outreach for the diocese.[9] As for the couples who married in April 1949, they had likely already been married civilly but were waiting for someone who spoke their language to perform the Catholic sacrament of marriage for them. It was improbable that the church held seven full weddings with a Mass in each on that April day, but rather, a priest carried out the marriage sacrament, including a nuptial blessing—considered one of the most important parts of the sacrament—for each couple. Their decision to wait to have this done until García was available shows how important it was to have a Spanish-speaking priest make their marriages official in the eyes of the church. The absence of a priest who spoke Spanish posed a challenge to Mexican migrants trying to re-create a familiar Catholic experience in Grand Rapids.

In 1951, the arrival of a new priest and an increase in Mexican migration to the area gave Mexican Catholics more standing to petition for a permanent space in the diocese. An ethnically Lithuanian priest, Father Titas Narbutes, arrived in Grand Rapids by way of Santiago, Chile, in the late 1940s.[10] A fluent Spanish speaker, Narbutes began saying Mass to Mexican Americans at St. Andrew's. The community grew fond of him. They affectionately called the pastor Father Tito, an endearing and diminutive Spanish moniker. Though he was not Mexican, Father Narbutes employed his Spanish-language skills to meet parishioner requests. Although in the 1950s Roman Catholic priests still said the Mass in Latin, a Spanish-speaking priest could deliver homilies that parishioners could understand, building a relationship between the priest and parishioners. Mexican congregations in the Midwest generally did not have a Spanish-speaking priest at this time. Many dioceses in the region compelled their priests to take short courses in Spanish to accommodate the growing demands of Mexican and later Puerto Rican parishioners.[11] The relentless work of the Mexican community and the cooperation of the diocese fashioned a place for Mexicans within the Catholic landscape of Grand Rapids.

Mexican migrants and immigrants also lobbied to have their own parish, like other ethnic groups in Grand Rapids. Church membership based on ethnicity was the typical model for immigrant groups that settled across the country, especially in the late 1800s and early 1900s. For example, the Polish immigrant community in Grand Rapids established at least three Polish Catholic churches by the early 1900s.[12] These churches had Polish-speaking priests and celebrated Polish Catholic traditions. The Catholic Church moved away from a preference for organizing ethnic churches by the 1940s to strengthen loyalty to the Catholic Church instead of to nationalities. By that time, the Catholic Church also had joined Americanization efforts, helping these European immigrants and their descendants transition into whiteness.[13] Even though the church no longer endorsed the approach, Catholics already in ethnic-specific parishes held onto a sense of belonging that lasted for generations. Having a church bestowed on their community would signal that Mexicans were a valid part of Grand Rapids' Catholic community. The Vargas and Vásquez families and other Mexican Catholics' insistence that Mexicans have their own church would bear fruit. In the early 1950s, the diocese instructed the Mexican community to begin fund-raising for a new church. They had asked the same of the other communities when they built churches some fifty years prior.[14] The Mexican community then hosted several fund-raising events in an effort to establish a parish and authenticate their presence in Grand Rapids. The local newspaper, the *Grand Rapids Press*, ran a story about one Mexican effort to raise funds "for the benefit of the chapel." Readers were informed of a "dinner . . . followed by a dance starting at 8 o'clock, featuring Mexican music. The public is invited to both the dinner and the dance."[15] Insisting that the diocese approve a space for Mexican Catholic devotion was an integral part of Mexican placemaking in Grand Rapids.

One year after Father Narbutes arrived in Grand Rapids, the community's efforts paid off. By 1952, the diocese purchased a house to convert into a chapel, just two blocks from St. Andrew's.[16] The money the Mexican community raised was for renovations. Among Mexicans, the chapel was known as the *capilla*. Father Narbutes approached Simon Aguilar about becoming the building's caretaker once it was completed. The Aguilars were migrant farmworkers from Laredo, Texas, who remained in Michigan only part of the year.[17] Accepting the caretaker position would guarantee housing for the family during the winter and an income to augment the money made from local farmwork. With the Aguilars taking care of and living at the new church, Mexicans saw it as their own. Virginia Moralez, the daughter of Daniel Vargas, recalled that the motivation for starting the chapel was so her parents and their contemporaries "would have a gathering place."[18] Father Leo Rosloniec, a Spanish-speaking Polish priest, was the congregation's priest from 1954 to 1956. A shortage of Latino, Spanish-speaking priests plagued dioceses around the country, and having a white, Spanish-speaking priest was common for churches with Mexican congregants.[19] Having Father Rosloniec and the *capilla*, although he was not a Mexican parish priest nor was the church newly built, confirmed Mexicans' place in Grand Rapids' Catholic landscape.

The Mexican Apostolate and the chapel provided some of the first social activities where people could form nonfamilial relationships. Examining marriage records reveals how the earliest migrants dealt with separation from their family network. Betrothed couples commonly chose family members or close friends as witnesses for their marriages, as demonstrated by the church's registrar. Migrants, with those networks out of reach, looked to other migrants to fill such roles. Of the seven couples who married in April 1949, many of them served as witnesses for one another. For instance, when Florencio Páez and María Luisa Araisa were wed, Gilberto García and Aurora González—also married that day—were their witnesses. In other cases, well-known couples would act as witnesses. Daniel and Guadalupe Vargas, already leaders in the community, served as witnesses for the wedding of Andrea Alvarado and Arturo Medina, both from Laredo, Texas. The Vargases performed the same function for three other couples over the next four years, showing their continued presence at the *capilla* and their readiness to welcome new parishioners.

Using the chapel and the cathedral's resources, the Mexican Catholic community hosted religious and secular events to welcome new migrants and immigrants. Mexican men formed the Sociedad Mutualista Círculo Mexicano, a mutual aid society, in the early 1940s. The group's interests overlapped with the Sociedad Guadalupana, a Catholic Mexican men's group. While hosting traditional religious activities like the celebration for the Día de la Virgen de Guadalupe on December 12 at the chapel, they also held more secular Christmas gatherings as well. For instance, families convened in St. Andrew's school gym in the late 1940s for a potluck-style celebration. One photo of the event shows over fifty children posing with both Father Leo Rosloniec and Santa Claus underneath a basketball hoop mounted on a brick wall.[20] Some of the children are dressed in folkloric attire for dancing. The Sociedad Mutualista Círculo Mexicano regularly planned dances for the chapel community. According to Daniel Vargas's daughter, Virginia, "they would have dances on Saturdays, they would collect the tickets and save the money, and they would sponsor different events through the year . . . with that money they would help families who were coming in, [with] clothing, food, housing."[21] With the chapel as a base for organizing and diversion, Mexicans worked diligently at placemaking in the diocese and Grand Rapids.

The Mexican community's efforts regarding the chapel and the overlap in some Catholic traditions between Mexicans and Puerto Ricans aided the latter group tremendously when they settled in Grand Rapids in the early 1950s. Like their Tejano and Mexican predecessors, Puerto Rican migrants also sought familiar institutions, and they were directed toward the Mexican Apostolate when they worshipped at the cathedral. To the migrants' relief, the *capilla* already practiced some of the Catholic traditions Puerto Ricans brought from the island. The presence of a Spanish-speaking priest at the chapel further aided Puerto Ricans in their transition. Also, some of the same youth opportunities were available at the chapel as in Puerto Rico, helping young people cope with their move to Michigan. As a young girl in Cagüitas, Puerto Rico, Rosalía Espíndola longed to participate in her church's Hijas de María group, a Catholic society for teenaged girls focused on supporting young women in maintaining their chastity. The organization started in the late 1800s in Mexico but then traveled throughout the Americas. Espíndola's family moved before she was old enough to join the hijas in Puerto Rico. But in Grand Rapids, the *capilla* hosted a Hijas de María group, giving her hope she could finally join and showing her the shared Catholic devotions of Mexicans and Puerto Ricans.[22] The small number of Puerto Ricans who arrived at the chapel in the early 1950s relied on the resources Mexicans had created. Their time in the chapel together began the long process of getting to know one another on a more intimate level as fellow parishioners. They engaged in this entente while simultaneously transforming the spaces around them from one that served Mexicans to one that served a pan-Latino congregation.

In the 1950s, there simply were not enough Puerto Rican families active in the church to put on their own events. However, they did not shy away from procuring space within Mexican Catholic festivities. Puerto Rican Dionisio Berríos, a devout Catholic who later was both a cantor and a lecturer at the church, was a leader in the community and advocated for Puerto Rican inclusion at Mexican events. He ensured that Mexican leaders "always incorporated Mexicans and Puerto Ricans" in events like the feast day of Our Lady of Guadalupe. For example, Puerto Ricans Rosalía Espíndola and Naida Vásquez were selected "para llevarle flores a la virgen" (to bring flowers to the Virgin), a custom that most Mexican communities perform on her feast day in December.[23] Espíndola later attributed their inclusion to Berríos. These small concessions fostered pan-Latino solidarity. However, the numerical imbalance among Mexicans and Puerto Ricans briefly took a toll on this budding relationship in the mid-1950s.

The transition to a pan-Latino space was not seamless. Part of the tension arose from the uneven power dynamics between the almost five hundred Mexicans and Mexican Americans and the one hundred Puerto Ricans living in Grand

Rapids in the early 1950s. The Diocese of Grand Rapids did not acknowledge the presence of Puerto Ricans even after they became active and engaged members of the *capilla*. The diocese still referred to the ministry that served both groups as the Mexican Apostolate well into the late 1950s and 1960s. Mexicans had arrived first and were the larger population, and the diocese did not take steps to become familiar with Puerto Ricans. The Diocese of Grand Rapids did not update the outreach program's name to the Hispanic Apostolate, reflecting a pan-Latino presence, until 1975.[24]

In the mid-1950s, friction occurred when the diocese designated the *capilla* an official parish in 1956. The conflict started when determining the name of the church. The diocese officially referred to the church as the Mexican Chapel, as the engraving on the side of the building still shows. According to Miguel Berríos—who migrated from Puerto Rico as a child along with his parents, Dionisio and Carmen—Puerto Ricans opposed this name, as it erased their presence. While Puerto Ricans were grateful for a place to worship where they could speak Spanish and practice some of their cultural Catholic traditions, this name did not reflect the shared parish that was well underway by the mid-1950s. The mix of Mexican and Puerto Rican parishioners decided to call the church Our Lady of Guadalupe. While she is largely associated with Mexico, this saint became the patroness of the Americas in the 1900s.[25] For Puerto Ricans, Our Lady of Guadalupe reflected their shared heritage.[26] The naming issue was a flashpoint of community tension that was driven by the diocese's erasure of Puerto Ricans. However, as a pan-Latino community, Mexicans and Puerto Ricans made a choice for themselves in how to name the parish that reflected their diversity. The parish went on to provide a place to interact and form relationships beyond their jobs and neighborhoods.

At Our Lady of Guadalupe, baptism and godparentage provided the formal occasions for the community to create and strengthen ethnic and cross-ethnic bonds. In theory, choosing godparents for one's children involved electing someone to guide them in the Catholic faith. The commitment also theoretically called for the godparents to care for the children if the parents were no longer able to raise them.[27] In practice, choosing *padrinos*, or godparents, for one's children linked families together as fictive kin, and the *padrinos* and the parents would become *compadres* and *comadres*. These terms describe the unique bond that connects the two families together in a semi-familial relationship. Social scientists have found that "choosing someone, especially a nonrelative, to serve as . . . [godparents] to one's child is considered a way to cement close friendships and make a public statement regarding the importance of the friendship."[28] In most baptisms from the mid-1940s to the mid-1950s, Mexican parents selected Mexican godparents, and Puerto Ricans selected Puerto Rican godparents for their children. However, by the mid-1950s, prominent Mexican leaders in the community also emerged as popular choices for Puerto Rican parents. Mexicans may have made suitable godparents because they were more well-established in the community, and they could open networks for their Puerto Rican *compadres* and *comadres*. For example, when Puerto Ricans Saturnino and Maira Ayala chose godparents for their child in 1954, they choose Daniel and Consuelo Vásquez—Daniel was a longtime community leader and founder of the Mexican Apostolate. In other cases, choosing godparents honored and solidified a relationship that grew outside of church.[29] Take for instance the case of Santiago Figueroa: his Puerto Rican parents, Leopoldo and Guadalupe Figueroa, chose Gregorio Chávez, who was Mexican, and Santa Sánchez, Leopoldo Figueroa's sister, as his godparents.[30] Chávez had helped the Sánchez family settle, and his generosity likely extended to Santa Sánchez's brother, Leopoldo. Baptism at Our Lady of Guadalupe allowed Mexicans and Puerto Ricans to cement the cross-ethnic bonds already forming among them.

The physical site for these cross-ethnic relationships changed in 1965. For reasons now unclear, Father Theodore "Ted" Kozlowkski, the chapel's Spanish-speaking priest who started there in 1958, left Our Lady of Guadalupe for St. Joseph the Worker on Rumsey Street off Grandville Avenue, one of the major corridors in southwestern Grand Rapids that would later be the center of Latino life in the 1970s. Not surprisingly, his loyal parishioners followed, stopping further development of Our Lady of Guadalupe for decades. The chapel opened and closed at various times well into the 1990s, while St. Joseph the Worker grew into a center of Latino Catholic life.[31] Kozlowski recalled that his transfer to St. Joseph the Worker was part of the regular rotation of priests the diocese regularly facilitated.[32] Some churchgoers, however, remembered that the diocese wanted to "mainstream" Latinos, which meant pushing the new migrants to assimilate, similar to how the church ceased forming new ethnic European churches in the 1940s.[33] However, Latinos eschewed assimilation for the process of cultural coalescence that allowed them to avail themselves of the resources of the diocese, but they still maintained their Mexican and Puerto Rican identities, and with that they formed a pan-Latino presence at St. Joseph. The parish was historically a Dutch Catholic parish but since the 1940s had grown into a cross section of various European nationalities and their descendants. However, after 1965, white parishioners at St. Joseph were scarce, while Mexicans, Puerto Ricans, and some Cubans filled the pews.

The congregation of St. Joseph the Worker in the late 1960s was emblematic of a pan-Latino identity and the changing housing dynamics in the southwestern section of the city. In the 1950s and early 1960s, the "ethnic" whites that worshiped there left the Grandville Avenue corridor for the exclusively white suburbs nearby, traveling back to the area for church on Sundays. In their stead, Latino and Black families moved into the neighborhoods off Grandville Avenue and near St. Joseph—areas that had excluded them just years earlier. One year after Our Lady of Guadalupe closed, those white families had all but disappeared from the parish. St. Joseph the Worker's parish baptism book reflected the change. In 1965 all the children baptized belonged to "ethnic" white families, but in 1966 only two of them did. In fact, after 1966, most children baptized at St. Joseph came from Latino families: twenty-eight out of thirty in 1966 and twenty-eight out of forty-two in 1967.[34] Every succeeding year, Latinos baptized their children at St. Joseph in greater numbers than any other group. Consequently, if the intention in transferring Father Kozlowski was to force Latinos to assimilate, share space with "ethnic" whites, and unite under Catholicism, white flight overturned this strategy.

Latino placemaking from St. Andrew's and Our Lady of Guadalupe to St. Joseph the Worker solidified Latinos' position in the diocese. Just as Italians and the Polish did in other areas of the city, Latinos now had a church that belonged to them.[35] Like most Catholic Churches in urban centers, St. Joseph operated as a "territorial" church serving the neighborhood around it, but changing housing dynamics resulted in St. Joseph becoming a de facto ethnic church, nonetheless.[36] Mexican, Puerto Rican, and Cuban parishioners who started attending St. Joseph in the 1960s did not get to build a brand new church like the European immigrants before them. However, they still claimed St. Joseph as their own. Located in the same neighborhood where Latinos lived and worked, the church became a part of the Latino landscape fashioned by these immigrants, migrants, and their descendants. In fact, parishioners in the 1970s started to call the church San José Obrero, the Spanish translation of St. Joseph the Worker. This diverse group of Latino parishioners even began drawing comparisons between Saint Joseph the Worker—the patron saint of workers—and themselves. St. Joseph resembled the "working-class immigrants" who belonged to the church, according to Verónica Quintino-Aranda, a parishioner who started attending St. Joseph in the 1980s.[37] While naming their previous *capilla* brought up challenges, in the 1970s the parishioners came together and chose to mold St. Joseph around a facet of their shared identity: their class. Latino religious placemaking since the 1940s established the foundation for pan-Latino relationships, activities, and how they would interact with non-Latinos.

"I DON'T FEEL MORE MEXICAN OR PUERTO RICAN—I'M BOTH": INTRA-LATINO MARRIAGES AND FAMILIES

Intermarriage deepened the bonds individuals formed at church and reflected the kinds of interpersonal choices Latinos pursued in Grand Rapids. While taking part in the baptism of one another's children was a way for Mexicans and Puerto Ricans to mingle, marriage represented the ultimate forging of family. Working, living, and worshiping in the same spaces allowed people to become acquainted and, for some, develop romantic relationships. These Mexican–Puerto Rican marriages provide further evidence that these two groups occupied similar positions in the local social and racial hierarchy.[38] Mexican and Puerto Rican unions far outnumbered other endogamous unions, reinforcing the notion that the two groups saw one another as social equals and thus suitable for marriage.[39] While quantifying the number of intra-Latino couples in Grand Rapids is difficult, I have identified people in eight couples who had come to the Midwest in the 1940s and 1950s, in each case arriving before they married. After the 1950s, the community grew beyond the stage of "when everyone knew everyone"—as one oral history participant referred to that era—and it became impossible to enumerate these marriages.[40] Thus, I derived the names of couples from oral history participants' memories. I offer a qualitative analysis of a few Mexican–Puerto Rican marriages and their MexiRican children.

For the first intra-Latino couples, relationships developed from the time spent in shared spaces. The rhythm of migrant labor dictated that work serve as a primary site for couples to meet. For example, one Mexican–Puerto Rican couple, Angelita Arizola and Marcial Hernández, followed a similar step migration, from Texas and Puerto Rico, respectively, to other Michigan agricultural towns, before finally settling in Grand Rapids. The Arizolas first brought their eight children, including Angelita, with them to Michigan in the 1930s.[41] They settled there in the late 1940s, though many of the Arizola children continued to perform migrant farmwork when they married and started their own families.[42] Marcial Hernández came from Aguas Buenas, Puerto Rico, to do farmwork in Michigan. Fields became a space for regular contact, which facilitated their relationship building.

Manufacturing work also produced Mexican and Puerto Rican couples. For example, Amelia Silva and Juan Báez met while living in a boardinghouse next to the manufacturing factory where they worked. Both Juan and Amelia had worked on the fields in Lake Odessa before coming to Grand Rapids, having never met on the migrant circuit. Báez worked on the fields briefly as he migrated throughout the state after arriving in the mid-1940s from Puerto Rico. Silva, however, traveled with her family of migrant farmworkers throughout the country and Michigan, though the family settled in Lake Odessa in the late 1940s. Around that time, Amelia's two sisters and father contracted tuberculosis. As the oldest sibling in a family of five girls, Amelia set out for Grand Rapids in search of a higher-paying job to help support her family during their recovery. She ended up finding work manufacturing cabinets at RCA, while Báez worked at a commercial bakery. Both Báez and Silva lived in a row house down the street from their jobs, where

Silva and other Mexican American women lived on the third floor while Báez and other Puerto Rican men stayed on the first floor. They married in 1954 and were one of the earliest intra-Latino marriages in West Michigan.[43]

Marriages like that of Juan and Amelia represent the beginnings of a pan-Latino community in Grand Rapids, but the reactions from their family members showed that the differences among Mexicans and Puerto Ricans still caused concern for some. Though Amelia Silva's sisters all supported her marriage to Juan Báez, Domingo Silva, her Mexico-born father, never quite supported his daughter's choice in a husband. Juan and Amelia's daughter, Carolina, recalled her grandfather's disapproval: "She married a Puerto Rican, and you didn't do that. You did not do that back then." To Domingo, a Mexican and Puerto Rican marriage was analogous to a "Black and white" marriage. Amelia and Juan's marriage might have seemed that way because Juan was Afro–Puerto Rican and Amelia had fair skin. That may have factored into how Silva saw the two groups as fundamentally different. He was not alone. Juan Báez's family also complained about his marriage to a Mexican woman. Carolina recalled that her mother, Amelia, did not "like how they treated her" and felt "like the outsider" when they visited Juan's family in Chicago. As a result, Juan, Amelia, and their children made the trip to Chicago only once a year. Back in Michigan, Carolina's grandfather did not treat her and her siblings poorly, and they even spent summers with her grandparents in Ionia, a nearby rural area. But she remembered her grandfather's dim view of her father. She felt like her dad "had to prove himself [for] many, many years." Indeed, he did. When he married Amelia, he promised that if she did not want to, she would never have to work another day in her life. He knew she had labored on the fields since her early childhood and had taken great care of her siblings and parents as the oldest daughter. Carolina stated that, once married, her mother worked sporadically and only when she chose to do so. The two were married nearly fifty years when Amelia died in 2000.[44]

In contrast, Angelita Arizola's father did not have a problem with her marrying Marcial, a Puerto Rican man; instead, other Puerto Rican women hesitated to accept Marcial's Mexican bride. Angelita's daughter-in-law, Josefina, recalled the family matriarch's struggle to gain acceptance from the women. After a few years and opportunities to get to know Angelita personally, however, the Puerto Rican women "got over it," accepted her as Marcial's wife, and befriended her.[45] With limited options for female friendships due especially to the small population of Puerto Ricans residing in Grand Rapids, Puerto Rican women recognized that becoming friends with Mexican women would vastly expand their social networks. Moreover, Angelita and Marcial's marriage also unified their two large Mexican and Puerto Rican families as well as the rest of the community. Their in-laws formed relationships and brought other friends into the fold, helping to shape the pan-ethnic Latino community. Puerto Rican Pete Gómez, a close friend of Marcial and someone also married to a Mexican woman, recalled that the Hernández-Arizola marriage allowed him to become close friends with Marcial's brother-in-law. He remarked, "We used to go to the bar. All three of us, then sometimes Marcial wouldn't come, and it would just be me and Jimmy Arizola. We ended up good friends."[46] These marriages, at times, were met with protest, but the Arizola-Hernández children did not recall any lasting ill feelings about the interethnic pairing and lifelong friendships formed from these couples' relationships.

These pairings not only crossed ethnic lines, but their children also represented the forging of a new ethnic identity: MexiRicans. Growing up, their families exposed them to both sides of their families, and as adults, they continued to self-identify as MexiRican. "I don't feel more Mexican or Puerto Rican—I'm both. I'm MexiRican," Rafael Hernández, Marcial and Angelita's son, explained. Juan and Amelia's daughter, Carolina Báez Anderson, recounted, "I never felt I fit in" with Mexicans or Puerto Ricans.[47] She was, however, quite comfortable socializing with the MexiRican Hernández children, who "were like cousins." Growing up, the Báez and Hernández children made a place for MexiRicans among one another. The eldest of them, now in their sixties, constitute the first generation of many MexiRicans that made Grand Rapids their home.

Mexican and Puerto Rican couples also provided the building blocks necessary to unite the larger communities. One Mexican–Puerto Rican couple, Cruzita and Pete Gómez, played extremely instrumental roles in merging the Mexican and Puerto Rican social networks. The Gómezes met and married in northwestern Indiana, in the 1950s—another confirmation of the Midwest's prominence as a site for Mexican–Puerto Rican relations. In Grand Rapids, the Gómezes bridged gaps among Mexicans and Puerto Ricans by reaching out to their respective ethnic group. Such efforts became increasingly important as the city grew, and pioneer families were no longer the only Latinos present. Pete and Cruzita helped reveal the commonalities between the groups. And more couples formed as people began spending more time with one another outside of work, both at church and in their neighborhoods. With the presence of intra-Latino families, many of the recreational venues Latinos sought out continued to foster pan-Latino friendships and, in some cases, more intimate relationships.

"YOU WENT AS A FAMILY": PAN-LATINO COMMUNITY RECREATION

The pan-Latino community in Grand Rapids borrowed Black and white spaces and created their own forums whenever possible. In addition to finding homes, jobs, and places to worship, they also desired spaces for recreational activities and engaging with their cultures. These dancehalls, salons, restaurants, and bars became integral parts of community life, especially since white spaces tended to discriminate against Latinos. As with churches, Mexican Americans built the first entertainment spaces that both Mexicans and Puerto Ricans would later enjoy. Mexicans and Puerto Ricans knowingly modified their activities to be welcoming to both groups. Family parties and community wide dances, a "Spanish" baseball league, and Mexican movie showings best exemplify how the communities encouraged a pan-Latino identity.

Dances, both public and private, provided Latinos with opportunities to freely engage with their culture with few compromises. Unlike work where Latinos were few among their coworkers or church where religious traditions and behavior were a must, dancing at a hall allowed Latinos to express themselves. Oral histories reveal that the earliest public dances happened in the late 1940s and early 1950s, when the community likely outgrew private gatherings in living rooms and the church basement. Though growing, the community remained relatively small and lacked the capital to purchase a private space. Latino-owned restaurants possibly provided small rooms for dances, but these were insufficient for larger parties. To hold a community dance, Mexican Americans often reached out to the owners of the Roma Hall, an Italian-owned entertainment venue. J. B. Russo owned the property on the corner of Wealthy Street and Division Avenue since the 1930s.[48] The Roma Hall was an open and welcoming place for those exploring musical entertainment outside of the mainstream.

Within walking distance from working-class neighborhoods, the Roma Hall had a reputation for being a reliable and safe place for African Americans and Latinos to let loose. Acts ranging from tap dancing to orchestras to jazz made it a trendy spot. Black Grand Rapidians could go there for jazz performances by other African Americans. Perhaps this signaled to Mexicans that they too would be welcome in the building—and they were. In the 1950s, Mexican bands played for packed audiences. Cruzita Gómez remembered family bands as the only musical option available for the community. The Ortega, Rincones, and Castillo family bands played a particular style of Texas conjunto that included the accordion, bass, drums, and the *bajo sexto* (sixth bass). After Santos Rincones worked his shift at Keebler, he and his brothers made up a four-man band. When his brothers quit the band, Santos later played with his sons. They also traveled to areas outside of Chicago and smaller cities in Indiana and Ohio to play for Mexican communities.[49] The community could count on one of these family conjunto bands for most of its events. Dances were regularly held as fund-raisers, holiday celebrations, or both. Valentine's Day, for example, provided the perfect reason to hold a dance and raise money at the same time. For Mexican Americans from Texas, these dances were like the *bailes* they would have attended in dance halls at home.[50] Holding them in Grand Rapids brought a familiar experience to an unfamiliar location.

When Puerto Ricans arrived in Grand Rapids, they too sought places to practice their culture. Though they also went to dances, the first parties and celebrations often occurred in living rooms. When the community consisted of about ten families in the early to mid-1950s, these gatherings were the easiest way to get together to reminisce about what they left behind and to discuss the lives they had started in Grand Rapids. At these get-togethers, Puerto Ricans held onto the traditions they practiced on the island. In particular, *parrandas*—literally "party" but specifically referencing Christmas parties in this context—were popular. In Puerto Rico, during *parrandas*, a group of people would walk to a family member's or neighbor's house to sing Christmas carols, and together they would travel to one home and then another until they all arrived at a predetermined, final destination for a party.[51] In Grand Rapids, continuing this tradition required some changes. Houses in Puerto Rico usually had only window screens, making it possible to hear people singing outside. Michigan winters—and glass windows—required that people coordinate within the community ahead of time to ensure that the *parranda* singers were not left out in the cold. During the earliest gatherings, many Puerto Ricans lived near one another, so walking door-to-door was possible. As the community grew, however, they turned to carpooling.

Preserving these traditions rested on people's ability to re-create these practices in Michigan. Bringing instruments with them to Michigan was an important step. With a *cuatro* (a type of guitar), maracas, a guiro, and claves in tow, Puerto Ricans could have performances just as lively as they were on the island. Food was another major part of celebrating the holidays. Take, for instance, Edwin Ramírez's earliest memories of *parrandas*. He was born in Grand Rapids after his Puerto Rican parents met there. He recalled the host usually provided food for parrandas, but a community member, Ana Doñez, traveled "with a chicken from the grocery store just in case the house we were at did not have anything to eat, [so she could] make arroz con pollo."[52] Doñez and other women guaranteed that this small community would not go hungry during their celebrations, which facilitated the placemaking process and supported its success.

Outside of Christmas events, the community mostly gathered in living rooms and occasionally at bars. Puerto Ricans played, danced, and sang along with *bombas* and *plenas*, traditional folkloric genres from the island. Record players also blasted familiar tunes from vinyl records, likely purchased on the island or in Chicago and brought to Grand Rapids.[53] These get-togethers helped Puerto Rican migrants form relationships for those who did not know each other or previously had limited interaction on the island. In time, they became *compais* and *comais*—the Puerto Rican terms for *compadres* and *comadres*. These small

Figure 2. Mexican and Puerto Rican women at a party at Juanita Murillo's home, 1960s. From left to right: Juanita Murillo, who was Mexican American; Rosa Pérez, who was Puerto Rican; Juanita Berríos, also Puerto Rican. Courtesy of Juanita Muñoz Murillo.

gatherings sustained the earliest Puerto Ricans, who were likely feeling culture shock during their first midwestern winters. It was even common for Mexican and Puerto Rican neighbors to join one another for living-room parties (fig. 2). Soon enough, however, the population would outgrow those living rooms. They also may have desired more social outings, extending beyond their closest family and friends. When that time came, in the mid-1950s, Mexican American *bailes* provided such opportunities.

In Grand Rapids, conjunto bands played for a mixed Mexican American and Puerto Rican crowd of all ages as well as for other residents. For example, Marilyn Vega, who was Black and white, attended with her Puerto Rican husband.[54] Young Puerto Rican men joined these events, often learning the steps to Mexican dances to aid in their romantic pursuit of Mexican women. Cruzita Gómez recalled that the conjunto bands played "a little mambo" to try to accommodate the Caribbeans in their diverse audience. Though likely appreciated, the lack of Puerto Rican music eventually motivated the community to bring salsa bands from Chicago in the late 1960s and early 1970s, when the community grew large enough to pool the required money together.[55] These Mexican and Puerto Rican dances also welcomed adults and children alike. In fact, many children did not have a choice on whether to attend. Carolina Báez Anderson explained: "You went as a family. Nobody got to stay home. When your mom and dad went out, you went with Mom and Dad."[56] If their parents allowed it, the kids danced with partners alongside their parents. From an early age, many of the community's children saw Mexican and Puerto Rican comingling as part of the Latino experience in Grand Rapids. Without many welcoming spaces, Latinos forged their own. Living rooms provided protection from the discrimination of the public eye for small groups of Latinos while renting dance halls large enough for the whole community required them to take chances on the assistance of non-Latinos.

Without the financial resources to own their own entertainment venues, Latinos continued to rent and borrow other spaces, claiming them temporarily, as was the case with movie theaters. Latinos had few signs that theater owners would welcome them, unlike their experience with the Roma Hall. Grand Rapids legally outlawed Jim Crow segregation based on a 1925 court case, which had centered on theater seating.[57] Yet Latinos were possibly still intimidated about attending theaters, especially those who arrived from segregated areas in Texas.[58] Moreover, monolingual Spanish speakers likely regarded English-language movies as unappealing. María Ysasi recalled how her mother-in-law, Aurora Chávez, a Mexican woman in the community, took it upon herself to persuade a local theater to let her play Mexican movies once a week. She ordered films from Mexico and brought them to the Liberty Theater, providing the community with an entertainment option in a language they could understand.[59] The theater was on Division Avenue, just south of Franklin, making it within walking distance for many Latino families. Chávez chose movies from Mexico's Golden Age of cinema that portrayed themes in Mexican culture, but they still offered a brief reprieve from listening to English for Mexican Americans and Puerto Ricans alike.

Community members of all ages, genders, and incomes sought entertainment at the movie theaters. Women often found delight in these outings. Older sisters, aunts, and mothers escorted young ladies to screenings, allowing them to get outside of their homes for a fun outing. Rosa Pérez, my great-aunt and a Puerto Rican who lived in Chicago and Grand Rapids during the 1960s, remembered frequenting the movie theaters with her female friends before she was married.[60] For an affordable night out, many married couples also went to the movies. The MexiRican couple, Cruzita and Pete Gómez, who both spoke English, usually went to the Town Theater on Grand Rapids' northwest side to watch films. In 1950, a third theater downtown started playing Spanish-language films on the weekends.[61] With multiple movie theaters willing to play these movies, perhaps Grand Rapids theater owners recognized the potential profit in catering to a growing population and the recognition of Latinos as legitimate residents with buying power. That Chávez and others in the Latino community pushed for these films also illustrates how people shaped the existing public entertainment landscape for their own desires.[62]

While Mexican movies, conjunto bands, and salsa music might have required that Latinos concede to learning about another culture's activities, baseball did not entail as many concessions. This was a pastime Tejanos and Puerto Ricans already enjoyed before moving to Michigan, and many Latino men organized games and leagues once they settled in Grand Rapids. The area boasted several all-white men's, white women's, and Negro men's leagues before Mexican migrants arrived. Perhaps the Mexican Americans who arrived in West Michigan in the 1940s did not see themselves as fitting into the racialized and gendered teams that existed. Or they knew clear communication would be necessary to play, and they wanted a setting in which their teammates all spoke the same language. Regardless of motivation, as early as the late 1940s, Mexican Americans formed their own team. They joined a league made up mostly of other Mexican teams from nearby rural areas. Staying for the summer, migrant farmworkers formed teams and played on weekends. Mexicans who had settled in Grand Rapids played against those teams in what was known as the "Mexican league."[63]

When Puerto Ricans arrived in the 1950s, the league transformed into the "Spanish league," a common way at the time of referring to Mexicans and Puerto Ricans alike. If anyone objected to including some of the new players, they may have reconsidered once they saw the talent they were acquiring. Many of the Puerto Ricans, including Juan Báez and Pete Gómez, played for company teams in prior years. Playing on a company baseball team, along with higher wages and less arduous work, drew Báez off the fields and into a canning factory in Lake Odessa. Gómez played in several leagues in East Chicago, Indiana, growing up. He boasted about his days playing against Orestes "Minnie" Miñoso, who later became a legendary Chicago White Sox player. With this depth of talent and the long-standing Mexican team, the community eventually developed its own "Spanish" leagues. They no longer needed to travel outside the city and named the baseball diamond at Rumsey Park their home field. Their use of the space showed how they staked claims to the area beyond baseball. Women earned extra money by selling food at the Sunday games. Oral history participants remembered that Luisa Fernández, my grandmother, made and sold *alcapurrias*, a traditional Puerto Rican snack, to the Spanish-speaking crowds. Mexican women sold beverages and candies as the baseball events attracted the youngest and oldest community members. Mexican and Puerto Rican men formed relationships with one another on the field while the crowd introduced new foods to one another. Anybody driving by the park would have seen Mexicans and Puerto Ricans enjoying a Sunday together.[64]

Claiming a field in southwestern Grand Rapids provided yet another sign that the neighborhood was becoming a Latino place. The park itself was at the bottom of the hill on Rumsey Street. It was within walking distance of their parish, St. Joseph the Worker; Franklin Elementary School, where a growing number of Latinos attended; and the industrial companies where Latinos worked. Not all streets in the neighborhood were accessible to Latinos at the time, but the changing nature of the public spaces helped to cement the perception that the area was a home for Latinos.

"FESTIVAL TO MARK INDEPENDENCE OF MEXICO": CELEBRATING IDENTITY, GENERATING REVENUE, AND CRAFTING AN IMAGE VIA FESTIVALS

From the late 1940s to the early 1970s, festivals, like other recreational activities, helped the Latino community achieve various goals. They allowed Latinos to celebrate their identities, served as fund-raisers for a cash-strapped community, and curated a neutral public image during the rising political tension in the early 1970s. The very first community-wide festivals promoted the retention of cultural practices. Women, for example, ensured that traditional foods and dances were showcased at these events. These festivals were also genuine attempts to teach people about their culture, which included teaching Mexicans and Puerto Ricans about one another. However, the Mexican pioneering generation originally organized the small festivals in the late 1940s and early 1960s with the notion of opening them up to greater Grand Rapids. Community leaders understood their position as a small minority with only a sliver of the capital and purchasing power possessed by white Grand Rapidians. Organizing committees extended invitations to non-Latinos for any events that doubled as fund-raisers, hoping to meet their monetary goals and teach white Grand Rapids about Latinos. This also led planners to police the image of the community they presented with the aim of not putting off any potential festival goers. Given the social norms of a majority white conservative city, the Cold War's pressure for conformity, and a growing backlash to Civil Rights efforts, these decisions, as a part of cultural coalescence, allowed the community to celebrate their identities while not attracting negative attention.

The earliest public Mexican celebrations in Grand Rapids reveal the interlocking gender dynamics among the organizers. The Sociedad Guadalupana and the Mexican Patriotic Committee (MPC) described their purpose as planning many of the community's social events that celebrated Catholic feast days and patriotic events. Since the groups' origins in the late 1930s, the groups had overlapped with many members belonging to both. Every year, the society and the MPC sponsored the Mexican Independence Day celebration. The image in

Figure 3. The Mexican Patriotic Committee, 1952. Courtesy of Grand Rapids History and Special Collections, Archives, Grand Rapids Public Library, Grand Rapids, Michigan. "Mexican Festival," folder 6, box 3-5, collection 321.

figure 3, however, is emblematic of the early interpersonal dynamics among the MPC members. The society permitted only men to join, so it is easy to assume some of the same men from the society also played prominent roles in the MPC. A close look at the picture reveals that women were also a part of this organization, though likely seen as less prominent members. Between the shoulders of the smiling men, one can see the foreheads and hair of women standing behind the men. In the photo—and in reality—these men often literally overshadowed women. The placement of the women, however, was not indicative of their commitment to the MPC and festivals. The interviews I conducted showed over and over that these festivals probably would not have happened if women had not taken part in the planning and the execution, as we see below.

In the mid-1950s, many members in the community valued men's involvement as important and worthy of recognition, and women's contributions as simply expected; therefore, women rarely received recognition for their work. Part of the first wave of Tejano migrants to settle in Grand Rapids, Maurelia Blakely, a Mexican and Irish woman from Texas, planned some of the first religious celebrations and community festivals. She worked diligently to help the community but recalled: "It was always the men in the public spotlight . . . in those days, women did a lot of work, but received little credit or attention."[65] Blakely saw the church and events within it as a place where women's contributions could be valued. However, strong gender norms convinced women who were active in the church to dismiss their labor as unimportant. For example, Guadalupe Vargas recalled that her husband, Daniel, was responsible for the success of these religious festivities. When asked if she helped with these events, Vargas replied, "They used to, not me. Dan, he used to have the festival—" but her daughter interjected, saying, "She used to help my dad all the time." She then listed all the ways that Guadalupe made the events in Grand Rapids realizations: "My mom did all the cooking. The women would get together and do all the cooking and all the cleanup."[66] These events were successful precisely because women provided clean and inviting spaces for people to gather and eat. Good cooking bolstered the celebrations as well, since many of these events were fund-raisers where attendees purchased food. With women's integral contributions, the festivals quickly flourished and became a staple event for Latinos.

Just as women were the hidden contributors in figure 3, Puerto Ricans functioned as the lesser-known organizers and attendees at these community events, even the Mexican patriotic celebrations. Although the archive doesn't name the people pictured in figure 3, community members I showed the photo to recognized Julio Vega as the man at far right. Vega was one of the first Puerto Ricans to come to the area, and he likely felt comfortable in spaces with Mexicans. He lived and worked alongside Mexicans the entire time he resided in Grand Rapids. As the Puerto Rican community grew, other Puerto Ricans joined, and they increased their presence at these events. Lea Tobar, a Puerto Rican woman married to a Mexican man, also joined the MPC in the late 1960s. That Puerto Ricans helped plan these festivals signified the important place they held in this pan-Latino community, even when they were a small minority of this population.

While Mexican Independence Day had no cultural meaning for Puerto Ricans, many of them participated in these events and included displays of Puerto Rican pride as well. For example, Puerto Rican girls learned both traditional Puerto Rican and Mexican dances. My Puerto Rican aunts, Nilda and Virginia Fernández, danced to Mexican folkloric routines alongside their Mexican and Puerto Rican friends in the mid-1960s during a Mexican Independence Day parade.[67] Some Puerto Ricans even attended the Mexican Independence Day Festival dressed in Puerto Rican traditional folkloric garb. For example, in one 1971 photo included in a Grand Rapids Public Library collection, a high school–aged young man is wearing white pants, a white shirt, and a red cotton kerchief around his neck— recognized as a traditional outfit for a *jíbaro*. This folkloric character represents the rural farmers in the mountains of Puerto Rico and evokes national pride.[68] The costumed teenager also held a large Puerto Rican flag in front of a van decorated with Mexican flags. Since there were not enough Puerto Ricans in Grand Rapids for them to have their own parade in the late 1960s, the Puerto Rican community carved out a place for themselves within Mexican celebrations. The revelers maintained their ethnic identities as either Mexicans or Puerto Ricans, but joint participation in Mexican festivals caused these two groups to spend more time together and celebrate one another. These events helped the two groups form the foundation of pan-Latino solidarity, and they also began to attract non-Latino Grand Rapidians.

Inviting non-Latinos to the Mexican Independence Day festival was part of ensuring that the event would grow into a successful fund-raiser. In fact, the community had invited the readers of the *Grand Rapids Press* to come to their events as early as the 1950s. For example, a 1951 *Grand Rapids Press* article highlighting how Mexican Americans settled in Grand Rapids served as an advertisement for that year's Mexican Independence Day festival. After describing the varying migration routes and neighborhoods in which Mexicans lived, the article informed readers that there would be tacos, enchiladas, and tamales available as well as a Mexican dance in the gymnasium of St. Andrew. It also ran a picture of a Mexican family dressed in folkloric attire.[69] Inviting all of Grand Rapids to partake in this festival might have indicated Mexicans' attempt to integrate into the wider Grand Rapids community, and it also could be that they understood how much more fund-raising they could collect from people outside of their groups. The advertising worked. Though the earliest celebrations in the 1940s attracted about a hundred people, mostly from within the community, more than five hundred people—Latino and non-Latino—attended the Mexican Independence Day festival by 1956. The local paper ran an article every year announcing the festival starting in the mid-1960s. A sample headline from 1970, the first time the festival was held on Calder Plaza, reads "Parade, Festival to Mark Independence of Mexico," and the article goes on to explain to white readers how the September 16 celebration is to Mexicans "what St. Patrick's Day is to the Irish American."[70] By the 1970s, thousands of people attended the annual event, which had also grown proportionally in prominence. Around this time, Mexican festivals around the country were also growing in popularity, as were European ethnic festivals as white Americans began to publicly celebrate their ethnic identities.[71] The festival's expanded format reflected its evolution. It now included a celebration of Mass, a parade, musical performances, food vendors, cultural activities, and a contest for festival queen. Organizers hoped they could provide something for all the festival attendees, Latino and non-Latino alike.

From the 1950s to the 1970s, the Mexican Independence Day Festival was the mechanism by which the rest of Grand Rapids learned that Latinos were a part of the city, that they were Americans, and that they belonged there. This was the most apparent in the 1971 festival. Every year the floats, logos, and other visual elements celebrated Mexican and Puerto Rican pride. However, in the 1970s, this community's allegiance to the United States was prominently displayed throughout this event, which was not uncommon during the Cold War, when fealty to the United States was part of a strategy in fending off accusations of communism.[72] For instance, the Fernández Bar Float highlighted in the introduction of this chapter recognized the pan-Latino community with Mexican and Puerto Rican flags, but they also demonstrated their U.S. identity by flying the Stars and Stripes. In another example, consider the Sociedad Mutualista Círculo Mexicano float, which boasted only a large U.S. flag. Other floats followed suit. Even the logo for the MPC, the festival sponsor, included both the Mexican and U.S. flags as it served as the backdrop for the mainstage. Housed in a Grand Rapids Public Library archive is the most revealing image of devotion to both the United States and Mexico—and their belonging in Michigan. This photo is of three Mexican men, two dressed in traditional vaquero attire and one in mariachi garb riding on horses during the parade. The photo shows one of them holding a U.S. flag, the other a Mexican flag, and the last one holding the Michigan state flag.[73] Parading down one of Grand Rapids' main corridors in such fashion was an outward sign that these Latinos belonged in Grand Rapids and that Michigan was their home. In addition, many parade-goers held U.S. citizenship as Mexican Americans or Puerto Ricans. In a prime example of cultural coalescence, these Latinos embraced their traditional culture, but they also chose deliberate imagery to let observers know that they too were American.

By the early 1970s, national events in the Chicano movement forced the MPC in Grand Rapids to reconsider the image the festival would portray to the rest of the city. Many Mexican Americans across the country during the late 1960s and early 1970s called for self-determination and referred to themselves as Chicano. Mexican Americans used this term to wholeheartedly reject assimilation into whiteness. The Chicano movement developed and spread, devoting special attention to issues involving the precarious position of Mexican American farmworkers and discrimination in housing, education, and jobs. The formation of the United Farm Workers (UFW) was central to the Chicano movement. Cesar Chávez, Dolores Huerta, and other activists organized farmworkers into recognized unions in California. They sought self-determination for Mexican American farmhands, who had long suffered under poor, abusive treatment from growers. In trying to have California grower E & J Gallo Winery recognize the UFW, the union called for a nationwide boycott of Gallo lettuce, table grapes, and wine, and a secondary boycott of stores that carried Gallo products in 1973. This campaign gained both international and national support. Some Mexican Americans in Grand Rapids also became deeply involved, owing to the long history of migrant farmworkers in the area. Marshall Chávez, a restaurateur and the son of Gregorio and Aurora

Chávez—Mexican pioneers in Grand Rapids—was an active UFW organizer, even getting to know Cesar Chávez personally through his involvement.[74] The 1974 Mexican Independence Day Festival seemed like the perfect event to publicize the boycotts.

The tone of the festival, however, clearly demonstrated a cautious stance that courted the support from Grand Rapidians rather than fully endorsing the UFW. For example, festival organizers discouraged all exhibitors and vendors from speaking about or providing information on or in support of the boycotts. In a sign of the MPC's hesitancy to align with the UFW, they officially invited, then uninvited, and finally re-invited the UFW to the 1974 festival. The MPC, as a condition for the UFW's inclusion, gave the UFW strict instructions about their presence and engagement at the festival. The UFW could attend the festival with banners and even talk briefly on the festival's stage. However, UFW organizer David Martínez was "bound not to urge support of secondary boycotts again at stores carrying the products in this area," indicating that one had already occurred.[75] The MPC was worried that continuing to encourage secondary boycotts would further sour relationships between Latinos and the local business community, a powerful entity in Grand Rapids that also helped sponsor the festival. To maintain the support from white Grand Rapidians, the MPC wanted the festival to remain neutral. In fact, the MPC president, Ramiro Wals, told the *Grand Rapids Press*, "this is not the time or the place for politics." While Mexican festivals and other community gatherings around the country might have served as a base for local activism, Latinos in Grand Rapids evaded the issue. Against the backdrop of civil unrest in the late 1960s and the early 1970s, the small Latino population worked tirelessly to craft a nonthreatening image of their community so as to not put off members of the majority white city in which they lived. Though they missed an opportunity to be in solidarity with farmworkers, the festival planners succeeded at forming relationships with city and business officials, which safeguarded the future of the festival and potentially opened avenues of social mobility for festival organizers. The social norms of the city and the larger political moment influenced the course of Latino placemaking from the 1940s to the 1970s. Latinos in Grand Rapids wanted to create opportunities to celebrate their cultures and gather with one another, but sometimes they had to censor these events and render them devoid of the struggles many Latinos faced.

NEGOTIATING PLACEMAKING

By the 1970s, Latinos had made a clear impact on the cultural landscape of Grand Rapids. Though they had been present in large numbers since the 1940s, it was not until the late 1960s and 1970s that they secured places dedicated to Latino use. Living, worshipping, working, playing, and partying alongside one another created a visible pan-Latino community in Grand Rapids. The religious and recreational events the community designed helped Mexicans and Puerto Ricans retain their ethnic identities, but they also built bonds with one another as part of a new group. That Mexicans and Puerto Ricans intermarried exemplifies the depths of the relationships they formed and the forging of a new MexiRican identity. From living rooms to public plazas, Latinos transformed spaces into meaningful places to accommodate the full lives they were living in Michigan. These interactions elevated their relationships from simply interacting with one another to a burgeoning pan-Latino solidarity.

For the most part, Mexicans and Puerto Ricans also resisted the assimilationist trends of the 1950s, which asked ethnic groups to shed their cultural markers and embrace conformity. Perhaps they believed that any attempts at assimilation would make no difference in the treatment they experienced in Grand Rapids. Instead, they made sure to retain and reproduce the cultural traditions that made them uniquely Mexican and Puerto Rican. Women were essential to upholding these practices; without women who cooked, cleaned, sewed costumes, and taught traditional dances, these festivities would have been impossible to hold. Due to their commitment to the community, Mexicans and Puerto Ricans taught each other about their cultures and jointly celebrated their events. However, as the population's needs grew, they sometimes made tough decisions on how best to use the Mexican Independence Day celebration in a way that helped their community, which resulted in trying to attract white festival goers.

As the festival expanded beyond Latinos, festival planners engaged in cultural coalescence and made concessions in the presentation of their image to the wider city to earn much needed money for the community. They chose to display a non-threatening outward identity that would attract white Grand Rapidians. Latinos thus adopted a position to keep potential consumers, who likely were uninterested in the challenges that Latinos faced and wanted only to engage with celebratory acts of culture like traditional food and dancing. These festivals, devoid of talk of oppression, conjured images of Latinos who had assimilated to the American dream in Grand Rapids. However, the material conditions of the community showed otherwise. Not all Latinos in the community supported the decisions about representation at the festival. Latino organizers and attendees held differing opinions on how they should proceed to make space for themselves and to garner changes in their treatment and conditions.

By the early 1970s, the stakes for such decisions went up as the community struggled. Economically, the onset of deindustrialization meant that Latino unemployment was higher than for their white counterparts. Other grievances also piled up. There were no interpreters at municipal offices or health-care facilities.

The number of Latinos not finishing high school increased each year. The local power structure, the City of Grand Rapids, had yet to acknowledge that Latinos were an underserved, marginalized population in Grand Rapids. In large part, they lumped their issues in with African Americans. There was some overlap, but these groups had separate problems that deserved separate resources. While the community engaged in making space for themselves and their cultural traditions, they also engaged in political placemaking through local politics. The end goal of such involvement was to guarantee better living conditions for Latinos in Grand Rapids. Questions quickly arose, though: who would lead this multigenerational, pan-Latino group of people, and how would they do it? Would they use the same strategies community leaders used to attract people to festivals? Might they only employ integrationist approaches? Would they embrace the Chicano or the Puerto Rican nationalist movements' rhetoric of revolt? Or would they find another strategy somewhere between those options?

– 4 –

Latins Want Parity

With few exceptions, the Grand Rapids Human Relations Commission (HRC) meetings only discussed issues that directly pertained to Mexican Americans and Puerto Ricans when Daniel Vargas was present in the late 1950s and 1960s. In 1958, Daniel Vargas was the first Latino to be appointed to that body, where he and the other commissioners were to help "foster mutual understanding and respect among all racial, religious, and nationality groups." The commission, which was comprised of Black and white representatives prior to Vargas's tenure, tended to focus on racial dynamics that were most relevant to their communities.[1] By the 1950s, Vargas, a native Mexican who traveled from Texas in the late 1930s with his wife, Guadalupe, became a community leader with a wealth of knowledge about the Latino experience in Grand Rapids. By welcoming Vargas onto the committee, the HRC perhaps wanted to understand the plight of Spanish-speaking people in Grand Rapids.

However, whenever Vargas was not present to push Latino interests, the commission assumed that Latinos did not hold pressing needs. Unless directly involved in the community, white commission members lacked a full understanding of Latinos' employment, language, housing, and educational needs. For their part, African Americans, who comprised 10 percent of the population in Grand Rapids, worked diligently to ensure that city officials addressed their community's grievances. Latino issues mirrored those of African Americans, except for language. The HRC's disregard for Latino issues also reflected the level of separation that Latinos experienced as minority residents. The appearance of a repeated disregard for the status of Latinos led to intense frustration on their part. By availing themselves of the opportunities from antipoverty programs, Vargas and other Latino activists cultivated their voice in city politics.

Since the 1920s, the city government and local social services agencies had ignored Latinos. They were excluded from influential positions in municipal agencies. No social service programs addressed their specific needs as ethnic and racial minorities or as a population with many non-English speakers. Thus, by the 1960s and 1970s, when Latinos made up 5 percent of the city and had a growing number of people in the community in poverty, they had to force various local, state, and federal representatives to acknowledge them as residents of Grand Rapids. As Grand Rapidians, they deserved the same services and resources other inhabitants of the city could access, regardless of race, ethnicity, or language ability. Though Latinos acknowledged that African Americans faced systemic racism in Grand Rapids, using the "politics of recognition" they worked to have white and Black middle-class leaders in Grand Rapids recognize that racist policies also affected Latinos and that their concerns needed remedying.

People of color have practiced the "politics of recognition" throughout the twentieth century to garner more civil and human rights through strategies that have ranged from gradualism to radicalism.[2] This process involved forcing the white majority in the United States to acknowledge that nonwhite people also belonged in the country and deserved to thrive as much as any group. Their tactics varied. For example, during the 1930s, the Puerto Rican Office of Employment and Identification issued identification cards to Puerto Ricans in New York to signal to employers that they were citizens.[3] This was especially important when they looked for jobs, and recruiters became confused as to whether they were foreigners or immigrants. In the late 1960s and 1970s, organizers gained recognition for their communities via social movements that adopted more radical and revolutionary approaches like large public demonstrations and boycotts. Another strategy included what scholar José E. Cruz cites as "demand-protest," which is a "reactive and contingent" method of gaining recognition. For example, when Puerto Ricans were left out of programs and opportunities, they staged protests to demand their inclusion.[4] They communicated their demands for change in immediate and unflinching terms and as incompatible with the current system. The Black Power movement, the Chicano movement, and the Puerto Rican nationalist movement all engaged in more confrontational methods of protest that also called for recognition along with self-determination.

Latinos in Grand Rapids most actively engaged with the politics of recognition via local participation in federal antipoverty programs. Lyndon B. Johnson's Great Society shepherded the passage of laws that protected civil rights and aided impoverished Americans through the Economic Opportunity Act of 1964. The creation of several programs that stressed the participation of the poor in administering funds to ameliorate poverty collectively became known as the war on poverty. The country elected Richard Nixon in 1968, and he chose to cut back funding—or simply not renew it—for many of the citizen-based war on poverty programs. Unfortunately, Grand Rapids gained access to those programs only in the late 1960s and early 1970s, when funding for them had begun to wane, increasing tensions among the programs' participants. Two of those programs, the Community Action Program (CAP) and the Model Cities Program (MCP), also known simply as Model Cities, were key sights of organizing for Latinos in Grand Rapids. Their participation in CAP and MCP helped to shift Latinos' quiet requests for recognition to demands for inclusion as there was less and less money available for programs that aided the poor and marginalized. In the late 1960s and early 1970s, this shrinking pool caused increased infighting and tensions among Latinos and between Latinos and African Americans.

Amid the turmoil, demanding recognition and thus participation in antipoverty programs forced Latinos to develop leaders and tools to advocate for their community. Though they previously had engaged in advocacy efforts, antipoverty programs provided the incentive to organize on a much grander scale. During a time of heightened nationalism among Mexican Americans and Puerto Ricans, their efforts also raised important ideological questions about the strategies and methods of protest. These debates often resulted in intra-racial and interethnic conflict. Specifically, this put Latinos at odds with African Americans, who had been in the city since the 1850s. They had long engaged with the respectability politics the city demanded.[5] As a result, middle-class African Americans created well-respected uplift organizations in their community and made inroads with antipoverty institutions. Latinos, in large part, attempted to follow suit in the 1950s, but by the late 1960s they started to engage with more radical strategies to achieve the moderate goal of inclusion. This shift caused tension with African Americans who wanted to protect their long sought-after antipoverty funding. It also threatened to divide some Mexicans and Puerto Ricans who held different ideas on how to achieve change, but long-standing members of the Grand Rapids community refused to abandon their pursuit of a pan-Latino solidarity. Gendered conflicts over leadership positions also arose, and women sharpened their community leadership skills through these debates. Nonetheless, Latinos worked to be heard and recognized as belonging in Grand Rapids.

During the late 1960s and early 1970s, Mexicans and Puerto Ricans in Grand Rapids used various forms of grassroots activism to force antipoverty program administrators to see them as legitimate social actors, a marginalized community, and deserving of aid. While strategically advocating for federal dollars to assist their communities, they also forced the City of Grand Rapids to confer on them the rights of first-class citizenship through equal treatment and equitable policies designed to meet their needs as a Spanish-speaking minority. This chapter argues that by seeking recognition as a distinct political entity in the city, Mexicans and

Puerto Ricans strived to attain a more visible, active, and pan-Latino presence in Grand Rapids. During the urban crisis—the concurrent phenomenon of poverty, deindustrialization, disinvestment, and structural racism during the 1960s and 1970s—Latinos articulated their specific conditions, and participation in CAP and MCP helped garner funding for the creation and sustaining of their own grassroots organization.

This chapter affirms scholarship on the war on poverty across the country: a lack of adequate funding, a call for maximum feasible representation, and participation of multiple minority groups often put communities at odds with one another. In examining Grand Rapids, a nuanced view on resistance to war on poverty programs emerges. The national narrative of "pulling oneself up by the bootstraps" to achieve economic and social progress meshed well with the local influence of Protestant Reformed conservative values—being modest, pious, and hardworking—to create resistance to implementing or expanding social welfare programming. In addition, local leaders' practice of "managerial racism" that equated to moderate, slow changes to discriminatory policies, while giving the appearance of racial progress and economic prosperity, prevented both Black and Latino communities from effectively using the limited antipoverty funds they received to address poverty.[6] Examining Grand Rapids, however, also shows us how communities dealt with tension that arose due to limited resources and how they worked through it or around it to affect change with whatever tools they had available.

"DEPRIVED MINORITIES": AN URBAN CRISIS FOR SOME, BUT NOT FOR ALL

Grand Rapids' economic climate by the mid-1960s only vaguely resembled that of other urban centers. The city witnessed some industrial decline but survived deindustrialization better than most other urban north cities.[7] During the postwar boom, the city and county governments' diversification efforts helped bolster Grand Rapids and the surrounding economies of the suburbs. The city suffered some business losses, but Kent County, the home of Grand Rapids, performed better than auto manufacturing-dependent areas. In an application for funding from an antipoverty program, which was supposed to highlight why Grand Rapids needed federal help, city officials boasted that Grand Rapids "has continued to diversify . . . to grow . . . to attract new people . . . to attract new industry, and . . . to expand as a market center." They remarked that Grand Rapids had maintained a "strong and healthy economy."[8] Growth for the suburbs and towns in Kent County helped to bolster greater Grand Rapids' reputation as an economically prosperous area for most of its residents, but not all.

Most of the growth was concentrated in burgeoning suburbs. Older, multi-story manufacturing facilities within the city center could not accommodate the streamlined production that companies now desired. Thus, manufacturing companies often looked to the suburbs, where larger plots of land could support their growth. In 1961, the new U.S. Route 131 highway connected the expanding suburbs to downtown Grand Rapids. This diverted traffic from the downtown area toward businesses that relocated to nearby locales like Wyoming and Walker. Initially, many companies failed to realize the immediate benefit of relocating to the suburbs, especially since rail lines and other resources remained in the city. But the burdens of municipal taxation in the wake of white flight and the increasing availability of nearby land led many to reconsider. Soon, many manufacturers established facilities immediately beyond city limits, including in the suburb of Wyoming—a fast-developing manufacturing hub.[9] Subsequently, General Electric, Steelcase, and other major companies all moved just south of Grand Rapids.[10] White Grand Rapidians who could afford to do so flocked to the suburban areas and closer to the new factories. For the local economy, manufacturing in the suburbs proved a positive factor for economic growth. But manufacturers' cost-saving did not trickle down to low-wage workers. Moreover, the close relationship between business and the local government foreshadowed the challenges ahead for activists who advocated for such workers.

As the area experienced economic growth, poor Black and Latino residents endured an economic downturn as they were shut out of the growing opportunities. Daniel Vargas raised this issue with the HRC after attending a Fair Employment Practices Committee conference in Lansing in the early 1960s. On his return, he reported the negative predictions for the condition of low-wage workers, many of whom were a part of the city's Black and Latino populations. He added, "the greater demand for skilled technicians would aggravate existing problems for 'economically . . . and . . . educationally deprived minorities.'"[11] By the late 1960s, the inadequate educational opportunities and several additional factors conspired to create a full-blown emergency in Grand Rapids: a wanton disregard for institutional inequality on behalf of the city and local agencies; the inability to address the various and unique needs of an expanding Latino and Black population; a lack of investment in minority neighborhoods; and a local economy that would not train Latino and Black workers for high-paying jobs.

While the city went through an economic boom, the most marginalized Black and Latino residents went through an urban crisis. The intersection of poor housing, underfunded schools, and a lack of high-paying jobs, among other issues, coalesced not just in Grand Rapids but in urban centers across the country, affecting both Black and Latino communities. Black Grand Rapidians experiences were more dismal than that of the smaller Latino population, in part because some Latinos managed to secure manufacturing jobs in the 1950s, while African Americans had been systematically excluded from postwar industrial jobs all together. Though it is difficult to achieve a commeasurable comparison, taken as a whole, their circumstances were similar. Some social service agencies paid closer attention to the larger, more established African American community as early as the 1930s and 1940s, producing telling statistics on their conditions and mostly through the lens of their experiences as compared to white Grand Rapidians. These same statistics are unavailable for the Latino community until the late 1960s, largely due to the use of the U.S. Census as a measure of poverty. Mexicans and Puerto Ricans were not clearly demarcated as groups that were not white or Black on the census until the 1960s.[12] Thus, the same entities that recorded and measured Black poverty did not recognize Latinos as a minority largely until the war on poverty began. Then, Latinos used funding to document their experiences. Despite a lack of commeasurable data, from what is available, it is clear that their experiences overlapped.

Black and Latino poverty, unemployment, housing, and education mirrored one another in Grand Rapids. They both experienced higher poverty rates than their white counterparts: in the 1960s white family incomes remained 65 percent higher than "nonwhite" families, according to a socioeconomic profile of the area.[13] About a decade after African Americans experienced a facet of poverty, so too did Latinos. Consider that by 1960, the majority of the Black southeast side residents lived below the poverty level, while in 1970, half of all families on the southwest side, where Latinos lived, had incomes below the poverty line.[14] Both groups also suffered from unemployment. While the total unemployment rate for the city in 1960 was 5.3 percent, Black unemployment was at 14 percent that year.[15] Though statistics on Latino unemployment in 1960 are not available, in 1970, unemployment for Latinos in Kent County was at 13.7 percent while it was at 12.6 percent and 5.4 percent for African Americans and whites, respectively.[16] In addition, In 1970, at least 77 percent of all Black homeowners owned properties that were built before 1939 as compared to 38 percent of white homeowners.[17] One in three Black-owned homes remained virtually uninhabitable in the 1970s as well.[18] In 1968, the HRC described Latino housing conditions in the same way: they were "occupying the older, more dilapidated, blighted housing in the core or central city, surrounding the downtown business district."[19] In addition, in 1960, only forty-nine Black high school seniors graduated out of over a thousand, mostly white, students in the district.[20] Like other data on Latinos, graduation rates in 1960 are unavailable, but in 1971, two out of three Latino students did not graduate high school. The larger narrative among these two communities shows that they were affected by the same elements of the urban crisis, even if to varying degrees.

In the summer of 1967, an urban uprising illustrated the frustration of the city's marginalized residents with their situation. However, the rebellion also reified the old notion that Grand Rapids' race and poverty issues existed solely on Black and white lines. The long train of 1960s uprisings that hit New York, Los Angeles, Chicago, and other urban areas arrived in Detroit on July 23, 1967, and a day later Grand Rapids police stopped Black teenagers driving a stolen car on the southeast side. Curious Black patrons at a bar nearby spilled onto the streets to observe the police stop and saw a white officer manhandle a teenager. Stories soon spread like wildfire about how the police roughed up the teenager, with some complaining that the police had assaulted him. This incident was part of a growing list of disturbances on July 24 that spilled over into the next day.[21] Coupled with their grievances regarding the city's crumbling infrastructure and severely under-resourced public schools, claims of police brutality pushed people to their breaking point. During the rebellion, patrolmen and business owners claimed that someone launched Molotov cocktails and rocks at cars and buildings.[22] In the hopes of quelling any further racial unrest, local authorities instituted a curfew, halted liquor and gasoline sales, and quarantined neighborhoods on the southeast side. Once the disturbances subsided and these conditions were lifted, antipoverty programs in the city paid more attention to the contributing factors that caused the uprising. In particular, middle-class African American leaders lobbied those organizations for more—and much-needed—funding to aid Black Grand Rapidians.

As Black organizers sought federal funding, Latinos walked a fine line in acknowledging the depths of poverty their Black counterparts lived in while also trying to advocate for their own needs. Though some Latinos lived alongside African Americans and even participated in the urban uprisings, the events of late July 1967 largely affected majority Black neighborhoods. However, Latinos' high rates of poverty obliged them to take part in the antipoverty programs alongside African Americans. But there was little representation of Latinos on antipoverty program boards, and, for the most part, the conversation around poverty centered on the African American experience. The national and local coverage of urban rebellions and poverty hardened the idea that, in the urban North, poverty and racism were Black issues. The dynamics of urban disturbances are hardly monolithic and depend on local racial and power relations, as historian Llana Barber observes in her scholarship focused on Latino-white relations during the urban crisis in Lawrence, Massachusetts.[23] To the rest of the Grand Rapidians, including the city administrators, what happened on the southeast side concerned African Americans only. Many Latino leaders, frustrated by this erasure, understood the need to get organized to gain recognition. They started by forming an organization to represent the growing number of Latinos in the city.

"TO SELECT OUR OWN REPRESENTATIVES": LATINO ORGANIZING IN THE LATE 1960S AND THE COMMUNITY ACTION PROGRAM

The founding of a grassroots organization, the Latin American Council (LAC), represented a watershed moment in the history of Latino social justice movements in Grand Rapids. Specifically, the establishment of the local organization helped Latinos to gain the visibility the Latino community needed and provided a medium to express their increasing grievances. Formed by some of the pioneering Mexican American families in Grand Rapids in the mid-1960s, the purpose of the organization was to "hire enough translators to work in the Latin American community."[24] The LAC, became a base for formal political organizing among Latinos to lobby for the resources they needed. It developed into the center of Latino cultural awareness, advocacy, and activism in Grand Rapids. This organization emerged as the culmination of decades of work. Building on the efforts of previous organizations like the Sociedad Mutualista Círculo Mexicano and the Mexican Patriotic Committee, the LAC went on to provide an informal space for Latino solidarity and placemaking efforts. Five Mexican Americans and two Puerto Ricans, all of whom arrived in Grand Rapids between 1945 and 1960, served as the inaugural members of the LAC Board of Directors. Though he had served as one of the pioneers and leaders in the community for decades, Daniel Vargas was noticeably missing from the city's first comprehensive service and advocacy organization, having resigned from the HRC in 1968. Vargas left to focus his energy on advocating for migrant farmworkers throughout Michigan. His departure from the HRC and his absence within the LAC marked a shift in Latino engagement with city officials. The new community leaders wanted representation on important municipal boards and to form coalitions with other activist organizations forming with federal antipoverty funding.[25]

By 1969, the LAC now served as the preeminent force for change among Latinos residing in the city, and its board of directors secured grants backed by the Diocese of Grand Rapids and the Grand Rapids Foundation for the purchase of a physical location for the council.[26] They chose a house on the city's southwest side in the Grandville Avenue area, which was increasingly becoming recognized as Latino space. While African Americans and poor whites still lived in the neighborhood, and some Latinos lived across the new U.S. Route 131 on the southeast side, Grandville Avenue was exactly where the council needed to be to formally demarcate the street as Latino space.[27] Having purchased the house, the LAC used the remaining funds to hire a director, though the organization relied heavily on a volunteer staff. At the outset, the council had two main goals: to serve as an umbrella organization for the city's multiple Latino cultural groups, and to arrange the social services that would improve Latino living conditions.

A concentrated focus on the latter goal would lead the LAC to actively engage in electoral politics.

Through their efforts to garner more funds for community service work, the LAC soon encountered the Grand Rapids Community Action Program. Usually, CAPs were social service organizations that applied for official designation under the federal program, then evolved into a distributor of war on poverty funds. Public and private organizations could apply to CAP, but only if they met the federal Office of Economic Opportunity's guidelines for receiving funds. Specifically, CAPs could allocate money to organizations in which "poor persons were themselves to be involved with the development and operations . . . that were intended to help them."[28] During the 1960s and early 1970s, CAPs around the country brought social services within reach of those who needed them most.[29] Daniel Vargas, while serving on the HRC in years prior, had forewarned Latinos that they would need to be involved with CAP if they wanted to make substantive changes in their living conditions. In a 1965 speech to the Michigan Welfare League, Vargas offered recommendations for Latino participation in urban planning committees, and he argued for "the opportunity to select our own representatives rather than having [CAP] decide who should represent the poor." He ended his speech with a plea for Latino representation "in large numbers," especially for the CAP Leadership Policy Committee.[30] Vargas's keen insight as to what the community needed only became more relevant after his departure from the HRC as the urban crisis deepened. The LAC heeded Vargas's advice and committed to transforming the local CAP into a more effective organization for Spanish speakers.

Latino leaders soon found themselves negotiating with the middle-class African American and white program coordinators who had been spearheading the Grand Rapids CAP since its inception in the mid-1960s. Middle-class African American leaders had grown highly experienced in running organizations that worked in tandem with the city government after decades of applying pressure. Founded in the 1920s, the local National Association of the Advancement of Colored People (NAACP), along with the Urban League, which was established in 1943, were forerunners among the city's Black activist community. Headed by members of the Black middle class, both the NAACP and the Urban League catered to the needs of the Black community, though at times class divisions and ideological issues threatened to divide Black Grand Rapidians. For example, inspired by the Black Power movement, some of the more radical members of the Black community referred to the Grand Rapids CAP as an "Uncle Tom institution" and one remarked to the press that CAP was "an extension of the white power structure, uninterested in drastic steps, like the redistribution of wealth."[31] Undeterred, CAP nonetheless remained an organization run by middle-class leaders. Raymond Tardy, a longtime community servant familiar with Grand Rapids' NAACP chapter and the Urban League, became CAP director in 1969, and his brother, Melvin Tardy, became planning director. Many of the conversations that Latinos had with CAP, they had through the Tardy brothers.

Prior to the Tardys' leadership over CAP, the LAC had requested to change the structure of CAP to include high-level positions for Latinos. In this way, council members adhered to Vargas's directives while achieving "maximum feasible participation" under CAP mandates. "Spanish Americans [must] be involved on all Committees and Boards that make decisions about human services that affect the lives of our people," the LAC argued. The term "Spanish Americans" was a popular way of referring to Latinos—including Mexican Americans and Puerto Ricans—in the 1960s and 1970s, though many members of both groups would later reject that label. Employing the language from the war on poverty requirements, they explicitly stated that they required CAP assistance to "guarantee that to the maximum possible degree Spanish Americans are participating in staff and committee positions." In addition, they asked CAP to encourage the city's social service agencies to examine their hiring policies in order to determine ways to incorporate "Spanish-Americans" into their administrations.[32] At the time, few social services agencies included bilingual or Spanish-speaking staff. Latinos, under the LAC, wanted assurances against being deprived of future opportunities to be employed at CAP or any social services agencies that Latinos used.

The Tardy brothers and other administrators insisted that CAP's programs served Latinos and African Americans equally, and thus they dismissed the LAC's claims to the contrary. Melvin Tardy argued that Latinos had access to the CAP-funded drug and alcohol rehabilitation center, the Upward Bound education program, the Neighborhood Youth Corps, job corps, and two social service complexes. According to CAP administrators, they already fulfilled the "maximum feasible participation" mandate because their programs cut across race and ethnicity.[33] For many Latinos, however, the established programming was largely inaccessible due to the absence of Spanish-speaking staff members.

Some LAC board members cautioned patience and opted for ongoing discussions with CAP leaders about how to integrate Latinos into existing antipoverty programs. Other members of the Latino community were increasingly frustrated by what seemed to be perpetual calls for patience, followed by endless waiting. CAP's leadership expressed resistance to any major organizational changes, refusing to address the structural issues that contributed to Latino exclusion. For example, even if the local CAP hired Spanish speakers for the purposes of interpretation, it would only alleviate part of the problem. Underlying the request for bilingual staff rested the idea that Latinos needed access to plan, design, and execute cultural programming aimed at Latino experiences. Frustrating conversations between CAP and the LAC continued into the mid-1970s, with limited progress made in convincing the former to hire Latinos for decision-making roles. While the LAC and CAP failed to arrive at a mutually agreeable solution to this issue, various other members of the community turned their attention to the newly launched Model Cities Program.

"SYSTEMATICALLY EXCLUDED": BLACK AND LATINO NEGOTIATIONS IN THE MODEL CITIES PROGRAM

Given the barriers inherent to joining CAP, LAC activists hoped that the recent establishment of MCP would secure them access to much-needed funds for the Latino community. As a program designed for urban areas, MCP aimed to give poor people the tools to participate in their local governments while also supporting community programs and renewal efforts. When MCP began taking applications in 1966, Grand Rapids did not quite meet program application criteria, which led to their rejection in April 1967. Compared to Chicago or Baltimore, for example, the urban crisis in Grand Rapids appeared as an aberration in an otherwise small and relatively peaceful city. The July 1967 urban uprising presented program officials a reason to reconsider whether Grand Rapids was a racial powder keg set to explode again. Consequently, when the City of Grand Rapids applied once more to Model Cities in 1968, the application was accepted. The city's application, however, offered no clarity on how Latinos would be incorporated into MCP efforts, given its characterization of poverty and unemployment as problems that pertained only to the Black community.

The content of the application foreshadowed the difficulty Latinos would face in the most recent antipoverty effort. Unsurprisingly, the language largely described racial dynamics and poverty as a Black and white issue. The 1967 Model Cities grant only once mentioned people from the United States "southwest," referring obliquely to Mexicans. The remainder of the application was generally devoid of detailed information regarding Mexican experiences. Puerto Ricans were excluded altogether. Instead, the application referred mostly to the "negro" population, "minorities," and "non-whites," with the context suggesting that the latter two terms were euphemisms for Black residents.[34] While antipoverty organizers appeared to be aware of the Mexican presence in the area, that was the extent of their knowledge. Moreover, the City of Grand Rapids, which submitted the grant, relied solely on census data regarding the local Black population, which exacerbated the disparity in the application because of the lack of aggregated data on Latinos. To access the funds available via MCP, Latinos first needed to make city officials and Black antipoverty leaders acknowledge their community as a legitimate constituency that required federal aid and deserved to access it.

Complicating Latinos' quest for inclusion, MCP underwent a rough start. Like CAP, MCP served as a parent organization that also funded projects throughout the city that met the program's requirements. As with many of the war on poverty initiatives around the country, implementation was challenging.[35] The first task for interested residents, many of whom possessed limited experience in governance, was to devise a leadership structure and appoint representatives who would serve as part of the Model Neighborhood Citizens Committee (MNCC).[36] Areas included in the MCP were divided by neighborhoods and referred to as "Model Neighborhoods." Representatives from each Model Neighborhood comprised the members of the MNCC. The MNCC controlled future funding decisions, rendering it incredibly powerful. Predictably, a struggle for control ensued.

Many poor Grand Rapidians worried about cooptation of control of the organization from middle-class reformers and from city officials. Poor Black, white, and Latino residents alike worried that the middle-class organizers would push their own ideas about how to alleviate poverty without having experienced it first-hand. Model Neighborhood residents also consistently accused "City Hall of trying to run the show."[37] Cooptation from local governments was a common complaint at this time about federal antipoverty programs from the intended beneficiaries.[38] Meanwhile, some of the MNCC representatives already worked for CAP or other organizations, including the small percentage of African Americans who held white-collar jobs but still lived in poorer neighborhoods as a result of Grand Rapids' intense racial segregation.[39] By late 1968, only months after the program started, MCP had not succeeded in integrating poor people into its rubric, nor had it come anywhere close to aiding the city's blighted areas.

While middle-class African Americans and whites dominated the MNCC, Mexican and Puerto Ricans fought for representation on the committee. To populate the forty-one-person committee, MCP leadership structure decided to hold elections, wherein over a hundred people ran, the majority of whom were African American and about half of which were women.[40] The elections never yielded more than one Latino winner. Instead, as the LAC membership pointed out, Black residents were the majority of those elected to the MNCC, in addition to holding positions of power in other programs like CAP.[41] African Americans made up 67 percent of the MNCC's electorate, whereas Mexicans and Puerto Ricans together totaled only 10 percent.[42] Thus, the MNCC statistically underrepresented the Latino community, and three or four Latino members, rather than one, would have made it more proportionate.

MCP administrators defended the imbalance by pointing to a lack of Latino participation in the MNCC elections. Representing the Latino community in these discussions, the LAC countered that the program had not encouraged their participation and the demographics of the MNCC had left the impression that it was not meant for them. After countless discussions about inclusion, the Latino community carried their complaints to the federal Department of Housing and Urban Development (HUD), which oversaw MCP. After filing a formal complaint about their exclusion, a HUD representative from the Chicago office visited the Grand Rapids' MCP branch. The HUD official affirmed the claims of Mexicans and Puerto Ricans and urged MCP to "improve the participation of Latin Americans within the program to prevent the public from thinking Model Cities here is catering only to Blacks."[43] While Latinos had hoped that MCP administrators would include them immediately, bureaucracy triumphed: another series of closed-door meetings ensued between the MNCC and the LAC, yielding no results. A segment of the Latino population responded by growing more vocal about their grievances while insisting that waiting patiently was no longer a viable strategy. Stepping out of the shadows, they publicized their demands for inclusion and decision-making roles on the MNCC.

No longer content to remain mere supplicants to the city's antipoverty administrators, Martín Morales, a recent transplant to Grand Rapids, led the way. Morales delivered a breath of fresh air to many Latino residents. Originally from the Rio Grande Valley, he arrived in Grand Rapids in 1968, the same year that the LAC had formed. According to newspaper articles on Morales, he left Rio Grande City, Texas, at nine years old and joined his uncle as a migrant worker traveling across the country because his mother could no longer support six children. At age fourteen, he enlisted in the army, but only after lying about his age, according to one exposé (though military records show that he enlisted at eighteen).[44] After his army discharge he settled in Mansfield, Ohio, where he worked for the transportation department and started a family. He then worked in the mayor's office for some years before making a solo trek to Grand Rapids after a divorce.

In 1968, having arrived in Grand Rapids to take a position with the Diocese of Grand Rapids, Morales quickly swayed local Latino organizing efforts. Morales became the director of the diocesan human relations commission (not to be confused with the city's HRC), which attempted to address racial, ethnic, and religious issues among Catholics in the city.[45] The changes Morales wanted were reformist in nature—inclusion in the city's power structure, including local war on poverty organizations—but his strategies were often radical and certainly a break from the norm in Grand Rapids. From the late 1960s until the late 1980s, he organized boycotts and pickets, shut down city meetings, and shocked city officials and residents alike with attention-grabbing stunts like riding a horse to city hall to protest educational inequality. Standing at six feet, two inches, his frame and over-the-top personality attracted a sizable following in the Latino community. Characteristically, a frustrated Morales once told Latino migrant workers in Grand Rapids who were waiting for food donations, "You have been living on your knees for too long. Stop praying and get out there and fight for your rights. . . . Get ready to march to the governor's office in Lansing."[46] This strong-arm attitude and unforgiving rhetoric was par for the course in other places during civil rights struggles. However, in Grand Rapids, where sit-down meetings were the norm, Morales represented the personification of radical organizing that many longtime Latino residents had feared.

Morales's radical activism prompted many in the Latino community to ask the question: had Mexican Americans and Puerto Ricans been too moderate in their push for greater civil rights? While acknowledging the slow pace of change and the political environment in Grand Rapids, many Latinos remained hopeful that gradualism would succeed. With Latinos representing just 5 percent of the city, many were reluctant to adopt confrontational politics. It seemed improbable that the large-scale public demonstrations that occurred in Los Angeles, New York, and Chicago could yield the same effect in Grand Rapids. As such a small population in a smaller city, Latinos were unlikely to draw national media coverage that helped in making larger protests successful. In addition, as a smaller group, they would have easily been overcome by the police—a well-known formidable force against eager protestors around the country. Business leaders and city administrators also colluded—with some operating simultaneously from both camps—increasing the likelihood of economic repercussions if protests grew too militant. In addition, many whites in Grand Rapids held conservative religious views that deemed sidestepping the legal system as imprudent. At best, Latinos were working at the margins, hoping for a seat at whatever tables they could access.

Given the environment, the people in power in Grand Rapids saw any Latino attempts at activism as radical. Historian Marc Rodríguez noted the same characteristics among Chicano student activism in the 1970s: their "demands were reformist—and the call for immediate reforms to the status quo was in itself radical."[47] Like Latinos around the country, those in Grand Rapids tried a variety of activist strategies, but they often chose institutional activism—or working with existing institutions—to achieve their desired outcomes. Consequently, when Morales arrived in Grand Rapids and employed his own spectacular tactics that did not work with existing institutions, some viewed it as too overblown and unnecessary. To others who saw institutional activism as not producing the desired results, Morales presented a much-needed answer.

Nevertheless, Morales's controversial organizing strategies and antics garnered press attention and raised questions about leadership within the Latino community. On two occasions between the 1970s and the 1980s, Morales became the focus of exposés that sensationalized his life story and what the press perceived as what would today be called a toxic masculinity. One reporter described Morales as "a six-foot, 230-pound Texan whose main lines of ancestry are Spanish and Indian."[48] Another reporter for the *Grand Rapids Press* likened him to a "tall broad shouldered man with a brown mestizo face and gravel voice" and as a "raging bull with a cause."[49] The press's portrayal of Morales played up his bravery, strength, and masculinity as well as exoticizing him with comments about his skin color and by playing to white stereotypes of male, Latino leadership by comparing him to an animal. Though there had been other leaders in this community, including less bellicose men and women, the press focused on Morales.

Morales's physicality, tactics, and rhetoric undeniably commanded attention among a diverse group of Latinos in Grand Rapids. In some cases, his support cut across various demographic categories. For example, his largest contingent of supporters were working-class men, younger people, and Mexican Americans. He had just turned forty when he arrived in Grand Rapids, and many Mexican American men who were his contemporaries also backed him. Daniel Vargas, a pioneer in the community, a trusted leader, and a lower-middle-class Mexican American, also supported Morales and even recommended Morales represent Latinos on the diocesan human relations commission. Vargas saw Morales as "an outsider who had not yet made enemies."[50] People outside of those categories welcomed his leadership as well. A much smaller group of women, middle-class Mexican Americans, and some Puerto Ricans across the socioeconomic spectrum also supported him. The clearest distinction between those who supported him and those who opposed him, however, derived from ideology. He drew in Latinos who believed there was a need for new ideas and strategies, but those who had faith that the systems in place would benefit the community did not ultimately support him. Vargas's comments signaled how strained political relationships had become in Grand Rapids by the time of Morales's arrival, and he quickly became one of the city's most polarizing figures. While many residents pursued the path of least resistance, Morales spent the next decade at the center of the struggle for Latino rights in Grand Rapids.

After years of being excluded from CAP and now MCP, some Latinos followed Morales's lead and embraced confrontational activism as a method of redress. Under Morales's direction, in December 1969, over sixty "Latins," as they were described in the press, disrupted a MNCC meeting to demand the appointment of four people from the Latino community to vacant seats on the forty-one-member commission. Cruzita and Pedro Gómez, a Mexican and Puerto Rican couple who had been in Grand Rapids since the 1950s, had gathered with other supporters that day. They went to that meeting because they knew funds were going to be distributed, but they wanted to know, as Cruzita recalled, "what about the Hispanic community?"[51] Standing before the committee, Morales appealed to the commonalities between African Americans and Latinos in Grand Rapids:

"we, like you, are tired of being errand boys and errand girls." However, he then insisted that the Latino community had "qualified people—that could teach you something."[52] In Morales's statements to everyone on the MNCC, Black and white alike, he was rejecting the idea that Latinos did not have ideas to offer such a committee. He and the other sixty Latinos at the meeting asserted that Latinos were valuable and capable of self-determination.

For their part, most of the MNCC was adamant about following MCP guidelines. Some MNCC members present at the meeting argued that the federal government could disqualify them from MCP if they appointed unelected people to an elected board. The precarious funding situation always weighed on the MNCC members' minds and often paralyzed their decision-making. Other MNCC members reminded their colleagues that, about a month prior, a HUD representative had criticized the MNCC for its lack of Latino representation—so perhaps it did not matter how Latinos joined the board. H. David Soet, a MNCC member, pointed out, "the day we walk into HUD and tell them we don't have any Latin Americans, we will be wrong regardless, whether we followed the right election procedures."[53] Furthermore, if the MNCC turned in its 1969 funding report without the addition of Latinos, they might risk government sanction. The committee faced mounting pressure to comply.

This confrontation forced African Americans to reconsider the demands of their Latino neighbors as well as how they related to them generally. Morales's exhortations resonated with at least one Black committee member, Phyllis Scott, who countered MNCC obstinance by offering, "What you are saying is what we have been saying to whites for years—'Let us have some policy-making power on your committees.'" Scott insisted that the MNCC take Latino demands into consideration given the similarities in their condition: "We should be the most understanding people in the city since we have been in that position before."[54] Scott also remarked that while she firmly believed people in Grand Rapids saw MCP "as a dream," she did not believe it could be successful "under the present leadership and certain committee members," signaling in-fighting within both MNCC and MCP.[55] The demonstration and chaotic meeting resulted in a much-needed conversation between Latinos and African Americans, and there was an opening to amend Latino underrepresentation in MCP.

Several days after Latinos attended the Model Cities meeting en masse, the MNCC added two Latinas—LAC board member Carolina Cantú and Ophelia Garza—to its ranks, adding to the few Latinos already on the MNCC. Cantú moved to the area in the post–World War II period and had been active with the LAC and with Our Lady of Guadalupe Church.[56] Garza was executive secretary for the LAC.[57] Their appointment foreshadowed the role Latinas would play in antipoverty programs in Grand Rapids. Yet, while the appointments of Cantú and

Garza helped to alleviate some frustration among Latinos, the move fell short of Morales's and his supporters' demands. They wanted Latinos in leadership positions. Latino organizers requested that, when it became available, the position of assistant chairman of MCP should go to Tomás Martínez, the first Mexican American MNCC member. The assistant chairman operated second only to the chairman, and the position paid a handsome $10,000 a year. Passing over Martínez, however, the committee chose Cedric Ward, an African American man who was already an MCP staff member. Hoping to assuage the concerns of their "Latin" constituents, they nevertheless created a part-time citizen participation specialist position that required the prospective candidates demonstrate fluency in Spanish. MCP chair Armond Robinson explained to the *Grand Rapids Press*, "Latins should not consider the [position] as a subterfuge of their demands." According to Robinson, the committee had devised the idea on December 8—two days before Morales showed up to the MNCC meeting with sixty people—and, on the surface, demonstrated an earnest gesture toward the local Latino community.[58] But Robinson's preemptive tactics only fanned the growing interracial tensions. While some Black MNCC members supported Morales in his quest for greater representation, his brash brand of organizing frustrated Black leaders, who became incensed by his refusal to respect the program's procedures.

Morales, by this time accepted as leader of this rebellion, balked at the temporary position that paid $6,500, pointing out that it held no decision-making responsibilities. Though Morales had resided in the city only for a little over a year, in a press interview he referenced a history wherein "Latins" were "overpowered" and "did not have a voice." He did not specify who was silencing them, but like other leaders in the community, Morales stressed how the language difference among Latinos and African Americans lay at the center of their dispute. "How can they claim to know what our problems are when they cannot even speak to us?" he asked, likely referring to the African Americans and the liberal whites who comprised the antipoverty machine in Grand Rapids.[59] In referencing the differences among African Americans and Latinos, Morales engaged a much-used political strategy that called attention to differences among these two groups as a way of garnering separate funding. This was a popular tactic in the 1960s and 1970s when federal funding was available but scarce enough to prevent substantial changes—ensuring that special interests fought for meager rewards. By stressing differences, Latinos or any other impoverished community could argue against sharing resources. The ideology behind the choices to separate varied. In Texas, African Americans and Mexicans saw themselves as racially distinct groups with little in common, mostly due to a popular notion among Mexican Americans that they held a higher status than African Americans on the social and racial hierarchy in Texas. As Mark Brilliant's work shows, "fighting their own battles" seemed the most sensible path for African Americans and Mexican Americans in Texas.[60] In New York City in the early 1970s, Puerto Ricans, who had a long history of coalitional work and a shared minority identity with African Americans, began to stress the differences from their former allies to demand more educational resources. Puerto Rican organizers took to arguing that African Americans and Latinos were different because Latinos spoke Spanish whereas their Black counterparts did not. Some even went so far as to insist that Puerto Ricans were "Hispanic," stressing their European roots. They regarded this identity as at odds with African Americans' Blackness.[61] The strategy had some success in securing funds, but it came at a great cost: it strained the decades' long relationships between African Americans and Puerto Ricans who had formed a cohesive, antiracist shared community up until that point.

For his part, Morales advocated for funding separate from that of African Americans, realizing that Latinos could acquire more funds this way as opposed to dividing them between the two groups. It was unclear whether Morales truly believed that African American and Latinos were fundamentally different. Nonetheless, it was a risky strategy. If his plan succeeded and administrators allotted more money to the city under MCP, benefits would accrue to both sides. If the plan failed, it could increase interracial tensions, prevent future coalitional work, and deprive Latinos and possibly African Americans of additional funds. It also ran the risk of alienating Afro-Latinos, who could conceivably see themselves as part of both groups.

Morales exacerbated the situation and increased the stakes of the fight because he offered a direct and more aggressive threat to local Grand Rapidian powerbrokers, who were more familiar with the conciliatory tone of the HRC's Daniel Vargas and various LAC leaders. "We feel like no one knows our problems like we have lived, and therefore, we will wage our war against any program that tends to exclude us and not recognize our problems," Morales exclaimed as part of his one-man battle against the frugality of antipoverty programs where Latinos were concerned.[62] Morales's statements matched the tone of the militant movements that were growing more popular around the country. He escalated his style to embrace an all-or-nothing strategy that left little room for negotiation. His rhetoric attracted people fed up with the slow pace of change, but it also infuriated many of the older, more established Latino organizers in the city. The latter group had put in considerable effort in forming networks that included city leaders, and Morales threatened their work. They publicly distanced themselves from him and tried to maintain their personal relationships with African Americans and white leadership. Even as activism across the nation acquired a more radical tone, this generation of leaders remained reluctant to support Morales's more confrontational strategies.

Despite their strategic differences, the LAC and Morales, who had yet to hold a leadership position in the organization, continued to exert pressure on MCP administrators. After the MCP denied Tomás Martínez the position of assistant chairman, members of the community undertook a strategic letter-writing campaign to inform prominent politicians across the country of the unequal distribution of power within the local MCP. The city's congressional representative and future president, Gerald R. Ford, American GI Forum founder, Dr. Hector García Pérez, and U.S. Senator Joseph Montoya of New Mexico all received letters. In addition to LAC members, representatives from several other local organizations—among the oldest and most active organizations serving Latinos in Grand Rapids—also signed the letters, including the Sociedad Mutualista Círculo Mexicano, the American GI Forum, the Raza Unida Party, and the Jalisco Club. The signatories argued that Latinos had "been systematically excluded from jobs and participation" in the war on poverty programs, while noting that "our candidates for employment are not given consideration . . . when we asked why we are not given consideration, we are immediately offered the lowest paying jobs available."[63]

More importantly, their letters called for an investigation into the administration of federal agencies in Grand Rapids, including CAP. Morales and his supporters charged Grand Rapids' antipoverty bureaucrats with racial discrimination against Latinos. They further demanded that all federal antipoverty program activities cease until the matter was fully investigated. While there is no record of an investigation, MCP administrators quickly set about hiring Latinos for other high-level positions after the letter-writing campaign. During the next election, Latinos also won twelve seats on the MNCC, reflecting not only the increased awareness among Latinos regarding MCP, but also the sheer extent and impact of organizing by the local leaders. Moreover, it also illustrated a newfound sense of agency that Latinos felt in their dealings with MCP. Yet, for Morales and his supporters, these additions hardly compensated for years of neglect and blatant disregard for Latino grievances. They desired a paid leadership position and more federal funds. Consequently, Morales went so far as to say that he was willing "to kill the MCP."[64] He called on Latinos to boycott the program until these demands were met, knowing that a lack of Latin American participation could get the MNCC in trouble with HUD and jeopardize its funding.

Black gatekeepers like the Tardy brothers and their Latino critics like Morales exposed the powerful toll that decades of exclusion had on the city's minorities. These issues also revealed the problems inherent to federal antipoverty programs—they were a flawed response to systemic racism, at best. For decades, Black middle-class residents demonstrated their worth to white leaders in Grand Rapids by upholding a religious respectability that they thought showed they belonged within the democratic politic of Grand Rapids. African Americans accomplished this feat by emphasizing their relationship to religious institutions and accepting supporting roles in white-run civic organizations in order to have some influence over the community funding. The hiring of Black administrators by the antipoverty programs implied that their decades of self-discipline and following the rules had paid off. When Latinos like Morales demanded inclusion and did so in a way that ran contrary to the respectability politics that held sway in the city, many African Americans perceived these actions as a threat. For their part, Black antipoverty leaders did not deny that Latinos suffered from racism. Their refusal to acquiesce to Morales's demands, however, showed how they safeguarded their hard-won positions in a white-dominated conservative space, fearing a loss of status if the process was overturned. Neither African Americans nor Latinos agreed with the hold white conservatives had over federal and local resources in Grand Rapids, but many felt that the current arrangement was their only option to address systemic racism. Black activists did what they needed to do within the system to receive the much-needed funding, also shunning more radical Black activists who tried strategies similar to Morales's. Black administrators felt that, if Latinos wanted to enjoy these resources as well, they would need to follow the same path.[65]

As for the Latino community, Morales's boycott was a step too far for some. Many argued that a boycott was out of the question, considering the job opportunities and funding for Latino-oriented programs that could be available through MCP. Latinas, who comprised a large percentage of first hires in MCP, most prominently articulated these concerns with the boycott. Across the United States, women obtained economic opportunities within war on poverty programs, which helped them to establish health clinics, Head Start programs, and welfare reform organizations.[66] For example, Black women in Mississippi who worked for Head Start often did so "in part because normative gender roles prescribed child rearing and teaching as women's work," long before federal funding became available for antipoverty programs. Women of color throughout the nation had supported and cared for their communities informally for decades through educating them at day cares and planning for their health care.[67] Grand Rapids was no exception. In the early spring of 1970 and in the immediate wake of the Latino protests against MCP in 1969, Irene Alba filled the citizen participation specialist position for MCP that Morales had scoffed at when the position was created. After relocating to Grand Rapids in the mid-1950s, Alba established a reputation for herself as one of the community's most vocal advocates.[68] She was also one of the founding members of the LAC. After Daniel Vargas resigned from the HRC in 1969, Alba joined the committee as one of Vargas's replacements, along with Francisco Vega, another founding member of the LAC.[69] Though there are scant records on Alba's life in Grand Rapids before the late 1960s, her appointment to the HRC signaled that she was enough of a presence in the community to represent them on this important board.

Officially the third "Latin" to serve on the HRC, Alba was the only Latina, demonstrating a shift in the status of women organizers in this community and their material advances during the war on poverty era.[70] Two Mexican American women, Ernestine Savala and Cruzita Gómez, also gained paid auxiliary positions in the local MCP around the same time. For Gómez, this appointment formalized the community work she had performed for decades, as her marriage to her Puerto Rican husband had opened the door for her to be involved in the Puerto Rican community as well as the Mexican community. Though she had supported Morales's campaign some months earlier, she did not agree with his boycott once Latinos started gaining paid positions. Instead, she regarded MCP as a conduit for her pursuit of an education. With the last of her eight children then in school, Gómez had started taking college classes in the field of education. And she was not alone. After experiencing firsthand how the program could offer resources and education to other members of the community, Latinas became strong advocates for MCP. Antipoverty programs, for the most part, legitimized the work that women had performed for years and established a way for women to make an immediate impact on their communities.

Eager to avail themselves of MCP's funds, Latino men and women continued to demand more resources. To meet their increasing demands, some activists encouraged the LAC to reach out to MCP for formal funding apart from other community groups. Some even floated the idea that perhaps the council could become its own federally funded organization. Morales opposed this suggestion, harboring concerns over cooptation from middle-class Black reformers or from white city hall administrators. Regardless of any opposition to the proposal, the LAC was in desperate need of additional funding.

Previously, the LAC depended on small grants and volunteers to serve the community. However, the local Latino population had since grown to eleven thousand people, which exhausted the LAC's budget. As local demographics continued to shift, the council also required restructuring to meet the evolving needs of recent transplants, including Mexicans relocating from the Southwest, Puerto Ricans migrating from New York and Chicago, many temporary migrant workers, and some exiled Cubans. With young people comprising a large percentage of the recent migrants, the LAC also needed to craft an approach that reflected the shifting political disposition of activists, falling somewhere between Vargas's gradualism and Morales's militancy.

"LATINOS DO NOT SUPPORT TÍO TACO": THE MODEL CITIES PROGRAM AND INTERETHNIC TENSION

The LAC's efforts to participate in MCP reveals that Latinos tailored the nationalist ideals of larger social movements to meet their circumstances, especially in an otherwise conservative climate. Mexican Americans and Puerto Ricans inscribed many meanings onto nationalism during the 1960s and 1970s. For some, it included committing to fostering ethnic and racial pride among Chicanos,

Boricuas, and other Latinos who identified as nonwhite. Mexicans and Puerto Ricans active in the LAC were fueled by pride in their identity and a sense of self-determination. While they demanded community control over social services, jobs, and education, they also nurtured spaces where they could grow more confident in their Latino identities. As the rest of this book shows, Latinos in Grand Rapids, with the assistance of the LAC, celebrated who they were through a bilingual community newspaper, educational activities that focused on sharing the history and accomplishments of Latinos and Latin Americans, and festivals that showcased Mexican and Puerto Rican foods and dances. The form of nationalism most Latinos in Grand Rapids embraced created an inclusive environment that celebrated their identities.

However, asserting nationalist pride had the potential to erase coalitional work and diversity while excluding people whose identities did not align with the dominant perceptions of Chicano or Puerto Rican identities. Morales and his supporters tapped into some of this exclusionary rhetoric of nationalism. During the Chicano movement, many nationalist organizers regarded loyalty to the cause as the most important factor for group cohesion and producing tangible gains for the community. Yet, this made it difficult for people with different approaches to challenge popular movement ideas. For example, Rodolfo "Corky" Gonzáles, an organizer in the late 1960s for the Crusade for Justice and the Chicano Youth Conference in Denver, Colorado, equated a former militant who took a job in an antipoverty program as "counter-revolutionary . . . not an ally . . . an enemy because he's contaminated," because he did not commit to working outside of the system.[71] Morales utilized similar language in Grand Rapids. When he discovered that some Latinos refused to boycott MCP, he labeled them "traitors." Within the framework political theorist Cristina Beltrán created to understand dissent in social movements, Morales—like Gonzáles—was branding his Latino opponents as "culturally and politically suspect."[72] He emphasized this characterization by using the term "Tío Taco," the Spanish version of "Uncle Tom," to describe people who didn't support the boycott. Morales rendered any difference in strategy as a betrayal to the cause, leaving little room for people to contemplate any opposition.

This rigid leadership style contributed to the emerging gendered conflicts within the movement. Mexican and Puerto Rican women's leadership in the antipoverty programs caused friction with Morales's group. As some of the first Latinos hired in MCP, women emerged as some of its most excited and fiercest supporters, despite their ongoing struggle for representation within the program. Two Puerto Rican women, Lea Tobar and Juanita Larriuz, displayed this pride when they posed in a photo for the MCP newsletter after they were hired as MCP community contact personnel. The photo shows the two women standing side by side and holding certificates indicating they had trained to teach mothers in their community about a nutrition program.[73] As these early hires proved, there were tremendous opportunities for women to be paid to do work that they enjoyed and found important. Many women thus opposed Morales's boycott. Morales and his supporters responded by calling them sellouts.

Men involved in nationalist movements often used this strategy to chastise women who ventured outside of traditional gender roles. Women taking paid leadership positions and openly defying an order from a Latino man fell into that category. Men also charged these women with deviating from the collective cause of self-determination when women accused the men of trying to silence them. This was a recurring problem across nationalist movements in the 1960s and 1970s. Many women involved in Black, Puerto Rican, and Chicano nationalist movements formed their own organizations exclusively for women because sexist attitudes in their coed groups stifled women's concerns and diminished their role in any major decision-making capacities.[74] In Grand Rapids, gendered tensions came to a head in March 1970, when Irene Alba's part-time MCP citizen participation specialist position tasked her with increasing Latino participation in the program. This would directly challenge Morales's boycott. However, Alba did not pause. One of her first plans to increase Latino participation within MCP was to gauge the community's interest in the LAC incorporating into MCP.

After the earlier public disagreements about the unequal representation between African Americans and Latinos under the program, one might have expected Latinos to jump at the chance to have the LAC receive federal funding. This would increase their decision-making power in Grand Rapids and perhaps result in additional funds for the Latino community's unique needs. However, Martín Morales and twenty supporters were prepared to leverage their boycott until MCP altered its leadership structure. Alba, on the other hand, proceeded to schedule a meeting where she hoped to inform Latinos about the benefits within Model Cities.

Alba and MCP administrators realized that Morales's attendance at the meeting would increase conflict. Numerous sit-downs, the letter-writing campaign, and the protests had strained relationships between Morales and the leadership at CAP and MCP. Hosting representatives from these groups in one room was tense enough, but Morales also had fallen out of favor with some of the old-guard Latino organizers, who found him unabashed and arrogant. Though these older activists remained frustrated with the unequal distribution of funds between Latinos and other groups, they favored an open dialogue with MCP officials, hoping it would produce more funding for LAC programs. However, Morales still charmed those who had grown impatient with MCP's painstakingly slow response to their needs. Should these diverse and outspoken constituencies all appear at the meeting, disruption was assured.

The events outside and inside the 1970 meeting that Alba planned exemplified the gendered, ethnic, and racial concerns that undergirded the debate about the MCP. Clad in heavy jackets appropriate for early spring in Michigan, Morales and about twenty other Latinos picketed near the entrance to Alba's MCP meeting on March 20. On the sidewalk near the brick Model Cities office building on the southeast side of the city, protestors held signs reading, "Latins Won't Take a Back Seat," "Brown Power, Viva La Raza," "Latinos Do Not Support Tío Taco," "Latins Want Parity, Not Charity," and "Latinos, Sí, Tío Taco, No!" Alfred Chambers, a frustrated African American MNCC member, told the group on his way into the meeting, "the problem with you people is that you don't speak English." This insult ignored both the signs in English and the protestors speaking in English. Perhaps Chambers's comment arose as a byproduct of Morales's strategy to accentuate the differences between African Americans and Latinos, especially when it came to language. Regardless, it added interracial tension to the already-present interethnic divides occurring outside of this meeting. As guests filed into the meeting, Morales stoked the flames of dissension by distributing an anonymously authored pamphlet that called into question Alba's leadership and the MCP: "We do not condemn her because her needs are as human as ours. We condemn the MCP that forces our people to such depths. Therefore, we ask a continuing boycott of the MCP. Beware of their Tricks! They still need our participation to get federal funds. Do not listen to anyone who comes to your door to offer second-class citizenship to our proud people. Boycott this evil program. We must not sell our souls, our culture, and our destiny for a crust of bread. Viva La Causa."[75]

The pamphlet author likened the fight against MCP to that of the Black freedom struggle and the labor movement, situating it within the rhetoric of other nationalist movements. "Second-class citizenship" was a phrase used throughout the Black freedom struggle to denote how citizenship did not guarantee equality for African Americans. For Mexican Americans and Puerto Ricans, for that matter, this underscored the notion that they were legally citizens, but were often treated as foreign without economic and political rights. The author cited this concept to illustrate how decision-making capabilities within MCP amounted to a privilege that Latinos could not access, despite their status as legitimate potential recipients of aid and residents of Grand Rapids. They tied their cause to the labor movement through the expression "crust of bread." During industrialization in the nineteenth century, workers demanded more than a "crust of bread," referencing the pittance of the profits that employers used to pay their workforce.[76] Boycotters accused MCP of distributing funds in the same manner. Moreover, positioning themselves as the laborers in this metaphor revealed how they viewed their struggle—as battling the capitalist class for a share of their excess wealth. In other disputes over antipoverty program funding, people likened the amounts they received to "breadcrumbs" as compared to the largesse of money spent abroad on the war in Vietnam. Lastly, adding "Viva La Causa" to the end of their message symbolically connected the fight with MCP to the United Farm Workers movement, who had popularized the phrase in this era. While the boycott of MCP arose from local conditions, the protestors understood it as a part of a long, nationwide history of injustice.

Alba refused to let Morales and the other picketers intimidate her. Bravely, she breached the picket line, followed by her supporters—men and women, Mexican and Puerto Rican, though there were slightly more women and more Puerto Ricans. Conducting the meeting in Spanish, Alba ensured that all Latinos would feel welcomed regardless of language abilities. Meanwhile, Cruzita Gómez, one of the Latinas first hired with MCP, offered an English interpretation. She translated Alba speaking about the action phase of the program: "Why shouldn't we take advantage of [the MCP's resources] . . . why should we be left out? Model Cities has said [more] Latin Americans will be hired." And Alba had no reason to doubt MCP administrators. With her petite frame, she commanded an entire room of onlookers, overshadowing the rising clamor just outside. "How can he represent the Latin community when he has been here only five months?," she asked, taking direct aim at Morales, who had arrived in Grand Rapids only two years prior. Alba, on the other hand, had resided in the city since the 1950s. Nationalists like Morales were not alone in employing the language of exclusion as Alba labeled Morales an outsider. Taking precaution against any possible repercussions from the protestors, Alba encouraged people not to be afraid as they exited the building but also to avoid engaging with the protestors.[77]

Morales's antics gained him coverage in the *Grand Rapids Press*, creating an opportunity for the city's conservative and white-run newspaper to showcase the dysfunction in local antipoverty efforts. "Latins Listening to Tough Guy Morales," read a byline for the *Grand Rapids Press*, while identifying Morales as the leader of the Latino community. In a statement sure to fan ethnic tensions, Mike Niemann, the columnist, insisted that Morales "was the catalyst for their tenuous unity," erasing the decades-long work of the community to cultivate a shared pan-Latino vision of social justice that included all the factions of the Latino community, not just Mexicans. The author also described how Puerto Ricans and newly arriving Cubans refused to fall in lockstep under the "Mexican banner."[78] Perhaps gratified by the attention, Morales did not refuse the title of community leader, nor did he refute the claim that Mexicans and Puerto Ricans just "did not mix," as Niemann claimed.

This assertion dismayed Dionisio Berríos in his capacity as a member of the LAC Board of Directors, as it did other Puerto Ricans. To Berríos's knowledge, no interethnic divisions threatened to undermine the greater Latino community or had prevented them from working together. Berríos knew more than most people about the community's strong interethnic ties, since he was a pioneering member himself. While Mexican Americans did possess the largest Latino presence in Grand Rapids and thus more of a political voice, Mexicans and Puerto Ricans alike had attended the MCP meeting that Morales picketed. Morales later doubled down on his criticisms against Alba, the LAC, and MCP by calling them "scabs." In his view, how dare they cross his picket line and assume paid positions within MCP? Sensing pressure from his base of support and outrage from other Latinos, Morales issued a public apology shortly after he made those comments. He claimed his goal was only "trying to unify our people to get justice for all." He then offered an apology in the "name of unity."[79] Some Puerto Ricans, like Berríos, accepted his apologies, but not all Puerto Ricans did. Either way, the incident fueled the public perception that Mexicans and Puerto Ricans were at odds. This observation failed to consider how tensions in the community often derived from competing egos and personalities instead of from ethnic differences.

Morales accurately noted the increased attendance of Puerto Ricans at the MCP meeting in March, but there were also more women than usual. In large part, they were recruited. Irene Alba, Cruzita Gómez, and other MCP employees had invited members of their various social circles and family members to hear about paid job opportunities. Given the nature of gendered friendships, Alba and Gómez told the women in their circles about the paid opportunities to help their communities. Cruzita's marriage to Pete Gómez, who was Puerto Rican, also offered her insight into the needs of the Puerto Rican community, more so than any other MCP staff member. And she specifically reached out to people she knew, many of whom were Puerto Rican.

The MCP meeting also attracted younger, Afro–Puerto Ricans seeking more of a voice in leading the community. Rubén Sánchez, a twentysomething Afro–Puerto Rican whose family was one of the first from the island to settle in the area, considered MCP a way to contribute. "I am one of the silent minority that is silent no more," Sánchez told a *Grand Rapids Press* reporter about his decision to attend the meeting. While Nixon campaigned on the "silent majority" as a reference to the growing conservative backlash to progressive gains during the 1960s, Latinos were often referred to as a "silent minority." It referenced their place as a minority but one whose voice was drowned out by African American political messaging. Sánchez added, "I have lived here twenty years and I want to help represent the Puerto Rican community," reframing his experience as part of a soon-to-be expanding minority.[80] MCP offered Latinos who may not have felt welcome a chance to help organize amid what seemed like a dual power struggle between Morales and Latinos who opposed him and Morales and the political establishment. Afro-Latinos like Sánchez and Latinas like Irene Alba, Cruzita Gómez, and others found that MCP had expanded to make room for their voices.

TRABAJANDO JUNTOS PARA PONERLO TODO JUNTO:
MAKING: A MODEL CITIES PROJECT

When the LAC relaunched many of their initiatives in August 1971, their stationery read: "The Latin American Council: Model Cities Project." After almost two years of resistance from Morales and others, the LAC Board of Directors had applied to MCP for federal funding and was quickly approved. Perhaps the increasing number of Latinos hired by MCP convinced the board members and the community to join. While many people initially supported Morales in what over time morphed into a one-man battle against MCP administrators, others distanced themselves from him, especially after his treatment of Alba. Former supporters witnessed his goal of providing more resources for the community slip away as his ego seemed to outpace his crusade. For example, when Miguel Navarro, a local Mexican American business owner, funded his Latino-oriented youth boxing program with MCP money, Morales "ribbed" him for taking the money and being a sellout in front of other Latinos at a bar to such an extent that Navarro returned the money.[81] Despite his at-times boorish behavior, a contingent of people stuck with Morales and understood him as well-intentioned in his effort to advocate for structural changes in MCP. Organizational tensions did not automatically disappear upon the LAC's acceptance into MCP, but many chose to forge ahead despite ongoing fears that the city government, which administered the program, would co-opt their organization.

The selection of the next director in 1971 exacerbated those fears. It is unclear why, but the council's previous director, José Álvarez, resigned in the fall of 1971. To remain compliant with federal funding requirements, the LAC had to replace him. MCP administrators suggested they hire Al Wilson to head the organization. Just recommending a successor felt like an overstep to many LAC members. Perhaps more importantly, Al Wilson was white. In a period when nationalist consciousness butted up against the intense white resistance that was surfacing in Grand Rapids and around the country at this time, this looked like a foolish move. But his résumé likely attracted the attention of MCP administrators. A trained social scientist, Al Wilson had lived and worked in Mexico City, Kenya, Nigeria, and Puerto Rico since the mid-1950s. Moreover, he had experience working with Mexican Americans elsewhere in Michigan through the U.S. Department of Labor. While working for HUD, he also evaluated the formation of the MCP in Lansing. Last, he held multiple degrees, including one from the Universidad de las Américas in Mexico City.[82]

Wilson had the credentials necessary to lead an organization receiving federal funds. He was familiar with the bureaucracy of the war on poverty and the federal government. Save for his racial background, he possessed the intercultural experience necessary to understand the plight of Latinos in the Midwest. Nevertheless,

Wilson agreed to take the position on a temporary basis and vowed to step down once the council was operating sufficiently. Wilson understood his particular position as a white man involved in the politics of minority representation in Grand Rapids. He knew his role would be temporary, and he promised not to make any decisions without advisement from the all-Latino board of directors. His stated intent was to lend his expertise in bureaucracy and to execute the wishes of the community. Many Latinos thought he was the right person to help the LAC access federal funding.

Still, Morales and a few of his supporters disapproved of Wilson. No extant records show who else applied for the position of director in 1971, but one might surmise that Martín Morales did. He continued to boycott the MCP and added the council to his list because it accepted money from MCP and hired Al Wilson. Morales's actions made it unclear what exactly the purpose of his campaign had been. To some people, oversight from the city government was why they resisted MCP, but most people had fought for equitable representation and funding. When the LAC became a Model Cities Project, it remedied the latter concern. Others felt the oversight was worth the trade-off, especially if they received the necessary aid.

Within a few short months, many of the concerns about Wilson, Morales, and infighting dissipated. The LAC started to receive the money it desperately needed, and it shifted from a group of volunteers to a full-scale social service provider, center of cultural awareness, and base for activism. Though the funds were modest, they also allowed for more full- and part-time positions. The tense working relationship between MCP, the CAP, and the LAC persisted, but it did not prevent the organizations from meeting the needs of the community. Irene Alba, Cruzita Gómez, and Lea Tobar took even more active roles in the LAC and MCP, revealing how antipoverty programs were instrumental in giving women more opportunities to lead. Mirroring trends within the expanding Black Liberation movement, younger Latinos also joined the fight, and a budding second generation of leadership emerged. The council's immediate success won over Morales and others as well. Cutting his losses, Morales continued to be an active part of the community. He dropped his boycott and eventually, when Wilson's term was up in 1973, Morales became the director, a position in which he stayed until 1978.

*   *   *

Federal antipoverty funds helped transform a group of volunteers into politicized organizers who demanded recognition for their plight and the resources to ameliorate it. The availability of federal money did generate some uncomfortable conversations about policies and equity between African Americans and

Latinos as well as among Latinos as a group. Through these discussions, however, the Latino community developed and identified leaders for the next round of battles, which involved clashing with Grand Rapids city officials. Organizing for recognition placed Latinos at odds with some African American leaders, who previously had maintained a firm grip on the limited funds distributed by the federal government.

Despite this friction, African Americans and Latinos—via CAP, MCP, and the LAC—had forged a working relationship within just a few years. Personality differences persisted among the administrators of these organizations, but when funding was not at stake these groups later demonstrated the benefits of a coalitional approach. They began to collaborate more and took on causes that mutually affected them, such as police brutality and the failing education system. As a sign of their progress, in 1972, MCP held a contest to create an emblem for the organization. The winning logo read, "Working Together to Put It All Together," with its Spanish translation, "Trabajando Juntos para Ponerlo Todo Junto." The logo depicted two hands shaking. Printed with black ink on white paper, one hand was filled in with black ink and the other was only outlined in black. Given the bilingual message, this could be interpreted as the filled-in hand representing African Americans, and the outlined hand representing Latinos or maybe even whites who were also involved in MCP. While the illustration could give the false impression that the categories of Black and Latino were mutually exclusive, it seemed that the two groups were trying to express, at the very least, that they were making a concerted effort to work together—and that years of organizing had resulted in Latinos' recognition within MCP.

Latinos gradually had gained visibility through tense discussions, pickets, and boycotts—fulfilling Daniel Vargas's vision that started in the early 1950s. Though Vargas's approach resembled gradualism, that was par for the course for organizers in the 1950s and early 1960s. Vargas's recommendation of Morales for the diocesan human relations commission perhaps signaled his acceptance of the need for more aggressive tactics. To be sure, these strategies had consequences. In 1970, Morales joined twenty-five Mexican Americans from across the state in a protest in Benton Harbor—a small city about seventy miles southwest of Grand Rapids. Deploying a strategy like the one he used in Grand Rapids, he and the others staged a sit-in to demand the reinstatement of a local fired Mexican CAP employee and the hiring of more Mexicans. Police promptly arrested fourteen protestors, including Morales.[83] Understanding the complexity of the consequences of organizing, Vargas's gradualism was part of an effort to teach Latinos to navigate the bureaucracy associated with accessing funds that poor people needed to survive while still maintaining working relationships. In retrospect, Latinos in Grand Rapids needed to employ a delicate mix of *both* gradual and more radical methods. Had they pursued solely one or the other, they would not have made as much progress. While gradualist methods sometimes led to more sit-down meetings without further action, radical methods alone might have led people to shut Latinos out of the conversation completely or led to sour relations between the community and CAP, as it did in Benton Harbor. Using both tactics ensured the federal antipoverty programs delivered on their promises.

As for Latino relationships, some of Morales's nationalist rhetoric threatened to dismantle the pan-Latino solidarity that the community had forged. However, the presence of organizers, mainly Latinas, with deep relationships to both Mexicans and Puerto Ricans helped to keep the community together and focused on improving their collective plight. Armed with federal funding, leaders turned their attention to alleviating poverty for Latinos in Grand Rapids. This process required less fighting among one another and more engagement with city administrators. Adding to those challenges, the war on poverty that Lyndon B. Johnson initiated was coming to an end under Richard Nixon. Though Nixon did not immediately end programs, he denied them federal dollars over the course of his term, leaving communities across the nation looking for ways to maintain their institutions without adequate funding. Under those circumstances, Latinos fluctuated between working within the system and pushing at its seams to make a place for themselves in this political landscape and to meet the community's needs.

– 5 –

Needs of the Community

Despite the tension and infighting that plagued the Latin American Council during the late 1960s, the LAC continued to play a significant role in the daily lives of many Latinos in Grand Rapids by the early 1970s. The organization especially influenced the Gómez family's sense of belonging and purpose in the predominantly white city, after they relocated from East Chicago, Indiana. For instance, when not working with the Model Cities Program, Cruzita Gómez provided interpreter services for the Spanish-speaking locals who frequented the council. She also worked with her husband, Pedro ("Pete"), to register voters through the LAC. The council's employment program helped Pete find a job at Pak-Sak, a local materials producer facility. Laura Gómez, Pete and Cruzita's daughter, attended various LAC youth activities.[1]

The Gómezes were not alone. The council had become a cornerstone of life for hundreds of Latinos in Grand Rapids. When surveyed, 69 percent of them agreed that the LAC "does an excellent job at providing services." Beyond the council's multiple social service initiatives, Latinos also gained insight about local politics through LAC-sponsored discussions and enjoyed the LAC's myriad of entertainment options. The LAC functioned as a space where Mexicans, Puerto Ricans, and even newly arrived Cubans continued to forge a pan-Latino solidarity, and it simultaneously emerged as a physical site of belonging outside of the home and church, as seen in previous chapters. MCP, which funded the council since 1971, declared the organization performed an "excellent job of meeting the needs of the community."[2]

But the exigencies of the national economy and President Nixon's tightening of the MCP's budget threatened the existence of the LAC. Ongoing federal spending on the war in Vietnam, a shift to the political right signaled by Nixon's election, and the tension arising from the slow progress in antipoverty programs coalesced to move national sentiments against locally administered antipoverty programs, leading to the loss of federal funding. While some cities had received Model Cities funding since the mid- to late-1960s, the LAC only started to accept funding in the early 1970s toward the tail end of the federal antipoverty initiatives. By allowing the funding for many of the Johnson-era programs to expire beyond their renewal dates, Nixon overhauled the fund distribution process, guided by his staunch opposition to sending federal money to local initiatives. For the few programs he left intact, he still greatly reduced the number of financial resources disbursed by the federal government. Instead, he recommended a "special revenue sharing" system that allocated federal funding with very few stipulations for how it was spent.[3] Most cities under this system technically would receive more money, but there would be no requirement that these monies went to fund any antipoverty programs.

Thus, while Latinos mounted a civil rights campaign, they did so with only a portion of the funds that the City of Grand Rapids dispersed to its other municipal functions. As a local journalist predicted in 1972, "projects not yet approved, such as the Latin-American Council . . . may be in for some trouble since they use almost 100 percent of Model Cities funds to operate."[4] To the frustration of the LAC, city officials tied the allocation of funds to the organization's ability to prove its efficacy in monthly, weekly, and even daily reports. Still, the LAC's budget withered, and they continuously sought ways to stretch their ever-shrinking coffers at a time when their community-controlled social services had finally started to have an impact.

Despite constant threats to their funding, Latinos involved with the LAC doubled down on its cross-ethnic solidarity efforts during the early 1970s, while also seeking creative responses to the LAC's limited budget. Mexicans and Puerto Ricans in Grand Rapids, like others around the country, fashioned a form of cultural nationalism that fostered Latinos' pride as a marginalized people and focused on improving the plight of their community. The decades of living and working together insulated these two factions from any attempts to privilege one group's needs over another's. Rather, they focused their joint efforts on transforming the city around them to meet the needs of all Latinos. They ensured that the LAC facility, located at 929 Grandville Avenue in a green two-story house with a basement, remained a sustainable physical space in the heart of a burgeoning Latino neighborhood. To help Latinos carve out a unique political and cultural identity in the mostly white and Black city, the LAC carefully curated events, programs, and a community newspaper that celebrated pan-Latino solidarity for Latino youths, adults, and elders.

Latinos also learned to practice institutional activism. This strategy encouraged improving Latinos' material conditions by working with already existing institutions. Their efforts produced lasting changes to the available prospects and resources for Latinos. Organizers around the country used similar strategies. For example, Puerto Ricans in New York used both identity politics and liberalism, seemingly contradictory frameworks, to demand that local government should meet their specific material needs, and thus brought about change to local community institutions receiving state aid.[5] While Latinos in Grand Rapids still suffered from glaring disparities in accessible social services, the council also established a wide variety of community-controlled programs to address those needs. In Grand Rapids, their services ranged from well-baby check-ups to employment services that assisted four hundred clients per month, facilitated by five full-time staff members, a handful of part-time employees, and volunteers.[6] The LAC also hosted political gatherings for many Latino youths and adults. Through the council, Latinos became knowledgeable about burgeoning social movements, fueled in great part by Chicano and Puerto Rican nationalism. The growing social movements and nationalist ideology prompted political organizing at the local level, and many Latinos now looked to electoral politics to make substantive changes to their conditions.

Popular memory of Latino and Black social movements of this period acknowledges a shift from integrationist frameworks toward calls for self-determination, separatism, and community control over resources.[7] However, the LAC enacted a form of advocacy that expands our understanding of political activism during the late 1960s and 1970s. Activists engaged in a dual approach that combined ongoing demands for integration within the context of community control that was more common than narratives of radical organizing describe.[8] In Grand Rapids, Mexicans worked together with Puerto Ricans and other members of the broader Latino community to gain access to local social service institutions, transforming these into spaces that grew more responsive to their communities. At times, their methods may have appeared conventional—or even somewhat conservative—in comparison to the more confrontational, direct-action tactics used in other locales. Nevertheless, in an era of political conservatism and reduced funding for social welfare programs, Latinos in Grand Rapids attempted to secure resources for their communities in a self-directed war on poverty but still radically insisted that social services represented entitlements that were long overdue for full-class citizens. Their increasing participation in the democratic processes of the city transformed local politics, which also provided leverage for their ongoing advocacy for all members of the Latino community.

The community defined their needs and what they saw they deserved of public funding to support themselves as citizens. Latinos in Grand Rapids created publicly funded initiatives that addressed the harms done by assimilation and thus focused on building pride in cultural identity. Others addressed material needs resulting from years of discrimination. By examining social welfare programs that formed via activism during a time of waning state funding in the 1970s, this chapter shows how people adapted and innovated when the federal government would not provide adequate funds for an equitable social safety net for all its citizens.[9]

The next section describes the LAC's ongoing fight for funding from 1971 to 1973. The remaining sections chronicle the initiatives the organization created while operating with a limited budget and engaging in a sustained battle for funding. These proposals included youth programs, a community newspaper, a social services program, and a base for Latino electoral politics.

"THEY DON'T WANT TO SEE THE LATIN AMERICANS GO FORWARD": THE CONTINUED FIGHT FOR RECOGNITION AND FUNDING

As federal funds waned for social programs, the LAC fought to convince the City of Grand Rapids that Latino residents needed and deserved funding.[10] Since 1971 when the organization first received funding from MCP, the council had difficulties funding its plethora of programs and services. As they attempted to execute their initiatives, the staff also investigated how to pull funding from other sources, including more money from MCP; the City of Grand Rapids, which oversaw the MCP budget; and the Kent Community Action Program (KCAP), a countywide distributor of antipoverty funding. Federal cutbacks to antipoverty programs plagued the LAC, which first led the organization to negotiate with MCP, the City of Grand Rapids, and KCAP for help meeting their operating needs. Specifically, the LAC asked for funding to carry out a Latino census of Grand Rapids and of the people who utilized its organization to prove its need and efficacy. When those agencies resisted, the council leaned on its allies in other social service and social justice-oriented organizations, not just across the city but also across Michigan and the Midwest. These efforts exemplified the challenges Latinos faced in trying to organize with the limited funding and increased bureaucracy that governed the early 1970s.

The Nixon administration's trimming of the federal budget resonated at the local level and furthered the need for a Latino census. In July 1971, just months after the LAC became a MCP affiliate, the federal Department of Housing and Urban Development (HUD) refused to fund three antipoverty organizations in Grand Rapids. With less and less money available, various levels of government in the Office of Economic Opportunity and HUD required accurate statistics to fund programs.[11] This motivated the LAC's desire for a Latino-specific census. City officials, both Black and white, did not support the LAC undertaking a separate census; they argued the 1970 U.S. Census already provided ample data. The LAC director, Al Wilson, countered: "initial attempts in 1970 by the U.S. Bureau of

Census to count the nation's Spanish speaking inhabitants have produced controversial results, and as such they are of only limited usefulness."[12] According to the LAC, the 1970 federal census estimate indicated that only 5,400 Latinos resided in Kent County, but the councils' estimate of the population in 1972 was 11,000—double the number of Latino residents reported in the census.[13] This finding fit the history of miscounting or inaccurately categorizing Latinos.[14] The council also had anecdotal evidence of the ways the city had failed Latino communities from their monthly and weekly reports. However, city officials insisted on relying on skewed empirical data and overly bureaucratic processes to determine funding allocations. This preference for quantitative data in antipoverty programs regularly discounted the experiences of marginalized people that could not be captured in statistics. In Grand Rapids, the data obfuscated Latinos' lived realities as a minority in the city. Yet, without such data, the LAC organizers possessed no means to lobby for the funding they desperately needed.

Documenting the presence of Latinos and continually putting pressure on city agencies developed into an essential strategy in securing a future for Latinos in Grand Rapids, where they were otherwise overlooked and underserved. The council soldiered on in attempting to find funds for a census. At a June 1972 meeting, the LAC implored city commissioners to think about the ramifications of such a miscount: "One result of this lack of precise population information is that Kent County Latin Americans have often met with resistance from local government and community agencies . . . for publicly funded governmental and community services as well as proportionate participation in the delivery of these services."[15] Still, the City of Grand Rapids responded by insisting that funding a survey was a wasted investment and advised the LAC to pursue other avenues. Patrick Barr, the second ward representative, remarked, "we have a tight budget and yet we're the only ones you're asking to provide cash."[16] Although he claimed to support the census in theory, he denied that it was the city's responsibility to provide the funding for it. The city's obvious disregard for the needs and voices of its Latino constituents did not deter the LAC from trying to convince the city's six commissioners to fund the survey. In one attempt to persuade the City of Grand Rapids, the LAC highlighted how a census could result in fund-raising from other lenders. The LAC reasoned that a city grant for the survey would lead to more accurate information, which would in turn aid them when applying for grants outside of the city, placing less of a financial burden on the city in the long run. Their quest for self-sufficiency required the cooperation of MCP and the City of Grand Rapids.

City officials eventually relented in late 1972 and supplied enough support for a preliminary census on the condition that residents living in the MCP target area were hired to help with the survey. This allowed the city and MCP to approve the project through their MCP budgets without earmarking additional funds to the LAC. With the limited funds, the LAC verified the addresses of a thousand Latino families in Kent County and found another thousand unverified addresses. However, they were unable to verify all the addresses without the proper funding. The LAC used the rest of its census budget to conduct in-depth interviews with a random sample of thirty-five families in Kent County. The Model Neighborhood residents worked on carrying out interviews, and the HRC offered to help the LAC hire Paul Aardsma, a professional sociologist and research director at a local foundation, to analyze the statistical data.[17] However, another threat to the LAC's funding emerged as the analysis of the census data was underway.

In late 1972, the LAC learned the application for their 1973 operating budget was denied due to MCP's funding stipulations, exacerbating the council's financial situation. MCP, a program designed to stop urban blight, allotted money for projects that served communities—which they called Model Neighborhoods—within the Grand Rapids city limits. The LAC, however, served clients that lived in and outside of its Model Neighborhood. Thus, MCP approved only $56,000 of the $116,000 the LAC requested for its 1973 operating budget. MPC director Ora Spady defended his position: "only about 20% of the Latin American community live in the Model Neighborhood [so we] felt we shouldn't be obliged to pay all the cost."[18] MCP and the City of Grand Rapids, which oversaw the MCP budget, committed only to funding the council based on the number of Latinos in the Model Neighborhood per MCP guidelines. Latinos, for their part, moved regularly between neighborhoods in Grand Rapids and from urban center to rural periphery due to migrant work schedules, layoffs, and the search for better wages or more affordable housing. Though Spady correctly assessed that only 20 percent of Latinos in Kent County lived in the Model Neighborhood, it held the highest concentrated population of Latinos in the county.[19] Beyond helping Latinos in Grand Rapids and its outskirts, the LAC also assisted anyone who came through its doors, even if they were not Latino. Given LAC's clientele and their specific needs, the money MCP directed to the LAC would simply not be enough. MCP administrators acknowledged the breadth of the LAC's services to those in the city and around the county, which taxed its small budget, but those officials did not believe MCP funds should support that outreach.[20] This setback dealt a major blow to the LAC's prospects of widening community service initiatives for Latinos and also threatened the organization's very existence.

In response, the LAC board members launched an expansive letter-writing campaign to the mayor and city commissioners to appeal for a larger operating budget for 1973. Other antipoverty organizations like the Urban League and the Grand Rapids' Tenant Union augmented the LAC's efforts by insisting that the city approve of the council's proposed budget.[21] Writing in solidarity, Chester Eagleman of the Grand Rapids Inter-Tribal Council wrote that "the local Indian community" was "familiar with a 'minor' minority attempting to upgrade the socioeconomic standard of our people" and supported the LAC's proposal of an increased budget.[22] Eagleman's use of "'minor' minority" references how marginalized groups criticized the disbursement of funds by Grand Rapids among the various oppressed groups, charging that the Black community received disproportionate amounts of funding (see chapter 4). Jane González, a local civil rights activist and city councilwoman in nearby Norton Shores, Michigan, wrote to support this cause. Her December 1972 letter stated that denying the LAC the funds it requested was tantamount to the city dismissing the work of the LAC for the past six years, which was "already well known, not only to [the] City Council, but throughout the Mid-west."[23] Shortly after the mayor received González's letter, Ricardo Parra of the Midwest Council of La Raza (MCLR), one of the largest Latino advocacy organizations in the Midwest, also wrote to support the LAC's "efforts to expand the 1973 budget to offer the Spanish speaking community of Grand Rapids true comprehensive services."[24] As the letter writers had discerned, the council's work had gained a regional reputation.

At city and county commission meetings, the LAC's board members and activists continued to hold the City of Grand Rapids and Kent County accountable for its lack of funding by drawing attention to local authorities' history of underserving the Latino community. In February 1973, Martín Morales, LAC's director at the time, accused city officials of "never [wanting] to help the Latin American people although many Latins live there . . . they don't want to see the Latin Americans go forward." Community organizers Richard Campos and David Rodríguez added that the refusal to adequately fund the LAC reflected "the city's usual treatment of Latinos."[25] They also decried the city's lack of progress in hiring an adequate number of bilingual or bicultural staff at its agencies, leaving it to the LAC to help Latinos. When KCAP also refused to add to the LAC budget, Morales reminded them, "the Council came into existence because of discrimination against Latin Americans," including KCAP's failure to hire any Spanish-speaking staff members within its own organization.[26] Organizers also pointed to the city's continued neglect of Latinos in the area and the hypocrisy in its refusal to adequately fund the LAC while not making any changes to city staff. Their relentless lobbying and continued acts of solidarity from the community succeeded in increasing the funds for their operating budget. The City of Grand Rapids granted an additional $19,000 to the LAC for 1973. Though nowhere near the original ask, it was still significantly higher than what MCP administration had first approved. The LAC now had to determine the best use for its limited resources to serve a growing clientele.

Within months of the new budget's approval, the results of the limited Latino census were ready, revealing what services people needed the most. Its coverage paled in comparison to what the LAC envisioned, but the census was a first step in documenting Latinos' presence. Relying mostly on the interview information they obtained, the LAC supplemented that research with the available public data. After Latinos had been in Grand Rapids for almost fifty years, the report the LAC produced, based on their census, was "the first scientifically collected data which reflect[ed] the unmet social and economic needs of the Latin American Community."[27] The results of this momentous undertaking revealed the precarious conditions for the Latino community. It found that in the Model Neighborhood, specifically the Grandville Avenue corridor wherein the council was located, 40 percent of the Latino population was under nineteen years old; 25 percent of them had graduated from high school (compared to 54 percent of whites); and about 17 percent were unemployed (compared to 6 percent of whites). Respondents reported their specific need for access to health care like dental care and interpreters at medical appointments. The Latino community also needed driving lessons, youth programming, English lessons, clothing, and job assistance.[28] The council now possessed the data to show that the young population did not have the basic social services they required. Moreover, the Latino community would need sustained educational efforts as well as immediate unemployment relief.

The council set to work improving its programming and devising even more innovative solutions to the challenges facing the community. While the LAC was not given the requested resources for the operating budget or the amount they needed for a comprehensive survey, they completed remarkable feats with what they had. Their persistent organizing and solidarity—with one another and other organizations—won them more self-determination. The LAC accomplished several initiatives from 1968 to 1973, all while fighting for adequate funding and resources.

A PLACE THEY "CAN CALL 'THEIR OWN'": YOUTH AND ADULT CULTURAL PROGRAMMING

By the early 1970s, LAC leaders had reached the limits of their patience with the City of Grand Rapids, which failed to provide adequate resources for its constituents. Yet, with few other options available, they realized that they still needed to work with city officials if they hoped to secure any funding at all. The cultural programming the LAC sponsored in the early 1970s reveals how the council balanced its desire to connect the struggle of Latinos in Grand Rapids to broader national movements while operating with a limited budget. The LAC sought to design a rich and robust curriculum for Latinos to try to offset an environment that had largely suppressed the celebration of Mexican and Puerto Rican identities. They did so by creatively harnessing the talents of their community members, many of them Latinas. They also wanted to incorporate programming that further promoted Black and Latino solidarity, which had blossomed among young people in the community, although a funding scarcity often compelled leaders to accentuate interracial differences to avoid being forced to share already limited resources. With the available tools at their disposal, the LAC generated compelling experiences for youths and adults in the early 1970s.

With 40 percent of the Latino population under the age of nineteen, Latino administrators rushed to build a space where young Mexicans and Puerto Ricans could express their cultural identities with pride. Al Wilson, then director of the LAC, relayed the communities' concerns to city officials, pleading for more money to fund the establishment of such a space and the salaries for LAC personnel. He justified the proposal on the idea that Latinos had "no center with permanent, on-going programs which they can call 'their own.'"[29] Indeed, there was no place in Grand Rapids where Latino youths could frequent and enjoy programming that centered on Latinos or provided bilingual services. The CAP sponsored social services for teen activities in two complexes located on the South Side of Grand Rapids, named the Franklin-Hall Complex and the Sheldon Complex, after the streets in which they were located. Latino and Black youths often attended at their leisure. However, young Latinos who did not speak English did not have the same experience as their English-speaking counterparts. One of the Latino community's greatest complaints about CAP services was that they employed almost no staff members who spoke Spanish. Wilson used this absence to argue for a paid youth coordinator. He pointed out that before the LAC joined MCP, the council boasted a youth group with at least seventy members who availed themselves of the chance to participate in recreational and service activities. However, the numbers fizzled out because the volunteers who ran the organization could not keep up with member demands while holding their full-time jobs.[30] With funding for a youth coordinator, they could host a club in the LAC's basement and extend programming for young people.

Wilson argued for the new council position based on the idea that Latinos represented a distinct racial group. Although Wilson was white, his training and field expertise as a sociologist guided his argument for why the LAC needed to create this position: "Youth need to identify 'with their own kind' in order to achieve a sufficiently, self-assured personality and social base from which, subsequently, to engage in interpersonal and intercultural tradeoffs with youths who are perceived by them, and who in turn perceive Latin American youth, as significantly different."[31] Without using the words "race," Wilson nonetheless highlighted some of the most pressing identity issues facing Mexicans and Puerto Ricans. For years,

"Mexican," "Puerto Rican," and "Latino" did not register on the spectrum of racial identities people in Grand Rapids recognized. Thus, their identity formation often forced them to choose from two well-known racial categories—Black or white—lest they be completely Othered, which many of them were.[32] This categorization left little room for Latinos to make claims to other racial and ethnic identities. For instance, Latinos could be both racially Black and ethnically Latino or racially white and ethnically Latino. To add to this dilemma, Black and white communities rejected or failed to acknowledge the Latinos who espoused dual identities. And city officials still tended to lump communities of color together.

For Wilson to explain to the nearly all-white city administration and MCP officials why young Latinos needed a place of their own with a full-time administrator to operate it, he had to stress the differences between African Americans and Latinos. Wilson, with his experience working in MCP programs in Lansing before coming to Grand Rapids, anticipated the critique MCP administrators would lob at his proposed youth program: they could label it a duplication of services given the other youth programs available at the Franklin-Hall and Sheldon Complexes. Like Martín Morales, the gregarious activist and future LAC director who fought with MCP over funding, Wilson decided to employ difference as a political strategy. He argued that Latino youths required a separate recreation center from the one that served African Americans. Engaging with the politics of recognition came with risks, as Morales had discovered. Elevating the visibility of Latinos' needs by distancing the entire group from African Americans had the potential to damage relationships with African Americans and erase Afro-Latinos. He couched his proposal to the city in not wanting to overtax already existing programs but also urged them to give Latino youths a space he felt they deserved. He found a strategy, although a problematic one. Underscoring the differences between Latino youths and "other cultural groups"—as he referred to them—Wilson explained, "the key element here is the unique ability of the Latin American Council to facilitate the satisfaction of those special bilingual and bicultural interpersonal needs which Latin American youth have." He then reassured MCP administrators: "it would seem that a full-blown youth program for Latin American youth . . . would not duplicate any existing youth programs either in the Model Neighborhood or elsewhere in Grand Rapids."[33]

These arguments were successful, yielding them one youth coordinator. With a permanent paid coordinator, the council officially hosted Latin American Youth in Action (LAYIA), a social group for area Latino teenagers, and provided space in the basement of the LAC building. Under the direction of the youth coordinator Rachel Campos, a Mexican American woman who was a part of the first generation of Latinos raised in the area, the LAC created a drop-in center where teens could come and hang out. No longer forced to congregate in their homes or on the streets, young people now enjoyed a safe, dedicated place of their own where they could play pool, listen to music, or simply enjoy supervised gatherings, much to their parents' approval. They also enjoyed LAYIA-sponsored events, participating in excursions and workshops, where they discussed issues of identity, social movements, and other topics of interest to teenagers, like dating.

LAYIA became a welcoming place for Latino youths of varying identities and attracted devotees for various reasons. For example, Victor Báez, a MexiRican teenager, served on LAYIA's executive board and did not live near the council, revealing the draw the youth organization had for Latinos across the city. During the 1970s, Rafael Hernández, who is also MexiRican, attended LAYIA as a teenager.[34] Though he lived in the Burton Heights, which was about ten minutes by car and much longer by foot, he visited the council when he spent time with his cousins on Grandville Avenue. In fact, about half of the young people who came to LAYIA did not live near the LAC.[35] However, those that lived on the southwest side near the council found the centrally located drop-in center to be an accessible meeting place for their Latino and non-Latino friends. Though Wilson employed the politics of recognition to garner funding for Latino youth experiences, that strategy did not affect Black youths' choices for leisure and entertainment. African American teenagers Billy Tappin and Malcolm Montgomery, who lived near the council, regularly frequented the drop-in center. Though Tappin could have gone to the Franklin-Hall or Sheldon Complexes for youth programming, the LAC was close to his house and his "friends went there." Tappin felt so welcome that he joined the executive board as LAYIA's sergeant at arms one year.[36] Youth programs like LAYIA made a difference for Black and Latino young people living in a majority-white city and region.

LAYIA members requested multiple types of programming, and women in the community used their expertise and time to craft Latino-centered cultural events and celebrations that were not regularly available in formal settings anywhere else. With over sixty registered members and, on average, twenty to thirty students attending weekly meetings, their interests ranged.[37] Some wanted to bring speakers to Grand Rapids to talk about the Chicano movement, while others wanted cooking classes and hair care classes. Rachel Campos relied on community members to provide enriching experiences for the teenagers. For example, a Planned Parenthood representative, Alice Garza, came to LAYIA's space in the basement of the LAC to host "kickbacks," or small gatherings, and give informational presentations. At the request of the students, Garza returned once a week for a one-hour drop-in session, where students felt comfortable raising all types of concerns, including issues related to reproductive health and sex. Campos also invited women from the community to lead Mexican, Puerto Rican, and Cuban cooking lessons. Carmen Fitte, a licensed cosmetologist and a Puerto Rican transplant form New York, taught students new hairstyles. Other women led additional workshops such as silk screening. Dance rehearsals, however, offered some of the most fun. Led by Rachel Campos and Sara Ramírez, a Puerto Rican LAC staff member, LAYIA youths learned traditional Mexican and Puerto Rican dances, which they performed at not only the Mexican Independence Day festival, but also Grand Rapids' Festival of the Arts—a popular annual festival that began in 1970.[38] These events, which depended greatly on women volunteers, posed little extra budgetary burden and were yet another example of the unpaid labor women provided for their communities. Their time and energy with the youths was highly valued, however. After years of forced assimilation in school, LAYIA events granted students a chance to explore their identities and connect with various elements of their cultures.

The LAC's facilities provided many opportunities for Latino adults to learn more about Latino histories and current issues, just as the youths did. LAC administrators understood the importance of organizing cultural events for their constituents. Previously, cultural traditions usually occurred in church basements, private homes, or in select entertainment venues. With its building in the Grandville Avenue neighborhood, the council could provide culturally relevant entertainment options that were both geographically and financially accessible. For example, the LAC boasted about its regularly scheduled events, including a free film series. Selected films included the canonical *Salt of the Earth*, and others that chronicled the Puerto Rican Young Lords Organization's activities, Cuba's campaign to eradicate illiteracy, and the guerrilla resistance in Guatemala.[39] A local college student group, La Lucha, selected films that portrayed a bit more of the radical leanings among young people as opposed to the more moderate stance the LAC usually embraced. The council walls formed a haven for Latinos to learn about the more revolutionary elements of their culture and history, as well as that of other Latino ethnic groups in a way that was often unattainable elsewhere in Grand Rapids. The later addition of a Latino library with culturally relevant literature and resources in 1973 (see chapter 7) expanded the enrichment possibilities accessible to the community. Augmented by LAYIA-centered events and services, the LAC financed occasions for Mexicans, Puerto Ricans, and other Latinos to continue learning about their individual histories and one another's cultures, strengthening their pan-Latino solidarity.

LA RAZA AND *QUÉ PASA*:
PAN-LATINO SOLIDARITY AND NATIONALISM IN A COMMUNITY PAPER

During the early 1970s, the LAC expanded its services for the growing Latino community to include a bilingual newspaper. *Qué Pasa*, a federally funded, community-run newspaper for the Latino community, added an avenue for cultural identity development during a period of heightened nationalism for midwestern

Latinos. As the first newspaper in Grand Rapids that directly served the Latino community, *Qué Pasa* serves as a lens into the formation of interethnic solidarity against Grand Rapids' conservative background. The newspaper was published and funded by the MCP from 1971 to 1974. As part of MCP's commitment to resident involvement in local politics, the newspaper fulfilled a requirement for MCP organizations like the LAC and kept the community informed.[40] Residents living in the Model Neighborhood received copies, and the LAC stocked copies for community members to read. This free publication functioned similarly to the community census, given that the articles also expressed the most pressing concerns for Latinos in a majority-white area: language loss, forced assimilation, and a shortage of cultural and financial resources. More importantly, the paper's editorials, columns, and advertisements reveal how Mexicans and Puerto Ricans wrestled with how to fashion their pan-Latino solidarity while considering the Chicano and Puerto Rican cultural nationalism emerging in the Southwest and New York, respectively, that at times stressed pride in one's national culture above all else. This process occurred differently in the Midwest than in other places—especially in Grand Rapids, where Latinos were a numerical minority in a conservative city. Even with all the challenges *Qué Pasa* faced, the newspaper, like the LAC, was a sign of placemaking and belonging to the Latino community.

The introduction of a bilingual newspaper in 1971 illustrates the significance of federal funding to the development of Latino political organizing in Grand Rapids. Compared to the emergence of Spanish-language news publications in the Southwest, New York City, and Florida—whose publications dated back to the turn of the twentieth century—Grand Rapids' Spanish-language paper arrived late.[41] Even midwestern locales such as Indiana Harbor, Indiana, published *El Amigo del Hogar* as early as the 1920s. However, prior to the 1970s, Latinos likely lacked access to the necessary capital to launch such a project in Grand Rapids. During their early settlement in Grand Rapids, Latinos were a tight-knit community, so they may not have seen the need for a large-scale publication. Church bulletins and early club newsletters likely were the most immediate instruments for disseminating information. With funding from MCP in the 1970s, the community could begin to circulate *Qué Pasa*. In an editorial for *Qué Pasa*, Paul Mitchell, a Chicano college student, suggested that "newspaper[s] [provided] a forum for ideas, a base for Chicano culture and the tool by which the seeds of unity can be planted."[42] The paper spread community news while centering Latino culture after decades of marginalization and exclusion.

As eager as Latino Grand Rapidians were to promote *Qué Pasa*, ideological differences and budget constraints threatened the paper's launch in 1971, revealing the precarity of the paper's existence. Per MCP's requirements, the LAC's funding was contingent on the publication of a newspaper, but it did not allocate the council a separate budget line for this endeavor. Council administrators thus staffed the paper with volunteers so they could direct their budget to other underfunded LAC programs. Irma Aguilar, a Mexican American woman who grew up in Grand Rapids, served as the volunteer editor of the paper when it started. Recognizing the constraints of running a paper with no money, she planned to produce the paper in English to give non-Spanish-speaking people in Grand Rapids information about the community, hoping to garner financial support from non-Latino readers. Utilizing the capital of other people and organizations was a tried-and-true survival strategy that Latinos had practiced in Grand Rapids for years. On the other hand, Lea Tobar, then a newly hired Puerto Rican assistant assigned to work with the LAC by the MCP, argued that the first Latino newspaper in Grand Rapids should be printed in Spanish to reach people who were often isolated due to their inability to speak English.[43] Tobar intended to prioritize monolingual Spanish readers and speakers, a far cry from their treatment in previous years. Moreover, MCP, which funded the LAC, stated that the council had a "contractual obligation" to print a Spanish-language newsletter.[44] Not surprisingly, Tobar and García settled on a bilingual paper, which both fulfilled MCP's requirement and appealed to a broader circulation.[45] Moreover, the articles in English likely reached the second-generation Mexicans and Puerto Ricans who spoke and understood Spanish, but could only read in English due to the lack of bilingual education in Michigan.[46] Some articles were in both Spanish and English, and others appeared in only one language. Having a bilingual paper allowed *Qué Pasa* staff to fund-raise and engage Latino readers with their thoughts on the nationalist movements occurring across the country.

Many of *Qué Pasa*'s articles and editorials related to the larger Chicano and Puerto Rican nationalist movements. Inspired by the Black Power movement, Puerto Ricans and Chicanos sought self-determination and cultural pride in the late 1960s and 1970s after centuries of racism and colonization. The Black Power movement, which proclaimed "Black is beautiful," gave members of the African diaspora a sense of intellectual, political, and cultural belonging. Chicanos and Puerto Ricans joined African Americans in protesting discrimination in jobs, housing, education, and health care. The formation of self-defense and advocacy groups like the Chicano Brown Berets and the Puerto Rican Young Lords, modeled after the Black Panthers, helped these groups celebrate their identities and fight for greater civil and human rights. *Qué Pasa* and the LAC recognized these nationwide movements and tried to connect those issues to their community. The paper ran news stories about Chicano movement conferences and sent its staff to them when possible. Other articles informed readers of the United Farm Worker boycotts and encouraged readers to help. For example, Richard Campos's essay in a November 1972 *Qué Pasa* called on Grand Rapids Latinos to boycott nonunion lettuce so that farmworkers could have a "decent life and a fair wage."[47] While he was referring to farmworkers who lived in California, this article and others connected residents to nationwide events that affected all Latinos. The LAC also tried to educate local Latinos with film screenings. For example, one issue of *Qué Pasa* included a notice of a film and presentation on the Young Lords in New York.[48] These actions helped Chicanos and Puerto Ricans in Grand Rapids associate their political circumstances to the larger nationalist movements happening elsewhere.

The concerns of the wider Chicano and Puerto Rican movements around language loss already resonated with some local Latinos, who expressed their concerns in *Qué Pasa* editorials and columns. Retaining Spanish as a connection to culture was a cornerstone of both social movements nationwide. The Young Lords in New York organized alongside parents to ensure Puerto Rican students had access to bilingual education, as did Chicanos in East Los Angeles. While language retention was a concern for most Latinos, organizers in Grand Rapids felt particularly worried given the demographics of the area. Walter Acevedo, an admissions counselor at Grand Valley State College and a *Qué Pasa* contributor, penned "Reflections on Our Language" in 1972. Due to the stigma of speaking Spanish in public in Grand Rapids, Acevedo stated his concern that Latinos in Michigan would lose their ability to speak the language at all. Originating from outside of the Midwest, Acevedo was shocked he could go "whole days [without] convers[ing] with an *hermano* in Spanish."[49] However, it was not the isolation that bothered him as much as the shunning of the language itself. "Language is a living, breathing, and vital part of my existence," Acevedo insisted, and without speaking Spanish regularly, he wondered if one could "murder a language." Acevedo's preoccupation with maintaining Spanish suited the Midwest setting, wherein Latinos were a minority and the opportunities to speak Spanish were limited. Indeed, many Mexicans and Puerto Ricans in Grand Rapids had been shamed into dropping the use of Spanish. *Qué Pasa's* staff and community members lamented the loss of Spanish because it meant detaching from a part of their identity—one they previously had been made to feel ashamed of but were currently celebrating with nationalist zeal.

Qué Pasa writers also underscored how Spanish was the foundation for the community's shared identity—the ability to speak the language is what had brought Mexicans and Puerto Ricans together in Grand Rapids and elsewhere across the country. This unifying characteristic held extra significance in the context of nationalist movements. Though the Chicano and Puerto Rican movements had overlapping aspects, they primarily energized and unified their respective ethnic groups. The Chicano movement rhetoric motivated Chicanos, and it was the same for Puerto Ricans involved in the Puerto Rican nationalist movement.

At times, the rhetoric used did not promote a pan-Latino identity. Thus, *Qué Pasa* writers faced a dilemma: how to engender the same level of unity that the Chicano Movement and Puerto Rican nationalist movements inspired in their separate communities in a city like Grand Rapids where Mexicans and Puerto Ricans organized together?

Mexicans and Puerto Rican Grand Rapidians overcame this impasse by rallying around their use of Spanish and their concept of race to bolster unity. To them, speaking Spanish and being Latino amounted to membership in *la raza*, which can mean in "the race" or "the people." While many Chicanos used this term to refer to Chicanos exclusively, *raza* in the Midwest became synonymous with "Latino" and generally referred to people who spoke Spanish.[50] The LAC and *Qué Pasa* staff, to partake in the 1960s and 1970s cultural nationalist movements, used *raza* to unite the Latino community under one category in a highly racially bifurcated Grand Rapids that recognized only white or Black identities. For example, Puerto Rican *Qué Pasa* columnist Sara Ramírez attended the Primer Congreso Nacional de Tierra y Cultura, a Chicano nationalist conference in Albuquerque, New Mexico, in 1972, and her time with Chicanos and Puerto Ricans at the conference invigorated her. She brought back a message for *Qué Pasa* readers: "Nuestra lengua es la razón de ser[,] el español es la raza, y el día que muera el español ese día muere la raza" (Our language is the reason for being, Spanish is the race and on the day that Spanish dies the race dies with it).[51] *Qué Pasa* subscribers received a clear lesson: *raza* and the Spanish language were intimately tied to one's identity. This framing pressured Mexicans and Puerto Ricans to maintain their use of Spanish to bolster their unity and strengthen their *raza*. During a time when racial identity dictated how other nonwhite groups such as African Americans were organizing, using a "racial" identity via *raza* and the Spanish language as an identifier further united Grand Rapids' Mexican and Puerto Rican communities in this nationalist moment. It also put them in conversation with other race-based movements.

Conceptualizing Latinos as a racial group predicated on the use of Spanish was problematic and fraught with the potential to exclude. This configuration of pan-Latino identity had the ability to homogenize Mexicans and Puerto Ricans along with their unique histories and lives. It also excluded non-Spanish-speaking Latinos and shunned monolingual, English-speaking Latinos whose parents chose to spare them the stigma associated with Spanish in Grand Rapids. Moreover, referring to Latinos as a distinct race had the potential to further erase Blackness from Latino identities because this framework made being racially Black and racially Latino mutually exclusive. This version of Latino identity left no room for Afro-Latinos. Against the backdrop of the nationalist movement and the racial dynamics in Grand Rapids, Latino leaders willingly disregarded the linguistic and racially complex identities of Latinos to carve out a space for a pan-Latino alliance amid the Black-white dichotomy in Grand Rapids.

While Chicanos across the country stressed their indigeneity and language, Acevedo's 1972 *Qué Pasa* article was consistent with some leaders' concern that Chicanos in Grand Rapids would adopt whiteness to gain acceptance in a white-majority city. His column argued that many Latinos who possessed lighter skin regarded speaking Spanish as the one aspect of their identity that prevented their assimilation into whiteness. He declared: "Hermanos, Spanish is the mainblood [*sic*] of our cultural survival as a definable article that will not melt easily into the 'American Melting Pot.' This aspect of our language is a vital part of our identity. . . . The Chicano can be assimilated too easily into the white, dominant society." Acevedo warned that it might be tempting for Chicanos to lose their language in "order to make it as a being in our society."[52] His fears may have been founded on the decades prior, when Mexican Americans did claim whiteness as a strategy against discrimination.[53] That Acevedo could see whiteness as a possibility for Chicanos perhaps reveals how Chicanos in Michigan differed from those elsewhere. Though full assimilation into whiteness was not possible for all Chicanos, he was still concerned that people would try it there. While part of Acevedo's editorial aimed at invoking solidarity among Mexicans and Puerto Ricans, these quotations demonstrate that he used *Qué Pasa* to address specific issues among Chicanos. This message to resist assimilation was not directed at the Latinos in Grand Rapids, both Mexican and Puerto Rican, who could never assimilate into whiteness because of the color of their skin, regardless of their skill with English or Spanish. It was for lighter-skinned Chicanos who considered assimilation. The presence of this editorial highlights the pressures on Chicanos in Grand Rapids to stop using Spanish and to abandon other cultural markers during a national movement that celebrated their ethnic identity.

Through their choices in advertisements and announcements, concerns about the precarity of funding, like the threat of language loss, was also ever present in *Qué Pasa*'s content. The cash-strapped LAC ran advertisements from organizations that could have been considered controversial in the Latino community during the 1970s. For example, recruiters for the army and navy advertised in *Qué Pasa*. One small announcement in 1972 read, "Captain José R. Ramos from Fort Sam Houston, San Antonio Texas would like to speak to all the young people over 15 years old about opportunities for both men and women to enroll in an officers['] school academy. He has a lot of information for the young people on how to continue their education through benefits from the Army Corps."[54] This announcement was representative of how the military targeted Latinos for enlistment. This advertisement also shows the line that Latinos in Grand Rapids walked: trying to provide opportunities for young Latinos while also engaging with nationalist movements that rejected military involvement, especially during the Vietnam War.[55] On a national level, Chicano antiwar activists pointed to the evidence that showed Latinos died in the war at a disproportionate amount compared to their percentage of the total population—a fact that emerged as a defining issue of the Chicano movement.[56] Puerto Ricans also worried aloud that their service in Vietnam would further serve to "protect the economic, military, and political interests of the colonizer," as Oscar López-Rivera, one of the most prolific modern Puerto Rican independence activists, warned.[57] While the antiwar narrative is well-known, scholars have also shown the Mexican American community's turn to protesting the war came on the heels of decades of patriotism and participation in World War II.[58] Thus, examining Latino engagement with the military while also engaging with nationalist rhetoric in Grand Rapids shows us the tensions between patriotism and protest that existed for this community. With diminishing revenues from MCP, LAC and the *Qué Pasa* editors may have thought that they had no other choice but to accept financial support from all manner of sources. Given the limited opportunities for Latino advancement in Grand Rapids, the editors might have also viewed this advertisement as a way to pass along critical information for Latinos seeking educational opportunities.

Meanwhile, government agencies possessed their own motives in forming a relationship with *Qué Pasa*, especially the local police department, which also ran advertisements for open positions. In the early 1970s, the Latino and African American communities were in the process of trying to transform the Grand Rapids Police Department through the enforcement of new federal affirmative action hiring policies that attempted to reduce discrimination by creating more opportunities for jobs for marginalized peoples. This often resulted in racist backlash. In 1969, the 371-person police department's staff remained almost all white, except for thirteen African American officers. There were zero Latinos on staff.[59] Whether or not the LAC solicited the police ads is unclear, but in May 1972, Officer Don Creswell, a member of the Community Affairs Unit, submitted an advertisement to *Qué Pasa* containing the department's listed job requirements for officers with information about how to apply. Like discussions about the military, the topic of policing usually invoked strong opinions within the Latino community, likely a result of the tense relationships between Latinos and law enforcement. Although much of the public focus on police brutality has centered on the relationship between predominantly white police departments and Black citizens, Latinos regularly encounter instances of police brutality, specifically in places where they have higher populations, like in Chicago, New York, or Los Angeles. These historically fraught relationships with the police rendered the thought of aspiring to be a police officer distasteful to some in the community.[60] Complaints of police brutality toward Latinos did occur in Grand Rapids. Yet, rather than snub the opportunity to join forces with the profession that brutalized them, Latino leaders imagined that more Latino police officers could help address their community concerns, including complaints about abuses of power.

The police and military advertisements show the varied ideologies that guided Latino pursuits of upward mobility and the newspaper's ability to reach different cross-sections of the community. Though some more radical members of the community might have seen the LAC as "selling out" to these institutions, the presence of other job ads and articles describing disproportionate Latino unemployment suggests that the advertisements for the military and the local police could have also been the LAC's way of trying to assist the unemployed at all costs. The inclusion of these ads, the discourse around loss of language, and the cultural nationalism all illustrate how organizations like the LAC and individual Latinos negotiated their varying identities in Grand Rapids with limited financial and cultural resources.

SERVING THE COMMUNITY

The LAC filled a cultural and social service void among Latinos in Grand Rapids by sponsoring LAYIA and offering *Qué Pasa*. However, with an expanding Latino population, the LAC discovered that it had to increase its level of advocacy to ensure that its constituents' basic needs were fulfilled. These needs escalated in proportion to the level of neglect they experienced from federal and local agencies, the latter of which had no Spanish-speaking employees. As a result, Latinos who did not speak English often were completely shut out of the country's social welfare system, receiving any of their benefits as U.S. citizens, or any assistance for meeting their basic needs unless they had a family or friend who could interpret for them. LAC directors Al Wilson (1971–73) and Martín Morales (1973–77) consistently lobbied the City of Grand Rapids and local agencies to convince them to hire more Latinos. Rank-and-file employees at the LAC used every available resource and formed relationships with other organizations to provide health care, general welfare, and unemployment services to up to four hundred Latinos every month.[61] The LAC thus emerged as a viable force in expanding Latinos' access and control over social services. Though there remained a scarcity of resources in the LAC, the efforts of council employees made it possible for Latinos to remain in Grand Rapids.

Outreach workers at the council performed an important function when they accompanied clients to appointments ranging from medical to governmental in order to interpret for them, turning what was once unpaid labor into a paid position that was acknowledged and valued. When the community was smaller in the 1950s and 1960s, Cruzita Gómez, Daniel Vargas and others escorted people to many such appointments. During the mid-1960s, Vargas worried: "In most agencies, Spanish speaking employees who could serve as interpreters are not available. . . . Many Latin-Americans have been unfairly treated and on numerous occasions. . . . [I have had to] personally serve as an interpreter without remuneration."[62] Consequently, he had demanded that the city hire Latinos in those agencies, holding multiple meetings with the Kent County Welfare Department and the Michigan Employment Securities Commission to discuss this very issue.[63] The LAC also coordinated with other local advocacy organizations, especially regarding migrant workers, including Michigan Migrant Opportunities and the Michigan Committee to Aid Farmworkers.[64] However, almost ten years later, the city's record on Latino employment remained dismal. Instead, it was LAC staff members who spent most of their work hours holding intake meetings with new clients, assessing their needs, making appointments for them, driving people there, and interpreting for them at those appointments. Without bilingual people at the most basic social service agencies, the LAC's community outreach center made the difference in people getting what they needed and showed city agencies' glaring lack of concern for Latinos.

Severely underdeveloped public resources for Spanish-speaking poor people led the council staff to help residents take the first steps in accessing entitlement benefits. Many of their clients were in the most desperate conditions. In a report on LAC activities, the director reflected on the challenges the council faced in helping those people "with unemployment increasing, and with migrants beginning to trickle into Grand Rapids . . . the most frequent problem our staff is dealing with are concerns and assistance in establishing eligibility for welfare and related social service benefits, establishing eligibility for unemployment compensation, and job screening."[65] These entitlement benefits could carry people over until they found jobs, which the council could also assist them with. One complication for the LAC was that applicants required valid identification to sign up for benefits. For former farmworker clients without IDs, the outreach worker had to contact the client's home state to request copies of the appropriate documents. From there, they could try to secure welfare, Medicare, and food stamps. Staff estimated that they spent at least eight hours with everyone who signed up. The process was cumbersome, but it often made the difference between Latinos having to leave Grand Rapids or being able to live and thrive there with the benefits they were entitled to as citizens.

From 1971 to 1973, the LAC employed several outreach workers, each possessing the blend of necessary skills to operate as social service advocates and community activists. Three outreach workers at the LAC in the early 1970s exemplified this skill set. Richard Campos, who was Mexican American and the brother of youth coordinator Rachel Campos, traveled to Chicano conferences and was involved in the United Farm Workers movement.[66] David Rodríguez, another Mexican American, worked for MCP, was the first Latino to be hired in the local employment recruitment office, and eventually was elected as one of the few Latino school board members.[67] Carmen Fitte, the Puerto Rican who relocated to Michigan from New York, lent her vision and skills to the outreach work of the council, subsequently emerging as one of the fiercest advocates for Latino education in Grand Rapids. Along with many others, these three workers managed many dockets, including educational concerns, commissioner meetings, and community-wide trainings. In addition to those responsibilities, they also identified reputable lawyers for people experiencing legal trouble and located dentists, obstetricians, and family physicians for LAC clients.[68] Grand Rapids lacked an expansive public transportation system, which LAC activists determined was a major obstacle to finding a job; thus, employees also taught people to drive. LAC employee Sara Ramírez, who was also a contributor for *Qué Pasa*, transported "needy persons" to other agencies and translated written drivers' exams for clients according to one LAC activity report. She spent hours with clients, chauffeuring them to driver's training, helping them register vehicles and purchase insurance for newly acquired cars, and even practicing with aspiring drivers.[69] Providing these community-controlled social services filled the yawning gaps in accessible municipal services for Latinos.

The council decided to redirect its energy beyond accompanying people to appointments and started offering social services at the council's building. For example, in 1970, with about a third of the Latino youths in Grand Rapids under five years old, there was high demand for pediatric providers and care, especially in Spanish.[70] The council director at the time, Al Wilson, convinced the Kent County Health Department and the Neighborhood Youth Corps to send nurse aides-in-training to the LAC to facilitate a monthly "well-baby" drop-in clinic where infants and toddlers would receive their regular checkups and immunizations. Utilizing the director's office for appointments, they stretched the resources of the LAC facility by repurposing his round conference table into an exam table. In one year alone, more than five hundred babies received checkups at the council. Outside of clinic hours, the council hosted small-group English classes and Alcoholics Anonymous meetings, which were led in Spanish and supported by the Kent County Health Department.[71] Extending its efficacy beyond the LAC facility, the council also offered free tickets to the circus and other local enterprises to cash-strapped parents looking for affordable family fun.[72] These piecemeal services together wove a social safety net, and Latinos in Grand Rapids came to count on the council for many of their unmet needs.

Perhaps the most pressing challenge facing Latinos at the time was how and where to secure employment; rather than depend on the slow pace of municipal services, the council opted to remedy the unemployment problem in-house. Like many cities during the postwar period, Grand Rapids underwent a wave of deindustrialization, leaving many in a serious quandary because they lacked the necessary skills to keep pace with the evolving economy. By 1970, unemployment for Latinos in Kent County was at 13.7 percent while it was at 12.6 percent and 5.4 percent for African Americans and whites, respectively.[73] Grand Rapids lost some industries to the southern and western regions of the country.[74] White residents may have struggled to a degree, but African American and Latino residents faced an uphill battle when attempting to locate employment as manufacturing jobs dried up. For monolingual Spanish speakers, the local economy was unforgiving. An LAC survey in 1973 found that about 20 percent of people needed help finding jobs. Latinos who migrated to Grand Rapids prior to the 1960s had expected their children to fare much better than they had under the difficult circumstances of settling into the city. Due to the lack of jobs in the long postwar period, parents and grandparents discovered that their children struggled harder to locate work than the first Latino residents. Plus, years of pleading on behalf of the LAC still had not resulted in one Spanish-speaking employee in the municipal unemployment office. Latinos sought work but simply could not locate jobs, nor was there an infrastructure to support their search. And, notwithstanding the financial importance of finding and sustaining a job, the LAC's "Unmet Economic and Social Needs" report determined that employment also represented the surest conduit toward acceptance and belonging for Latinos. The report asserted that "employment is a necessity for a person to take his or her place in the community."[75]

Stepping in to fill the gap left by municipal services, the LAC morphed into its own employment agency, so to speak. Prior to 1972, the LAC assigned outreach workers to assess a client's eligibility for jobs sponsored by the unemployment office, where they often served as interpreters for job seekers. As community members increasingly relied on this support, the LAC realized that offering this service within its facility would help clients bypass the bureaucracy of the city agency and its seeming disregard for the unique needs of Latino community members. Consequently, in 1972, the LAC opened its own employment services division in its building on Grandville Avenue, a neighborhood where most of the city's Latinos lived. Eager to avail themselves of the opportunity to locate work—while also being treated with dignity and respect—between 150 and 200 people sought these services annually. On arriving at the LAC, clients were screened to determine their proficiency in English as well as their financial needs and goals. Clients also disclosed the length of time they had resided in the city, details about their work records, and whether they had access to transportation. The employment officer subsequently attempted to place the person in a position that aligned with their individual needs. From 1972–73, the sole staff member working on un-employment had 167 inquiries from people needing a job, set up 111 interviews, and helped 60 secure jobs. While this under-resourced program was unable to assist everyone, the combined income of LAC's placements totaled $396,500 a year, according to organizational reports.[76] Emphasizing that it was performing much-needed work with little support from the local unemployment office, the LAC reasoned that it had saved the city of Grand Rapids a substantial amount of money; local Latinos relied more heavily upon LAC services than the relatively few options originating with the city.

This community-controlled employment program depended on strong rela-tionships between LAC staff and local employers. In 1972, Rudy Pérez, an em-ployment officer, visited some of the remaining industrial employers, introduced himself, and informed them about Latinos looking for jobs. When clients came in, he called those employers to inquire about openings and to pitch his clients.[77] For blue-collar, monolingual workers, LAC employment officers located positions at Rapistan, a supply chain company. They also guided them toward jobs at K and R Construction, Lear Siegler (an automotive parts manufacturer), Interstate Trucking, and Baker Furniture.[78] For the many bilingual job seekers who relied on LAC's employment services, officers directed them toward jobs within the Grand Rapids Board of Education, the Community Action Program, and the Michigan Employment Security Commission. Recognizing where their clients' strengths lay and utilizing networks as effectively as possible allowed the LAC to grow into an improvised, comprehensive social service agency. If the municipal unemployment office continued to refuse the LAC's demands for a Latino hire, LAC's service work ensured that its constituents would not be forgotten or aban-doned as an integral part of the Grand Rapids community. The LAC had again reinforced its position as a central entity in Latino life while laying the necessary groundwork for engaging with local politics.

"RAZA CANDIDATES" AND ELECTORAL POLITICS

Given the City of Grand Rapids' resistance to funding the LAC, some Latinos looked to running for office to make substantive changes. MCP provided many Latinos with their first experiences running for office. In the early 1970s, a few Mexicans and Puerto Ricans ran for the Model Neighborhood Citizens Com-mittee with hopes of garnering more funds for the LAC. They also used these elections to highlight their pan-Latino solidarity. Expanding their vision beyond the MNCC, Mexicans and Puerto Ricans began to seek public office. Many com-munity members expected that, with more Latino representatives, the commu-nity would receive more attention and funding. Though operating at a numerical disadvantage, the Latino community organized behind candidates displaying a keen interest in issues that affected their community. Meanwhile, the council served as a base for many campaigns and as a conduit for candidates to reach their constituents. Through their participation in politics, Latino leaders sought to safeguard a place in the present and in the future for Latinos in a mostly white city.

The MNCC election furnished Latinos with experience in running for office and helped them to secure a voice in the MCP, which became the funding agency for the LAC. Up until 1969, African American and white candidates dominated the MNCC (see chapter 4). The influence and community work of the council convinced more and more Latinos to invest in MCP. Many residents hoped that, if Latinos secured positions on the MNCC, they could direct more funding to the LAC. In 1972, seven Latinos ran for positions on the MNCC. Demonstrating the growing sense of solidarity and "race pride" in predominantly white Grand Rapids, *Qué Pasa* showcased each of the "raza candidates" in a one-page announcement.[79] The roster of candidates included three Mexican Americans: José Pérez, Margarita Morales, and Félix Ybarra. It also included two well-regarded Puerto Ricans: Pedro "Pete" Gómez and Orlando Carrión. Pedro's daughter, Laura Gómez, represented the upcoming generation of MexiRicans, and Josefina González represented not only Mexicans but also the city's youths; both ran for "teenager-at-large." The teenage candidates aspired to a newly created position designed to increase political engagement among young people. In the context of an election where white and Black candidates dominated, *Qué Pasa*'s use of the term *raza* called attention to the Latino identity of the candidates, a factor that they hoped would compel Mexicans and Puerto Ricans to vote as a bloc, signifying the pan-Latino solidarity that the LAC and the larger Latino community espoused.

While elections for the antipoverty program offered Latinos the opportunity to exercise solidarity, municipal elections revealed just how excluded Latinos were from the body politic. Unlike MCP elections, Grand Rapids' municipal contests were not confined to the low-income neighborhoods where Latinos lived. As a numerical minority, Latinos found it incredibly challenging to have their voices heard in the local government. Since the 1910s, Grand Rapids adhered to a council-manager system structure that prevented most residents from directly influencing decisions. Under this system, residents voted for a mayor and councilmembers, which were also called commissioners. Elected commissioners subsequently chose a city manager who was tasked with more of the administrative decisions. Despite being elected democratically, mayors were more of a figurehead in comparison to the unelected city manager. For all intents and purposes, the commissioners wielded more executive power than the mayor because they selected the city manager. In this way, city officials were insulated from the direct input of residents, further marginalizing Latino voices.

Residents of Grand Rapids held the most sway in the election of commissioners, but the boundaries of the city's wards and Latinos' small population limited Latinos' chances at ever electing a *raza* candidate as a commissioner. Each of the city's three wards selected two commissioners. Until 1973, the first ward covered northwestern Grand Rapids, where Polish and other Eastern Europeans immigrants and their descendants lived. The second ward encompassed northeastern Grand Rapids. Segregation patterns kept the second ward mostly white. The third ward covered southern Grand Rapids, where many African Americans and some Latinos lived. In the early 1970s, parts of the third ward became part of the first ward, splitting large swaths of those groups into two separate wards.[80] Essentially, the ward configuration both before and after the shift has yielded only a few minority commissioners except for the few Black commissioners out of the third ward. For example, the first African American commissioner, Lyman Parks, emerged from the third ward in 1975. Since then, there have been seven other Black commissioners, all in the same ward as Parks.[81] As dismal as the numbers are for African Americans, commissioner elections have resulted in even worse results for Latinos, who have only won one seat in Grand Rapids' history. It was only as recently as 2019 that the second ward elected Mexican American Milinda Ysasi, the great-granddaughter of Simon and Juana Aguilar, who migrated to the area during the 1940s.[82] With such a small Latino population compared to the larger white population, there was a very limited chance that Latinos could elect a representative out of their ward. Instead, the community focused on finding candidates who were sympathetic to their causes and canvassed for them, hoping they would reward their efforts by prioritizing Latino interests after the election.

Despite the challenges inherent to seeking electoral representation, Latinos dedicated themselves to municipal elections as a way of advocating for their interests. The LAC became a hub of voter registration and the neighborhood's engagement with local politics. Almost a third of people the LAC surveyed in 1973 about their unmet needs requested assistance from the council with voter registration, signaling a deep commitment to voting among Latinos. In the 1950s, Daniel Vásquez, one of the pioneering Mexican men in the city, heard from local commissioners that, if Latinos wanted change, they needed to vote. As Vásquez recalled, they told him, "you got to vote to count."[83] He devoted himself toward that issue well into the 1960s. By the 1970s, Pete and Cruzita Gómez, who were regular LAC volunteers and general advocates for the community, held many meetings with city commissioners on how to increase Latino influence in city hall. Cruzita recalled that the commissioners implored them to vote. She and her husband took the call seriously and started registering people. They also met with commission candidates to learn their positions on issues. The Gómezes told their neighbors that it was even more important for those who could vote to do so, on behalf of those who lacked the franchise, recognizing that there were members of the Latino community who could not. She remarked, hypothetically, "You could say there are 40,000 [Latinos], but if only 15,000 vote, then the city looks at the 15,000. . . . Maybe those other 25,000 can't vote if they're not here legally."[84] For this reason, the Gómezes expanded their voter registration drives beyond the LAC facility and engaged in door-to-door canvassing in the community. To achieve any semblance of community control, voter outreach became an essential part of the LAC's advocacy. The willingness exhibited by Latinos participating in Grand Rapids' electoral politics illustrates their placemaking work to transform their city into one that met their needs.

Even with the numerical and systemic disadvantages to running for office, some Latinos committed to overcoming the hurdle of their outsider status in politics. Frustrated with their limited political power, Grand Rapids residents of all races called for a review of the Grand Rapids City Charter in 1971, which mandated the council-manager style of governance. Then Mayor C. H. Sonneveldt wanted to expand the powers of the mayor to balance out the city manager's power. This proposed change required a revision to the city's charter. Voters then elected nine people to sit on the Grand Rapids Charter Revision Commission, which was tasked with reviewing the charter and offering a recommendation for legislation to change it.[85] My maternal grandfather, Porfirio Murillo, who worked for the American Seating Company, and Miguel Navarro, the owner of the local El Matador Tortilla Company, were among the ninety-eight candidates who ran for the nine seats. Both Murillo and Navarro worked as farmworkers before settling in Grand Rapids. Having any working-class, nonwhite representation on the commission would have revolutionized the composition of city government. Navarro and Murillo lost their election bids, however. Murillo garnered 1,836 votes, or about 2 percent of the total, and Navarro earned 5,170 votes, or 5 percent of the total. Neither approached the 9,000 votes for former city manager Donald Oakes, or the 12,000 votes for former deputy city attorney Thomas Shear. The other positions were filled by white men: former city commissioners, a police chief, an engineer, and a teacher.[86] The 1971 bid to change the charter failed, and Grand Rapids continued with the council-manager form of local government and three wards represented on the commission. Despite these setbacks, Latinos refused to crumble under the white power structure that disenfranchised so many and robbed them of a voice. Licking their wounds, they instead found alternative strategies to claim space in Grand Rapids and improve their material conditions.

THE RELENTLESS FIGHT FOR *LA RAZA*

While acknowledging the difficulties the LAC encountered, it is indisputable that the organization dramatically improved the quality of life for Latinos in Grand Rapids. It filled a necessary role and became the organization that adamantly represented Latinos in the early 1970s. Indeed, Latinos affirmed this in a survey of the council's efforts. When asked which social service organization could best represent Latinos, "the Latin American Council was selected by a majority of the people."[87] To families like the Gómezes, the council not only represented their values as a civically engaged Mexican and Puerto Rican household, but it also channeled their energy and passion into formally helping the community they cared for so deeply. The LAC was also the pinnacle of organizing in Grand Rapids that called for Latinos to be integrated into the city's social fabric. They fought to deliver to Latinos the services they deserved as residents of the city and stressed that Latinos should be hired and paid to respond to the unique needs of their community. Through the council's relentless fights for funding, outreach workers and administrators succeeded in working to help Latinos, causing both the local and federal governments to acknowledge their inefficacies. The people who so desperately needed this assistance could take solace that there was a dedicated and creative staff that would find the means to help. From teenagers who had a safe and welcoming place to celebrate their identities, to a former migrant worker looking for a job in a new city, to a mother needing a check-up for her child, the LAC was a center for Latino placemaking in a city that had operated within a Black-versus-white binary for decades.

Continuing to nurture pan-Latino solidarity and celebrate Latino identities motivated the LAC administrators and staff members alike. As a director from 1971 to 1973, Al Wilson stressed the importance of a burgeoning pan-Latino identity among Mexican and Puerto Rican youths. Young Latinos required a place of their own to learn community-building skills. Thoughtfully curated youth and adult programming celebrated both Mexican and Puerto Rican culture while also incorporating elements of other Latino ethnic groups. Just four years prior, in 1969, the council suffered an internal struggle so severe it appeared in the *Grand Rapids Press*, which blamed it on the inability of Puerto Ricans and Mexicans to unite in a common cause. Yet, the city witnessed numerous examples of cooperation and productivity within the LAC during the 1970s, proving those outside observers wrong. The LAC's use of *raza* and the Spanish language as a cultural touchstone, while problematic and exclusionary in some ways, functioned as a uniting concept, which helped the community to refocus on increasing their pan-Latino solidarity. Retaining Spanish turned into a means to resist the temptation of assimilating for upward mobility. These issues, openly discussed in *Qué Pasa*, revealed how Latinos negotiated their position in Grand Rapids. The LAC granted many Latinos the ability to reclaim some sense of culture—a sentiment that many thought they had lost while living in a majority-white city. The council literally created a space for Latinos in a place where their needs were often ignored and neglected.

While the relationship with the city was fraught with tension over funding and control, Latinos defined their own interests and identities with the help of committed community members and other resources. The war on poverty also legitimized the work that Latinos did, especially Cruzita Gómez, Rachel Campos, Sara Ramírez, and other Latinas, signaling to women and to future generations the value and necessity in aiding one another. While the official war on poverty ended with Nixon, the concept of paid community workers has stayed with our society until the present, even if programs are underfunded. With money and collaboration attached to these long-practiced acts of survival, antipoverty programs like MCP and the LAC helped cement the idea that guaranteeing people's basic needs was work in which the government should invest. Through these programs and their own innovation, Latinos created their own social safety net in Grand Rapids.

Without the avenues for radical political resistance or electoral success to alleviate Latino living conditions, advocacy became a form of activism in Grand Rapids. The movement looked different in every geographical and social context around the country, but examining the work of people outside of the Southwest and the Northeast shows how ordinary people found ways to subvert local hierarchies. It also reveals how Latinos in Grand Rapids treated the meeting of people's basic needs as the core of activism. The LAC could not have accomplished many of its goals without the sometimes-reluctant cooperation from city agencies, corporations, local businesses, and foundations. To take their activism further, Latinos in Grand Rapids developed their institutional activism as they took aim at some of the largest structural barriers that oppressed them: discrimination in police hiring and an education system that failed them. Like other midwestern activists that merged their interests with institutions, Latinos attempted to further the work of structural change from within the system.

– 6 –

Tangled with the Police

In 1970, Community Action Program executive Melvin Tardy penned a letter to the mayor of Grand Rapids demanding that the city hire more Black and Latino police officers. Having worked closely with Black and Latino youths in his position as programming director, Tardy recognized the importance of hiring officers who were directly familiar with the communities they served. "The fact is," Tardy began, "that the young drop-out who has tangled with the police himself, who speaks Spanish or the street-language, is potentially exactly the man who can relate to that part of the community."[1] He also criticized the Grand Rapids Police Department (GRPD) for maintaining hiring standards that immediately disqualified the people who, but for their academic experiences, would nevertheless stand as ideal candidates for policing jobs. The GRPD required that candidates possess high school diplomas, pass a civil service exam, and have no criminal record. Additionally, they also must have claimed U.S. citizenship, which disqualified some Latino residents.[2] These requirements stopped many Latinos from even applying for police positions. A history of distrust between communities of color and the GRPD also caused African Americans and Latinos to expect the worst about the likelihood of their being placed in such positions of authority in a predominantly white city. As of 1969, the department boasted a dismal record of employing African Americans and Latinos, with only thirteen of the former and zero of the latter out of the 371-person GRPD and no plan to improve such disproportionate numbers.[3] Municipal leaders in the 1970s refused to relinquish white men's century-long rule over policing.

To Tardy and other Black, Latino, and white activists who emerged in the late 1960s and early 1970s, altering the hiring process would ensure that more Black and Latino officers would be eligible for positions within the GRPD. In turn, they argued that their increased representation would improve community relations between the police and communities of color. While these efforts failed to target structural racism, the focus on policing called attention to the overall racial imbalance of power between white residents and communities with a sizeable constituency of African Americans and Latinos. With the Black and Latino population representing 15 percent of the city, concerns over policing continued to grow in Grand Rapids, as they did throughout the nation. A coalition of mostly middle-class Latino and Black activists and organizers from the Latin American Council, the Urban League, CAP Complexes, the Human Relations Commission, and a variety of religious organizations worked toward change. Speaking on behalf of the Latino community, Al Wilson, Martín Morales, and Juan Maldonado, among others, and many in the Black community, including Melvin Tardy and Kathy Phillips, advocated for changes to the GRPD. Together they pursued a path of lobbying within the system to address over-policing and the job discrimination that barred Black and Latino potential officers from the force.

Black and Latino activists' pursuit of changing the police department was inspired by the nationwide shift toward radical organizing in the late 1960s and early 1970s, though local activists realized they needed to amend their approach. As a direct outgrowth of Black nationalist campaigns against police violence, the Black Panthers popularized the notion of "armed self-defense" against police brutality that both Chicanos in the Brown Berets and Puerto Ricans in the Young Lords Party and Young Lords Organization adopted. However, this strategy did not always work for Latinos in smaller midwestern cities. Thus, Latinos and African Americans used institutional activism, just as they did to serve their community during the period of waning funding for antipoverty programs. Organizers in Grand Rapids carried out studies, held meetings, tried to enforce federal policies, and even brought lawsuits against the city. These tactics aligned more with those of Latinos in South Bend, Indiana. There, the Midwest Council of La Raza worked with the University of Notre Dame's Institute for Urban Studies to back social change programming.[4] When challenging discriminatory hiring within the GRPD, an institution that represented the city and held so much authority, Latinos and their allies chose to operate within the system, viewing it as the strategy with the most potential.

Both moderate and radical forms of activism alike engendered white resistance at the national and local level. In 1968, presidential candidate Richard Nixon called for "law and order" to put an end to urban uprisings and backed the police departments that enforced this pledge. Nixon's "silent majority" strategy sought to appeal to frustrated white Americans who felt that they were left out of the social "revolution."[5] Whites saw the wellspring of activists' demands across the country as an affront to the racial and social order. At the same time, they recognized a growing need to conceal open racial animosity. Many white detractors to social progress stopped using ethnic slurs and engaged in, as political sociologist Eduardo Bonilla-Silva argues, "racism without racists."[6] To avoid the language used in decades and centuries past, white people adopted terms such as "reverse discrimination" to criticize any shifts in local hierarchies of power. In Grand Rapids, resistance emanated from white residents and the Fraternal Order of Police (FOP), which acted as a union for the police until the 1980s. Both white residents and the FOP characterized any response to police issues from Black and Latino community as "unnecessary" and an "overreaction." This strategy permitted the majority white community and the FOP to deny allegations of racist motivations in the most traditional sense, though their objections were rooted in racism.[7] This resistance posed a formidable challenge to Latinos' plan to reduce police brutality through more representation in the GRPD.

Interethnic and interracial coalitions developed as a natural response to white resistance. Mexicans and Puerto Ricans trusted in their interethnic solidarity for this fight. Their decades of work together in informal recreational spaces and their time at the LAC facilitated their presentation of a united front when confronting such high stakes. Their pan-ethnic solidarity was so embedded into their rhetoric that, while discussing the hiring of Latino police officers, no one differentiated among how many Mexicans or Puerto Ricans should be hired. They simply wanted Latino officers, particularly those who spoke Spanish so they could communicate with monolingual Spanish-speaking residents.

This interethnic solidarity mirrored the interracial solidarity that Black and Latino leaders and community members showed in these discussions, generating a more successful campaign. As earlier chapters have shown, African Americans and Latinos often lived next to one another, occasionally intermarried, and formed friendships—just as Mexicans and Puerto Ricans did. Their shared experiences with over-policing and police brutality also made their relationships ripe for interracial organizing. This demonstration of unity for policing and jobs was in stark contrast to the tension between Mexicans and Puerto Ricans and between Latinos and African Americans over antipoverty resources. Noticeably, the discussion over federal funding and the local battle for representation in municipal offices, including the police, happened concurrently. Though it appeared as if leaders employed paradoxical strategies in these two fights, both communities understood what was at stake in antipoverty funding and policing. Stressing their ethnic and racial differences garnered each group more of the limited federal antipoverty funding when resources were scarce. Coordinating at the local level increased their communities' power when arguing against the City of Grand Rapids' racially discriminatory practices. They chose strategies that would most effectively gain the resources they desired from the white power structure at varying levels of government.

Black and white leaders played integral roles in leading this fight that also affected and benefited Latinos. Black leaders from the NAACP, the Urban League, and the HRC of Grand Rapids had long dealt with the issue of policing, and some made room for Latinos in this fight. As Sonia Lee points out in her history of Black and Puerto Rican organizing, "by emphasizing the multiple overlaps that existed between the world's racial and colonial subjects, African American leaders opened up a way through which various groups of people could create a common language of protest with them. Identifying with the Black freedom struggle did not require a primordial link to an African ancestry but only a broad political orientation opposed to America's capitalist and imperialist practices."[8] Black leaders followed this path in Grand Rapids, inviting Latinos to imagine a city government that represented them as well. White allies who listened to Black and Latino communities were also integral to making change in a white-majority city. Though some political issues would highlight these groups' differences, rallying the city to hire more minorities required solidarity with one another. This strategy improved the odds for all involved, given the limited individual power these groups possessed.

Unlike organizers in larger, more liberal cities, Black, Latino, and white activists and advocates in Grand Rapids eschewed more radical protest methods in favor of more institutional activism to obtain more Black and Latino representation in the police department. They joined together against over-policing and police brutality. While some activists wanted community control over the police department, most organizers settled for representation as a feasible goal and a strategy that could protect them from more harm done by an all-white police force.

White resistance to social progress in the 1970s changed and adapted in rhetoric and strategies. Although managerial racism can be just as harmful as outright denials of progress, people of color can leverage their collective power in a situation that has afforded them very little. They used successful and viable strategies to amplify one another's voices and gain support. White allies also played an important role in a conservative, majority-white city in aiding social progress, doing so without overstepping their boundaries.

"THE OFFICERS ACTED ACCORDING TO ESTABLISHED STANDARDS": A BRIEF HISTORY OF COMPLAINTS AGAINST THE POLICE

Ongoing tensions between Black and Latino community members and the predominantly white GRPD did not emerge overnight and, as was the case elsewhere in the United States, originated from soured race relations that dated back to the

1920s or earlier. In what was supposed to show good faith between the police department and the city's Black residents, the GRPD hired its first African American police officer, Walter Coe, in 1922. While many Black community members celebrated what really amounted to a token hire, others argued that Coe's appointment was no more than a ploy on the part of the GRPD to increase surveillance and control over Black and Latino neighborhoods.[9] By claiming that their measures aimed to control drinking and other forms of vice during Prohibition, Coe and his fellow white police officers actually "overpoliced" Black neighborhoods in a manner that mirrors late twentieth- and early twenty-first-century policing practices in large cities.[10] Historian Randal Jelks references members of the Black community who claimed they were arrested five to six times more than "their percentage of the population would warrant."[11] Over the years, Black community organizations like the Urban League tried to hold the GRPD and its near-lily-white staff accountable for profiling and brutality, but had little success. Tensions between Black and Latino residents and local police officers would reach a fever pitch by the late 1960s.

The 1967 urban uprising (see chapter 4) was emblematic of the frustration Black Grand Rapidians felt regarding police misconduct. The July rebellion, which started just a day after civil unrest exploded in nearby Detroit, ignited when the community claimed local police officers roughed up a Black teenager upon apprehending him and others. Spurred to action by the protests that followed, more Black residents lodged complaints with the Michigan Civil Rights Commission (MCRC), a statewide agency charged with investigating matters of discrimination. MCRC complaints pointed to various forms of intimidations and excessive force including chokeholds. In most instances, the MCRC cleared police officers of any wrongdoing, arguing that "the officers acted according to the established standards under the circumstances."[12]

Latinos endured their own issues with the GRPD. Early Mexican migrants who arrived during the first half of the twentieth century often encountered similar experiences with policing as African Americans. The small Mexican American railroad worker community in the pre–World War II era were arrested proportionate to their population, but they were picked up for similar crimes as African Americans, such as drinking, gambling, and vagrancy, the latter of which was more likely for those working temporarily in the area.[13] As the Latino community expanded, the rate of complaints about policing among Latinos also increased, with many insisting that the GRPD was starting to use more violent methods.

Language barriers were often blamed for incidents between the police and Latinos. For example, in 1958, Daniel Vargas responded to the concerns of a Puerto Rican couple after a seemingly racially motivated confrontation with police. At the time, Vargas, the sole Latino on the HRC, held a leadership role within the

Catholic Latino community, and regularly helped new migrants settle in Grand Rapids (see chapters 2 and 3). One Saturday, police were called to break up a fight taking place outside of the Franklin Bar, which was located on the southeast side in a mostly Black neighborhood with some Latino residents. A crowd had gathered, but the fight was over when the police showed up. However, the police began to "shove the spectators standing on the walk and struck several persons with their night sticks." Officers struck a Puerto Rican man while he proclaimed his innocence. When his wife tried to intervene, the police "pushed her to the walk." Although the couple was later determined innocent, the GRPD simply dismissed the incident as a misunderstanding resulting from a language barrier between the couple and their municipal-employee assailants. Having already had several decades' worth of questionable run-ins with the local police, Latino community members refused to accept the GRPD's version of events. Vargas relayed to the HRC that Latinos viewed their treatment as the perpetuation of a "dual system of justice." Since African Americans suffered prior acts of police brutality, including the events that sparked the 1967 uprising, it was clear to many residents that the attack on the Latino couple did not stem simply from language barriers that conveniently placed the onus of understanding on Latinos and not their would-be protectors. Vargas asserted that the police officers' actions in the case of the couple outside of the Franklin Bar was "precipitate and excessive . . . and was directed at the Latin-American group."[14] The HRC director, an African American man named Alfred Cowles, echoed Vargas's concerns some seven years later. Cowles recognized that Latinos were often "questioned, searched and detained" unnecessarily because the force did not have Spanish-speaking police officers.[15] Vargas, Cowles, and others posited that these interactions between Latinos and the police would continue.

Though individual acts of police violence exposed a type of inherent racism within a community that regarded Latinos, Blacks, and other nonwhite groups as outsiders, local Black activists soon realized that structural racism also accounted for their disparate treatment by the police. Drawing inspiration from the Black Panther Party, whose Ten-Point Program included demands for "an immediate end to police brutality and the murder of Black people," in 1967 local Black activists presented the City of Grand Rapids with thirty-two demands of their own that called for more representation in education and city management. One demand identified the need for "the establishment of a Civilian Review Board to investigate charges of police brutality."[16] They reasoned that the review board would offer a check on the city's system of policing that, up until then, went largely unexamined. While Black leaders like the Reverend Lyman Parks, a local African Methodist Episcopal (AME) pastor, Melvin Tardy, a CAP program director, and his brother Raymond Tardy, also a program director, were speaking on behalf of a "Negro Leadership Committee," many of their demands, especially the review board, would benefit Latinos as well. The police department responded to these requests by charging that the activists lacked legitimacy as representatives of the community. Police chief William A. Johnson, who served from 1956 to 1969, went further in minimizing their demands when he described it as merely the "yipping" of "a small part and parcel of the Negro community who don't know what they're talking about." One lieutenant argued that, "if anything, an officer hesitates to use undue force" in dealing with offenders. He added, "the police, if anyone, are at a disadvantage."[17] Citing this "disadvantage," the GRPD refused to establish a community review board. The department's meager compromise was to offer "ride-alongs" and the occasional role-playing events, which they offered to convince community members of the difficulty of their position.[18] However, none of those activities addressed the way the police treated citizens, and the department's views on police brutality remained the same. Chief Johnson revealed this intractable attitude when he stated that "'police brutality' is anything they don't agree with."[19] With this response, many Latinos and African Americans concluded that the only way to gain any influence was from within the department itself.

"THESE EXAMINATIONS SHOULD BE DESIGNED TO GET PEOPLE INTO THE DEPARTMENT, NOT KEEP THEM OUT": BARRIERS TO MINORITY REPRESENTATION ON THE POLICE FORCE

By the late 1960s and early 1970s, middle-class Black and Latino activists pursued a path to increase their representation in one of the city's most important entities, which they hoped would give them some input into police behavior. The GRPD constantly told the community that, if they had a problem with policing, then "the way to correct that is simple—join the department and work with us rather than simply criticize us from the outside."[20] However, many community members who tried to become officers were rejected. Even though the job requirements for police officers never mentioned anything specific to race, the list of standards conjured an image of eligible candidates as tall, white males with a large frame. As of 1965, eligibility for police work—and even for work as a firefighter—remained contingent on one's citizenship status, and more specifically, one had to be 5'10" or taller, weigh at least 160 pounds, hold a high school diploma, possess a valid driver's license, and pass a written civil service exam. GEDs did not qualify. Additionally, eligible candidates needed to have a clear criminal record, a limited traffic record, and pass a physical exam.[21] Though there were no stated gender restrictions, male candidates were exclusively hired for patrol work until the mid-1970s.

Taking into consideration the GRPD's emphasis on educational achievement alone, most of the hiring standards represented a direct bias against Latinos and African Americans because a large percentage of residents from both groups had only limited access to educational opportunities, as outlined in previous chapters. Grand Rapids Public Schools were not sites of academic success for Black and Latino students in the 1960s and 1970s. Teachers and administrators actively discouraged these students from pursuing higher education and steered them toward vocational tracks. In 1960, of the thousand-plus graduating seniors in the district, only forty-nine were Black and most of them came from one segregated high school.[22] By 1968, two-thirds of Latinos did not graduate from high school.[23] Thus, Latino and Black men were more likely to have earned a GED than a diploma. The civil service exam's difficulty also blocked even the best-prepared candidates. In commenting on the test, Melvin Tardy, CAP director and community advocate, expressed that the exam itself "should be designed to get people into the department, not keep them out."[24] However, at least half of the candidates—of all races—needed to retake the civil service exam, adding to the already burdensome requirements.[25] Latino and Black applicants further argued that barring those with a criminal record unjustly disqualified them. As the Black community had long documented, over-policing had prompted more interactions with police and resulted in more arrests of Black residents. Meanwhile, many Latinos could not communicate with the monolingual English-speaking police—or GRPD officers refused to listen—and they contended this led to more arrests. To all appearances, systemic barriers kept them out of the department.

Two other requirements excluded many Latinos and discouraged others from applying, which were not altogether unrelated to the distinct experiences of those who lacked English-language fluency and did not fit the Westernized image of the "able" male. First, the citizenship status of many Latinos remained in question. While Puerto Ricans and Mexican Americans comprised most of this population and enjoyed a nominal U.S. citizenship, Mexican nationals and Cubans, for example, could not apply to the police department. Some also argued that the height requirement also disqualified many Latino men.[26] In 1965, Latino activists demanded that the police department lower the requirement from 5'10" to 5'7", with city officials finally agreeing to 5'8".[27] While New York, Chicago, Philadelphia, and other urban police departments adjusted their height requirements to 5'7", Grand Rapids refused to follow suit. At least, this is what the MCRC found in a report published in 1968.[28] Prevailing knowledge at the time on the average height by race indicated that "the average height of a Mexican American man is 5 ft 6."[29] Thus, Latino residents insisted that the difference of two inches kept people from applying for positions with the GRPD. Between the height and citizenship requirements, it was no surprise that there remained zero Latino police officers on the force.

The police department in Grand Rapids remained almost entirely white by the end of the 1960s. Tensions between the department and the community, not surprisingly, had not dissipated. To make matters worse, the police hired two of its largest classes of recruits in 1967 and 1968—both groups were nearly entirely white.[30] Between 1940 and 1970, the number of African American and Latino residents grew exponentially: over 700 percent and 2,000 percent, respectively, yet their representation in the department stayed stagnant at 2.5 percent and 0 percent of the 371-person police department.[31] Data from around the country revealed similar trends. Departments in Baltimore, Chicago, Cleveland, New York, Philadelphia, and Newark employed fewer minority officers than white ones even though the Black and Latino populations were growing in those cities. For example, though Baltimore was about 50 percent African American, its police force of about 3,000 had about 245 Black police officers, or just 8 percent of the department.[32] The statistics, however, fail to convey how significant these positions were to communities that the predominantly white police force served. Black and Latino people in Grand Rapids argued that, without any representation and little recourse to redress their concerns, the predominantly white GRPD would continue to over-police and brutalize people of color. Given the decades of inaction on the part of men like Chief Johnson and the officers working under him, challenging the current hiring practices proved arduous. Even more, it was becoming harder and harder to convince the city to consider it a priority.

"IF THIS ISN'T A RACIST CITY THEN WHAT IS IT?"
THE PUSH FOR MORE BLACK AND LATINO POLICE OFFICERS

Rather than wait for what appeared an inconceivable change under the current conservative environment in Grand Rapids, Latinos and African Americans pushed forward with their demands and made more proposals to the city and the GRPD about how to reform the requirements for becoming a police officer. These leaders collaborated with white members of the HRC and allied city commissioners. Together they prepared studies, held face-to-face talks with city officials, and initiated proposals to convince the city that their police hiring policies were outdated and, more to the point, racist. However, the GRPD, the mayor, the city manager, and many white residents wholeheartedly rejected any demographic changes to the police department. Using colorblind language and coopting the rhetoric of the civil rights movement, these groups argued that relations between the GRPD and Latino and Black residents were nothing less than harmonious and rejected any responsibility for remedying any of the decades-old problems.

By the mid-1960s, a coalition of Black and Brown activists along with the HRC prepared to bring these issues up with the City of Grand Rapids. As a city entity without enforcement power, the HRC had researched issues of discrimination in Grand Rapids since 1958 when the commission was founded. On the issue of job discrimination within the city, the HRC had gathered anecdotal evidence from aggrieved community members. It also carried out a study of the city's hiring patterns. After the completion of its review, the HRC issued a report that revealed what it called a "'passive' racial discrimination in city employment," which included the GRPD. The HRC characterized this behavior as "acts of 'omission' rather than commission, which tend to 'solidify the status quo.'"[33] Todd Robinson, a scholar of Black Grand Rapids, has referred to this same phenomenon as "managerial racism."[34] The HRC also gathered information on the civil service exams and hiring practices for six major cities across the country, noting more open hiring policies in places like New York City.[35] The information gathered by the HRC only confirmed what community members had known for years: the City of Grand Rapids used discriminatory hiring practices. In its stated list of proposals, the HRC insisted that the city put minorities on appointive committees, send targeted notices of job openings to minority outreach organizations, and hire a special recruitment officer to facilitate this process.

It took the mayor and the city manager over six months to publicly respond to the HRC, and when they did, they wholeheartedly rejected the proposal. In March 1967 at a city commission meeting, Mayor C. H. Sonneveldt and the city manager, Henry Nabers, balked at the very suggestion of job discrimination and decried the HRC's findings as inaccurate. "It seems to me," the mayor said, "that what they [HRC officials] really are talking about is special employment privileges."[36] Mayor Sonneveldt went on to accuse the HRC of exaggerating its conclusions: "I would hope our own Human Relations Commission would be more factual." The mayor's comments revealed his disbelief that Grand Rapids had unequal hiring patterns and thus saw no need for the city to remedy them. This reaction also willfully obfuscated the plentiful affirmative action policies that had benefited whites in the United States for generations.[37] Echoing the mayor's sentiments, Nabers charged that the HRC's recommendations sounded like "some of the gobbledygook that comes out of fair employment."[38] This statement highlighted the city management's judgment that the federal-level changes to alleviate employment discrimination were nonsense. Moreover, when asking Nabers why the city had not hired a Black administrative assistant to the city manager, a journalist summarized his response this way: "He has actively sought Negroes as assistants in his office but does not know of one Negro anywhere in the country who is studying or involved in city management."[39] This unfounded claim exposed Nabers's racist opinion of the capabilities of Black people. In many cases, the City of Grand Rapids did the bare minimum to comply with civil rights legislation, but in this case, the city's representatives showed open hostility to antidiscrimination efforts.

With the HRC's findings all but ignored, activists devised alternative ways to wrest power away from the GRPD. The July 1967 urban uprising did not mark the end of clashes between the police and Black residents. Over the next few years, small skirmishes laid bare a level of racial discord that contradicted the police chief's claims regarding the city's harmonious race relations. An incident in April 1970 motivated the Black community to renew their calls for police reform after neighbors had observed a police cruiser nearly run over two Black boys during their regular patrol on the southeast side.[40] Previously, residents had complained about the constant patrolling, and many regarded this latest incident as additional evidence that the police were unfairly targeting minority communities as sites of criminal activity. While mainly Black activists organized around this issue, any gains that they made for representation in the police department would have ramifications for Latinos as well because they resided in the same neighborhoods.

In response to this event and as a preventive measure, Black activists announced several demands to try to diminish the unbridled control of the GRPD. First, they insisted that the department keep its tactical unit out of Black neighborhoods. Such units had officers with specialized training for dealing with more violent situations than police normally handle. They also demanded that the department only send Black officers to Black neighborhoods. Last, they proposed the hiring of an "aware" Black administrative assistant to the chief of police's staff.[41] They hoped this assistant would implement changes that prevented mistreatment from white officers and also shield them from the harm that an "unaware" Black administrator might cause. Given the community's previous experiences with Walter Coe, the GRPD's first Black officer, many members of the Black community were all too familiar with Black police officers who did not appear to have the best interests of communities of color at heart. After all, Coe was complicit when many Mexican Americans were rounded up and arrested for offenses as innocuous as vagrancy. Placing someone who remained sympathetic to the concerns of marginalized groups in a city where whites held the most power—and someone who might dare to shatter the force's wall of silence by refusing to provide cover for police brutality—would ensure that African Americans and Latinos could find redress against such abuses. The presence of a Black administrative assistant might also inspire the GRPD to study its problematic policies toward minority recruitment. Taken together, these proposals would grant African Americans some power over the policing practices that affected them every day.

Black activists sought a restructuring of the GRPD that addressed the discrimination and abuses that Black and Latino communities suffered at the hands of the police. In the spring of 1970, while still the director of programming for CAP, Melvin Tardy emerged as one of the most vocal advocates for coalitional representation among Blacks and Latinos. He proposed that the special assistant to the chief of police be attuned to issues that affected both communities. There was good reason for him to do so. Because of Tardy's position in CAP, which distributed antipoverty resources, he witnessed firsthand how hard Latinos fought to secure federal funding for their initiatives and the problems they faced in Grand Rapids, as seen in chapter 4. Thus, Tardy understood that Latinos, who also had a stake in changing the police department, would make valuable allies. In a letter to Mayor Sonneveldt, he suggested the GRPD hire a Black office manager and a Latino assistant manager to work with the superintendent of police and a community oversight committee. Howard Rienstra, a white ally to minorities and third ward commissioner, also echoed the call for an assistant. He insisted that the "person should be aware of the sensitivity necessary for Black and Latin Americans," illustrating that Rienstra recognized Latinos as part of the affected groups.[42] A history professor at Calvin College in Grand Rapids, Rienstra had a reputation as a champion of the civil rights movement. As a white man, his constituency in the third ward was largely Black and included the burgeoning Latino neighborhood at this time. In calling for both Black and Latino administrators in the police department, Rienstra displayed public support for his constituents. He also emerged as a powerful voice of reason during discussions about antipoverty funding and the lack of municipal support for Latinos. Rienstra pointedly used his privilege as a white commissioner to amplify the voices of the Black and Latino communities on police reform.

In addition to increasing the representation of Black and Latino officers through the GRPD's hiring practices, some organizers wanted fundamental changes to the department's policies. This campaign echoed the calls from Latinos for community-controlled education and social services, but reforming the police was their most ambitious endeavor. In a report Tardy penned on the issue of policing in May 1970, he imagined that the committee could plan the police orientation program and thus "the community itself will become totally familiar with the police department . . . [it] would take part in it . . . so that there is much greater involvement of the inner city community."[43] Known for his over-the-top demeanor and outlandish organizing strategies, Martín Morales chimed in to suggest that "greater efforts [could] be put toward hiring more minorities and poor whites," which demonstrated his willingness to move beyond a focus on race and ethnicity by centering class as a unifying characteristic of those left out of the GRPD's ranks. Focusing on the challenges that Latinos and Blacks confronted when applying for positions with restrictive educational and height requirements, Morales also recommended that the city alter the civil service requirements for police and firefighter examinations so that "more ethnic groups can be recruited."[44] His concerns for the unique challenges that Latinos faced and his shrewd skills as an organizer were clear in his proposal that bilingual candidates receive extra points on their application. He surmised this plan would ensure a better relationship between monolingual Spanish speakers and the police department in the future. By 1970, Morales and Tardy concluded that structural changes to the policies and systems that excluded and endangered Brown and Black communities were key to helping the entire minority population in Grand Rapids.

In May 1970, it briefly looked as if the Black community had won some concessions from the police department. Fearing ongoing stonewalling on the part of the city, superintendent Robert Anderson, city commissioners, and various representatives of local Black churches and the Urban League held a meeting to discuss recent issues of police misconduct. Under the direction of Kathy Miles of the Urban League and other Urban League administrators, the community had secured a promise from city commissioners to hire a Black assistant to the superintendent of police and to pull patrol officers out of the southeast side for two weeks—over the objections of past and present police officers. For example, former police superintendent, William A. Johnson, patronizingly stated that he could not blame the recently elected commissioners who made this decision due to "their total lack of experience, their amateurishness, their ineptness."[45] Johnson, who was working for Grand Valley State College's police department at the time, clearly felt that siding with the Black community over the police department could only occur because of political inexperience or naïveté. Within days of agreeing to the concessions, the city retracted its position and returned to its stall tactics.

This renunciation was likely due to ongoing pressure from the police and residents. The former police superintendent also questioned the credibility of the leaders of this movement, stoking tension within the Black community and adding to the pressure on the city to reconsider its decision. Regarding Miles and others from the Urban League, Johnson asked, "Do [they] speak for the black community? I'd say for perhaps 5 percent of the black community."[46] Delegitimizing the leadership of this movement and speaking for the "silent majority" were part of the power structure's strategy to quell resistance. After the May meeting, the *Grand Rapids Press* ran stories of African Americans who did not agree with this movement.[47] As part of this series, the newspaper interviewed Walter Mathis, a thirty-year-old Black man who worked for the federally funded legal aid office, about the proposed changes to the police department. While he agreed with many of the demands, the press made sure to include his thoughts on the leadership in the Black community. Journalist Ed Kotlar wrote that "Mathis said they are not speaking for everyone." Then Kotlar quoted Mathis as saying "Where are the good black folks? Why don't they go to the City Commission meeting and speak up?"[48] In running the story on Mathis, Kotlar and the press capitalized on the tension about advocacy and leadership within Grand Rapids' Black community. Including this quote also implicitly posited that there were "good" Black folks like Mathis and there were others who were not good, which left open the inference that Mathis meant Miles. It is unclear if city administrators read this article or others like it, but they eventually caved to mounting pressure. In a quick turn of events, municipal authorities demonstrated their commitment to maintaining their seemingly absolute power over policing. Rather than appoint an assistant outright, Mayor Robert Boelens, who succeeded Sonneveldt, argued that whether to make the appointment was still negotiable and insisted that representatives of the Black community must communicate with the FOP prior to any final decision from the city. As a union for police officers, the fraternal organization declared its right to offer input.

Activists, especially Black women, used the FOP's resistance to showcase the bureaucratic failings of municipal governance. Kathy Miles, as the head of the appointed committee, refused to meet with the FOP and, in her refusal, illuminated the power dynamics governing Grand Rapids. "We, the citizens of the black community, do not feel it necessary to meet with the Fraternal Order of Police and mayor's committee due to the fact that we have stated our position and made our demands to the highest authority in the city, which is the city commission—we thought," Miles reasoned somewhat sarcastically in a public statement. "Now the question arises who is really the authority in the community—the police or city commission; it seems it's the FOP."[49] Miles's perceptive statement summarized the Black community's frustrations. They had gathered everyone who had a formal role at the May meeting according to stated hiring procedures. Yet, for all their efforts, they continued to be pushed around by municipal authorities, likely in the hopes that activists would abandon their campaign or capitulate to the FOP's terms. In refusing to meet with the FOP, Miles shined a light on the bureaucratic inefficiency of the city's response to ongoing instances of police brutality. In a sleight of hand, however, Miles brilliantly pitted two distinct and powerful municipal entities against each other: the city commission and the FOP. As someone who did not have the authority to formally impact city issues, Miles inventively reversed the power dynamic between the Black community and the City of Grand Rapids.

For its part, the FOP staunchly rejected any of the proposed changes to policing, but it especially disparaged the idea of a special assistant, viewing any form of "special treatment" toward minority groups as unnecessary. The GRPD committed itself to a "colorblind" approach to hiring, meaning that their policies were absent overt discussions of race. Even when asked about hiring more minority officers in the years prior to the 1970 meeting, the department's representative exclaimed that the FOP was "not interested in the man who feels he should be a police officer and receive special treatment just because he is a member of a minority group."[50] The suggestion of a special assistant received nothing but harsh criticism from FOP president Robert Row. In a May 1970 letter to the mayor, Row insisted that any agreement to hire the special assistant would only lend "credence to the charges of police brutality." The FOP leadership viewed any concessions to activists as an admission of guilt that they preferred to ignore and, at times, deny. The FOP portrayed the special assistant position as a "symptomatic overreaction" to minority complaints. The FOP leadership fell back on the "slippery slope" argument, alleging that granting the Black community a special assistant would see the department besieged by demands from every ethnic group, including "Japanese, Chinese, Dutch, Polish, Puerto Rican, Anglo-Saxon" residents. In reality, "Anglo Saxon," Dutch, and Polish residents were already represented by the near-lily-white police force.[51]

White residents echoed the FOP's sentiments in their letters to the mayor, activists, commissioners, and the press. Many of them added that minorities were undeserving of structural changes. Robert Denick, a white resident of southeastern Grand Rapids, wrote in May 1970 that it would be unfair for Latinos and Blacks to receive "things they are too lazy to work for."[52] Using this rhetoric, white people suggested that merit, as opposed to structural racism, accounted for their social and economic mobility. This framework made it easy for white Grand Rapidians to dismiss any proposed changes as unnecessary. For instance, Mrs. Doug Riemersma wrote that "we have to stop bending over backwards," while implying that white residents never enjoyed systemic advantages. She also regarded Black and Latino people as unworthy of any assistance and believed that the city should ignore minority demands. Some residents clearly deemed equitable hiring policies as a threat to their control over the GRPD and other municipal entities. Using a pseudonym, one person wrote that "n-----s [are] . . . trying to dictate policy to the white taxpayers."[53] While the language in this letter was the harshest of all the letters I reviewed, and therefore an outlier, the other correspondences displayed similar sentiments, even if they did not use the same racial slur. "If the city commission is willing to give in to the colored people on the police question, then I think it is only fair to withhold fire protection too," another resident wrote. "In fact, maybe that should be a part of the agreement," he added, suggesting that minorities deserved any harm that occurred because of their demands. According to this logic, if Black and Latino Grand Rapidians would not accept the flawed state of the public safety services, then they deserved none. Deeply racist beliefs undergirded the resistance to making the police department more representative.

Latinos encountered that same racist rhetoric when they tried once more to convince the police department to alter its hiring practices. Juan Maldonado, one of the only Latino teachers in Grand Rapids at the time and later a lawyer, repeated what the police department told him in front of the city commission in April 1971. Maldonado claimed that, during his meeting with the GRPD, he was told they could not do "anything special to assure the recruitment of Latin Americans" into the police department, according to an interview he did with the *Grand Rapids Press*.[54] "Everybody can make it in this society if they want to try," the GRPD assured Maldonado, displaying its adherence to colorblind rhetoric and a pull-yourself-up-by-your-bootstraps mentality to deny opportunities to people of color. Maldonado interpreted the GRPD's rebuttal as implying that Latinos were not trying hard enough to succeed, which discounted the entire history of their recruitment to Michigan specifically to fill labor needs. In his statement to the commission and to the fifty Mexicans and Puerto Ricans in attendance at the meeting, Maldonado referenced the other Michigan cities that had hired Latino police officers, asking, "so why not Grand Rapids?" He observed that Latinos' work ethic was not the problem—the problem was structural racism. Attempting to further delay, Mayor Boelens proposed another study to investigate the matter. "We don't need no more studies. We want a commitment," Martín Morales replied, in his typical bellicose fashion. "When are you going to give us Latin-American policemen?," he asked in an aggravated tone that summarized the growing frustration of the activists working on community-controlled policing. He then exclaimed: "If this isn't a racist city, what is it?"[55] In response, the mayor promised that more minorities would be hired, but he could not say in what capacity and when.

Frustrated by such bureaucratic maneuvering, activists subsequently weaponized the city's affirmative action policies to force the city to hire more Black and Latino police officers. In 1970, municipal officials had adopted an affirmative action plan for contractors after the Grand Rapids Coalition of Minorities (GRCM), a group that formed to address job discrimination, pressured them into developing one. GRCM efforts resulted in a policy that required companies to have at least 8 percent of their workforce identify as minorities if they wanted to do more than $10,000 worth of business with the city annually.[56] Though hardly the 15 percent that the GRCM had asked for, activists were undeterred and next turned their attention to the city itself.[57] They charged Grand Rapids was failing to comply with federal affirmative action recommendations because it had no formal plan to hire more minorities. An affirmative action plan for outside contractors was a step forward but encouraging the city to embrace a plan for city employees would improve upon the dismal number of minority employees working within municipal offices. Activists also hoped to use a hiring agreement to compel the city to hire more minority police officers.

The city's lack of an affirmative action plan came to a head at a commission meeting in 1971, when one of the few Black city employees called out local officials for their neglect. Harold Oliver, an African American man and the manpower programs coordinator who managed the distribution of federal programs for jobs for the City of Grand Rapids, offered a blistering critique of the municipal government's discussion of affirmative action in city contracts. Referencing a manpower report that he prepared, which recommended hiring more Black and Latino police officers and firefighters until the numbers reached "reasonably representative integration," Oliver insisted that the city "set its own house in order before demanding that private businesses hire minority group employees."[58] Accordingly, he recommended that the City of Grand Rapids should "quickly take steps to be a shining example" of affirmative action compliance for other municipal governments.[59] Oliver pointed out the hypocrisy of the city not addressing its own discriminatory hiring practices while regulating businesses to ensure they complied with the necessary affirmative action quotas to contract with the city. He urged the city to refrain from its usual "passive" manner in recruiting and become more proactive in order to create "upward mobility for minority persons."[60] In demanding that the city amend its policies to remedy the negative consequences its earlier actions had on Black and Latino Grand Rapidians, Oliver's comments revealed a radical take on the responsibility of local government to aid minorities in their advancement. Juan Maldonado, a Puerto Rican activist, echoed Oliver. "The report says what we have been saying for 35 years," he exclaimed during the tense meeting.[61] Maldonado and Oliver received an uproarious applause from the coalition of Black and Latino community members in the audience. However, Mayor Boelens did not feel the same enthusiasm.

Likely hoping to avoid a white political backlash in his first years of office, Mayor Boelens dismissed Oliver's suggestion and tried to distance himself from any plan to impose affirmative action policies on the police or fire departments. Boelens stated that Oliver's report was "only a recommendation" and declared there was no room in the budget for more police officers or firefighters. Nevertheless, the Reverend Lyman Parks refused to let Boelens off the hook. As the commissioner for the Third Ward and the only African American on the commission, Reverend Parks exclaimed, "My God, what do we need to do to prove we are citizens?" Parks went on to tell the mayor, "I am a little shocked. I don't believe that three Latin Americans out of 10 is asking too much. I don't believe that asking three Blacks out of 10 is too much."[62] Parks's statements reiterated the extent to which Grand Rapids had Othered Black and Latino people. These groups had been facing questions about their citizenship and belonging in the United States for the past two centuries by this time.[63] Parks's comments also revealed the level of exhaustion and frustration he, and likely many others, felt, since nothing they accomplished or argued convinced the city to hire them.

From his position of power, Parks tried to hold Boelens accountable to the residents he was supposed to represent. The meeting then turned into a shouting match between Parks and Boelens. After calling out the second-class treatment that Latinos and Blacks endured from city officials, Parks directed his ire toward the mayor: "Before we had this report, you told these people that we had to do something for the minorities in this community. Don't start hedging now." An agitated Boelens denied Parks's claim. Boelens's response resulted in an abrupt end to the meeting, without the city taking an official stand on minority hiring.

Despite Oliver's and Park's urging, the city continued to stall changes in the GRPD's hiring policies for the foreseeable future. Although city officials had enacted an affirmative action plan in July 1971, the plan lacked provisions for enforcement and thus failed to spur any progress in hiring. As for Mayor Boelens, he was either "hedging" as Parks claimed or he was being duplicitous. He vaguely promised more hires to the Black and Latino community, but whenever he was pushed to act, he did nothing. After multiple urban uprisings in the city expanded the white backlash in Grand Rapids—a pattern that occurred around the country wherever people of color actively challenged inequality and second-class citizenship—Mayor Boelens resigned in June 1971, citing only his poor health as the reason. Boelens appeared to understand the conservative nature of Grand Rapids and often acted accordingly. With police reform, he chose inaction to support the status quo, and later he even switched political parties to win approval in Grand Rapids. Though he was a Democrat for most of his life, Boelens ran as a Republican in the 1973 election for Gerald R. Ford's vacant seat in the U.S. House of Representatives.[64] Regardless of Boelens's motivations or political aspirations, his resignation created an unanticipated opening for a leadership position in the city. Left with the decision to appoint a commissioner as acting mayor, the nearly all-white city commission chose the Third Ward's Lyman Parks, the only Black commissioner, as interim mayor in 1971. Some of the commissioners who had elected Parks were less conservative than the other members. Both Howard Rienstra and the Reverend Harold Dekker were professors: as already noted, Rienstra was a history professor at Calvin College, a local Christian college, and Dekker was a professor of missions at Calvin Theological Seminary. They represented the "liberal" wing in a largely conservative body. Grand Rapids' residents elected Parks themselves in 1973. Parks's appointment and subsequent election to mayor marked the first—and to date only—time a Black person has served in that office in Grand Rapids' history and one of twenty or so Black mayors in the country at the time.

Although Parks's elevation may seem like a radical move for such a socially conservative city, Parks himself represented the myths about race and ideology that many in Grand Rapids held dear. City representatives stressed that though there were some radical African Americans in Grand Rapids, they constituted a small minority among the Black community. Parks was, in Walter Mathis's language, one of the "good Black folks."[65] White people believed that Parks, and Mathis for that matter, represented the opinions of most of the local Black community. Parks was an AME pastor who idolized Martin Luther King Jr. and Booker T. Washington instead of more radical leaders like W. E. B. Du Bois and Malcom X. As Todd Robinson, a scholar of Black Grand Rapids, astutely assesses, Parks was rather conservative. He approved of the progress made in the civil rights movement, but he stated that, by the late 1960s, "perhaps we'd reached the point where we need to sit down and assess where we had come, and evaluate it on the basis of what this meant for the future, rather than continue to push for 'freedom now.'"[66] That idea fell in line with those of many of the commissioners and other white Grand Rapidians. His 1973 election marked an increase in racial diversity of city leaders, but it was hardly an ideological shift. Standing up to Boelens at the 1971 commission meeting was one of his few acts that seemed to challenge the white supremacy at the root of Grand Rapids' municipal government. Though Black residents may have hoped that an African American mayor would make substantial changes to the police department or other city departments, Parks did not. Even if he had a more radical vision, under the restrictive council-manager format of governance, Parks had one vote—the same as the commissioners.[67] His election was not a victory for radical organizers and can best be understood as a morale boost for middle-class activists who favored institutional activism as the path to more representation in municipal government.

Black and Latino community advocates tried and failed to persuade city officials to end discriminatory hiring practices. The most powerful political entities in the City of Grand Rapids showed no interest in changing the demographics of the department. Neither did many of the city's white residents. Most simply they dismissed the campaign as outside their responsibility to remedy the city's racist policing and hiring practices. The refusal of these powerful municipal authorities to act ended up merely safeguarding the power and authority the GRPD wielded in already disenfranchised communities. In early 1972, the police and fire departments reaffirmed their opposition to reforms when they carried out a round of hiring that netted no Black or Latino hires, despite the pleas emanating from communities of color.[68] In years past, such recalcitrance might have dissuaded Latino and Black communities from implementing a more radical strategy to achieve their goals. However, fueled by the rhetoric of the civil rights movement, activists dug in their heels and readied themselves for an ongoing battle that would change the composition of the police department.

"AND ALL OTHER PERSONS OF THEIR MINORITY GROUP": FORGING A PATH FOR CHANGING POLICE HIRING THROUGH THE FIRE DEPARTMENT

In the fall of 1972, a coalition of Black, Latino, and white advocates devised a plan to alter the requirements for hiring within the police department while avoiding a direct appeal to the GRPD, which had just demonstrated its unwillingness to submit to outside pressure. The Grand Rapids Fire Department (GRFD) relied on similar hiring standards as the police department, which also had resulted in a homogeneous group of firefighters. In the 294-person fire department in the late 1960s, there were only six Black firefighters and no Latinos.[69] Observing this pattern, Al Wilson, director of the LAC and a white ally to the Black and Latino coalition, set about challenging the hiring requirements in the GRFD. He specifically targeted the validity of the civil service exam, arguing that the exam failed to predict job performance. Working on behalf of a Mexican American man and an African American man from the community—respectively, Pablo Martínez and James Ragsdale—Wilson launched a case in 1972 against the Civil Service Board of Grand Rapids, hoping to dismantle the unfair requirements to be a firefighter. Other activists hoped that a favorable ruling in *Martínez and Ragsdale v. Civil Service Board* would establish a precedent that could invalidate the police department's civil service exam to ultimately deliver the change in police hiring they desired.

The outcry among white Grand Rapidians over the proposed affirmative action hiring policies for the GRPD pushed Black and Latino activists to redirect their energy; they hoped challenging the fire department would avoid similar levels of resistance from their white neighbors. The police department's hiring policies and racist practices only reinforced the local racial and social hierarchy that many white residents benefitted from and supported. By not increasing African American and Latino representation on the GRPD, municipal officials exposed their belief that these communities remained undeserving of high levels of authority in Grand Rapids and that they also lacked the wherewithal to police themselves. However, the fire department offered a different discourse because it did not prop up the racial or social order, or at least it appeared that way on the surface. Minority residents had not launched any prior complaints of inequitable treatment on the part of the fire department, although their reasons for not doing so may have varied. Certainly, in New York, Black and Latino residents observed a level of neglect from the fire department and ambulances that suggested a lower regard for Black and Latino life than was held for the lives of white residents. These communities often criticized these municipal services for responding to minority calls with less urgency.[70] Yet, this did not seem to be a prominent concern among Blacks and Latinos in Grand Rapids. White residents also appeared less concerned about a Black and/or Latino "invasion" of the fire department because, unlike with the debate around the GRPD, few made any public statements denouncing minority firefighters who might benefit from "special privileges" under the city's hiring practices. However, given that the department had no Latinos on staff and that Black firefighters made up only 2 percent of the force when they were 10 percent of the city's population, the hiring procedures were clearly racially biased.

Operating on behalf of the LAC and the city's 15 percent of minority residents, Wilson sought a lawsuit against the fire department after multiple failed attempts to educate white city officials and residents about the structural racism that governed hiring policies in the police and fire departments. Furthermore, when the GRPD recruited new officers again in 1972 without netting any minority officers, the police department responded simply by offering white officers "Negro history" and Spanish courses. Commissioners once again considered adding a recruitment officer who would specialize in working with minority applicants. An unnamed citizen wrote an editorial in the *Grand Rapids Press* warning readers that a recruiter would not work because "the drive must come from within the minorities' own community."[71] Wilson took this as an opportunity to critique both the op-ed and the city's policies. Wilson wrote a three-page response to the editorial, but the *Grand Rapids Press* did not publish it—so he forwarded it to Mayor Parks. In his unpublished letter, Wilson asked how "the Grand Rapids Police Department can justify the effort and expense of sending a dozen of its Anglo officers to take intensive Spanish language instruction at Grand Valley State College, but cannot justify the effort and expense of training Spanish-surnamed and Black officer candidates to increase their skills in recognizing geometric shapes and in using the white majority dialect of English?"[72] Echoing Wilson, Martín Morales, in his usual sardonic fashion, said that "learning Spanish does not make [police officers] Latin American," when later providing a comment for the *Grand Rapids Press*.[73] These activists recognized the double standard at play regarding how the department used its resources to ensure the success of certain police officers and recruits.

Wilson also questioned the legitimacy of colorblind hiring procedures in his letter to the press. In the editorial that provoked Wilson, the writer supported the city's refusal to change any hiring procedures: "Standards should not be lowered to permit anyone, of any race or color, to qualify for service in either branch of the city government, especially since the emphasis in such departments around the country is to raise standards," the author argued, referring to the standards of both the police and fire departments.[74] In response, Wilson suggested the writer needed "an introduction to institutional discrimination before attempting his next analysis of minority problems."[75] Next, he explained the futility of the current policing standards:

How relevant to policing and firefighting is the acquisition of an extensive 'proper' English vocabulary, or the ability to identify and remember esoteric names for various geometric shapes? Or for that matter, how relevant to the adequate performance of a wide range of City jobs is the ability to perform well on a written (or verbal) examination of any sort? These skills, including the exam-taking skill itself, are behaviors acquired as young people pass through our school system—a system which still today harbors countless obstacles to motivation and successful learning on the part of the colored and economically underprivileged students.[76]

Wilson understood that the culturally biased examinations could never be fair to racial and ethnic minorities in Grand Rapids. In his response, he also laid out a multilayered attack against the interconnected social structures that kept Blacks and Latinos on the margins. As a white man, Wilson used his position of privilege to educate his peers, though it yielded no immediate results. His fixation on the civil service test, however, would pay off.

While Wilson considered his response to the editorial, he also searched for plaintiffs in a suit against the Civil Service Board of Grand Rapids. At first, he had located a Mexican American man, Pablo Martínez, and asked Martínez if he knew of any Black candidates who had been rejected due to the civil service exam. Eventually Martínez met James Ragsdale after one of the practice tests and introduced him to Wilson. The choice in plaintiffs was emblematic of the multiracial path of organizing that Wilson and others had embraced for this fight. By ensuring that there were both Latino and African American plaintiffs, Wilson underscored the importance of unity among these groups in this fight against the city. He then secured a grant from the Steelcase Corporation to hire a local labor lawyer, Rhett Pinsky. At thirty-five years old, Pinsky had just started his own practice where he represented workers and their families. Discrimination in hiring was at the core of this case, which was one of his areas of expertise.[77] In the lawsuit against the fire department, Pinsky argued that the civil service test was not an accurate predictor of job performance. Instead, as Wilson had outlined in his response to the editorial, the exam was designed for "white, middle-class persons of good education."[78]

Focusing on the hardships that Pablo Martínez and James Ragsdale faced while applying for positions in the GRFD, Wilson and Pinsky exposed the degree to which racism stood as a formidable obstacle, even under the otherwise "colorblind" hiring system. Martínez and Ragsdale were both Vietnam War veterans. At the height of the war, in which poor minorities were disproportionately represented as soldiers, the fire department's rejection of their application was characterized as even more egregious. Martínez worked at the LAC, which had provided him with employment after he left the army and was unable to secure a job. He performed various jobs around the council, but his hopes for more stable employment were dashed after he failed the fire department's civil service exam. On retaking the exam, Martínez met Vietnam War veteran James Ragsdale, who had previously failed the exam as well. Both men aspired to more than menial work and knew they were capable. For example, Ragsdale attended Grand Rapids Community College, where he made the honors list while working two jobs, one of which was as an instructional aide at an elementary school. Despite demonstrating great potential, both men regarded the test as unusually difficult. Ragsdale was shocked that, even with his résumé and his impeccable grades, he did not pass. He remarked, "that says a lot about these tests."[79] Martínez, for his part, earned his high school degree while he was in the U.S. Marine Corps and was interested in being the first Mexican to be employed with the fire department.

With the plaintiffs in place, Pinsky filed a complaint with the U.S. District Court for the Western District of Michigan in June 1972 on behalf of Martínez, Ragsdale, and "all other persons of their minority groups." The suit charged that the department's hiring standards were not "'job related'" and tended to "screen out lower-income persons." The Civil Service Board, its chief examiner Andrew Vanderveen, and Fire Chief Robert Veit were all named as defendants in the class action suit. Judge Noel P. Fox set a trial date for December 4, 1972.[80] Fox, appointed by John F. Kennedy, had a liberal reputation in Michigan. Beyond this case, he later sided with Native Americans in a fight to allow them fishing rights on Michigan's Great Lakes.[81] Activists felt some hope when Fox affirmed Pinsky's request for an injunction against the GRFD, which prevented any hiring while the case was underway.

Pinsky's strategy relied heavily on the verdicts in similar cases and department statistics that reflected the GRFD's discriminatory hiring policies. One case, *Carter v. Gallagher* (1970), involved the Minneapolis fire department. At the time of the case, not a single African American or Native American firefighter was employed in its 540-person department, even though they represented a combined 6 percent of the population. In that case, the judge banned the diploma requirement and ordered an entirely new entrance exam. Pinsky also referenced *Griggs v. Duke Power Co.* (1971), a U.S. Supreme Court case centering on the Duke Power Co., which set the standard in North Carolina and elsewhere for challenging aptitude tests and the requirement of a high school diploma. The court ruled in favor of Willie Griggs, finding that the energy company relied on aptitude tests and a diploma merely as measures to maintain a lily-white workforce, a practice that now violated title 7 of the Civil Rights Act of 1964. These cases established that the presence of racial disparities in a department provided the grounds for a prima facie case for discrimination; that is, given the racial disparities, Pinsky could argue that racial bias in hiring existed until he was disproven. These two cases, among others, also placed the onus on the defendants—the representatives of the city in this case—to prove its hiring tools accurately measured job performance. Thus, *Martínez and Ragsdale v. Civil Service Board* could rest on the gross underrepresentation of minorities as an indication of racial discrimination in the GRFD's hiring procedures.

About six months after Pinsky and Wilson filed, the parties settled and signed a consent decree. Without admitting guilt, the commissioners, as the body representing the city, agreed to the terms Pinsky asked for—the first tangible sign of progress in a fight for more representation in municipal offices. Judge Fox oversaw the conditions of the consent decree on the case that incorporated many of the Black and Latino activists' demands. On January 22, 1973, the City of Grand Rapids agreed to cease discriminating against Blacks and Latinos in hiring for the fire department. To ensure compliance, the city agreed to the following terms: establish a civil service appeal board for denied applicants, undertake an affirmative action program to integrate the department, set up recruiting stations in minority communities, consult with agencies and groups that had direct contact with minority communities, and provide pretest tutoring to applicants. Most importantly, however, the commissioners agreed that the civil service test must be validated by an outside firm to ensure that it could accurately predict a firefighter's job performance.[82]

Though the consent decree went into effect immediately, it took over a year for the city to implement a hiring plan that Judge Fox approved. Between 1973 and 1974, city administrators started making changes and putting into place an equitable hiring program. Rather than require candidates to hold a high school diploma, the GRFD agreed that potential recruits only needed to be able to read and write. The age requirement was also lowered to eighteen. The city quickly selected an outside firm to certify that its civil service test was pertinent to the job description.[83] In February 1974, the city personnel director, Andrew Vanderveen, promised that an intensive recruitment program would begin within several weeks of the ruling and that it would focus on Latino, Black, and Native American firefighters, the last of whom were about 1 percent of the county's population but had skilled activists fighting for their representation in Grand Rapids.[84] Judge Fox approved the city's plan, and as a result of these changes, the fire department hired twenty-two recruits in September 1974; nine were Black, six were Latino, and two were Native American.[85] With the consent decree issued and a plan for increasing minority hiring in place for the GRFD, local activists began to consider how they might apply the verdict to police hiring. "I don't think the city has any defense," Martín Morales insisted. "It's using the same biased testing in the Police Department," he added. Foreshadowing the activists' next steps, one *Grand Rapids Press* journalist reported that "some officials think the Fire Department plan will have an impact on other city hiring, particularly the Police Department."[86]

Almost two years after Wilson and Pinsky filed suit against the fire department, the police department started to make changes to its hiring policies in May 1974. Before announcing the 1974 plan, the police department hired two Latino officers, perhaps sensing they would soon have to change its policies as well. Then in June 1974, it began the process of hiring two more Latino officers: Miguel Berríos, son of one of the first Puerto Rican couples to settle in the area, and Reyes Carrasco, a Tejano from San Antonio.[87] Even with these hires, there were still only seven nonwhite officers in the entire department.[88] Using the fire department's consent decree and program for increasing minorities as a guide, the police department announced it would hire ten "minority persons" through a program in which recruits would start as aides prior to transitioning into full-time positions in the police department. Deputy Chief Francis Pierce explained that the program was being implemented "to comply with the recent court decisions, including a federal court ruling here and subsequent resolution aimed at bringing more minority persons into the Fire Department."[89] Though these hires were monumental in the context of the department's history of resistance, the number of minority officers was hardly proportionate to their population in the city.

The GRPD then learned that it needed to continue hiring minority officers after the federal government denied the department a grant under the Law Enforcement Assistance Administration (LEAA) in late 1974 for failing to comply with the equal-opportunity guidelines. The LEAA gave federal monies to financially struggling departments, but funding was contingent on compliance with federal affirmative action mandates. Thus, in 1975, the police department continued its training program and hired two more Latino police officers, Daniel Flores and Vladimir Sáenz, and three other minority veterans: Marvin Smith, Percy Brown, and Larry Moore.[90] It also hired its first-ever women patrol officers. Each of the 1975 new hires was fresh from the training program.[91] For decades, Black, white, and Latino activists worked tirelessly to achieve representation in the police department. It took a federal court ruling and being forced to comply with a federal program's guidelines before it finally hired minority officers. Nevertheless, the groundswell of backlash that appeared among white residents during the initial attempts to diversify the police and fire departments had not entirely dissipated.

AFTERMATH

Even after the fire department launched its affirmative action hiring program, potential recruits faced intransigent resistance from white Grand Rapidians who intended to preserve the racial status quo by any means. For example, though he was one of the plaintiffs in *Martínez and Ragsdale v. Civil Service Board*, Pablo

Martínez was reluctant to reapply for a position in the GRFD when he learned from allies in the department that it could be dangerous for him to do so given the resentment from white firefighters toward the lawsuit. In fact, after the lawsuit it took him eight years to reapply for the fire department. He eventually joined the GRFD in 1980, starting a long and decorated career as one of the City of Grand Rapids' first Latino firefighters and the first Latino fire investigator. He held the latter position for eighteen years, prior to his retirement in 2008.[92] James R. Ragsdale never joined the fire department, though it remains unclear what happened to him after the trial. Though the case forced the city to rework the civil service exam to ensure that it was related to the job description, the new tests, in many respects, represented another form of gatekeeping. As David Goldberg, a scholar of Black firefighters in New York, has found, the tests could be validated by outside agencies but still contain biases. Once they were approved, the exams codified those biases while giving the appearance "that the new tests were facially neutral."[93]

Minority police officers continued to encounter more obstacles. Shortly after the 1975 cohort of minority recruits were hired, the FOP demanded that the GRPD stop hiring minority candidates. They deemed the recruit program as unfair because all the department's recent hires were nonwhite. Meanwhile, in 1978, the U.S. Supreme Court invalidated the use of racial quotas in affirmative action with the decision in *Regents of the University of California v. Bakke*, which led the GRPD to preemptively cancel the recruit program. Those minority officers who joined the department also faced additional hurdles. In the mid-1980s, nineteen minority officers filed suit against the police department for discriminatory practices regarding promotions.[94] The plaintiffs won, but the backlash persisted.

For every stride the community made to improve race relations between white, Black, and Latino communities in the late 1960s and early 1970s, the predominantly white city government and white citizens of Grand Rapids strenuously resisted change. The requirements for municipal jobs had ensured that Black and Latino applicants were barred from some of the most coveted positions in Grand Rapids, which thwarted their upward mobility. The fight to uphold the hiring standards signified the white leadership's commitment to preserving the power dynamics between the authorities and residents as well as between the white and nonwhite communities. White residents, city administrators, and the police department, especially the FOP, cloaked their resistance in colorblind rhetoric, disguising their racist ideas and firm belief that minorities were "undeserving" of assistance. Meanwhile, they dismissed minorities' claims that whites had enjoyed additional privilege, a position that failed to reckon with the history of Grand Rapids, the state of Michigan, and the United States. For its part, the city government often enforced the bare minimum of the requirements to stay in compliance with federal mandates. Overall, municipal officials moved at a snail's pace toward measurable change.

Given the entrenched racism in Grand Rapids, Black and Latino leaders settled on fighting for representation when what many truly desired was community control. In the early 1960s, Black activists had called for community-controlled policing that would challenge the systemic issues they faced. Their demands for the appointment of a Black aide to the superintendent of police, for the withdrawal of white patrolmen from Black neighborhoods, and for the hiring of "aware" Black officers would have transformed the nature of policing Black communities. With the intractable resistance from the FOP and the city, some activists decided to put their energy into gaining a foothold in the GRPD. Placing members of their communities in the most powerful departments seemed their best chance at changing their lived experience. To that end, they implemented strategies to fit the circumstances of Grand Rapids' fierce backlash to racial progress. They organized in coalitions, carried out studies, used resources from other organizations, developed research-backed proposals, utilized federal policies like affirmative action, and ultimately carried their complaints to the U.S. District Court for the Western District of Michigan, all to gain some control over their interactions with the local government.

In the struggle to gain representation in municipal employment, Black organizers played key roles in creating the opportunity for an interracial coalition. To be sure, in the late 1960s, police brutality and department policies disproportionately affected the Black community in Grand Rapids. Kathy Miles, Melvin Tardy, and other middle-class Black leaders joined others to place constant pressure on the police department to give the community a semblance of control over the policing they experienced. Specifically, their demand for a Black aide to the superintendent of police created an opportunity for other Black, Latino, and white organizers to reimagine the possibilities for community intervention in municipal hiring. Melvin Tardy, Martín Morales, and Al Wilson were among those who recognized that the Black community needed representation and so too did Latinos. Opening the discussion on what was possible within the police department cleared a path for these organizers to engage and support one another along with their respective communities.

To achieve their demands for a role within the GRPD, Black and Latino residents needed interracial organizing. While working toward greater access to CAP and MCP funding in the years prior, African Americans and Latinos had stressed their differences. The battle for municipal employment, however, could not rely on that previous strategy because it was ineffective in the long term. Even Martín Morales, who in 1968 stressed that African Americans and Latinos possessed very different needs, supported this burgeoning coalition. As a man who had a reputation for antagonizing any attempts at interethnic and interracial solidarity, his letters supporting more minority hires—and not just Latino hires—shows how well he understood the dynamics of political organizing in Grand Rapids. The coalition among Black and Latino communities cooperated to lobby for small, incremental gains, like slowly trying to delegitimize the height requirement, and coordinated some of their larger actions like filing a joint lawsuit.

White allies also played an integral role in this struggle. In his work on behalf of marginalized communities, Al Wilson condemned the hiring standards for the GRPD with both Latinos and African Americans in mind. Wilson exemplified how white allies could use their privilege and resources to help minorities. Oral histories with Latino activists from the 1970s praised Wilson for his efforts, absent the critiques often leveled at white allies. He listened to their desires for self-determination and facilitated their access to outside support without overstepping or centering himself. Black and Latino communities also benefited from allies on the city commission. Howard Rienstra and Reverend Dekker used their positions to vote on issues that mattered most to Black and Latino residents.

Together, Black and Latino leadership—along with the communities that supported and validated them—took aim at their exclusion in what many residents viewed as an important challenge to structural racism in Grand Rapids. Obtaining jobs in public safety would not only legitimize them—in the eyes of their white neighbors—as residents of Grand Rapids, but it would also allow these communities to live more peacefully and with less fear of police interactions. This fight morphed into an attempt to safeguard a future for these communities. While inequalities remain, the need for a coalitional approach to fighting for dignified lives, representation, and true community control continues to this day. As was the case with policing, Black and Latino coalitions also became important to transforming another inequitable system—education.

– 7 –

Justice for Our Kids

By the end of junior high, Rosa Collazo all but abandoned any interest in schooling. The curriculum did not appeal to her, and more significantly, she never quite felt welcomed. As a young Puerto Rican teenager with curls that defied gravity, hazel eyes, and light skin, she had been deemed too white by the African American girls in her neighborhood. Yet, she also appeared too Black for her white classmates at Burton Junior High. She tried to explain to all parties that she was Puerto Rican, but this only confounded them further. Later, when Collazo reflected painfully on that period, she recalled that she lacked a full understanding of her racial and ethnic identity.[1] The public school system in Grand Rapids had not furnished her with many opportunities to learn about her culture. Additionally, her parents neglected to disclose any information about their lives back in Puerto Rico, though she later discovered that they had endured much hardship in what was, for all intents and purposes, a U.S. colony.

The appreciation she developed for Latino culture was gained from participating in the Latin American Council's youth programming during the early 1970s. Like other teenagers who visited the LAC, Collazo enjoyed access to a community library that housed all types of books about Puerto Ricans, Mexicans, Cubans, and other Latinos. To help cope with feelings of alienation that they may have felt as part of Grand Rapids' minority Latino community, teenagers like Collazo also benefitted from the center's cultural and educational programming, which they offered free of charge. There were many Latino students who felt like Collazo. In fact, almost 69 percent of Latino high schoolers left the Grand Rapids Public Schools (GRPS) system before graduating in the early 1970s.[2] As part of a grassroots effort to reduce these numbers, the LAC played an essential role in the educational development and socialization of Latino youths in Grand Rapids via the formation of the Neighborhood Education Center (NEC), or El Centro de Educación. A community-run public school, the NEC was also fondly regarded by students as El Centro for short, and it became a place where Latino students like Collazo could attend and feel welcomed.

The youth services at the LAC and El Centro's establishment grew in direct response to the expanding needs of Latino youths, whom the public schools had failed. By the 1970s, the problems plaguing Latinos in the GRPS were similar to those in many urban school districts across the country. For example, schools in Chicago and Los Angeles relied on racist and discriminatory educational policies that corralled Latino students into vocational tracks.[3] Despite the overwhelming presence of Spanish-speaking students in these cities, many schools required that English be the only language of instruction. Prioritizing Eurocentric curriculum that devalued their cultural histories also left students like Collazo feeling detached and uninterested in school. As a result, 71 percent of Puerto Rican students in Chicago stopped going to school altogether. In East Los Angeles, which boasted a large concentration of Mexicans and Mexican Americans, at least 50 percent of Chicano students were systematically "pushed out" of school as well.[4] The expression "push out" instead of "drop out" emphasizes the structural factors that cause students to leave school: this phenomenon is not an individual choice devoid of systemic inequalities. Given the nation's history of racial exclusion, Latino educational activists argued that these appalling rates of attrition arose from the consequences of structural racism and were not due to students' lack of ability. A combination of segregationist policies, biased evaluation methods, and unequal schooling all conspired to circumscribe the opportunities available to Latino youths.[5] Activist Martín Morales summarizes the feelings of the community by describing the formation of the NEC as "finally getting justice for our kids."[6]

Latino communities around the country reacted in various ways to such inequities. Students held walkouts to protest their educational experiences in large cities like Los Angeles and small cities like Lansing. The creation of the NEC most resembled the independent school movement of the 1960s and 1970s. While Afrocentric schools are the most well-known of these institutions, Chicanos also formed independent schools in this era. Unlike the NEC, most of these independent schools were funded through private dollars. This put the NEC among the few schools of this kind in the Midwest. It also was one of the few schools in the country to deliver ethnicity-focused, community-controlled education with public funding.[7]

Although scholars have often focused on education reform of the 1960s and 1970s through the lens of creating separate, private institutions or forcing change through radical organizing, in fact Latino Grand Rapidians transformed grassroots remedies into institutional solutions to create space for themselves in a majority-white school district and institute community control over Latino students' educational experiences. A cross-section of Mexican and Puerto Rican educational activists in Grand Rapids were inspired by the powerful rhetoric of self-determination of the 1960s' and 1970s' social movements, which stressed the importance of identity formation and knowing one's cultural and ethnic history. Organizers sought to address three major concerns that parents and children identified: a lack of Latino teachers, the need for Latino counselors, and the development of a bicultural and bilingual curriculum. Without these resources, the community argued that their students would not interact with people who could relate to their specific challenges as students or to their position in society as Latinos. Educators and activists from the LAC created a range of grassroots solutions to these issues, including encouraging community members to be paraprofessionals in the classroom, creating a one-on-one counseling program, and starting a cultural library. Their greatest achievement, however, was founding the NEC, which encompassed all those services and more. This space allowed students to celebrate their ethnic identities and nurture their pan-Latino solidarity. To finance their school, Latino educational advocates in Grand Rapids applied for a grant from the State of Michigan's Neighborhood Education Authority—a program that was created and administered by Black educators—to address the inequitable education Latino students received. Though the NEC and the LAC each experienced an untimely, but intertwined demise, Latino educational advocates in Grand Rapids succeeded in creating the equitable educational opportunities that many of their parents and grandparents had dreamed of when they relocated.

Coalitions among people from various racial backgrounds and with varying degrees of power can be successful in helping the most marginalized. During a period of backlash to efforts to provide equitable education, like busing for integration or attempts at creating more inclusive curriculum, a creative group of community organizers addressed the immediate needs of their students to change their educational experiences. Through institutionalizing their efforts, they were able to preserve quality education as a public good for Latinos in a region that had largely failed to do so.

"THERE IS A GREAT NEED": GRASSROOTS SOLUTIONS TO STRUCTURAL INEQUITIES

Since its inception, the LAC had viewed education as the cornerstone for improving Latinos' lives in Grand Rapids. In 1968, the council employed youth specialists and educational specialists who worked together to provide solutions to the pressing issues that young Latinos faced. Carmen Fitte, a Puerto Rican transplant from New York City who arrived to Grand Rapids in 1965, was one of the education specialists at the LAC. David Rodríguez and Richard Campos, both Chicanos from Grand Rapids, joined her as well as Rachel Campos, Richard's sister. These organizers as well as the LAC directors, Al Wilson (1971–73) and Martín Morales (1973–77), served as advocates for the Latino community's discussions with the GRPS on how to meet Latino students' educational and social needs. La Lucha, a student group at nearby Grand Valley State College comprised of former GRPS students, also assisted these efforts. Inspired by their own experience of attending the predominantly white public schools in Grand Rapids, they hoped to devise strategies that would help Latino students complete high school. Thus, where the school district fell short, the grassroots efforts of the LAC and its supporters filled in—providing students with Latino paraprofessionals, a counseling program run by people they could relate to, a rudimentary bilingual education program, and a cultural library that could fill in the gaps and correct the erroneous information in the local schools' curriculum on Latinos.

In the 1970s, GRPS had a disproportionately low number of Latinos on staff, severely limiting the chance that Latino students would interact with adults with whom they could relate. By this time, there were about 750 Latino students who needed bilingual services in the Grand Rapids school system, with Mexicans as the majority and fewer Puerto Ricans and Cubans.[8] Latinos made up higher concentrations in certain schools in their neighborhoods as compared to others. To serve them there were only six bilingual and bicultural Latino teachers and only one administrator throughout the entire school system. Although GRPS officials hired additional Latino teachers at times, the retention rate for Latino teachers was nearly as bad as it was for Latino students. In addition, there were no Latino secretaries, no bus drivers, and only two custodial workers. The low numbers of Latinos across various positions hinted at a systemic barrier that kept Latinos out of GRPS. The consequences of these unequal numbers were devastating. Young people between the ages of one and eighteen constituted a large swath of the Latino community, and without the possibility of delivering bilingual or bicultural education, an entire generation ran the risk of being pushed out of school.[9]

GPRS officials often blamed the dismal retention rate of Latino teachers and staff on a lack of capable teachers they could hire, not on the district's unwillingness to step up their recruitment efforts. In May 1972, LAC director Al Wilson, youth coordinator Rachel Campos, outreach workers Carmen Fitte and Richard Campos, and Henry Vásquez, part-time LAC employee and student activist with La Lucha, met with school administrators to devise ways to increase academic interest among Latino students. In the meeting, GRPS officials admitted that they were unable to locate and retain certified Latino teachers, though they would agree that "the demand for Latin American educators is great." Yet, they insisted that there were few Latinos in colleges and universities whom they could recruit. Faced with a low reserve of what they considered to be qualified educators in Grand Rapids, they often lured teachers from Texas and other Latino-dominated areas, but these recruits chose not to stay. They determined at the meeting that the only long-term solution was to conduct teacher recruitment among "people from the local area who intend to stay."[10]

Still, public educational officials failed to realize that until they addressed the push-out rate among younger Latinos, recruitment would continue to be a problem. With almost two-thirds of Latinos not earning a high school degree, there was a much smaller pool of college-educated Latinos from which to draw teachers. Universities also failed to provide white students who desired to teach with the cultural competency necessary to educate nonwhite students. Meanwhile, school officials would have to encourage those college-bound Latinos to pursue degrees in education and become teachers. Each year, the cycle repeated, so the number of available Latino and/or Spanish-speaking instructors remained low, a fact that underscored why the school system needed to prioritize Latino student needs immediately.

After that 1972 meeting, the district promised to go to great lengths to identify, hire, and retain Latino teachers. Serving as the personnel director for the GRPS, Don Schriemer promised "more effective Latin American teacher recruitment" by making inroads with local colleges and universities.[11] Recognizing that it would take time to construct a pipeline of Latino educators, community members sought alternative routes to having a Latino presence inside the classroom. Lacking formally trained Latino teachers, they invited GRPS to hire community members who would serve in "short term instructional capacities."[12] This solution, which turned into the LAC's paraprofessional recruitment program, would allow Latino students to rely on having Latino adults in their classrooms and perhaps sustain or even heighten their interest in school, even without having Latinos hired as full-time teachers. The LAC employment program (see chapter 5) sent eligible and interested Latinos to elementary schools to work as paraprofessionals along with some LAC employees who also worked as part-time paraprofessionals.

The LAC did not regard the paraprofessional program as a panacea for the problems in the GRPS. There was the potential that the GRPS might go the route of New York City schools, where entrenched segregation and an unequal distribution of resources resulted in the use of certified teachers in white schools and noncertified teachers in Black and Puerto Rican schools, particularly in the Bronx.[13] Nevertheless, in Grand Rapids, where Latino students were in the minority within a majority-white school district, the presence of Latinos in positions of authority could make a difference in allowing students to see they were welcome, regardless of whether the teachers were certified. LAC activists also formulated a plan for GRPS to follow, which included the immediate hiring of bilingual, bi-cultural staff and administrative personnel.[14] Buoyed by a nationwide movement led by other Latino and Black activists to have greater control over education, the LAC helped GRPS recognize the unique insights that Latino community members possessed, regardless of whether they had obtained certifications or college degrees.

Educational activists also pushed for the hiring of more Latino counselors since GRPS employed none, which had lingering consequences to students' development. Much as with the qualifications for teachers, counseling positions required, at minimum, a bachelor's degree, though candidates with master's degrees enjoyed a considerable edge over others. Without an available pool of Latino college graduates in Grand Rapids, the district could not find counselors who could relate to the unique experiences of Latinos.[15] Yet, according to La Lucha's research from collecting data on Latinos in high school, a lack of counselors was a contributing factor to the low student retention rate. In 1971, the organization conducted a study on the experiences of Latino high school students in Grand Rapids (tenth through twelfth grades). They reported that, of the 108 students they interviewed, counselors failed to build relationships with at least half of them. Among those who did report some interaction with their counselors, some relayed the meetings had left them "discouraged from [attending] college."[16] One Mexican American student, José Reyna, revealed deep inefficiencies in the high school counseling program. Reyna recalled how his counselor encouraged him "to sign up for the military," even though he was an excellent student and a talented wrestler. "[The counselor] was also recommending that the girls become secretaries" and forgo college as well, he added. Latino students around the country echoed these complaints about counselors, describing how they were forced into vocational classes like air-conditioning repair and typing.[17] In Grand Rapids and elsewhere, counselors replicated the existing social hierarchy by steering Latino students away from college.

Rather than rely on public school officials to prioritize their concerns, Latino residents turned inward to solve their issue with the non-Latino counselors. Drawing on decades of organizing and programming experience, the LAC used their already overstretched staff and resources to launch an academic program that offered one-on-one counseling services for students who had stopped going to school before they graduated. In her role as the LAC's youth coordinator, Rachel Campos began holding "dropout and disciplinary interventions" on her own, in addition to organizing programming for the youths. Working with administrators, parents, and pupils, Campos prevented three young people from leaving school in February 1972, according to her monthly activity logs for the

LAC. Later that year, in another monthly report, she detailed how she arranged for English-language classes for three students and for the part-time employment of two others.[18] Though this might not seem like many students, Campos's efforts made a difference in the lives of Latinos who otherwise had no other resources and helped to situate the LAC as a reputable organization for educational efforts. According to David Rodríguez, an education specialist with the LAC, school officials even began referring youths to the LAC, noting in one of his monthly reports that the "the principals of Hall, Burton, and Central Schools especially have been very co-operative in referring problems of Latino students to us."[19] The growing popularity of this program helped to illustrate how much value students placed on talking to someone who might understand their lived experiences. Despite their earnest attempts, however, the model was not a sustainable one. Without proper funding to hire more interventionists like Campos and Rodríguez—even though both continued to work on this issue well into the 1970s—the attrition rate among Latino high schoolers continued to rise.

Counselors could not address the lack of bilingual and bicultural instruction, which derailed many Latino students' educational pursuits. Functioning as GRPS's bilingual coordinator and the sole Latino administrator, Luis Murillo pleaded for the district to implement a wide-reaching bilingual education plan in 1968. As a result, GRPS introduced a limited bilingual program at one elementary school. However, only 120 students participated in this curriculum of the 750 Latinos who needed bilingual education throughout the school system; the program barely covered the needs of elementary schoolchildren and altogether ignored the needs of high schoolers. This initiative depended on teachers' aides, who extracted monolingual Spanish-speaking students from their regular academic classes and tutored them one-on-one. However, the paraprofessionals involved in this program admitted that not only were these methods inadequate, but they also stigmatized the children removed from the English-speaking classroom.[20] Though well-intentioned, this program was not the comprehensive, bilingual education program that students needed. Three years after GRPS launched the program, Murillo recognized the "inadequacy of the present programs" and pushed for more support with little result.

Rather than wait interminably for GRPS to gather the resources for a bilingual education plan, Murillo and LAC staff members drew on the community to establish a bilingual program. Utilizing LAC facilities, Murillo taught English-language classes on Saturdays, reaching youth who could not access the bilingual education program but still needed those services. In one month, he taught sixteen children, "none of whom [had] a rudimentary skill in English," as he wrote in a report for the council.[21] Still, this strategy only covered less than 1 percent of the students in the area who needed bilingual education.[22] Murillo and the LAC's attempt, if meager given the size of the problem, was an example of the grassroots activists' commitment to helping monolingual students.

Just as bilingual services were lacking, GRPS offered few bicultural and empowering educational materials. The curriculum, including the textbooks, disappointed education activists for not engendering pride in being Latino. The LAC found that many local schools used textbooks with outdated and incorrect information on Latinos, if such information appeared at all. The materials used in GRPS also contained gross misinterpretations of African Americans in history and contemporarily. Even the district's white social studies coordinator thought their current materials were "unsound and racist." African American organizing in the early 1970s yielded new elementary and secondary materials with updated information on African Americans. These resources corrected the distorted characterizations of Black life in America, but these same books still presented outdated material on Latin Americans.[23] For example, published as recently as 1975, *The People of Michigan* textbook included misleading errors. One of the section titles, "Latin American Settlers in Transition," failed to capture an accurate portrait of Latino relocation and settlement in the United States. Although Mexicans had settled in Michigan since at least the 1920s, the textbook perpetuated the myth that Latinos first arrived in the 1970s. Additionally, some textbooks had "misspellings of Spanish words," which called attention to the low respect publishers and school officials held for Latino culture and the Spanish language, which had served as a major point of forming a Latino identity among Mexicans and Puerto Ricans. Meanwhile, most books wholly omitted that Puerto Ricans and Cubans have distinct Latino identities. Not surprisingly, these transgressions offended activists and the communities they represented.[24] No longer willing to tolerate the general disregard for Latino experiences, educational advocates stepped in to take up the slack left by culturally insensitive materials and school officials.

In designing a grassroots approach to education, the LAC concluded that the most effective way of educating the masses involved promoting an increasing appreciation for Latino culture through youth and adult programming.[25] With federal antipoverty funding, LAC members showcased films like *The People Are Rising*, about the Young Lords Party, and *Historia de una batalla*, which focused on the Bay of Pigs invasion, at various community hotspots, including Latino-owned bars and restaurants. In the classes that the LAC hosted in its building, instructors facilitated Head Start and adult education classes from a bilingual and bicultural perspective.[26]

By far, the community library's founding in 1971 was the LAC's most inventive approach to recovering Latino history and promoting it among the community. Carmen Fitte assumed leadership over the library, reflecting her leadership among educational advocates. With the help of the Kent County Library technical assistants, Fitte and her team purchased a wide array of materials and established the procedures for book borrowing.[27] Not content to simply replicate school libraries' collections, the LAC's library provided access to titles like *Reveille for Radicals*. Written by nationally known organizer Saul Alinksy, this text is a handbook for achieving social change.[28] The LAC also purchased 175 English-language books and 50 Spanish-language books to stock the shelves, concentrating on literature and other works by Mexican, Cuban, and Puerto Rican authors.[29] The topics varied: poetry from Pablo Neruda, children's picture books, and nonfiction books ranging from sexual education to sociological studies on the plight of minorities in the United States.[30] With little power to change their district and the urgency of improving Latino student engagement, the LAC provided culturally competent education within its own facilities. The council succeeded in establishing another location for Latinos to increase their cultural awareness, sense of solidarity, and pride.

Despite the hard work from activists throughout the state, the rate of attrition among Latinos in Michigan and in Grand Rapids remained high. Their calculated attacks on the three reasons identified as to why Latino students left school before graduating—the lack of Latino teachers, the lack of culturally competent counselors, and the unavailability of bilingual instruction and bicultural content—had not made the lasting changes they desired. By 1973, the district had not provided bilingual education to all students; there had not been any major increases in the number of Latino teachers; and the curriculum had not changed, though it might have gotten worse from the textbooks the GRPS chose. Finally, in 1974 came the U.S. Supreme Court decision in *Lau v. Nichols* that schools must offer bilingual education if they received federal funding.[31] Endeavoring to fill the void in bilingual and bicultural education for all K–12 students, Latino educational advocates imagined new and inclusive pan-Latino programs and of expanding the LAC's educational and cultural offerings. Latino leaders went to great lengths to make bilingual, bicultural education and counseling available to their children. Nevertheless, they needed additional resources to truly stem the push-out rate.

"TO PROVIDE AN ALTERNATIVE EDUCATION SETTING": THE NEIGHBORHOOD EDUCATION AUTHORITY

Faced with limited resources at the local level, LAC administrators turned to the state to seek alternative solutions. Up until now, the State of Michigan could boast no large-scale curricular changes that might reduce the attrition rate among Latino students. However, through mounting pressure from various educational advocates and parents, the governor approved the Neighborhood Education

Authority (NEA) in 1970. Administered through the Michigan Department of Education, the main objective of the NEA involved "continu[ing] the education of those young individuals throughout the state who, for whatever reason, have been unable to complete their high school education."[32] To accomplish this task, the NEA also included provisions in its plan for NECs, like the one Latinos in Grand Rapids started. With approval from Governor William G. Milliken and a few African American education administrators, the NEA transformed the educational experiences of marginalized students through the spread of NECs. These state-funded schools gave parents and local activists control over their students' education, all without the need to raise independent funds for the school or upsetting the racial and social dynamics in local school districts. The program, while it provided much-needed resources, did propagate the problematic notion of education as an escape from poverty—an idea that emphasizes individual achievement as a remedy to systemic barriers. Regardless of its flaws, the NEA's pilot program in Pontiac yielded positive results, leading to its expansion across the state.

The first Black administrators in the Michigan Department of Education ushered in an approach to schooling that welcomed the creation of the NEA, which Latino educators eventually used to create an NEC in Grand Rapids. In 1969, John Porter, at the age of twenty-six, became the youngest and first Black employee in the Michigan Department of Education and rose through the organization into a leadership position. Like many administrators, Porter began his career as a teacher in Detroit and Lansing. Just ten years later, he was appointed to the superintendent of instruction position. He continued to break additional records when he became the youngest person in the nation to be named the head of a state school system and the first Black state superintendent in the country since Reconstruction.[33] In this position, he appointed other Black professionals, including Elisha Delbert Gray, who returned to the field of education as the head of the NEA after a brief stint as an entrepreneur.[34] It was also under Porter's administration that the state board of education allowed for the formation of the La Raza Advisory Committee (LRAC), a statewide organization consisting of teachers, parents, and educational advocates endeavoring to improve the experience of Latinos in Michigan schools. This new committee in the late 1960s and early 1970s created opportunities for parents and community members to curate educational experiences and spaces for marginalized students.

The changes Porter, Gray, and the NEA implemented were accomplished by working within the system. State officials did not force local school districts to alter the curriculum, even in places where students of color represented the majority population. Admittedly, establishing an NEC apart from GRPS perhaps reaffirmed the notion that traditional public schools needed to conform to white, middle-class standards rather than incorporate more diverse backgrounds. That white students constituted the majority population in Michigan schools was just one reason that minority students were underserved in most areas. During a time of intense white resistance to the changes made by the civil rights movement and the progressive reforms proposed by nationalist organizations, Black administrators discovered a way to secure additional resources for the state's most marginalized students—without disturbing the state's racial power dynamics. Running alternative programs that were independent of the local public school system provided a way for NEC staff, which included parents and organizers, to circumvent the bureaucracy and proven conservatism of Grand Rapids' public school system. The NEA provided outreach to students who were pushed out of GRPS, even if only through back channels. White backlash against the Latino mandate and other progressive educational policy shifts did not deter local Latino activists, who managed to preserve the ideal of education as a public good by making it accessible to marginalized students.

In choosing a location for the NEC's pilot program, applicants petitioned the NEA by conjuring images of students in dire need of alternative education. In 1971, NEA administrators selected Pontiac, a struggling suburb of Detroit, as the site for the first NEC. Black and Latino families made up about 28 percent of the population. One-third of the Latino and Black populations residing in Pontiac lived below the poverty line in 1970.[35] These communities were exactly the type that the NEA hoped to help. The NEA had identified its ideal student as anyone whose "assets [were] few in number as far as basic fundamentals necessary to achieve success in our middle-class oriented society." As such, the grant writers hoped to exemplify the necessity of such a program in Pontiac. However, when pointing to the challenges that students faced, they foregrounded some of the most stereotypical issues. Pontiac's application for funds for an NEC, for instance, identified "unwed mothers" as the source of the devastating economic conditions among the affected populations. They also described behavior that they characterized as "poor social adjustment," which led to violence and crime; they detailed the harmful effects of drug use as common practices and the ever-present opportunities to engage in criminal activities.[36] While these administrators wanted to help the Black and Latino youths in their district, their application pathologized their plight while nearly blaming Black and Brown students for the challenges they faced. This was likely in hopes of showing the most need and appealing to NEA administrators' liberal notions that education alone could overcome poverty. But as many Black and Latino graduates knew well, structural racism prevented them from accessing opportunities regardless of their education level. It was clear that undoing deep-seated institutional inequalities lay beyond the bounds of the NEA's concerns, but officials who recognized these limitations still hoped to equip students with the tools they required to lessen the impact of systemic racism. Given the shrinking federal budget for education and social services, the best the NEA could hope for was the type of immediate relief that would address some of the community's short-term needs.

Problematic justifications for state funding notwithstanding, the NEA engaged in multifaceted approaches to the problems impacting minority communities. Small class sizes and individualized instruction ensured that students would "progress at a rate that is comfortable" for each pupil. The Pontiac NEC offered traditional courses like English, math, and science, but it also offered adult education classes in business math, typing, and bookkeeping. The center also specifically designed some classes for Spanish-speaking English learners. To heighten its chances of success, the NEC employed counselors to help students navigate personal and school-related issues as well as assisting with post-completion plans. Information on both vocational training and financial aid packages for college offered students more control over their future than the tracking that many minority students experienced in public schools. Whenever possible, the Pontiac NEC administrators encouraged students to find their way back to traditional educational routes, hoping they would go on to graduate and earn a high school diploma. Students for whom regular school no longer appeared to be an option were steered toward GEDs, for which the NEC helped to prepare them. A quantitative assessment of the Pontiac pilot program revealed its success. Within less than two years, the NEC helped return eighty-five students to traditional schools, leading to twelve graduations, five college enrollments, three vocational training enrollments, and seven to admission in the military, where students hoped to complete their education.[37] After two years of success with running the pilot program, the NEA subsequently solicited applications from communities other than Pontiac. Soon, Latinos in Grand Rapids took advantage of the opportunity to form a school that could replicate similar successes for their students.

"FINALLY GETTING JUSTICE FOR OUR KIDS": EL CENTRO DE EDUCACIÓN

With the success in Pontiac, the NEA expanded elsewhere in Michigan. In Grand Rapids, Latino organizers and their allies, including Carmen Fitte, helped to apply for a grant to form an NEC. Education activists relished in the opportunity to provide bilingual and bicultural content, instruction, and counseling. Fitte, who arrived in Grand Rapids in 1965 with her husband, gravitated toward an interest in education through her work with the LAC and as a paraprofessional. She recalled the difficulties of transitioning from the school system in Puerto Rico to New York during the late 1950s and early 1960s as a teenager. "It was really hard going to high school and not knowing the language," Fitte explained. "I learned the hard way . . . I didn't have tutors or anything like that," she remembered. Fitte set her sights on helping to ensure others avoided similar challenges.[38] Using the state's funding, she and other organizers sidestepped local politics and white resistance to garner much-needed resources for Latino high school students whose academic plans remained in jeopardy. Building on the programs and services the community offered through the LAC, the NEC (El Centro) recruited community members to be instructors. In turn, these educators helped students celebrate their Latino identities, which opened a gateway to reach disaffected students. The program provided the first Latino community-controlled educational facilities in the district.

Securing guidance at the state level heightened the chances for the LAC's advocates to win an NEA grant. Frustrated by her experiences with the GRPS, Carmen Fitte contacted the Michigan Department of Education twice, first unsuccessfully in 1971 and again in 1972. R. Michael Haviland, a white ally who worked for the LAC, assisted her. Fitte admitted, "at that time, I did not have much knowledge of how it all worked" in terms of securing a state grant, but working closely with Elisha Gray, the NEA director, she quickly learned to navigate the NEA's bureaucratic process. In 1973, Gray's office awarded the LAC its first seed grant to implement an alternative high school for Latino students who had been pushed out of school. "I thought we were blessed to have someone there . . . who was interested in helping the kids in this area," Fitte remembered, expressing relief.[39] After years of resistance at the local level, the cooperation from the state administrators and state-level programs was very encouraging to the beleaguered staff of the LAC.

The idea of a Latino-operated school appealed to local activists. For the first time ever, Latino parents would not have to struggle with the school board, teachers, and administrators over their children's educational needs. NEA director Gray, perhaps with Superintendent John Porter's approval, seemed to purposefully avoid any tension with school boards. In deciding on funding allocations, the NEA specifically looked for groups that were not associated with local districts, sidestepping local administrators and politicians. This circumvention of the school district in Grand Rapids alleviated the need to battle with public school officials about finding and hiring experienced bilingual teachers. Additionally, the parents and organizers could design a curriculum and teach what they wanted, without any interference from GRPS. Partnering with the NEA also lifted an extreme financial burden for the council. Up until then, members had stretched the LAC's budget for educational outreach after the dissipation of federal antipoverty funds. Now, the LAC did not have to fund-raise for this project. Also, district officials could not interfere because the NEC funds were guaranteed by the state.

With an $85,000 grant, Carmen Fitte and other NEC employees searched for a building to house El Centro de Educación, while simultaneously recruiting students. Fitte's first recruitment stop was Central High School, which a large portion of the city's Latino youths attended. After multiple visits, Fitte discovered students who were on the verge of dropping out and many who possessed no clue as to their future. For instance, José Reyna attended Central, where the guidance counselor was disregarding his excellent academic record in recommending his next step after high school. Reyna received guidance from Fitte at the NEC and an educational setting that understood the steps he needed to take to matriculate into a bachelor's program. After some time hunting for a physical building, the LAC secured a room in the basement of Fountain Street Church, a nondenominational liberal religious institution in downtown Grand Rapids. In May 1973, El Centro expanded into Maplewood Elementary School and even secured recreational and administrative space at Franklin Elementary School, facilities that were already familiar to the community because many of the newest recruits once attended those two schools.[40]

Students who attended El Centro had an educational experience that considered and accounted for all the obstacles they faced. At the program's inauguration, seventeen students (between fourteen and eighteen years old) attended El Centro. Enrollment skyrocketed to eighty-five within just a few years.[41] Some attended to make up credits that would allow their reentry to mainstream schools. Others took advantage of the GED preparation courses, while still others were there to explore multiple career options. Beyond traditional subjects, students also participated in planned excursions to local businesses, where they learned about postsecondary opportunities. The NEC's untraditional approach to education became a magnet for the city's newest arriving, Spanish-speaking students, who traveled directly from Mexico, Puerto Rico, and other places to reunite with family members. Many of the Tejano migrant workers who settled in West Michigan also availed themselves of the opportunities El Centro offered. These new students included a twenty-year-old who had left junior high in Puerto Rico and subsequently enrolled in the general education development program in Grand Rapids. While attending El Centro, the young man helped coordinate athletic activities for the school and the LAC, and he enjoyed learning there because the "teachers won't flunk you if you're slow," as he recalled.[42] Instead of overlooking students with unique needs or shuffling them aside, El Centro specialized in working with students that traditional schools were ill-equipped to help.

The NEC also provided culturally competent counseling, with Carmen Fitte serving as the postsecondary career counselor. Though Fitte lacked a degree in the field, her wealth of experience working in social services for the LAC provided her with the expertise necessary to work with El Centro students. As she recalled, she was both "bilingual and mature"—which were optimal qualities for those working with bilingual or monolingual Spanish-speaking students. Fitte warmly recalled the excellent rapport she developed with the students, who "took to [her]" and respected her, which helped her guide them through their education and their post-completion plans. It was not always an easy job, Fitte admitted. She recalled breaking up fights among the students, which would have resulted in suspension or expulsion in GRPS.[43] She made every effort to secure those students the resources they needed when that happened. Though the counselors in other schools may have held degrees, they likely worked with hundreds of students. Fitte, however, could tailor her meetings to the individual—just what students long neglected by mainstream society needed.

The NEC also offered students the chance to be taught by Latino teachers, one of their most frequent requests. Though white teachers also worked at the NEC, a variety of Latino community members served as instructors over the course of the NEC's existence. Ruth Drummond and Pedro Roman, Mexican American and Puerto Rican, respectively, were two of the first people to sign up to teach. They were joined by Spanish teachers Sara Ferguson and Richard Rosales, who both attended Grand Valley State College. Ferguson recently had relocated from Lima, Peru, while Rosales was a Grand Rapids native. Teaching art at NEC was José Narezo, an accomplished Mexican American artist, also from the area, whose work illuminated Latino cultural themes.[44] "The kids were really growing and learning" in this setting, Fitte recalled excitedly.[45] El Centro teachers drew great pride from working with Latino students and participating in the NEC's mission.

Teachers relied on their personal expertise to develop engaging curriculum and often allowed students to assume responsibility for their course of study. For example, Rosa Collazo discovered her love of dance at the NEC. Though she had always frequented the *bailes* in Grand Rapids, one of her new El Centro dance teachers introduced her to modern dance as a genre—an experience she might have missed while attending GRPS.[46] In another case, a teacher marshaled her background in English and drama to help students produce a play focusing on prejudice. Students were excited that their new school offered this possibility as a part of the curriculum. According to her pupils, Sara Ferguson taught Spanish in a way that taught students to "be proud" of their cultural background.[47] José Reyna recalled that Carmen Fitte created an individualized curriculum for each of the students whenever possible. Fitte asserted that traditional schooling produced an environment that closely monitored students and promoted assimilation, which led many Latino students to be unsuccessful in the GRPS. As she remembered, there was value in letting the students "think for themselves . . . we learned to do that."[48] Decades later, when José Reyna reflected on his experiences at El Centro, this sentiment is exactly what he treasured most. He credited the teacher's support and encouragement in pushing him to recite poems in Spanish or Spanglish, to produce book reports on Latin America, and to analyze rock and roll and other contemporary music trends.[49] Along the lines of this framework, if students so desired, they could choose content for reading and art that reflected their culture. Within this independent school, the staff met the bilingual and bicultural demands of its students because that is what made them successful.

El Centro's summer program demonstrated how in tune staff members were with the students' financial, cultural, and educational needs. El Centro administrators partnered with students in the Comprehensive Employment and Training Act (CETA) program, a federally funded program that helped young people locate jobs in public service.[50] Students enrolled in the program devoted part of their day working for compensation and part of the day in an academic setting. In the summer of 1975, under the direction of art teacher José Narezo, a group of Latino and Black teenagers were paid to paint a cultural mural on Grandville Avenue (fig. 4). Utilizing mathematical skills and artistic abilities, these students learned how to position colorful murals on walls by utilizing a standard piece of paper to plot their designs. As José Reyna recalled, Narezo created a process of painting that made students feel like they were "putting themselves into the

Figure 4. NEC mural first created by José Narezo and students in 1975. This photo depicts updates made in 1978. Courtesy of Steff Rosalez (on behalf of Grandville Avenue Arts and Humanities).

mural"—one of the first times many of the students ever felt included in a formal educational activity.

With their teacher, the NEC and CETA students painted one of the Latino community's first large cultural products that encapsulated pan-Latino solidarity, interracial solidarity, and elements of pride that social movements ushered in during the 1970s. The mural is on the south-facing wall of a large building on Grandville Avenue, in the heart of the bustling Latino neighborhood. The main figure in the painting by the students and Narezo is their interpretation of the Aztec symbol of the sun. Mexican and Puerto Rican flags figure prominently between several of the sun's golden rays. A Cuban flag was added to the mural a couple of years after its initial unveiling. Also depicted is the black, red, and green pan-African flag with a Black power fist over the flag, demonstrating the racially and ethnically diverse minorities' efforts to bridge what, at times, were competing cultural identities. The stars and stripes of the U.S. flag appear in the next two spots, with a glyph representing women over the left portion of the flag. Over the right portion of the flag is the bust of a brown-skinned person with dark long hair, possibly depicting an Indigenous person. Images of Latino men in traditional clothing are also interspersed throughout the mural. This collaborative project became one of the earliest permanent representations of Latinos on Grandville Avenue. This mural acted as the figurative and literal symbol of the decades of organizing that led to the creation of the NEC. In one public work of art, one could see the inspiration of the social movements that taught Latinos to value their ethnic identity and recognize the shared struggle of marginalized people that El Centro's multiethnic curriculum espoused. It also highlights the working-class struggle of Latinos who had worked to build the NEC and the LAC along with committed Latina leaders. As one GRPS administrator remarked, this program was really one of a kind: "None of the other alternative education institutions in the city are geared to specifically assist bilingual and bicultural high school students."[51]

After struggling to overcome years of neglect from the GRPS, then director of the LAC Martín Morales remarked that, with the NEC, "we are finally getting justice for our kids and a decent education for our kids."[52] A dedicated physical space for Latino education with a curriculum designed to address their needs supplied an equitable remedy to the indifference demonstrated by mainstream schools. Between 1973 and 1978, the NEC helped hundreds of students complete high school or achieve their GED. Many of these students also advanced to postsecondary training programs and nearby colleges. Drawing from the community-controlled model of education the LAC and La Lucha envisioned, Latino education advocates and activists formalized the programs they had launched with meager resources, which paved the way for the success of the NEC.

THE NEC AND THE LAC'S INTERTWINED DECLINE

The NEC provided five years of high-quality, bilingual and bicultural content instruction and counseling before it closed—for reasons mainly out of its control. As the NEC endeavored to be more effective and expand its offerings, GRPS in 1975 started to offer additional resources and services to staff and students. While these were welcomed at the time, this assistance would eventually undermine the NEC's argument for its independence, which set up the NEC for co-optation. Another situation that would lead to the NEC's decline stemmed from the LAC's formal connection to it. In 1975, the LAC rebranded itself as the Latin American Council and Education and Cultural Center (LACECC). In this new form, the LACECC housed both the LAC and NEC. While it is unclear from their records why these institutions came together under a new umbrella organization, it was likely proposed to allow them to share resources and to streamline the educational services they both offered. A host of problems at the LAC—ranging from mismanagement of funds, leadership transitions, and a scandal—all contributed to the dissolution of the LACECC, depriving Latino Grand Rapidians of the LAC and the NEC.

Changes at El Centro following the merger moved the organization away from its stated mission of being an independent, bilingual, and bicultural education provider. First, in the new relationship between the NEC and the LAC, the NEC staff maintained authority over programming and general direction of the organization, but they had to report to the LACECC directors and share a budget and building with the LAC. With more students needing services, this concession appeared well worth the reorganization. In previous years, the NEC helped fewer than 100 students, but during the 1975–76 school year, the NEC served an average of 156 students each quarter with secondary education and 135 people through adult education.[53] By 1976, the NEC also accepted financial help from GRPS to better meet the needs of its growing student population. While the NEA, their grantor, gave them $70,000 a year, the GRPS contributed another $52,000 in 1975. This allowed the "city to claim Latino students enrolled there on their citywide headcounts, used to determine the amount of state aid," according to Carmen Fitte.[54] Now that such a substantial amount of their budget originated from GRPS, the NEC was beholden to the local school system, which pushed the group to open its services to non-Latinos. This mandate led the NEC's founder and leader, Carmen Fitte, to leave the organization in 1977. Though there had always been both Black and white students at El Centro because they lived near the school, Fitte felt that this made it harder to devote the full weight of the organization's resources to its bilingual and bicultural focus—the school's purpose at its founding. These changes, coupled with the problems emerging from the LAC side of the partnership, led to the NEC's downfall.

The LAC's decline began in 1976 due to internal financial issues, which undermined the public's confidence in the organization. The council had a long history of struggling to garner funds for its operation, but those battles intensified in 1976, when the City of Grand Rapids, the council's largest financial supporter, accused the organization of mismanaging its funds. The issue centered on a $12,000 loan the city issued to the LAC to pay the IRS for back payroll taxes. The city had not asked to collect on the loan in 1975, but one year later, the city wanted it paid before giving the council additional funding.[55] Though there was no evidence of corrupt intentions, the council did suffer from a lack of accounting experience. It took a year for Martín Morales, the controversial director of the council, to work out a repayment schedule with the City of Grand Rapids. Then in January 1977 he resigned, leaving the LAC in flux.

The search for a director added to an already brewing intraorganizational tension at the council. The expanding and diversifying Latino community had stretched the LAC's ability to promote pan-Latino identity. Moreover, with increasingly limited resources, it was not prepared to serve the influx of Latino immigrants and migrants who arrived in the late 1970s. Mexican nationals, more Puerto Ricans from the East Coast and the island, and succeeding waves of Cubans joined the already established Latino community to bring the population from eleven thousand in the early 1970s to nearly twenty thousand by 1980.[56] The council's infrastructure—used to handling small influxes of migrants into the area—struggled to meet the needs of its growing constituency, which was exacerbated by an inopportune leadership transition. The council selected Francisco Cruz as the new director shortly after Morales resigned. He was a Puerto Rican educator and belonged to a growing contingent of middle- and upper-class Puerto Ricans who had recently moved to Grand Rapids.

His selection marked a substantial shift in LAC leadership. While apparently not a pressing concern, community members could not ignore that Cruz was the first Puerto Rican to be LAC's director. More importantly, unlike Fitte and other leaders of both Chicano and Puerto Rican descent, Cruz did not have a long history in the community, or the relationships needed to support his directorship. Working relationships in the LAC were often predicated on friendships among Latinos that had formed in shared neighborhoods and through religious and recreational activities (see chapters 4 and 5). With just one year in Grand Rapids, Cruz did not have those deep friendships and relationships. In addition, Cruz was unlike the working-class base that propelled the very first Latino organizing efforts. All of this made Cruz technically qualified for the role but highly critiqued by the community.

Just months after his selection, a scandal that centered on Cruz brought unwanted attention to the LAC and showcased class tensions among Latino Grand Rapidians. In March 1977, Cruz was accused of creating a diploma mill, or a pay-for-credit scheme. Though it was unclear who first brought these allegations to the public, the City of Grand Rapids began investigating. One woman came forward to reveal that when she told Cruz she only needed a couple of more credits to finish her bachelor's degree, he informed her he could help her finish her degree for $75 per credit through Latin American University. This institution in Puerto Rico, which he had created in 1976 before moving to Grand Rapids, was supposedly a religious university backed by the Seventh Day Adventist Church. It became accredited, however, through a loophole, when the Puerto Rican government went through a transition period in administering its universities.[57] Ultimately, investigations into Cruz revealed he broke no Michigan laws. The controversy, however, added to disruptions among growing factions. Working-class Mexicans and Puerto Ricans charged middle- and upper-class Puerto Ricans with trying to take over the council. Then, in 1978, when elections to replace Cruz as director ended with one of his close confidants, Honorato Rosa, as the winner, other LAC members charged Rosa and Cruz with foul play.[58] The divisive elections resulted in a fist fight between the factions, the police being called, and heavy press coverage of the event.

The damage was irreparable. Soon after, daily operations at the council came to a halt. By 1978, private and public sponsorship for the LACECC dwindled. The diploma mill scandal and elections led many organizations to cease funding the council. The Citizens Council for Community Development, the United Way, and the City of Grand Rapids all began to pull their support by the end of 1978.[59] The council waned and ceased to exist by January of 1979. While the LAC's model for serving Latinos in Grand Rapids had functioned well from 1968 to 1978, the context that had made it successful quickly changed within its ten years of operation. The organization, dependent on federal funding, had targeted a growing but still relatively small Latino population, and relied on the shared class background among organizers as well as long-standing personal relationships to smooth over any disagreements. Given the more ethnically, racially, educationally, and ideologically diverse Latino migrants arriving in Grand Rapids, it was impossible for one organization alone to unite this community, especially given the funding constraints the LAC faced.

The scandal had specific ramifications for the NEC. Once the pay-for-credit controversy came to light in 1977, the State of Michigan demanded that the LAC and NEC separate or risk losing their funding. The educational scandal had tainted the NEC and it struggled to recover without the administrative support from the LAC. As a response, in 1978, Elisha Gray, head of the NEA, ordered the NEC to hand over daily operations to the GRPS—the very school district that had failed to meet Latino student needs several years earlier. When the LAC ceded the Centro de Educación, the local press noted that it started "without any city school help."[60] The NEC formed as a community-based attempt to provide bilingual and bicultural curriculum after Latino students were pushed out of GRPS, and it ended with GRPS regaining control over those students' education. While the NEC was operating, the GRPS started to develop a more comprehensive bilingual education program, but it would be almost two decades until students at the high school level saw both bilingual *and* bicultural programming again.

A LASTING IMPACT

While Rosa Collazo found solace at the NEC after years of feeling like an outcast in her mostly Black and white junior high, she left the program without a high school diploma. After an early marriage and children, she could not continue to take classes. Undeterred, however, she later prepared for and passed the GED examination. Though she did not finish at the NEC, she remembered her time there warmly.[61] Surely, the experience kept her interested in completing school as the NEC's organizers had intended. Along with the LAC, the NEC marked an intellectual, emotional, and physical place in which she could be herself in Grand Rapids. After building up her sense of identity, she built stronger relationships with other Latinos and African Americans. Al Wilson, the LAC's director from 1970 until 1973, predicted that this would happen after he requested funds from the city for more youth-oriented programs. He argued that Latino youths need a place of their own to build a strong sense of self. For Collazo, while graduating was surely the goal, there was much to be gained from going to a community-led school that offered bilingual and bicultural content, counselors, and teachers.

The vision for this school was the culmination of all the strategies that Latino education activists had been implementing on smaller levels in Grand Rapids for decades. Before El Centro, they had advocated for community members to serve as teachers and created independent content and programs. The NEC realized these goals by maintaining small student-to-adult ratios, which in turn increased the effectiveness of counseling and instruction. The NEC, as a program and as a physical place, was the result of placemaking via community spaces, political placemaking that forced educational officials to recognize Latino needs were not being met, and a fierce cultural identity formation and placemaking that centered Latino lived experiences.

Activists worked tirelessly and deployed various strategies to provide Latino children the kind of education they deserved. Earlier experiences with civil disobedience taught them that they might be more successful if they chose an alternative route: activism *within* the system might yield more immediate positive results. Creating a uniquely Latino educational space was a logical extension of the civil rights organizing Latinos had previously practiced in Grand Rapids.

Building relationships with experienced African American educators was part of that process. Previously, Latinos had stressed their cultural differences with African Americans to garner more funds as two separate—albeit at times, overlapping—minority groups. In education, this strategy would be consistent, given that Latino needs in schooling largely rested on the issue of language—a tangible difference that often separated Latinos from African Americans. However, in contrast to the situation with antipoverty funds, Latinos and African Americans were not splitting the same funds. Instead, African Americans had used institutional gains to create programs that Latinos and African Americans, among other minority groups, could use. This example of cooperation gives credence to the idea that stressing the difference among Latinos and African Americans (see chapter 4) was deployed by Latinos as a political strategy in response to the contrived competition between minorities in Grand Rapids and not a reflection of any monolithic views either group held. The NEC's success in helping hundreds of students between 1973 and 1978 is in large part due to this interracial collaboration.

While the LAC's and NEC's closures were devastating to the community, as they were the first and only Latino-controlled organizations with comprehensive programming, their closings made room for other institutions to emerge and respond to Latino needs. In 1978, the same year that the LAC began dissolving, the Hispanic Center of West Michigan (HCWM) opened as a clearinghouse for social services that catered to Latinos, following in the tradition of the council. As a separate organization without an overlap in leadership with the LAC, the HCWM was able to secure grants and start again.[62] For over forty years, HCWM has been a mainstay as a Latino serving-institution in Kent County. However, it is not the only provider. When Latin American Services also opened in 1978, it started offering social services to the growing Latino community and now specializes in elderly support services throughout Kent County.[63] In regard to educational programming, it took decades for GRPS to truly respond to Latino student needs. In 1996, Adelante High School formed as a school for bilingual and monolingual Spanish-speaking students aged fifteen to nineteen who were in danger of not completing their education. Echoing statements that NEC students made in the past, Isaacson Velez, a seventeen-year-old Puerto Rican student at Adelante, remarked of his teachers, "They make you understand better. They don't go so fast."[64] Though the school closed in 2012, the emergence of another dual-immersion Spanish-English institution offering instruction from preschool to twelfth grade is one of the latest efforts of Latino educational advocates to fill the gap the NEC has left. While the Grand Rapids Latino community has changed in the last forty years, Latinos continue to work tirelessly to create new spaces for themselves and protect the ones they have.

Epilogue

Fighting Gentrification in the Twenty-First Century

When Eleazar López arrived in Grand Rapids in the late 1990s, he encountered the same music, sports, and food he had enjoyed in his native Mexico and his subsequent home in Texas. Because, as he recalled, "llegue en una comunidad Latina" (I moved to a Latino community).[1] Most of his social interactions were with other Latinos, shielding him from the discriminatory treatment he might face at other establishments where he would be in the minority. Although López knows that discrimination exists in Grand Rapids, as he reveals, he just "has not felt it," likely due in part to the expanding population and cultural resources that Latinos now enjoy in and around the city. In the historically Latino community along Grandville Avenue and in the Burton Heights—an area that emerged as a hub for Latino residents and commerce in the 1980s—López and others file their tax returns, receive haircuts, purchase groceries, frequent bakeries, shop for clothes, and have their cars repaired, all while speaking Spanish. Latinos enjoy meals at numerous *pupuserías*, *taquerias*, and other restaurants that showcase the rich diversity of this community. Unlike my grandparents' generation of migrants—who relocated to the area in the 1950s and 1960s, helped friends and family members find homes, and served as interpeters for them—Latinos who currently reside in the greater Grand Rapids area have a wealth of cultural resources. They also have access to a variety of health, social, economic, and educational institutions that serve them due to decades of ongoing placemaking.

Indeed, after decades of exclusion from the local body politic and social imaginary, Latinos have built a thriving community in Grand Rapids. When newer Latino groups arrived in the Grandville Avenue area in the 1980s and 1990s, they discovered a neighborhood with a reputation for vice and danger, characteristics that were largely due to local and federal government disinvestment. However, as a community, Latinos helped to revitalize this area by founding Latino businesses, which pumped much-needed dollars into the local economy. As these businesses expanded, so too did the community. People from Honduras, Guatemala, El Salvador, the Dominican Republic, Puerto Rico, Cuba, numerous countries in South America, and various states in Mexico now constitute the more than thirty thousand Latinos who populate the area. Given the subsequent waves of Latino immigration and migration to Grand Rapids, it's clear that the arduous place-making and activism Latinos engaged in from the 1920s to the 1970s has not only made the area into a more welcoming place but also laid the groundwork for more placemaking done by subsequent waves of immigrants and migrants. However, gentrification and other powerful forces currently threaten Latinos with displacement. Since the 2000s, the redevelopment of downtown Grand Rapids has placed poorer Latinos at the risk of losing the neighborhoods they spent decades building.

Efforts to reimagine downtown Grand Rapids, which had been the center of the city and county governments, as a thriving business center originally started in the early 2000s with the creation and expansion of two key industries: education and medicine. Grand Valley State University's downtown campus, eleven miles from the main campus in rural Allendale, has spread across the near northwestern section. Moreover, various health systems have built hospitals in the near northeastern area close to university-backed research facilities. The growth of these various educational and medical campuses has caused both displacement via eminent domain laws and a loss of affordable, quality housing. This has been in part due to the city's attempts to attract capital investors to provide entertainment. With the expansion of downtown's amenities, the families and businesses located in the southwestern part of the city, and specifically along the Grandville Avenue corridor, are at immediate risk.

While many residents celebrate the new opportunities for leisure, others lament the disproportionate nature of this "successful" renovation. For example, city officials and residents have recently embraced the city's new nickname—"Beer City, USA"—in homage to the expanding number of small breweries that have begun to populate the downtown landscape. However, African Americans and Latinos have largely been excluded from Beer City's success. In fact, Tracy Evans, a Black employee at Founders Brewery, a nationally known brand located in southwestern Grand Rapids, filed a lawsuit against the company in 2018 in response to the persistent racial discrimination and harassment he experienced while working at the brewery.[2] Meanwhile, African Americans who reside in the southeastern area have been disproportionately affected by displacement because of their proximity to downtown and the city's redevelopment efforts.[3] The retail and residential developments, along with an increase in the number of entertainment venues, now occupy the entire downtown area, as well as the near southeastern section of the city. As a result, "renewal" projects or a wave of gentrification, depending on perspective, has moved southwest, nearing the Grandville Avenue corridor.

During the early 2000s, signs of a gentrifying city were already evident after the Roman Catholic Diocese of Grand Rapids relocated St. Joseph the Worker Church in 2007, a central institution in the Grandville Avenue area (see chapter 3,) to a nearby suburb that was falling into economic decline. After being the host for Latinos' celebrations of mass and sacraments for over forty years, the deconsecrated building that once housed the parish of St. Joseph the Worker would have various other religious occupants after 2007. The building laid vacant in the early 2010s, but community organizations held outdoor events there in recognition that it had long been a gathering place for the community.

Another threat to the community activities at the church's former site came with the introduction of two large nonprofits to the neighborhood. In 2013, Habitat for Humanity began the purchase of over five acres of houses and land near the Grandville Avenue corridor, eventually also buying the former site of St. Joseph the Worker. Quickly thereafter, ArtPrize had a presence in the neighborhood. Since 2009, Grand Rapids' annual ArtPrize contest—an international competition designed by Rick DeVos, son of Betsy DeVos and heir to the Amway empire—has invited both amateur and professional artists to enter pieces at various exhibition spaces for its two hundred thousand visitors each year.[4] In 2015, Habitat invited ArtPrize to host art installations on the site of the former church. Strong criticism of the contest came when ArtPrize allowed SiteLab, a "nomadic all-volunteer artist initiative" that created installments in "underutilized spaces," to use St. Joseph the Worker's former building for their entry.

Their installation ushered in discussions about space and belonging. This included conversations about which spaces qualify as underutilized, given that although St. Joseph the Worker was no longer housed there, the community who patronized the church still lived in the area and saw the space as their own. Moreover, while ArtPrize's mission is rooted in "celebrating artists"—it does so every year with monetary prizes—it also claims that ArtPrize "transforms urban space" as one of its principles. This is at the core of the problematic relationship the organization has had with Black and Latino communities, who have already transformed urban space in Grand Rapids to fit their needs for decades and faced resistance from residents and the local government for doing so. Between Habitat for Humanity, ArtPrize, and the SiteLab installation, it was very clear gentrification efforts that had succeeded downtown and in the near southeastern area were now intruding into southwestern Grand Rapids.

The SiteLab installations for the 2015 ArtPrize contest housed at St. Joseph did not foster a welcoming feeling for Latino residents. Instead, the installation exacerbated the tension among community groups and nonprofits and called attention to issues with gentrification. Though the *Relocations* exhibit, which locally based Italian artist Filippo Tagliati constructed, did pay homage to the church's history, the other entries at the site did not resonate with the community.[5] Veronica Quintino-Aranda had migrated with her parents to Grand Rapids during the 1980s and soon became a member of St. Joseph. The changes made during the 2015 ArtPrize left her feeling excluded from the physical space where she met her husband, became engaged, and said a final good-bye to her brother at his funeral in the church. "This space is sacred," she insisted, as she stood on the steps of the deconsecrated church.[6] For Quintino-Aranda, and admittedly for me, as I had attended this church as a child and visited the site during the 2015 competition, it was disorienting to observe swarms of people, likely coming from well outside the area, viewing art unrelated to the lived experiences of Latinos in a space that was still "sacred" to the Latino community. After fighting to establish a separate parish, Latino Grand Rapidians had gathered for decades in that building for religious and secular reasons, including cultural celebrations, mourning services, and the daily activities that were essential to the community's placemaking. The transformations that had already occurred in downtown and southeastern Grand Rapids, the tendency for gentrification to target nonwhite places that developers and the city curiously labeled as "abandoned," the area's proximity to Founders Brewery and other downtown venues, and ArtPrize's use of this site all alarmed the community and its defenders. Without missing a beat, Latino activists mounted a fight to demarcate the area as a Latino space that had welcomed lower-income Latinos in recent decades.

Using strategies of placemaking similar to those deployed by the earlier Latino community, Cultura Collective emerged as a powerful voice to contest gentrification. Steffanie Rosalez, a local activist who directs the decades-old Grandville Avenue Arts and Humanities, which houses a community library and arts programming for local youths, formed the Cultura Collective. Composed of both Black and Latinx artists and community members, the Cultura Collective was created to "start dialogue about race and identity in Grand Rapids."[7] As a part of their activities, they critiqued ArtPrize and SiteLab's 2015 exhibit as an "act of gentrification."[8] In hopes of remedying the previous year's mistakes, ArtPrize then issued Rosalez a curatorial fellowship to create an exhibit in the following year's competition, with a promise that it would be on Rumsey Street, the quarter-mile street where St. Joseph, its rectory, and school stood. Instead, as the 2016 competition approached, Rosalez learned that ArtPrize would again host non-Latino artists in the collective's promised site. The Cultura Collective's exhibition space was moved farther into the neighborhood and about a half-mile from the contested site on Rumsey Street. Discouraged but not dismayed, the collective debuted at the new location what amounted to an award-winning, community-based multiple exhibit project: *This Place Is Not Abandoned.*[9] The title itself challenged a centuries-long impulse among white people to colonize places based on their dubious claim that the spaces are "underutilized," even though locals still use and view these spaces as vital to their community. As Steffanie Rosalez's curatorial statement states, "this exhibit welcomes viewers to think critically about what it really means to 'make a place,' and for whom these places are being made."[10] *This Place Is Not Abandoned* included several installations that showcase community artists' photography, paintings, fashion, music, theatrical performance, sonic exhibits, and a mural.

Though produced just before the 2016 ArtPrize competition, the mural is reminiscent of the 1975 mural that showcased the community's representation of their pan-Latino community (see chapter 7). Mirroring the efforts of Latino youths from the Latin American Council and the Neighborhood Education Center who had painted the older mural, teenagers collaborated with the Hispanic Center of West Michigan to construct the panoramic mural. Like the LAC and NEC mural, the Cultura Collective installation features multiple flags, though the latter has nine Latin American flags—a representation of the various Latinos who have called this neighborhood home over the past forty years. Both murals incorporate artistic interpretations of the sun. And while the 1975 mural, which has faded over time, features working-class representations of the community iconic to the 1970s, the Cultura Collective mural contains portraits of Latino youths.

Figure 5. Mural at 912 Grandville Avenue, created in 2016 by the Cultura Collective. Courtesy of Steff Rosalez (on behalf of Grandville Avenue Arts and Humanities). Cultura Collective, "912 Grandville Avenue Mural," Cultura Collective, October 12, 2016, https://culturacollective .com/2016/10/12/912-grandville-ave-mural/.

The mural clearly gestures toward Latino futurity—the imagining of Latinos in this space for years to come. Both murals represent efforts to safeguard Latino placemaking from encroaching gentrification.

In 2017, Rosalez and Cultura Collective continued their fight to save the forlorn church and the other buildings on Rumsey Street from gentrification and demolition, though both seemed imminent. In what they viewed as a "proper sendoff" to the church, Cultura Collective debuted *Undocumented/Indocumentado* in the 2017 ArtPrize competition. The name references both the neighborhood residents who lived in the area without documentation, as well as the untold stories of the neighborhood. It served as another critique of ArtPrize and the gentrification that rendered areas like Rumsey Street as vacant or meaningless. *Undocumented/Indocumentado* reclaimed the church as community space. Complete with an *ofrenda*, which is often used on the Day of the Dead to remember loved ones who have passed, the exhibit also played prerecorded video interviews of people who grew up in the church and lived in the neighborhood. Cultura Collective also brought pews back into the site to "reclaim the church" and the decades-long role it played in the community.[11] Entries in the other buildings on Rumsey Street referenced gentrification and highlighted the story of a Black family in the area who lost their home to eminent domain. Incredibly, ArtPrize accidentally omitted Cultura Collective's exhibit from the venue map that year. Though they later issued an apology, this was emblematic of the collective's experience in trying to work with the institution.[12] Cultura Collective's 2017 exhibit was well-received, and Rosalez briefly believed their work in bringing attention to the St. Joseph site would help in its preservation and reimagining as another community space. However, within four months of the 2017 ArtPrize competition, in a plan to help stave off gentrification in the area, Habitat for Humanity razed all the buildings on Rumsey Street, including the church, to the community's discontent.

Habitat's goal in this effort was to benefit the community by strengthening housing options with the installation of a plaza complete with mixed-income housing and their income-based Habitat homes along with other amenities. However, activists and neighbors have had to work diligently to ensure that they are heard in the process. Habitat insists that its ideas for this project, including the mixed-income housing and Habitat homes, were developed in concert with community members.[13] Rosalez, as an interested community member and organizer, remembers this differently: "They came up with the ideas and then asked the neighbors about them after. A historically white-led, faith-based institution defines community engagement in ways that support their work and mission, not in ways that center our neighbors." To work collaboratively, she noted the need for future "decision makers to have the relationships with the people they serve."[14] Since the inception of the project, however, the community has engaged in a struggle to ensure that they have an authentic relationship with Habitat and that their ideas are taken seriously as from an equal partner. The Latino community wanted to drive the development of this area after decades of placemaking. Regardless, Habitat's construction went forward. Adopting the name Plaza Roosevelt—referencing a historical moniker of this area that predates Latinos in this neighborhood—Habitat developed a multiuse space incorporating health care, education, mixed-income housing, and green space. While the plan has many benefits, it did not develop with all the community's concerns in mind—namely, their fears about gentrification.

The mix of fear of displacement and excitement about the new amenities available in the Grandville Avenue corridor characterizes the tension that has emerged since the development of Plaza Roosevelt. Indeed, Habitat developed the project with hopes of stymying gentrification and protecting the Grandville Avenue area. However, residents feel that some of the nonprofit's good intentions have resulted in unintended, negative consequences. Even though some of the apartments and Habitat homes have income caps, landlords outside of the plaza have begun increasing the rent in anticipation of higher-earning tenants who might desire to live near a new development. Some families have already begun to leave the area, fearing that they will eventually be pushed out anyway. Those that have stayed welcome the first pharmacy in many years to appear in the neighborhood. It is planned as an extension of Clínica Santa María. Located adjacent to the plaza, the clinic is a culturally competent health clinic that opened in the early 2000s to reduce the distance that poor and working-class Latinos traveled to receive care. Parents and other community members also successfully lobbied Habitat and GRPS to develop a bilingual, bicultural school—Southwest Middle High School–Academia Bilingue. This school, which opened in 2020, is an extension of Southwest Elementary–Academia Bilingue, a dual-immersion facility established in the early 2000s.[15] The elementary building stands just three blocks from Plaza Roosevelt and the new high school. Together the elementary, middle, and high schools serve more than eight hundred students. After more than forty years of sustained activism by community members who demanded K–12 bilingual and bicultural instruction for Latino children, the high school brings these efforts to fruition. Along with the bilingual schools, the 2022 change of Grandville Avenue's name to Cesar E. Chávez Avenue illustrates a recognition of this area as Latino space.[16] Parents hope they can continue to stay in the Grandville Avenue/César Chávez area to ensure their children can attend bilingual schools for the duration of their public education.

Community members continue to grapple with how to ensure that these developments do not eventually force them out of their neighborhood while also guaranteeing that nonprofits hear their voices before making decisions about future projects. These organizers, especially Rosalez, are part of a long line of Latino activists who must make tough decisions on how to influence white-led institutions to implement policies that will have equitable outcomes for Latinos. Just as their 1970s counterparts at the LAC fought for self-determination and resources from the City of Grand Rapids, present-day community organizers do the same with nonprofit organizations. This difficult task has been central to ensuring Latinos have a place in Grand Rapids, both in the past and in the future.

* * *

Rather than view the century-long history of Latinos in Grand Rapids as a tragic story of exclusion and displacement, *Making the MexiRican City* encourages researchers to use local and hyperlocal lenses to see the intimate, quotidian underpinnings of friendships and romantic relationships that help undergird political alliances among Latinos and non-Latinos alike. For those wishing to understand the formation of cross-racial or cross-ethnic alliances or any seemingly disparate alliance, it is not enough to draw attention to parallel experiences alone. Understanding the intricate ways that peoples' lives have intersected and overlapped is important, along with recognizing the power dynamics among groups that have emerged because of such experiences. This book takes seriously the ways community members circumvented the local power structure, as well as the avenues of engagement they pursued to resolve disagreements and reconcile differences. This information is necessary for current communities to understand not only how neighbors find common ground, but also how they are able to build sustainable—even if complicated—forms of organizing. *Making the MexiRican City* also demonstrates the myriad priorities of Latinos living in urban spaces. It reveals how, within social justice movements, there is no universally correct way to protest: people will invoke a variety of tools to address the multifaceted layers of oppression they face. More studies are needed on how marginalized people survive, thrive, and gain access to economic, political, social, and cultural resources when their environment affords them little opportunities.

Transforming Grand Rapids into a place where Latinos feel welcomed and enjoy genuine opportunities for social mobility has been an arduous task for successive generations of Latinos. For over a century, colonialism, economic exploitation, and U.S. intervention in Latin America have forced immigrants and their descendants to retreat from their native lands and abandon any hope of return. Nevertheless, relocation to Grand Rapids was not entirely a consequence of "push" factors; it was also a consequence of the human desire to reconnect with family and friends who continue to travel to and transform the area through their strong and distinct presence. For years, the local Latino community has depended on intra- and interethnic relationships to combat discrimination and to lessen the load of placemaking, although new challenges will emerge as the city continues to undergo demographic shifts. Political conservatism and white resistance to racial progress have remained consistent, but Black and white allies have become integral partners in Latino quests for greater civil rights, equity, and inclusion. Mexicans and Puerto Ricans, among other groups, made a place for themselves and successive generations. Continued migration of Latinos to the area, persistent placemaking, and the use of institutional methods like those used by their predecessors are helping Latinos maintain their homes and community, even as they continue to fight for belonging.

Notes

Abbreviations

GRCARC	Grand Rapids City Archives and Records Center
GRHSC	Grand Rapids History and Special Collections, Grand Rapids Public Library
HRCR	Human Relations Commission Records, 1965–1970, Equal Opportunity Department, Grand Rapids Archive and Records Center
LAC/MC	Latin American Council, Model Cities, PN-20, Latin American Council, box 202, 4/12/4/1, Grand Rapids City Archives and Records Center
LWM	Latinos in Western Michigan, collection 321, Grand Rapids History and Special Collections, Grand Rapids Public Library
NARA	National Archives and Records Administration
RG	Record group

Introduction

1. Bratt, *Dutch Calvinism in Modern America*, 13–19.

2. Dennis Hoekstra and Ted Rottman, "The Grand Rapids Inner City and the Christian Reformed Church," 1–10, folder 14, box 5, collection 308, Helen Claytor Civil Rights Collection, GRHSC.

3. Kleiman, "Great Strike," 91.

4. Ibid., 119.

5. Ibid., 115.

6. Ibid., 148.

7. On respectability politics, see Jelks, *African Americans*, and Robinson, *City within a City*. On the Black Midwest, see McDuffie, "New Day"; McDuffie, "Diasporic Journeys of Louise Little"; Lang, *Grassroots at the Gateway*; Pierce, *Polite Protest*.

8. HoSang, "Changing Valence," 117.

9. Hoekstra and Rottman, "Grand Rapids Inner City," 13.

10. Robinson, *City within a City*, xi.

11. Ibid., 96.

12. Molina, *How Race Is Made*, 3.

13. Dennis Nodín Valdés, *Al Norte*; Findlay, *We Are Left*.

14. See Innis-Jiménez, *Steel Barrio*; Pérez, *Near Northwest Side Story*.

15. See Dennis Nodín Valdés: *Al Norte*, *Mexicans in Minnesota*, *Organized Agriculture*, and *Barrios Norteños*.

16. Garcilazo, *Traqueros*.

17. Marc Simon Rodríguez, *Tejano Diaspora*.

18. On post–World War II Latino migration, see Lilia Fernández, *Brown in the Windy City*; Whalen, *From Puerto Rico to Philadelphia*.

19. García-Colón, *Colonial Migrants*.

20. Arredondo, *Mexican Chicago*; Rúa, *Grounded Identity*; Valerio-Jiménez, Vaquera-Vásquez, and Fox, *Latina/o Midwest Reader*.

21. Grossman, *Land of Hope*; Lemann, *Promised Land*.

22. Delgadillo, *Latina Lives in Milwaukee*; Hinojosa, *Latino Mennonites*; Mitchell and Pollack, "Making the 'International City Home.'"

23. Valerio-Jiménez, Vaquera-Vásquez, and Fox, *Latina/o Midwest Reader*; Delgadillo et al., *Building Sustainable Worlds*.

24. Balassiano and Maria, "Placemaking," 646.

25. hooks, *Yearning*, 42.

26. Lara, *Latino Placemaking and Planning*.

27. See, for instance, Ruiz, *From Out of the Shadows*; Gardner, *Qualities of a Citizen*; Lee, *Building*.

28. I draw from scholars of slavery in understanding the power of everyday resistance. See Holden, *Surviving Southampton*. For resistance in a Latino context, see Ricourt and Danta, *Hispanas de Queens*.

29. Johanna Fernández, *Young Lords*; Oropeza, *¡Raza Sí!*; Patiño, *Raza Sí, Migra No*.

30. Barber, *Latino City*; Contreras, *Latinos and the Liberal City*; Cruz, *Liberalism and Identity Politics*; and Marc Simon Rodríguez, *Rethinking the Chicano Movement*, 56–80.

31. Cárdenas, *La Causa*; Wiggins, "Women"; Wiggins, "Planting the Uprooted Ones"; Pierce, *Polite Protest*.

32. I draw from the "long civil rights movement" analytical framework, which encourages historians to consider the Black freedom struggle more broadly across time and space to make this argument. See Dowd Hall, "Long Civil Rights Movement."

33. Aparicio, *Negotiating Latinidad*; Aparicio, *Cultural Twins and National Others*; Aparicio and Chávez-Silverman, *Tropicalizations*; Padilla, *Latino Ethnic Consciousness*; Summers Sandoval, *Latinos at the Golden Gate*.

34. For a selection of scholars who examine how, why, and when people of various Latino ethnic groups come together as one group, see Beltrán, *Trouble with Unity*; G. Cristina Mora, *Making Hispanics*; Padilla, *Latino Ethnic Consciousness*; Oboler, *Ethnic Labels, Latino Lives*.

35. Contreras, *Latinos and the Liberal City*.

36. Mike Niemann, "It's Latins Picketing Latins at Model Cities Meeting Here," *Grand Rapids Press*, March 20, 1970, B1.

37. See Figueroa, *Decolonizing Diasporas*, for a much-needed discussion on how Afro-Latinos have been situated at the periphery of discourses of Latinidad. See also Vanessa K. Valdés, *Diasporic Blackness*, and Jiménez Román and Flores, *Afro-Latin@ Reader*.

38. Molina, *How Race Is Made*, 18.

39. Opie, *Upsetting the Apple Cart*, 3.

40. Ribeiro, "Forgotten Residents Fighting Back"; Ribeiro, "Asking Them and Protesting."

41. Cruz, *Liberalism and Identity Politics*; Lee, *Building*; Thomas, *Puerto Rican Citizen*.

42. I searched for Spanish surnames through collections of addresses on jail records, tax files, and city directories. Though this was a problematic methodology because not all Latinos have Spanish surnames and not all with Spanish surnames are Latinos, given that there was no other way that Latinos could be quantified, I used context clues to determine what information was applicable to my study. I also cross-referenced sources with one another when possible.

43. Guadalupe Vargas, interview with Gordon Olson, December 18, 1997, GRHSC.

44. In the 1960s, some Cubans fleeing Fidel Castro's revolution were placed in communities across the Midwest via religious organization sponsorships. For the most part, they did not share the same working-class background as most Mexicans and Puerto Ricans in the region. Instead, those elite Cubans often blended in with their white, Christian sponsors. Working-class Cubans didn't arrive in the United States until the 1970s, when they joined Latino communities in the Midwest; see chapters 4–7.

45. Durand and Massey, "Evolution."

Chapter 1. Trained and Tractable Labor

1. *Proceedings*, 1948, 25–27. These proceedings do not mention the recruitment of African Americans for agricultural labor. In our March 2012 telephone conversation, Bob Reed, whose father owned the Lake Odessa Canning Company, revealed that migrants from Pascagoula, Mississippi, came to harvest crops and work in the canning company during World War II and after. African American agricultural migration is well-documented in Hahamovitch, *Fruits of Their Labor*.

2. Findlay, *We Are Left*, shows us that these groups did in fact protest their conditions.

3. *Proceedings*, 26.

4. Findlay, *We Are Left*; Marc Simon Rodríguez, *Tejano Diaspora*; Dennis Nodín Valdés, *Al Norte*; Vargas, *Proletarians of the North*.

5. Jefferson, "Thomas Jefferson to the Governor of Virginia."

6. For more on the Mexican-American War, see Eisenhower, *So Far from God*; Guardino, *Dead March*.

7. The concept of "legally white, socially non-white" comes from Gómez, *Manifest Destinies*.

8. Gómez, *Manifest Destinies*, 165.

9. Carrigan and Webb, *Forgotten Dead*, 231.

10. See González and Fernández, "Empire," for their discussion on imperialism's role on migration that influenced this phenomenon before and after the Mexican Revolution. For information on the revolution's aftermath, its effects on immigration, and the resulting changing dynamics in Texas, see Johnson, *Revolution in Texas*. For a discussion of U.S. imperialism and resistance to it in Mexico before and during the revolution, see Knight, "U.S. Anti-Imperialism."

11. For more on the Great Depression in Mexico, see Knight, "Character and Consequences." For more on what Mexican Americans faced when repatriated to Mexico during the Depression, see Balderrama and Rodríguez, *Decade of Betrayal*.

12. For more on the war and its consequences, see Hoganson, *Fighting for American Manhood*. See also Erman, *Almost Citizens*.

13. See Meléndez, *Sponsored Migration*, 29, for discussion of how Puerto Rico's status as a commonwealth granted only limited autonomy to the island. Any choices Puerto Rican administrators had were made within the constraints of U.S. imperial control.

14. To see what Allen planned for Puerto Rico, see Allen, *First Annual Report*.

15. Arrington, *Beet Sugar in the West*, 54–55.

16. See also Whalen, *From Puerto Rico to Philadelphia*, 18–28, for discussion on the transition of Puerto Rico's diverse rural economy to that of one dependent on sugar.

17. See Dietz, *Economic History of Puerto Rico*, 89–99.

18. Dietz, *Economic History of Puerto Rico*, 105.

19. Ibid., 111.

20. Luisa Fernández, interview with Kate Schramm, Grand Rapids, 2001, folder 1, box 2, coll. 292, GRHSC.

21. Dietz, *Economic History of Puerto Rico*, 142. See also Amador, "Caring for Labor History."

22. Dietz, *Economic History of Puerto Rico*, 136.

23. This tension is best seen in the clashes between the U.S. government and Puerto Rican nationalists. In this era, the Ponce Massacre in 1937 is the most recognizable example. See Meyer, "Pedro Albizu Campos."

24. Maldonado, *Teodoro Moscoso*, 48.

25. See chapter 2 in Whalen, *From Puerto Rico to Philadelphia*, for more information on internal migration and later migration to the States.

26. Orozco, *No Mexicans*, 20.

27. For more information on the threat of mechanization in Texas, see Menefee and Cassmore, *Pecan Shellers of San Antonio*.

28. San Miguel, *Brown, Not White*; Behnken, *Fighting Their Own Battles*.

29. Carrigan and Webb, *Forgotten Dead*, 16.

30. For information on Mexican resistance to white Texans and the violence that ensued after, see Johnson, *Revolution in Texas*.

31. Guadalupe Vargas, interview with Gordon Olson, Grand Rapids, 1997, box 4, LWM.

32. For a full history on Mexican repatriation, see Balderrama and Rodríguez, *Decade of Betrayal*. For a history of Mexican repatriation in Michigan, see Vargas, *Proletarians of the North*.

33. Garcilazo, *Traqueros*, 68.

34. Jim Mercanelli, "Hispanic Seniors Pick Couple of the Year," *Grand Rapids Press*, May 23, 1988, 133. Daniel Vásquez, interview with Gordon Olson, Grand Rapids, [n.d.], box 4, LWM.

35. Albert Aguirre, Ysmael Flores, Epitosio Duarte, Joseph Zaragosa, Joseph Valdez, boxes 1–4, CA, 1924–1961, 1913–1974, fingerprint cards, Police Records Division, GRCARC.

36. Juanita and Santos Rincones, interview with Gordon Olson, Grand Rapids, 2000, box 4, LWM.

37. Vargas, *Proletarians of the North*, 51.

38. Rosales, "This Street."

39. Mapes, *Sweet Tyranny*, 66.

40. Juan I. Mora, "Latino Encounters."

41. National Defense Migration, Hearings before the Select Committee Investigating National Defense Migration, House of Representatives, Seventy-Seventh Congress, First Session Pursuant to H. Res. 113: Resolution to Inquire Further into the Interstate Migration of Citizens, Emphasizing the Present and Potential Consequences of the Migration Caused by the National Defense Program, Part 11, Washington D.C. March 24, 25, 26, 1941.

42. Luciano Cerda, 1930 Manuscript Census, 1930, Grand Rapids, Kent, Michigan, roll 1002, 2B, enumeration district 0075, image 985.0, FHL microfilm 2340737, 1930, Bureau of the Census, NARA.

43. See Escobedo, *From Coveralls to Zoot Suits*, for a discussion on the Equal Employment Opportunity Commission and Mexican Americans.

44. "Estimated Agricultural Labor Requirements for Michigan," 1943, RG 211, Records of the War: Manpower Commission; Records of the Bureau of Placement, Records of the industrial allocation division, records of labor recruitment and transportation section, State (MD-MICH) entry 198, NARA. See Rosas, *Abrazando el Espíritu*, for more information on how these strict contract requirements affected Mexican families left behind.

45. Dennis Nodín Valdés, *Al Norte*, 93. Braceros who came to Michigan often ended up in tiny towns across the state and received poor treatment. The Mexican consulate in Detroit received reports of "mal trato" from braceros around the state. They, like other braceros nationwide, reported unhygienic accommodations, long workdays, shorted paychecks, and local bars and restaurants prohibited them from entering. These conditions likely led them to abandon the area. There is little evidence that braceros came to and stayed in Grand Rapids in the 1940s.

46. Mason, "Aftermath of the Bracero," 239. While across the country Mexican national farmworkers were targeted for deportation during Operation Wetback in the mid-1950s, in the Midwest authorities concentrated their campaign in large cities like Chicago and Detroit. See Dennis Nodín Valdés, *Al Norte*, 140.

47. Grove, "Mexican Farm Labor Program," 311.

48. Whalen and Vázquez-Hernández, *Puerto Rican Diaspora*, 2.

49. Whalen, *From Puerto Rico to Philadelphia*, 52. Gilbert G. González and Fernández, "Empire," 15.

50. Whalen, *From Puerto Rico to Philadelphia*, 55.

51. Whalen and Vázquez-Hernández, *Puerto Rican Diaspora*, 2.

52. Sánchez Korrol, *From Colonia to Community*, 225.

53. Meléndez, *Sponsored Migration*, 203.

54. Ibid, 82.

55. *Emigración: Un librito para el pueblo*, no. 8 (Puerto Rico, 1955), Divisíon de Educacíon de la Comunidad, DIVEDCO) and "Managing Migration: The Government of Puerto Rico and Puerto Ricans in New York City, 1948—1968," both in caja 1207, Fondo Oficina del Gobernador, Archivo General de Puerto Rico.

56. These locations are derived from letters that Puerto Rican workers sent to the governor. Tarea 96-20, caja 454, Fondo Oficina del Gobernador, Archivo General de Puerto Rico; "Request for Workers to Romeo, Michigan," September 26, 1967, Luís A. Delgado, director, Lake Erie Operations to Carlos Gómez, acting director, Agricultural Program; "Migration Division, Agricultural Program: Transmittal of Checks," November 28, 1966; Employer Records Cards, folder 11, Correspondence 1967–1971, box 2402, Chicago Regional Office, Center for Puerto Rican Studies, Office of the Government of Puerto Rico.

57. "Plane with 65 Goes Down," *Chicago Daily Tribune*, June 6, 1950, 1.

58. "Puerto Rican Survivors Here, Still Shaky from Air Tragedy," *Saginaw News*, June 10, 1950, 5.

59. "Airline to San Juan Faces Permit Loss," *New York Times*, June 6, 1950, 55.

60. Walter Ruch, "His Wages 'Minus', Migrant Relates," *New York Times*, September 13, 1950, 30.

61. Leonard Jackson, "Puerto Rican Toils for Seven Weeks for 20 Cents," *Bay City (MI) Times*, August 7, 1950; Leonard Jackson "Puerto Rican Farm Workers Embittered by Deplorable Plight," *Bay City (MI) Times*, August 8, 1950.

62. "Puerto Rico Seeks Workers' Return," *New York Times*, August 20, 1950, 32.

63. "Describen Horrores en Campos de Michigan," *El Imparcial*, July 9, 1950; translation by the author.

64. Jackson, "Puerto Rican Toils."

65. Sara Ramírez, interview with the author, Gurabo, Puerto Rico, November 3, 2016.

66. Eileen Findlay includes an in-depth analysis of the workers' responses to the issues they faced on the fields. She explains their actions as a part of a larger process of *bregando* (struggling or negotiating) with both the Puerto Rican government and their position as colonial subjects. See chapter 4 in Findlay, *We Are Left*. Eduardo Meléndez, *Sponsored Migration*, also offers an insightful examination of key actors and policies in the debacle in Saginaw and Bay City, Michigan.

67. Ramírez interview.

68. Pedro López, arrest book 1, Police Records Division, GRCARC.

69. "Net Paid Circulation by Counties as of December 31, 1940," *Covered Best: Michigan Farmers* (Detroit, MI, 1942), RG 21, Records of the War: Manpower Commission, State (MD-MICH), entry 198, box 26, NARA.

70. "Migratory Agricultural Labor Requirements in Michigan," RG 211, Records of the War: Manpower Commission, Records of the Bureau of Placement, Records of the Rural

Industries Division, General Records of the Farm Placement Service, 1939–1946, 2, subject (M–O), entry 198, box 26, NARA.

71. María Ysasi, interview with the author, Grand Rapids, 2012.

72. Juan Báez, interview with the author, Grand Rapids, 2011.

73. Informe Mensual, July 1955, folder 13, box 2744, Center for Puerto Rican Studies, Office of the Government of Puerto Rico. The Migration Division took notice of the area in a monthly report and mentioned that not a single Puerto Rican quit his job in 1953.

74. Bob Reed, personal correspondence, March 2012.

75. Báez interview.

76. Rubén Sánchez, interview with the author, Kissimmee, FL, 2017.

77. Jim Mencarelli, "The First Ones," *Grand Rapids Press*, July 28, 1986, E3.

78. Olson, *Grand Rapids Sampler*, 176.

79. Jim Mencarelli, "A Life of Illusion and Fear: The Number of Illegal Aliens in West Michigan Is Growing," *Grand Rapids Press*, July 28, 1986, A1.

80. Alice C. Larson, *Michigan Migrant Seasonal Farmworker Enumeration Profiles Study 2013*, State of Michigan Interagency Migrant Services Committee, 2013, www.michigan. gov/mdcr/divisions/community-engagement/migrant-seasonal-farmworkers, accessed May 2, 2022. Theresa Hendricks, interview with the author, Lansing, 2020.

81. Vargas interview.

Chapter 2. Families Helped Each Other

1. Rudy Castro, Baptism Records, 1948–1951, Cathedral of Saint Andrew.

2. Parts of this chapter appear in Delia Fernández, "Rethinking."

3. Julio Vega, R. L. Polk Grand Rapids City Directory, 1958, and Rafael Berríos, R. L. Polk Grand Rapids City Directory, 1956, both in GRHSC.

4. "Reports Nonwhite Rise Here Higher than in Nearby Cities," *Grand Rapids Press*, January 18, 1957, 17.

5. Kent County, Social Explorer Tables, Census 1930 County Only Set, U.S. Census Bureau.

6. On the HOLC and FHA, see Rothstein, *Color of Law*.

7. Jelks, *African Americans*, xvi. Prior to World War II, the Klan operated publicly in Grand Rapids, as it did in many northern cities. African Americans had to challenge segregation in public establishments via the courts. Moreover, African Americans practiced a middle-class respectability that was expected of them in West Michigan. Still, race relations were relatively calm there before the first and second Great Migrations compared to other places.

8. For information on how Mexicans and Puerto Ricans dealt with racial binaries, see Arredondo, *Mexican Chicago* and Thomas, *Puerto Rican Citizen*.

9. Guadalupe Vargas, interview with Gordon Olson, Grand Rapids, December 18, 1997, GRHSC.

10. Jelks, "Making Opportunity," 27.

11. Gómez, *Manifest Destinies*, 165.

12. Pascoe, *What Comes Naturally*, 210–15.

13. Ibid., 207.

14. Pascoe, *What Comes Naturally*, details the connection between antimiscegenation laws and protecting white womanhood, white supremacy, and white purity. See also Feimster, *Southern Horrors*.

15. Cecil San Miguel and Betty Parish, Marriage Records, 1942–1949, Cathedral of Saint Andrew.

16. See Olivas, *Colored Men and Hombres Aquí*.

17. Many of the arrests in this period stemmed from interpersonal conflicts within the community, including fighting with family members or the failure to pay child support. On how Mexican American women used nonsupport and bastardy laws to exercise agency in Grand Rapids, see Delia Fernández, "Becoming Latino."

18. This confirms Thomas Guglielmo's thesis on Italians and race (*White on Arrival*, 8).

19. Albert Aguirre, Ysmael Flores, Epitosio Duarte, Joseph Zaragosa, Joseph Valdez, box 1-4, CA, 1924–1961, 1913–1974, Fingerprint Cards, Police Records Division, GRCARC.

20. Frank Acevedo Baltierrez, box 1-4, CA, 1924–1961, 1913–1974, Fingerprint Cards, Police Records Division.

21. Pearl Brown, Louie Hildreth, Lila Lett arrest records, Arrest Book 1, Police Records Division.

22. "Legal and Civil Rights Committee Meeting Minutes," January 20, 1964, series 13–14, box 1-3,HRCR.

23. Puerto Ricans use a variety of terms to indicate a spectrum of skin colors on the island. The government took up the concept of "La Gran Familia" as a nation-building project, which touted mixed-race heritage as the standard for Puerto Ricans, thereby erasing Afro–Puerto Ricans and the privileges white Puerto Ricans hold. See Lloréns, *Imaging*.

24. Thomas, *Puerto Rican Citizen*, 89.

25. Rubén Sánchez, interview with the author, Kissimmee, FL, 2017.

26. Rosa Collazo, interview with the author, Grand Rapids, 2018.

27. Juan Báez, interview with the author, Grand Rapids, 2011.

28. See Rothstein, *Color of Law*, for an in-depth analysis of how both local and federal governments created segregation where previously there was none and enforced it for much of the twentieth century.

29. In the Midwest, it was common for railroad workers and their families to live near the tracks or even in boxcars. See Arredondo, *Mexican Chicago*; Vargas, *Proletarians of the North*; Innis-Jiménez, *Steel Barrio*.

30. Kleiman and Grand Rapids Historical Commission, *Strike!*, 22.

31. Rosendo Fernández, R. L. Polk Grand Rapids City Directory, 1936, GRHSC.

32. Louis Fernández, 1930 Manuscript Census, 1930, Grand Rapids, Kent, Michigan, roll 1002, 2B, enumeration district 0075, image 985.0, FHL microfilm 2340737, 1930, Bureau of the Census, NARA. Due to the legacy of colonialism, I assume that the Catholic Church was a familiar institution for these Mexican migrants; however, I did not have access to records from the 1920s and 1930s from the Catholic Diocese of Grand Rapids to confirm this.

33. Rothstein, *Color of Law*, 133.

34. "Abstract of Title of Property," in *The Grand Rapids Inner City and the Christian Reformed Church: A Summary Statement*, folder 14, box 5, collection 308, Helen Claytor Civil Rights Collection, GRHSC.

35. There are no aggregated data recorded from the 1940s and 1950s on Latinos and housing, in part because they were not tracked as a group in the U.S. Census until the 1960s. No social service agencies in Grand Rapids paid close enough attention to their housing patterns to generate reports. The data for Latino housing choices come from oral histories, city directories, and the 1940 census. This makes it difficult to trace Latinos movements, but with the help of my Mexican American History course students, we plotted the addresses of over a hundred families to try to determine movement over time. The 1950 census, which was not available to researchers at the time of this writing, will likely reveal a clearer housing pattern that might disprove the research that I undertook here.

36. Bratt and Meehan, *Gathered at the River*, 205.

37. Rothstein, *Color of Law*, 64.

38. Shelly Stephans, "The History of Mexican-Americans in Grand Rapids," senior thesis, Calvin College, 1992, 3–5, folder 34, Hispanic Apostolate, Grand Rapids Diocese; Darlene Bos, "Isabel Navarro: Journey to Grand Rapids, Oral Histories of Mexican-American Senior Citizen Women in Grand Rapids," 1998, box 1, LWM.

39. Irma and Simon Aguilar, interview with the author, Grand Rapids, 2014.

40. Sánchez interview.

41. "Survey on Whether People Will Rent to Negroes," box 2, series 13-14, HRCR.

42. Luisa Fernández, interview with Kate Schramm, Grand Rapids, 2001, folder 1, box 2, coll. 292, GRHSC.

43. Home buying was rather accessible for a variety of people in Grand Rapids. Since the early 1900s, union organizers surmised that because working-class laborers could buy homes and sought stable jobs to make their payments, they were less radical than people who did not own homes. As other authors, particularly Randal Jelks and Todd Robinson, have shown, banks would loan Black families mortgages but not for properties near where white families lived, severely curtailing their attempts at home buying.

44. Vargas interview.

45. Daniel Vásquez, R. L. Polk Grand Rapids City Directory, 1941, GRHSC. Elías San Miguel, Narciso San Miguel, Cecil San Miguel, R. L. Polk Grand Rapids City Directory, 1946, GRHSC.

46. Sánchez interview.

47. Rothstein, *Color of Law*, 60.

48. Dionisio Berríos, R. L. Polk Grand Rapids City Directory 1954, GRHSC.

49. Irene Agosto, R. L. Polk Grand Rapids City Directory, 1955, GRHSC.

50. Julio Vega, R. L. Polk Grand Rapids City Directory, 1958, GRHSC.

51. Pedro Gómez, in ibid.

52. Marcial Hernández, R. L. Polk Grand Rapids City Directory, 1959, GRHSC.

53. Fernández interview.

54. Olson, *Grand Rapids*, 6.

55. Ibid., 6.

56. Juanita and Santos Rincones, interview with Gordon Olson, Grand Rapids, 2000, LWM.

57. Daniel Vásquez, interview with Gordon Olson, Grand Rapids, undated, box 4, LWM.

58. Rincones interview.

59. I examined fifty Spanish-surnamed families listed in the R. L. Polk Grand Rapids City Directory and recorded their listed employment to calculate these data. R. L. Polk Grand Rapids City Directory, 1946–1949,GRHSC.

60. Carmen Berríos, interview with the author, 2012; Dionisio Berríos, R. L. Polk Grand Rapids City Directory, 1955, 1956, GRHSC; Julio Vega, R. L. Polk Grand Rapids City Directory, 1957.

61. Pío Fernández and Rafael Pérez, both in R. L. Polk Grand Rapids City Directory, 1956.

62. Nicolas Escribano, R. L. Polk Grand Rapids City Directory, 1956, GRHSC.

63. Obituary of Juan Báez, *Grand Rapids Press*, August 13, 2017.

64. Rincones interview.

65. Juanita Baltierrez, interview with Gordon Olson, Grand Rapids, 2001, LWM.

66. Vargas interview.

67. Laverne Davis, interview with the author, Grand Rapids, 2017. Hattie Beverly, who was African American and Dutch, is recognized as the area's first Black teacher in the late 1800s, but it would be decades after she resigned in the early 1900s before another Black teacher was hired.

68. Case 76028, Roque Bueno, Felonies, Police Court, 26-27--28-29, 333–500, GRCARC.

69. Carmen Berríos interview; translation by the author.

70. Jason Blyveis, phone interview with the author, March 2, 2015. Blyveis, the grandson of the founder, indicated that these women would have needed specialized training to perform their job duties. He also noted that the small company still has extended family networks among its employees.

71. Carmen Berríos interview.

72. See Escobedo, *From Coveralls to Zoot Suits*, 77–80.

73. Baltierrez interview.

74. Lila García, interview with the author, Lansing, 2015.

75. For a robust discussion on how women functioned outside of the family wage system during the post war period, see Meyerowitz, *Not June Cleaver*.

76. On women in the agricultural packing and canning industries, see Alamillo, *Making Lemonade out of Lemons*; Ruiz, *Cannery Women, Cannery Lives*.

77. García interview.

78. Maria Zambrana, interview with the author, Grand Rapids, 2012.

79. Rafael Hernández, interview with the author, Grand Rapids, 2013.

80. Rosalía Espíndola, interview with the author, Lansing, 2020.

81. José Flores, interview via the Community House Senior Histories program, Grand Rapids, 2016.

82. Darlene Bos, "Isabel Navarro: Journey to Grand Rapids, Oral Histories of Mexican-American Senior Citizen Women in Grand Rapids," 1998, box 1, LWM.

83. Flores interview.

84. García interview.

85. Flores interview.

86. Board of Education, "Enrollment in Grand Rapids Public Schools, White and Non-White Pupils, 1951–1956," Board of Education Statistics, Equal Opportunity Series 13-4, folder 8, box 20, Community Relations Commission Records, 1950–1956, Equal Opportunity Department, GRCARC.

87. Irma and Simon Aguilar, interview with Laura Retherford and Christian Miller, Grand Rapids, 2001, LWM.

88. Rincones interview.

89. Espíndola interview.

90. Aguilar interview, 2001.

91. Ibid.

Chapter 3. A Gathering Place

1. On conformity during the Cold War, see Avila, *Popular Culture*; May, *Homeward Bound*.

2. Whiteness studies is an evolving field. See a selection of work in this field: Guglielmo, *White on Arrival*; Jacobson, *Whiteness of a Different Color*; Ignatiev, *How the Irish Became White*; Olden, *Racial Uncertainties*.

3. The literature on Mexican Americans' pursuits of whiteness and the plethora of reasons why it is not a wholly successful pursuit is voluminous. See, for example, Foley, "Partly Colored or Other White"; Guglielmo, "Fighting for Caucasian Rights"; Johnson, "Cosmic Race in Texas." On Mexican American identity formation, see the canonical text, Sánchez, *Becoming Mexican American*.

4. See Ruiz, *From Out of the Shadows*, xiv.

5. Aparicio, *Negotiating Latinidad*.

6. Latino Protestants followed a similar trajectory and used homes as their first places of worship in Grand Rapids. The lack of space and small population meant that living rooms were a regular part of community formation for both Latino Catholics and Protestants. The Reverend Leonard Ortiz launched a Baptist church in his home on the southeast side in the late 1940s. There were a few other in-home church options for the few hundred non-Catholic Latinos in the 1950s. See Leonard Ortiz, R. L. Polk Grand Rapids City Directory, 1960, GRHSC; "Obituary for Leonard Ortiz," *Grand Rapids Press*, November 5, 1998, C7. This does not come as a surprise as the Baptist faith was popular among Tejanos. See Ruiz, *From Out of the Shadows*. Though not on Baptists specifically, Hinojosa, *Latino Mennonites*, illuminates the history of non-Catholic Latinos in Texas and the Midwest. For Latino religious histories, see Kanter, *Chicago Católico*; Matovina, *Latino Catholicism*; Hinojosa, Elmore, and González, *Faith and Power*.

7. Shelly Stephans, "The History of Mexican-Americans in Grand Rapids," senior thesis, Calvin College, 1992, 3–5, folder 34, Hispanic Apostolate, Diocese of Grand Rapids.

8. Rafael Benítez and María Barajas; Arturo Medina and Andrea Alvarado; Gilberto García and Aurora González; Florencio Páez and María Luisa Araiza; Abelardo García and Isabel Stella James; Conrado Cantú and Josephine de la Rosa; Manuel Ruiz and Alicia Villapando; all in Marriage Records 1942–1953, Cathedral of Saint Andrew.

9. "Mexicans Fete Plans Shaped," *Grand Rapids Press*, July 11, 1950, 21.

10. Titas Narbutes, 1949, arrival in New York City, microfilm serial T715, 1897–1957, line 4, p. 12; "Priests of the Diocese of Panevėžys Who Left Lithuania the Summer of 1944 as the Bolsheviks Returned to Lithuania," *Chronicle of the Catholic Church in Lithuania*, no. 65 (January 6, 1985): 50.

11. See also Dolan, *American Catholic Experience*; Kanter, *Chicago Católico*; Orsi, *Madonna of 115th Street*.

12. Erdmans, "Poles, the Dutch"; Kanter, *Chicago Católico*; Kanter, "Faith and Family"; Kanter, "Making Mexican Parishes."

13. Shaw, *Catholic Parish*.

14. Erdmans, "Poles, the Dutch."

15. "Obtain House for Chapel," *Grand Rapids Press*, February 14, 1952, 23.

16. *Sanborn Fire Insurance Map from Grand Rapids, Kent County, Michigan, 319*, Sanborn Map Company, vol. 3, 1913, www.loc.gov/item/sanborn04023_009/. Mexicans were to share the house with Latvian refugees who were resettled in Grand Rapids as a part of a larger movement of Latvians escaping Soviet advancement in the post–World War II period.

17. María Ysasi, interview with the author, Grand Rapids, 2012.

18. Guadalupe Vargas, interview with Gordon Olson, December 18, 1997, GRHSC.

19. On the development of Spanish-speaking clergy, see also Pitti, "To 'Hear about God."

20. Photo 3967, folder 5, box 3.5, LWM.

21. Vargas interview.

22. Rosalía Espíndola, interview with the author, Lansing, 2020; Matovina and Riebe-Estrella, *Horizons of the Sacred*, 30; Matovina and Poyo, *Presente!*, 253.

23. Espíndola interview.

24. Zulema Moret, "A Life of Surrender," Diocese of Grand Rapids, https://grdiocese.org/a-life-of-self-surrender/, accessed November 2, 2020.

25. Odem, "Our Lady of Guadalupe"; Poole, *Our Lady of Guadalupe*.

26. Rt. Rev. Mnsr. Joseph C. Walen and Helen Black, eds., *The Information Guide and Directory of the Diocese of Grand Rapids*, vol. 2, *August 1, 1956, to July 31, 1958*, GRHSC.

27. Ebaugh and Curry, "Fictive Kin as Social Capital," 196.

28. Ibid.

29. Priscilla Ayala, Baptism Records, Cathedral of Saint Andrew.

30. Santiago Figueroa, Baptism Records, Cathedral of Saint Andrew.

31. Tanda Gmiter, "Hispanic Parishioners Feel Double Loss," *Grand Rapids Press*, August 4, 1994, B1.

32. Theodore Kozlowski, interview with the author, Grand Rapids, 2011. Cathie Bloom, "Ubaldina Paiz: She's the Heart of the Community," *Grand Rapids Press*, July 22, 1987, A15.

33. Miguel Berríos, interview with the author, Grand Rapids, 2011.

34. St. Joseph the Worker Baptismal Records, 1960–1970, St. Joseph the Worker Parish, Diocese of Grand Rapids.

35. This was a typical phenomenon. For more information on ethnic Catholic churches, see Orsi, *Madonna of 115th Street.*

36. Kanter, "Making Mexican Parishes," 36.

37. Michelle Jokisch Polo, "Rumsey Street: Leaving Behind a History of Sacred Space," Rapid Growth Media, October 19, 2017, www.rapidgrowthmedia.com/features/101917-OTG6-grandville.aspx.

38. Many of these marriages were between Puerto Rican men and Mexican American women. This gender and ethnicity pattern is likely due to these groups' migratory trends. Often, Puerto Rican men came to West Michigan as bachelors, while Mexican Americans came in a familial unit. Some of the earlier Puerto Rican–Mexican marriages were between Puerto Rican men and Mexican women who traveled to Michigan with their parents and siblings.

39. In the Cathedral of St. Andrew record books, of fifty records of baptisms, only three were of Mexican and white unions and only one was of a Puerto Rican and Black union. There were no entries for Mexican and Black marriages or Puerto Rican and white unions. This could suggest that, if interracial marriages did occur, they either did not happen among Catholics, or they were not viewed as socially acceptable enough to be recognized in church ceremonies. Interracial marriages did occur among Mexican and Polish Catholics in Chicago in the early twentieth century, however. Arredondo, *Mexican Chicago*, points to the gender imbalance in both communities that led Mexican men who traveled to Chicago alone to seek out Polish women. This was likely not the case in Grand Rapids, as families rather than single men migrated together.

40. Vargas interview; Juanita and Santos Rincones, interview with Gordon Olson, Grand Rapids, 2000, LWM.

41. Angelita Arizola, "Manuscript Census, 1940," Gillespie, Texas, roll m-t0627-04040, p. 10B, enumeration district 86-5, Bureau of the Census, Fifteenth Census of the United States, NARA.

42. Hernández interview.

43. Carolina Báez Anderson, interview with the author, Grand Rapids, 2013.

44. Amelia Báez, June 18, 2000, Social Security Administration, Washington, DC, Social Security Death Index, Master File;, Báez Anderson interview.

45. Hernández interview.

46. Cruzita and Pedro Gómez, interview with the author, Grand Rapids, 2013.

47. For more on MexiRicans, see Aparicio and Chávez-Silverman, *Tropicalizations*; Potowski and Matts, "MexiRicans"; Rúa, "Colao Subjectivities." Guevara, *Becoming Mexipino*, looks at people who are both Mexican and Filipino.

48. "Roma Hall Story," West Michigan Music Hysterical Society, An Interactive Archival Database for West Michigan Music History, accessed May 18, 2015.

49. Rincones interview.

50. See Sánchez-Korral, *From Colonia to Community*, 77–8; Ruiz, *From Out of the Shadows*, 51–69.

51. On how parrandas help people adjust to new environments see, Martínez, "Echoes of Familiar Rhythms." On the cultural significance of parrandas, see Gleason, "La Parranda Puertorriqueña."

52. Edwin Ramírez Carrión, correspondence with the author, March 7, 2015.

53. Espíndola interview.

54. Marilyn Vega, interview with the author, Grand Rapids, 2013.

55. Cruzita and Pedro Gómez interview, 2013.

56. Báez Anderson interview.

57. Jelks, *African Americans*, 75–77.

58. Irma and Simon Aguilar, interview with the author, Grand Rapids, 2014.

59. Ysasi interview.

60. Rosa Pérez interview with the author, Grand Rapids, 2011.

61. "Mexicans Find New Home," *Grand Rapids Press*, February 2, 1956: 13.

62. For more information on chaperonage and outings, see Ruiz, *From Out of the Shadows*, 52.

63. Ysasi interview.

64. Cruzita and Pedro Gómez, interview with the author, Grand Rapids, 2011.

65. Darlene Bos, "Maurelia Blakely Ortiz: Journey to Grand Rapids, Oral Histories of Mexican-American Senior Citizen Women in Grand Rapids," 1998, box 1, LWM.

66. Vargas interview; Rincones interview.

67. See the photo at Delia Fernández, "Becoming Latino," 73.

68. For a racial and class-based analysis of nationalism and the *jíbaro* icon, see Lillian Guerra, *Popular Expression and National Identity*.

69. "Mexicans Find New Home."

70. "Parade, Festival to Mark Independence of Mexico," *Grand Rapids Press*, August 27, 1970, 1C.

71. For the context that birthed the resurgence of white ethnic festivals, see Jacobson, *Roots Too*. On Mexican festivals in the region, see Juan Ramon García, *Mexicans in the Midwest*.

72. On conformity and identity during the Cold War, see Wall, *Inventing the American Way*.

73. Festival 1970/1971 Original Color Photos, folder 6, box 3.5, LWM.

74. "Obituary for Marshall Chávez," Pederson Funeral Home, April 21, 2017, www.pedersonfuneralhome.com.

75. Mary Kramer, "Mexican Fiesta Parade to Include Farm Union," *Grand Rapids Press*, September 12, 1974, 4C.

Chapter 4. Latins Want Parity

1. "Committee Study Racial Imbalance in the Grand Rapids Public School System 1965–1970," June 1, 1961, 2, series 13-14, box 2, HRCR.

2. See Cruz, *Liberalism and Identity Politics*; Lee, *Building*; Thomas, *Puerto Rican Citizen*.

3. Thomas, *Puerto Rican Citizen*, 67.

4. Cruz, *Liberalism and Identity Politics*.

5. See Jelks, *African Americans* for an overview on respectability among African Americans in the pre–World War II period.

6. Robinson, *City within a City*, 6.

7. On the urban crisis in Michigan, see Sugrue, *Origins of the Urban Crisis*; Highsmith, *Demolition Means Progress*.

8. "Model Cities Application," 1967, p. 1 of 16, series 38, Housing and Urban Development, Model Cities Program, National Advisory Commission on Civil Disorders, Dayton–Grand Rapids, LBJ Library.

9. Olson, *Grand Rapids*.

10. Ibid., 23.

11. Meeting Minutes, Human Relations Commission, January 28, 1960, folder 2, box 2, series 13-14, HRCR.

12. In 1960, census records demarcated Mexican Americans as "white" on the census due to the history of Mexicans' legal designation of white since 1848. An accurate count of the Mexican population thus became impractical. On the other hand, data on Puerto Ricans, first recorded in mainland census history in 1960, revealed a small population of less than a hundred in the city, even though there were an estimated one thousand residing in the city by 1965, according to community records.

13. "Socio-Economic Profile of Grand Rapids, Michigan," October 9, 1967, 1–2, RG 220, National Advisory Commission on Civil Disorders, Investigations, Englewood–The Englewood Police Department Report to New Haven—Socio-Economic Profile, Grand Rapids Memos; Field Research Reports, 25, Field Interview Folders, box E-49, Grand Rapids–Grand Rapids Team Interview Report to Grand Rapids-Arrest Record, Dayton–Grand Rapids, both in the LBJ Library.

14. U.S. Census Bureau, "Population Characteristics by Race, 1970," census tract 26, Kent County, Michigan.

15. Robinson, *City within a City*, 96.

16. U.S. Bureau of the Census, Unemployment Rate for Spanish Population, Unemployment Rate for Black Population, Unemployment Rate for White Population, Grand Rapids, Michigan, 1970.

17. U.S. Bureau of the Census, Selected Characteristics of Persons and Families by Residence in Census Tracts with Poverty Rate 20% or More, 1970, table B-2, SMSA 1-22.

18. Problem Description and Analysis, "Model Cities Application," 1967, part 2, p. 14 of 29.

19. *Ethnic and Racial Background of Newcomers to the City of Grand Rapids*, 1965–1970, folder 2, box 2, series 13-14, HRCR.

20. Robinson, *City within a City*, 95. Central High School Yearbook, 1960; Creston High School Yearbook, 1960; Ottawa High School Yearbook, 1960; South High School Yearbook, 1960; Union High School Yearbook, 1960, all in coll. 316, GRHSC.

21. Reconnaissance Survey, 25, Field Interview folders, box E-49, Grand Rapids–Grand Rapids Team Interview Report to Grand Rapids—Arrest Record, Dayton–Grand Rapids, LBJ Library.

224 · NOTES TO CHAPTER 4

22. "Court to Trim Bond on Some Riot Violators," *Grand Rapids Press*, July 31, 1967, A1. Tom LaBelle, "Driver Finds S. Division Wrong Place for Car Trouble," *Grand Rapids Press*, July 25, 1967, 19. Mike Niemann, "Police Find Moving Mob Calls for Mobile Tactics," *Grand Rapids Press*, July 25, 1967, 19.

23. On white violence toward Latinos during the urban crisis, see Barber, *Latino City*.

24. Cathie Bloom, "Ubaldina Paiz: She's the Heart of the Community," *Grand Rapids Press*, July 22, 1987, A15.

25. Vargas devoted his time to working with Mexican migrant workers. Vargas's obituary states that Michigan governor George Romney appointed him to the state's commission on migrant labor in 1964, and twenty years later Pope John Paul II honored him for his dedication to Michigan's migrant workers. "A Minister to the Migrants: Daniel Vargas dies at 85," *Grand Rapids Press*, December 9, 1992, A2.

26. "Our History," Grand Rapids Community Foundation, www.grfoundation.org/about/our-history, accessed 2018.

27. Al Wilson to the *Grand Rapids Press*, February 23, 1972, LAC/MC.

28. Debra Newman, "Preliminary Inventory of the Records of the Office of Economic Opportunity," 1977, 2, Administration History, Records of the Community Service Administration, NARA.

29. Jackson, "State, the Movement," 419.

30. Daniel Vargas, "Giving the Poor a Voice in Their Own Destiny," speech at the Michigan Welfare League Conference, November 16, 1965, folder 2, box 2, series 13-14, HRCR.

31. "Model Cities Body Will Accept Grant," *Grand Rapids Press*, April 30, 1969, G1.

32. Latin American Council, "Request to UFCS and Community Action Program Executive Committees," June 23, 1969, Model Cities Files, LAC/MC.

33. Bob Holden, "Five Years and $5.2 Million Later . . .," *Grand Rapids Press*, January 23, 1971, 4-A.

34. "Model Cities Application," 1967, part 2, p. 19 of 29.

35. For a history of Model Cities programs, see Burke and Jeffries, *Portland Black Panthers*; Fine, *Violence in the Model City*; Heineman, "Model City"; Siegel, "Dominant Decision-Making Authority"; Weber and Wallace, "Revealing the Empowerment Revolution."

36. Mike Niemann, "It's Off Again, on Again for Model Cities," *Grand Rapids Press*, October 18, 1968, 19.

37. "Model Cities Group Picks Lewis as Chief," *Grand Rapids Press*, November 11, 1968, 45.

38. Ashmore, *Carry It On*; Bauman, *Race and the War*; Behnken, *Civil Rights and Beyond*; Clayson, *Freedom Is Not Enough*; Hawkins, *Everybody's Problem*; Navarro, *Mexican American Youth Organization*; Sanders, *Chance for Change*; Ward and Geiger, *Out in the Rural*; Woodsworth, *Battle for Bed-Stuy*.

39. *Survey on Whether People Will Rent to Negroes*, 1965–1970, folder 2, box 2, series 13-14, HRCR.

40. Mike Niemann, "Model Cities Election Most Unusual in Area," *Grand Rapids Press*, March 13, 1968, 41.

41. "Model Cities Body."

42. U.S. Bureau of the Census, "Population Characteristics by Race, 1970."

43. Steve Vibregg, "Model Cities Fills $15,000 Position," *Grand Rapids Press*, November 14, 1969, B1.

44. Martin R. Morales, *U.S., World War II Army Enlistment Records, 1938–1946*, Ancestry.com, original data: Electronic Army Serial Number Merged File, 1938–1946; ARC 1263923, World War II Army Enlistment Records, NARA. Mike Niemann, "The Latins' Voice Grows Louder Here," *Grand Rapids Press*, June 14, 1970, B1.

45. Niemann, "Latins' Voice Grows Louder."

46. Mike Niemann, "Below Normal Cherry Crop Hits Migrants Hard," *Grand Rapids Press*, July 16, 1970, A2.

47. Marc Simon Rodríguez, *Rethinking the Chicano Movement*, 66.

48. Niemann, "Latins' Voice Grows Louder."

49. Jim Mencarelli, "Martin Morales: Community Leader is Hispanic—And Proud of It." *Grand Rapids Press*, E1.

50. Niemann, "Latins' Voice Grows Louder."

51. Cruzita and Pedro Gómez, interview with the author, Grand Rapids, 2011.

52. Steve Vibregg, "Latin Threat Nets 2 Model Cities Seats," *Grand Rapids Press*, December 10, 1969, B1.

53. Ibid.

54. Ibid.

55. "Mrs. Scott Quits Model Cities Post," *Grand Rapids Press*, January 5, 1970, C1.

56. Carolina Cantú, interview with Darlene Bos, Grand Rapids, 1997, box 1, LWM.

57. "Clubs List Events," *Grand Rapids Press*, September 15, 1969, 5B.

58. Steve Vibregg, "Model Cities Refuses to Appoint Latin," *Grand Rapids Press*, December 29, 1969, B1.

59. Mike Lloyd, "Latin-Black Arbitration?," *Grand Rapids Press*, March 18, 1970, B1. For a discussion on Latino exclusion in the war on poverty and Latinos' negotiation with African Americans, see Bauman, *Race and the War*; Clayson, "War on Poverty." Clayson notes that the middle-class nature of the agencies limited poor people's ability to work within them.

60. Behnken, *Fighting Their Own Battles*.

61. On how Puerto Ricans have distanced themselves from African Americans as political strategy, see Lee, *Building*; Thomas and Lauria-Santiago, *Rethinking the Struggle*.

62. "To Floyd Hyde from Representatives from Latino Community," January 2, 1970, Committee on the Spanish-Speaking, General Correspondence, folder 14, box 24, NARA; "Latins Demand Federal Probe of Model Cities," *Grand Rapids Press*, December 30, 1969, B1.

63. "To Floyd Hyde."

64. Mike Niemann, "Latins Demand 'Audit,'" *Grand Rapids Press*, March 11, 1970, B1.

65. See Robinson, *City within a City*, chapter 4.

66. For an overview of community organizing during the war on poverty, see Orleck and Hazirjian, *War on Poverty*.

67. Sanders, *Chance for Change*, 4.

68. Irene Alba, *R. L. Polk Grand Rapid City Directory*, 1956, GRHSC; Irene Alba, Jesse Alba, Texas Department of State Health Services: Austin, Texas, Texas Divorce Index, 1968–2014; Mike Niemann, "It's Latins Picketing Latins at Model Cities Meeting Here," *Grand Rapids Press*, March 20, 1970, B1.

69. Bloom, "Ubaldina Paiz."

70. "Meeting Minutes," Human Relations Commission, May 27, 1968, and August 28, 1969, box 2, series 13-14, HRCR.

71. Beltrán, *Trouble with Unity*, 46.

72. As political scientist Cristina Beltrán aptly explains in *Trouble with Unity*, "the movements' perception of conflict as something external and unnatural to the community meant that those who challenged norms and traditions become culturally and politically suspect" (56).

73. Photo of Juanita Larriuz and Leah Tobar, *Grand Rapids Model Neighborhood News* 4, no. 4 (June 1971): 4.

74. See Blackwell, *Chicana Power!*

75. Niemann, "It's Latins Picketing Latins."

76. "Crust of bread" was commonly evoked in the labor movement of the late 1800s and early 1900s, especially by John L. Lewis, leader of the United Mine Workers, who often used it in his speeches. See Sulzberger, *Sit Down*.

77. Niemann, "It's Latins Picketing Latins."

78. Niemann, "Latins' Voice Grows Louder."

79. Mike Niemann, "Morales 'Regrets' Charges," *Grand Rapids Press*, June 23, 1970, B1.

80. Ibid.

81. Al Wilson to Leonard Ortega, Subject: Background Comments on Roosevelt Lodge Boxing Equipment, February 15, 1972, LAC/MC.

82. Paul Aadrsma and Al Wilson, "Proposal and Study Plan: For a Census and Socio-Economic Survey of the Latin American Population of Kent County," LAC/MC.

83. "Chicanos Arrested in BH as Tri-Cap Trespassers," *Benton Harbor (MI) News-Palladium*, November 19, 1970.

Chapter 5. Needs of the Community

1. Cruzita and Pedro Gómez, interview with the author, Grand Rapids, 2011. "Persons Hired and Place of Employment Report," August 1973, LAC/MC.

2. "First Year Evaluation: Latin American Council," June 20, 1972, 10, Model Cities Program, Grand Rapids, Michigan, LAC/MC.

3. Frieden and Kaplan, *Politics of Neglect*, 239.

4. Liz Hyman, "Model Cities Faces Project Cuts," *Grand Rapids Press*, February 19, 1972, B1.

5. Cruz, *Liberalism and Identity Politics*.

6. Hyman, "Model Cities."

7. Jolly, *By Our Own Strength*; Price, *Dreaming Blackness*; Andrés Torres and Velázquez, *Puerto Rican Movement*, 12.

8. See Marc Simon Rodríguez, *Rethinking the Chicano Movement*, 66, for a discussion of how more radical organizing often existed alongside institutional approaches.

9. Understanding activism for social welfare in the 1970s helps to put in perspective welfare activism in the 1990s during the Clinton administration's cutbacks. See Reese, *They Say Cut Back*.

10. Meeting Minutes, Community Relations Commission, July 28, 1971, 2, series 13-4, box 7, 1965–1970, Community Relations General Subject File, Michigan-NAIRO, Community Relations Commission, Equal Opportunity Department, GRCARC. In 1968, the Human Relations Commission changed its name to the Community Relations Commission.

11. On how cities dealt with the waning funding from the OEO, see Chávez, *Eastside Landmark*.

12. Wilson, "Grand Rapids Latin American Population." The LAC arrived at the 11,000 figure after working with a geography graduate student, Gene Smith, from Western Michigan University, who used the average growth rate of the community over the course of twenty-five years to estimate the community's population of 11,000 by 1972. Paul Aadrsma and Al Wilson, "Proposal and Study Plan: For a Census and Socio-Economic Survey of the Latin American Population of Kent County," August 15, 1972, 2, LAC/MC.

13. "Doubling of Local Latin Population Spurs Bid for More Aid," *Grand Rapids Press*, June 14, 1972, E2.

14. See Clara E. Rodríguez, *Changing Race*.

15. Aadrsma and Wilson, "Proposal and Study Plan."

16. Liz Hyman, "City Shies from Footing Bill for Latin Census," *Grand Rapids Press*, August 2, 1972, B3.

17. Meeting Minutes, Community Relations Commission, November 19, 1970, series 13-4, box 7, 1965–1970, Community Relations General Subject File, Michigan-NAIRO, Community Relations Commission, Equal Opportunity Department, GRCARC.

18. "Latins' Protest Over Budget Gains Them $19,000," *Grand Rapids Press*, February 7, 1973, 1-D.

19. Michael R. Haviland and Martín Morales, "Unmet Economic and Social Needs of the Latin American Community in Grand Rapids," October 10, 1973, 8, HRCR.

20. "Latin-Americans Carry Budget Fight into City Hall," *Grand Rapids Press*, January 3, 1973, 1-B.

21. Francisco Vega to Lyman Parks, December 28, 1972; Jo Willis to Lyman Parks, December 27, 1972, both in box 7, series 28-2, 1970–1975, K–Ma, Mayor's General File (Lyman Parks), Executive Office—Mayor, GRCARC.

22. To Mayor Lyman Parks from Chester J. Eagleman, Inter-Tribal Council, box 7, series 28-2, 1970–1975.

23. Jane González to Lyman Parks, December 28, 1972, box 7, series 28-2, 1970–1975.

24. Ricardo Parra to Lyman Parks, December 29, 1972, box 7, series 28-2, 1970–1975.

25. Liz Hyman, "Model Cities."

26. Maury De Jonge, "Latin-Americans Ask Kent for Cash," *Grand Rapids Press*, May 15, 1973, 2-D.

27. Haviland and Morales, "Unmet Economic and Social Needs."

28. Ibid.

29. Al Wilson to Gus Breymann, November 9, 1971, 2, LAC/MC.

30. Ibid.

31. Ibid.

32. Native Americans were also kept off this identity spectrum, though the area had a large Native population around Michigan. For work about Detroit, see Mays, *City of Dispossessions*.

33. Wilson to Breymann.

34. *Qué Pasa* 1, no. 2 (May 1972); *Qué Pasa* 2, no. 3 (September 1972): 1; *Qué Pasa* 2, no. 2 (November 1972), all in LAC/MC.

35. Haviland and Morales, "Unmet Economic and Social Needs."

36. William "Billy" Tappin, interview with the author, Lansing, April 2015.

37. Monthly Narrative Report, Latin American Council, November 1971, LAC/MC.

38. Monthly Narrative Report, Latin American Council, May 1972, LAC/MC; "Festival History," Festival of the Arts, accessed April 12, 2018, https://festivalgr.org/history.

39. Monthly Narrative Report, Latin American Council, January 1972, LAC/MC.

40. Chicano movement newspapers were common at the time. For more on newspapers, see Josue Estrada, "Chicano Newspapers and Periodicals, 1966–1979," Mapping American Social Movements Project, https://depts.washington.edu/moves/Chicano_news_map .shtml, accessed December 15, 2021.

41. See Aguilar, "Pursuit of Representation."

42. Paul Mitchell, editor's column, *Qué Pasa* 2, no. 3 (September 1972), LAC/MC.

43. Leonard Ortega to Al Wilson, Publication of a Monthly Newsletter in Spanish by the Latin American Council, March 20, 1972, LAC/MC.

44. Ora W. Spady to MNCC Executive Director, "Attention Armond M. Robinson, Inter-Departmental Letter: Latin American Council," March 20, 1972, LAC/MC.

45. Irma and Simon Aguilar, interview with the author, Grand Rapids, 2014.

46. See Blanton, *Strange Career of Bilingual Education*; Crawford, *Bilingual Education*. See Zentella, *Growing Up Bilingual*, for the experiences of Puerto Ricans growing up bilingual in the 1980s and 1990s. Zentella's subjects also had difficulty reading and writing in Spanish though they spoke both English and Spanish.

47. Richard Campos, "Farmworkers," *Qué Pasa* 2, no. 2 (November 1972), LAC/MC.

48. *Qué Pasa* 2, no. 3 (September 1972), LAC/MC.

49. Walter Acevedo, "Reflections on Our Language," *Qué Pasa* 2, no. 2 (November 1972), LAC/MC.

50. See Wiggins, "Women." Latinos even used "Spanish" itself as a unifying moniker for both groups, dating back to the 1950s when, for example, the joint baseball league made up of teams of Mexicans and Puerto Ricans called themselves the "Spanish league."

51. Sara Ramírez, "La Columna de Sara," *Qué Pasa* 2, no. 2 (November 1972), LAC/MC; translation by the author.

52. Acevedo, "Reflections on Our Language."

53. Scholars of Mexican Americans and race have thoroughly examined how Mexican Americans have attempted to use their racial ambiguity to claim whiteness through a variety of social and legal avenues. For a very detailed overview of this process in New

Mexico immediately following the Mexican-American War, see Gómez, *Manifest Destinies*. See also Foley, *Quest for Equality*; Foley, *White Scourge*.

54. "Opportunity," *Qué Pasa* 2, no. 3 (September 1972), LAC/MC.

55. Latinos have had a historically complex relationship with the U.S. military, although many proudly served during World War II and the Korean War. While some returning soldiers enjoyed warm receptions after the war, others struggled to find equality post-deployment.

56. For a summary of the politics of Mexican American participation in World War II and Vietnam, see Escobedo, *From Coveralls to Zoot Suits*; Oropeza, *¡Raza Sí!*

57. López-Rivera and Headley, "Who Is the Terrorist?" See also Whalen, "Radical Contexts," 221.

58. Oropeza, *¡Raza Sí!* See the introduction for a discussion on patriotism.

59. "Ethnic Survey," May 8, 1969, "Miscellaneous, May 1969–Ca. September 1969" folder, box 2, series 13-14, HRCR.

60. See Johanna Fernández, *Young Lords*; Lilia Fernández, *Brown in the Windy City*; Haney-López, *Racism on Trial*.

61. Monthly narrative, Latin American Council, March 1972, LAC/MC.

62. Meeting Minutes, HRCR, April 22, 1965, series 13-14, box 1-3, HRCR.

63. Ibid.

64. Roy Fuentes, "Problems of the Migrant Workers in Michigan," 10, Michigan Civil Rights Commission, March 1968, series 13-14, box 1-3, HRCR. Charles Johnson, "Aid for Migrants: Interested Groups Form Council for Kent Area," *Grand Rapids Press*, May 19, 1965, 70. The history of activism by migrant farmworkers and on behalf of them in Michigan in the 1960s and 1970s has been well documented. On migrant workers from the 1950s to the 1970s in Michigan, see Fine, *Expanding the Frontier*; Findlay, *We Are Left*; Juan Mora, "Latino Encounters"; Salas, "Anti-Colonialism"; Salas, "Pablo's Problem"; Dennis Nodín Valdés, *Al Norte*.

65. LAC, Monitor Report, April 1, 1973–April 30, 1973, LAC/MC.

66. Campos, "Farmworkers"; Richard Campos, Southwest Program Development Corporation Certificate, November 3, 1972, possession of Richard Campos.

67. "Manpower Aid Fill Latin-American Post (David Rodríguez)," *Grand Rapids Press*, June 20, 1972, 1H; Doug Guthrie, "Hispanic Center Rejects Issue of Racism, Defends Firing Dow," *Grand Rapids Press*, March 1, 1983, 1A; "The WLAV Race," *Model Neighborhood News* 5, no. 3 (July–August 1972).

68. Carmen Fitte's Activities for October 15–31, 1973; David Rodríguez's Activities for October 15–31, 1973; Richard Campos's Activities for October 15–31, 1973, all in LAC/MC.

69. Leonard Ortega to Gus Breymann, Latin American Council Weekly Report, March 12, 1973–March 16, 1973, LAC/MC.

70. Haviland and Morales, "Unmet Economic and Social Needs."

71. Monthly Narrative Report, Latin American Council, January 1972, LAC/MC.

72. Sara Ramírez, "Circus Tickets," LAC/MC.

73. U.S. Bureau of the Census, Unemployment Rate for Spanish Population, Unemployment Rate for Black Population, Unemployment Rate for White Population, Grand Rapids, Michigan, 1970.

74. Donaker and Olson, *Grand Rapids and Its People*, 74.

75. Haviland and Morales, "Unmet Economic and Social Needs," 43.

76. Ibid., 44.

77. Monthly Narrative Report, Latin American Council, May 1972, LAC/MC.

78. "Persons Hired and Place of Employment Report," August 1972; "Persons Hired and Place of Employment Report," October 1972, both in LAC/MC.

79. *Qué Pasa* 1, no. 2 (May 1972).

80. Brian Malone, "City Reapportions, Expands 1st Ward," *Grand Rapids Press*, March 27, 1973, 1.

81. Matt Vande Bunte, "For First Time This Century, Black Candidates on Grand Rapids Mayoral Ballot," *Grand Rapids Press*, April 3, 2019.

82. "City Commissioners, 1945–1971," Grand Rapids Historical Commission, " History Grand Rapids, www.historygrandrapids.org/article/2231/city-commissioners-19451971, accessed February 12, 2013; "City Commissioners Terms of Office," All City Officials Past and Present Terms, 6, City of Grand Rapids, www.grandrapidsmi.gov/files/assets/public/departments/city-clerk/files/carc/all-city-officials-past-and-present-terms.pdf, accessed May 9, 2022.

83. Daniel Vásquez, interview with Gordon Olson, Grand Rapids, undated, box 4, LWM.

84. Cruzita and Pedro Gómez interview, 2011.

85. Zeemering, "Grand Rapids."

86. School Elections, City of Grand Rapids, Kent County, Michigan, Monday, June 11, 1973; Cumulative Report: Wards 1–3; City Clerk, series 2-32, Election Documentation File, 1970–1975; acc. 13, box 3, City of Grand Rapids, Kent County, Michigan, April 6, 1970, City Clerk, series 2-32, Election Documentation File, 1970–1975, GRPD General Election, KISD General Election, all in GRCARC.

87. "First Year Evaluation."

Chapter 6. Tangled with the Police

1. Melvin Tardy, "Police Program," June 25, 1970, folder 12, box 3, series 28-2, 1970–1971, MAY-PRO, Mayor's General Subject File Robert Boelens, Mayor, Executive Office, GRCARC.

2. "Police Officer Qualifications," Police Community Relations" folder, box 17, schedule 27-5, General Subject File, Police Clip-Police Traffic, Executive City Manager, GRCARC.

3. "Ethnic Survey," May 8, 1969, "Miscellaneous, May 1969–Ca. September 1969" folder, box 2, series 13-14, HRCR.

4. Ramos, foreword, vii–x. This is not to say that radical Chicanismo could not be found in Michigan. Chicanos in Detroit and in Lansing practiced radical organizing characterized by protests, demonstrations, and more confrontational strategies. See Salas, "Anti-Colonialism."

5. Lassiter, *Silent Majority Suburban Politics*.

6. Bonilla-Silva, *Racism without Racists*.

7. See Self, *American Babylon*.

8. Lee, *Building*, 10.

9. Laverne Davis, interview with the author, Grand Rapids, 2017.

10. On proactive policing and policing practices of the twentieth century, see Hahn and Jeffries, *Urban America and Its Police*, 105.

11. Jelks, *African Americans*, 96.

12. "City Police Cleared of Brutality," *Grand Rapids Press*, June 27, 1968, 2.

13. The following men were arrested for gambling on May 23, 1931: Antonio Arrellano, box 118/8/2/2 (A–f), CA 1924–1961; Peter Cortez, box 118/8/2/2 (A–f), CA 1924–1961; Guadalupe Trevino, box 118/8/1/2 (S–Z), CA 1924–1961, all in book 1, Arrest Records, Police Records Division, GRCARC.

14. Human Relations Commission Meeting Minutes, September 22, 1958, box 1, series 13-14, HRCR.

15. To Miss Kathy Post from Alfred E. Cowles, May 17, 1965, folder 5, box 7, series 13-4, Camps-Correspond, Community Relations General Subject File, Equal Opportunity Department, GRCARC.

16. Robert Alt, "Group Asks City Changes to Involve More Negroes in Governing Body," *Grand Rapids Press*, August 4, 1967, 17; "Special Sub-Committee Meeting Re Latin American Problems," box 1, series 13-4, Camps-Correspond. On the Black Panther Party's Ten-Point Program and demands for community control, see Hilliard, *Black Panther Party*, 74–77; Foner, *Black Panthers Speak*, 19, 40, 179.

17. "Johnson Opposes Police Review Board," *Grand Rapids Press*, August 5, 1967, 13.

18. Robert Alt, "Friendly Smile Dissolves Hostility," *Grand Rapids Press*, April 14, 1967, 13; Robert Alt, "You Have to Learn to Live Together," *Grand Rapids Press*, April 13, 1967, 35.

19. "Johnson Opposes Police Review Board."

20. "Police Seek Recruits from Minority Groups," *Grand Rapids Press*, August 28, 1968, 3.

21. "Police Officer Qualifications," 1969.

22. Robinson, *City within a City*, 95. Central High School Yearbook, 1960; Creston High School Yearbook, 1960; Ottawa High School, 1960; South High School, 1960; Union High School, 1960, all in coll. 316, GRHSC.

23. La Lucha, "Latin American Student Attitudes in Grand Rapids High Schools (An Exploratory Study)," 1971, author's personal collection.

24. Robert Alt, "Police Try to Recruit More Negroes—What's Been Going on in Grand Rapids since Last July?," *Grand Rapids Press*, May 1, 1968, 13.

25. Civil Service and Personnel Office, "A Report on Recruitment Practices and Hiring Procedures as Applied to the Position of Police Patrolman," April 1, 1966, "Police Recruiting" folder, box 17, schedule 27-5, General Subject File, Police Clip-Police Traffic.

26. Irma and Simon Aguilar, interview with the author, Grand Rapids, 2014.

27. "Mexico-American Opened Door to Hispanic Firefighters in L.A.," EFE News Service, August 6, 2010.

28. Thomas E. Johnson, "Minority Recruitment in Six Major Cities," May 9, 1968, "Police Recruiting" folder.

29. Roy H. Beck, "Shorter Men Get a Break," *Grand Rapids Press*, April 9, 1973, 26. The discourse around body types and race is reminiscent of Beliso-De Jesús, "Jungle Academy."

30. "19 Men Sworn in as Officers," *Grand Rapids Press*, May 18, 1967, 29; "33 Recruits Join Force: Biggest Police Class Graduates," *Grand Rapids Press*, May 25, 1968, 15.

31. Kent County, Social Explorer Tables, Census 1940 County Only Set; Kent County, Social Explorer Tables, Census 1970 County Only Set, both in Social Explorer and U.S. Census Bureau. See chapter 4 for a thorough discussion about Latino population estimates.

32. Johnson, "Minority Recruitment."

33. "City Gets 10-Point Program to End 'Passive' Discrimination in Hiring," *Grand Rapids Press*, August 31, 1966, 15.

34. Robinson discusses this in detail in *City within a City*, 24–50.

35. Johnson, "Minority Recruitment."

36. Floyd Allbaugh, "Mayor Defends City Job Policy," *Grand Rapids Press*, March 15, 1967, 27.

37. See Katznelson, *When Affirmative Action Was White* for a complete discussion on federal policies that have helped white Americans since the New Deal.

38. Allbaugh, "Mayor Defends City Job Policy."

39. Alt, "Group Asks City Changes."

40. Ed Kotlar, "Black Group Protests Police Treatment in Predawn Meet" *Grand Rapids Press*, April 30, 1970, 2D.

41. "Position Paper," folder 12, box 3, series 28-2, 1970–1971, MAY-PRO.

42. M. Howard Rienstra to Mayor Robert Boelens, Black Administrative Assistant to the Police Chief, August 21, 1970, folder 12, Police Dept, box 3, series 28-2, 1970–1971, MAY-PRO.

43. Tardy, "Police Program."

44. Martín Morales to Mayor Boelens, June 8, 1970, Executive Files, Mayor's General File (Robert Boelens), box 1, series 28-2, 1970–1971, App-Con, GRCARC.

45. "Ex-Chief Charges Police Harassment," *Grand Rapids Press*, May 8, 1970, 1.

46. Ibid.

47. Mike Lloyd, "Boelens Pledges Action to Curb Violence in the City," *Grand Rapid Press*, May 13, 1970, F1.

48. Ed Kotlar, "'Speaking for Many' Black Gives Views on Tense Police Issue," *Grand Rapids Press*, May 2, 1970, B1.

49. Kathy Miles quoted in Mike Lloyd, "Blacks Boycotting Police-Race Talks," *Grand Rapids Press*, May 7, 1970, 1.

50. Alt, "Police Try to Recruit."

51. Charles V. Probert, Legal Adviser to the Fraternal Order of Police, to Mayor Robert Boelens, September 3, 1970; Robert Row, President FOP, Norman Visser, Recording Secretary, "A Position Paper to the City Commission—May 5, 1970," both in Executive Files, Mayor's General File (Robert Boelens).

52. Mrs. Douglas Riemersma to Mayor Boelens, May 8, 1970; Robert Denick to Mayor Boelens, May 8, 1970; Robert Row, "A Position Paper to the City Commission," May 5, 1970, all in Executive Files, Mayor's General File (Robert Boelens).

53. Töten Schwartzen to John Toliver, June 1970, folder 12, box 3, series 28-2, 1970–1971, MAY-PRO.

54. Black Police Officer Survey, August 18, 1970, "Police Recruiting" folder.

55. Robert Holden, "Latin-Americans Demand Police Jobs," *Grand Rapids Press*, April 7, 1971, 21.

56. To City Manager from Joseph Zainea, Affirmative Action Report, December 11, 1970, box 2, series 13-14, HRCR.

57. "Jobs Demanded for Minorities" *Grand Rapids Press*, November 25, 1970, B1.

58. Exhibit A, *Martínez and Ragsdale v Civil Service Board of the City of Grand Rapids*, no. G-178-72A, July 10, 1972, box 12, RM CH 18-09, RG 21, 21-80-0009, USDC Grand Rapids, Civil Case Files, 178-72 CA, NARA.

59. Mike Lloyd, "City Would Speed House Demolition," *Grand Rapids Press*, April 28, 1971, 1-C.

60. Mike Lloyd, "City Job Policy Found Not Fully Unbiased," *Grand Rapids Press*, April 13, 1971, 1-B.

61. Lloyd, "City Would Speed House Demolition."

62. Ibid.

63. On Black and Latino exclusion from the privileges of full citizenship, see Jones, *Birthright Citizens*; Thomas, *Puerto Rican Citizen*; Gómez, *Manifest Destinies*.

64. "GOP Pros Fear Disaster in '74," *Human Events* 34, no. 2 (January 12, 1974): 3.

65. Kotlar, "'Speaking for Many' Black."

66. Robinson, *City within a City*, 173–74.

67. Parks's election could be considered a "hollow prize," as political scientist H. Paul Friesema described. He understood that minority mayors elected in the 1960s to the 1970s inherited struggling urban centers when turmoil from white flight and fiscal shortages emerged. See Kraus and Swanstrom, "Minority Mayors," 99.

68. "City Jobs for Minorities," op-ed, *Grand Rapids Press*, February 15, 1972, 12-A.

69. "Ethnic Survey," May 8, 1969.

70. Fernández, *Young Lords*, 104.

71. "City Jobs for Minorities."

72. Al Wilson letter to the editor, February 23, 1972, Editorial Page Editor, February 23, 1972, LAC/MC.

73. "Morales Decries Police, Fire Hiring," *Grand Rapids Press*, February 9, 1972, 1-C.

74. "City Jobs for Minorities."

75. Wilson letter to the editor, February 23, 1972.

76. Ibid.

77. Rhett Pinsky interview with the author, Grand Rapids, 2018.

78. Wilson letter to the editor, February 23, 1972.

79. Linda Hendershot, "Fireman Jobs Beckon Winners of Bias Suit," *Grand Rapids Press*, February 13, 1974, 2B.

80. "City Halts Firemen Hiring," *Qué Pasa* 2, no. 2 (November 1972), LAC/MC.

81. "Noel P. Fox, 76, Dies; Former Federal Judge," *New York Times*, June 5, 1987, D16.

82. Steve Aulie, "Stop Discriminating in Hiring, Testing Firemen, City Ordered," *Grand Rapids Press*, January 22, 1973, 1.

83. Brian Malone, "Minneapolis Firm Favored for Firemen Test Evaluation," *Grand Rapids Press*, January 3, 1972, 2B.

84. Hendershot, "Fireman Jobs Beckon Winners"; Linda Hendershot, "Judge Fox Oks Hiring Plan for 23 Minority Firemen," *Grand Rapids Press*, February 2, 1974, 1-A.

85. Linda Hendershot, "Most New City Firemen Are Minority Persons," *Grand Rapids Press*, September 23, 1974, 1-B.

86. "Police Push Plan to Hire Minorities," *Grand Rapids Press*, May 8, 1974, 60.

87. Miguel Berríos, interview with the author, Grand Rapids, 2011.

88. "Police Push Plan"; Hendershot, "Fireman Jobs Beckon Winners."

89. "Police Push Plan."

90. Ed Kotlar, "Women Begin Police Patrol Roles," *Grand Rapids Press*, August 20, 1975, 1-E.

91. Joel Clark, "City Police Plan Bias-Free Hiring," *Grand Rapids Press*, August 24, 1974, 2-B.

92. "Fire Calls Tough—But Rewarding," *Grand Rapids Press*, May 31, 2008, A2.

93. Goldberg, *Black Firefighters and the FDNY*, 221.

94. Stephen R. Drew and Ann M. Cooper, interview with the author, Grand Rapids, 2018.

Chapter 7. Justice for Our Kids

1. Rosa Collazo, interview with the author, Grand Rapids, 2018.

2. La Lucha, "Latin American Student Attitudes in Grand Rapids High Schools (An Exploratory Study), 1971, personal collection of the author.

3. On educators forcing Mexican American students into vocational tracts, see González, *Chicano Education*, 77–93. On how schools devalued the Spanish language as a language for instruction, see Maciel and Gonzales-Berry, *Contested Homeland*. On the devaluing of Mexican American culture in educational settings, see Valenzuela, *Subtractive Schooling*.

4. Lucas and Chicago IL Council on Urban Education, *Puerto Rican Dropouts*; Salazar, *Border Correspondent*, 202.

5. San Miguel and Donato, "Latino Education," 39.

6. Joel Clark, "Latins Celebrate School, Cultural Center," *Grand Rapids Press*, January 30, 1975, 2-B.

7. San Miguel, *Chicana/o Struggles for Education*, 125–29; Rickford. *We Are an African People*, 12–15. An exception is the Cuban exile community that arrived in Miami in the 1960s. Due to the Cold War, the U.S. government invested financial resources in the exiled Cuban community that other Latinos did not receive on arrival to the United States. Thus, Cuban parents requested funds for community-controlled, Spanish-language schools in the 1960s in Miami. Their method of delivery of instruction and the funding they received to do so is like that of the NEC. However, the NEC needed to use a circumnavigation to access this funding, while federal funding was made available to Cuban immigrants with relative ease. On the Cuban exile experience, including education, see Eckstein, *Immigrant Divide*; Maria de los Angeles Torres, *In the Land of Mirrors*.

8. "38 Racially Impacted School Districts," State of Michigan, Racial Census Summary, 1970–1971 (by district), La Raza Advisory Committee, proposal ndd, correspondence, 1972, folder 8, box 2, acc. no. 87-21, lot 120, Hispanic Education Files, Archives of Michigan.

9. Michael R. Haviland and Martín Morales, "Unmet Economic and Social Needs of the Latin American Community in Grand Rapids," October 10, 1973, 8, HRCR.

10. "Meeting with Personnel Department of the Board of Education and the Latin American Council Representatives," Latin American Council, May 22, 1972, LAC/MC.

11. Monthly Narrative Report, Latin American Council, January 1972, LAC/MC.

12. "Meeting with Personnel Department."

13. See Fuentes, "Struggle for Local Political Control," 111—20; Lee, *Building*.

14. Mr. Alfred Wilson to Mr. Philip Runkel, Superintendent of Schools, director of the Latin American Council, "ACTION MODEL to reduce Latin-American Drop Out Rate," May 16, 1972, LAC/MC.

15. "Meeting with Personnel Department."

16. "'La Lucha' Works," *Lanthorn* 5 no 6, (January 4, 1973): 3, Special Collections and University Archives, University Libraries, Grand Valley State University.

17. Gilbert González, *Chicano Education*, 77–93.

18. Monthly Narrative Report, Latin American Council, February 1972, LAC/MC.

19. David Rodríguez, "November Narrative—Education Department—Latin American Council," November 1972, LAC/MC.

20. Ladson-Billings, "Getting to Sesame Street?," uses the lenses of anthropology, education, and cultural studies, to examine methods of bilingual education since 1965.

21. The fight for bilingual education occurring across the country included a demand for bicultural teachers. Communities asked for teachers who not only spoke the language but understood their children. See Lee, *Building*, 179–99.

22. The 1 percent number seems to be based on the number of Spanish-surnamed students in the district (about 875). It does not consider the growing number of students who were increasingly raised as monolingual English speakers because their parents recognized their school system did not support bilingual learning.

23. "Meeting with Personnel Department."

24. Graff, "Latin Americans."

25. Demands for representation in textbooks resonated with Latino communities across the country. The student walkouts in East Los Angeles are the most well-known action taken to address Mexican Americans' erasure in textbooks. See Acuña, *Occupied America*; Haney-López, *Racism on Trial*.

26. Monthly Narrative Report, Latin American Council, April 1972, LAC/MC.

27. Monthly Narrative Report, Latin American Council, December 1971, LAC/MC.

28. Monthly Narrative Report, Latin American Council, July 1972, LAC/MC.

29. Lucy Maillette, "Latin American Council Creates Library to Promote More Latino Awareness," *Grand Rapids Press*, March 25, 1972, 7-B. Monthly Narrative Report, Latin American Council, January 1972, LAC/MC.

30. Monthly Narrative Report, Latin American Council, June 1972, LAC/MC.

31. See Olivas and Schneider, *Education Law Stories*; chapter 5 contains a detailed examination of *Lau v. Nichols*.

32. "Goals and Objectives," 1, folder 4, box 24, 80–41, 75, Education Superintendent, Subject Files, M–N, 1865–1972, Archives of Michigan.

33. Obituary of John Porter, *Ann Arbor News*, June 27, 2012.

34. A. J. Williams, "Former Business Leader Delbert Gray Dies," *Detroit Michigan Chronicle*, February 13, 2014, https://michiganchronicle.com/2014/02/19/former-business-leader-delbert-gray-dies/, accessed May 23, 2022.

35. "Poverty, 1970," Pontiac, Michigan, Social Explorer Tables (SE), Census 1970, Tracts Only Set, Social Explorer and U.S. Census Bureau.

36. "Pontiac Application," folder 4, box 24, 80–41, 75, Education Superintendent, Subject Files, M–N, 1865–1972, Archives of Michigan.

37. *Child Is Father to Man* (Lansing, Mich: Michigan Dept. of Education, Neighborhood Education Authority, 1970), Library of Michigan.

38. Carmen Fitte, interview with the author, Grand Rapids, 2016.

39. Ibid.

40. Joel Clark, "Latin Twist for Basic Education," *Grand Rapids Press*, November 8, 1974, B1.

41. Tamara Cooke, "Latin Dropouts Given 2nd Chance at School," *Grand Rapids Press*, February 26, 1974, 1-B.

42. Tamara Cooke, "Neighborhood Education Center: Understanding Spoken, Taught Here," *Grand Rapids Press*, May 27, 1974, 1-B.

43. Fitte interview.

44. Kate Nagengast, "Celebrated Local Artist José Narezo Dies at 63," *Grand Rapids Press*, December 18, 2008.

45. Fitte interview.

46. Collazo interview.

47. Cooke, "Neighborhood Education Center."

48. Fitte interview.

49. José Reyna, interview with the author, Grand Rapids, 2016.

50. See Patton, *Lockheed, Atlanta*, 150, for more on CETA's role in desegregating Atlanta's industries.

51. "Proposal," 7, folder 1, box 3, Reverend Harrold Dekker Papers, GRCARC.

52. Joel Clark, "Latins Celebrate School, Cultural Center," *Grand Rapids Press*, January 30, 1975, 2-B.

53. "Services in Direct Contact with Beneficiaries," folder 1, box 3, 1967, Latin American Council, CETA records, Direct Services, Human Resource Department (Later Grant Management), GRCARC.

54. Fitte interview.

55. "All Funds Agency, Budget for the LAC, 1976–1977," folder 1, box 3, 1967, Latin American Council, CETA records.

56. Jim Mencarelli, "A Story of Pride and Hope," *Grand Rapids Press*, July 27, 1986, E1.

57. Paul Chaffee, "Latino Leader Is Focus of Diploma Mill Inquiry," *Grand Rapids Press*, November 18, 1977, A1.

58. "Factional Tensions Erupt in a Melee at Meeting of Latin American Council," *Grand Rapids Press*, May 31, 1978, B1.

59. J. C. Bosworth to City Manager, Joseph Zainea: Current Status of Latin American Council, July 22, 1977; Mr. Ricardo García from Mary Alice Williams, Community Development Citizens' Committee, February 8, 1979, both in "Latin American Council" folder, box 1, Project Files, A–S, Human Resources Department, GRCARC.

60. Mary Kramer, "Latin-American Council Must Separate Office, High School," *Grand Rapids Press*, March 2, 1977, B3.

61. Collazo interview.

62. "About," Hispanic Center of West Michigan, https://hispanic-center.org/about/ #about-us, accessed January 25, 2021.

63. "Hearing Set for Agency Funding," *Grand Rapids Press*, June 28, 1979, B4.

64. Ronald Wilkerson, "School Helps Hispanics 'Adelante,'" *Grand Rapids Press*, October 20, 1997, A23.

Epilogue

1. Eleazar López, interview with Estephanie López, Grand Rapids, 2015.

2. Tom Perkins, "Now Founders Is Being Sued for Racial Discrimination," *Detroit Metro Times*, October 4, 2018, www.metrotimes.com/food-drink/now-founders-is-being-sued-for -racial-discrimination-16158524, accessed May 23, 2022. Though there have been modest increases in Black- and Latinx-owned breweries, inequality remains in this industry.

3. Tom Henderson, "A Grand Culmination; Market in Downtown Grand Rapids Brings Surrounding Area Back to Life," *Crain's Detroit Business*, May 21, 2018, 8. Matt Vande Bunte, "Gentrification Fears Stoked by Developers $60M Grand Rapids Proposal," *Grand Rapids Press*, April 2, 2019, www.mlive.com/news/grand-rapids/2016/03/gentrification _fears_stoked_by.html, accessed May 23, 2022.

4. "SiTE:LAB," Art Prize, www.artprize.org/sitelab, accessed January 25, 2021.

5. Filippo Tagliati, "Relocations—Art Prize 2015," *Filippo Tagliati*, https://filippotagliati .com/projects/relocations/, accessed January 25, 2021.

6. Michelle Jokisch Polo, "Rumsey Street: Leaving Behind a History of Sacred Space," *Rapid Growth Media*, October 19, 2017, www.rapidgrowthmedia.com/features/101917 -OTG6-grandville.aspx, accessed May 23, 2022.

7. "About," Cultural Collective, https://culturacollective.com/about/, accessed January 25, 2021. The founder identified the participants as Latinx.

8. Steffanie Rosalez, interview with the author, Lansing, 2021.

9. "About," Cultural Collective.

10. Rosalez interview.

11. Ibid.

12. Noah Fromson, "ArtPrize Apologize to Grand Rapids Artist Group," 13 On Your Side, October 2, 2017, www.wzzm13.com/article/news/local/art-prize/artprize-apologizes -to-grand-rapids-artist-group/69-480289876, accessed May 23, 2022.

13. "Plaza Roosevelt: Building with Our Neighbors," Habitat for Humanity of Kent County, www.habitatkent.org/plazaroosevelt/, accessed January 25, 2021.

14. Rosalez interview.

15. The school was previously known as Southwest Community Campus.

16. The city also renamed Franklin Street as Martin Luther King Jr. Street. "Martin Luther King Jr. Street and César E. Chávez Avenue," City of Grand Rapids, www.grand rapidsmi.gov/Government/Departments/Engineering-Department/MLKCh%C3%A1vez -Street-Name-Changes, accessed May 13, 2022.

Bibliography

Interviews by the Author

Irma and Simon Aguilar (2014)
Juan Báez
Carolina Báez Anderson
Carmen Berríos
Miguel Berríos
Jason Blyveis
Richard Campos
Rosa Collazo
Laverne Davis
Stephen R. Drew and Ann M. Cooper
Rosalía Espíndola
Carmen Fitte
Lila García
Cruzita and Pedro Gómez
Theresa Hendricks
Rafael Hernández
Theodore Kozlowski
Rosa Pérez
Rhett Pinsky
Sara Ramírez
Bob Reed
José Reyna
Steffanie Rosalez
Rubén Sánchez
Billy Tappin
Marilyn Vega

María Ysasi
María Zambrana

Other Interviews

Irma and Simon Aguilar (2001)
Juanita Baltierrez
Carolina Cantú
Luisa Fernández
José Flores
Eleazar López
Isabel Navarro
Juanita and Santos Rincones
Guadalupe Vargas
Daniel Vásquez

Journal Articles, Books, Book Chapters, and Dissertations

Acuña, Rodolfo. *Occupied America: A History of Chicanos.* New York: Harper Collins, 1988.

Aguilar, Emiliano, Jr. "The Pursuit of Representation in East Chicago, Indiana." In *Building Sustainable Worlds: Latinx Placemaking in the Midwest,* edited by Theresa Delgadillo, Ramón H. Rivera-Servera, Geraldo L. Cadava, and Claire F. Fox, 204–23. Urbana: University of Illinois Press, 2022.

Alamillo, Jose. *Making Lemonade out of Lemons: Mexican American Labor and Leisure in a California Town, 1880–1960.* Urbana: University of Illinois Press, 2006.

Allen, Charles H. *First Annual Report of Charles H. Allen, Governor of Porto Rico: Covering the Period from May 1, 1900 to May 1, 1901.* Washington, DC: Government Printing Office, 1901. Microfilm.

Amador, Emma. "Caring for Labor History." *Labor* 17, no. 4 (January 1, 2020): 65–69.

Aparicio, Frances R. "Cultural Twins and National Others: Allegories of Intralatino/a Subjectivities." *Identities* 16, no. 5 (September/October 2009): 622–41.

———. *Negotiating Latinidad: Intralatina/o Lives in Chicago.* Champaign: University of Illinois Press, 2019.

Aparicio, Frances R., and Susana Chávez-Silverman, eds. *Tropicalizations: Transcultural Representations of Latinidad.* Hanover, NH: University Press of New England, 1997.

Arredondo, Gabriela F. *Mexican Chicago: Race, Identity, and Nation, 1916–39.* Urbana: University of Illinois Press, 2008.

Arrington, Leonard J. *Beet Sugar in the West: A History of the Utah-Idaho Sugar Company, 1891–1966.* Seattle: University of Washington Press, 1966.

Ashmore, Susan Y. *Carry It On: The War on Poverty and the Civil Rights Movement in Alabama, 1964–1972.* Athens: University of Georgia Press, 2008.

Avila, Eric. *Popular Culture in the Age of White Flight: Fear and Fantasy in Suburban Los Angeles.* Berkeley: University of California Press, 2004.

Balassiano, Katia, and Marta Maria Maldonado. "Placemaking in Rural New Gateway Communities." *Community Development Journal* 50, no. 4 (October 1, 2015): 644–60.

Balderrama, Francisco E., and Raymond Rodríguez. *Decade of Betrayal: Mexican Repatriation in the 1930s.* Rev. ed. Albuquerque: University of New Mexico Press, 2006.

Barber, Llana. *Latino City: Immigration and Urban Crisis in Lawrence, Massachusetts, 1945–2000.* Chapel Hill: University of North Carolina Press, 2017.

Bauman, Robert. *Race and the War on Poverty From Watts to East L.A.* Norman: University of Oklahoma Press, 2014.

Behnken, Brian. *Fighting Their Own Battles: Mexican Americans, African Americans, and the Struggle for Civil Rights in Texas.* Chapel Hill: University of North Carolina Press, 2011.

———, ed. *Civil Rights and Beyond: African American and Latino/a Activism in the Twentieth-Century United States.* Athens: University of Georgia Press, 2016.

Beliso-De Jesús, A. M. "The Jungle Academy: Molding White Supremacy in American Police Recruits." *American Anthropologist* 122 (2020): 143–56.

Beltrán, Cristina. *The Trouble with Unity: Latino Politics and the Creation of Identity.* New York: Oxford University Press, 2010.

Blanton, Carlos Kevin. *The Strange Career of Bilingual Education in Texas, 1836–1981.* College Station: Texas A&M University Press, 2004.

Bonilla-Silva, Eduardo. *Racism without Racists: Color-Blind Racism and the Persistence of Racial Inequality in America.* Lanham, MD: Rowman & Littlefield, 2018.

Bratt, James D. *Dutch Calvinism in Modern America: A History of a Conservative Subculture.* Grand Rapids, MI: W. B. Eerdmans, 1978.

Bratt, James D., and Christopher H. Meehan. *Gathered at the River: Grand Rapids, Michigan and Its People of Faith.* Grand Rapids, MI: Grand Rapids Area Council for the Humanities: William B. Eerdmans, 1993.

Burke, Lucas N. N., and Judson L. Jeffries. *The Portland Black Panthers: Empowering Albina and Remaking a City.* Seattle: University of Washington Press, 2016.

Cárdenas, Gilberto, ed. *La Causa: Civil Rights, Social Justice, and the Struggle for Equality in the Midwest.* Houston: Arte Público Press, 2004.

Carrigan, William D., and Clive Webb. *Forgotten Dead: Mob Violence against Mexicans in the United States, 1848–1928.* Oxford: Oxford University Press, 2013.

Carter, Thomas P. *Mexican Americans in Schools: A History of Educational Neglect.* New York: College Entrance Examination Board, 1970.

Chávez, John R. *Eastside Landmark: A History of the East Los Angeles Community Union, 1968–1993.* Stanford, CA: Stanford University Press, 1998.

Clayson, William S. *Freedom Is Not Enough: The War on Poverty and the Civil Rights Movement in Texas.* Austin: University of Texas Press, 2011.

———. "The War on Poverty and the Chicano Movement in Texas: Confronting 'Tio Tomás' and the 'Gringo Pseudoliberals.'" In *The War on Poverty: A New Grassroots History, 1964–1980,* edited by Annelise Orleck and Lisa Gayle Hazirjian, 334–36. Athens: University of Georgia Press, 2011.

Contreras, Eduardo. *Latinos and the Liberal City: Politics and Protest in San Francisco.* Philadelphia: University of Pennsylvania Press, 2019.

Crawford, James. *Bilingual Education: History, Politics, Theory, and Practice.* Los Angeles: Bilingual Educational Services, 1999.

Cruz, José E. *Liberalism and Identity Politics: Puerto Rican Community Organizations and Collective Action in New York City.* New York: Centro Press, 2019.

Delgadillo, Theresa. *Latina Lives in Milwaukee.* Urbana: University of Illinois Press, 2015.

Delgadillo, Theresa, Ramón H. Rivera-Servera, Geraldo L. Cadava, and Claire F. Fox, eds. *Building Sustainable Worlds: Latinx Placemaking in the Midwest.* Urbana: University of Illinois Press, 2022.

Dietz, James L. *Economic History of Puerto Rico: Institutional Change and Capitalist Development.* Princeton, NJ: Princeton University Press, 1986.

Dolan, Jay P. *The American Catholic Experience: A History from Colonial Times to the Present.* Garden City, NY: Doubleday, 1985.

Donaker, April, and Gordon L. Olson. *Grand Rapids and Its People.* Grand Rapids, MI: Grand Rapids Historical Commission, 2003.

Dowd Hall, Jacquelyn. "The Long Civil Rights Movement and the Political Uses of the Past." *Journal of American History* 91, no. 4 (March 2005): 1233–63.

Durand, Jorge, and Douglas S. Massey. "Evolution of the Mexico-U.S. Migration System: Insights from the Mexican Migration Project." *Annals of the American Academy of Political and Social Science* 684, no. 1 (July 2019): 21–42.

Ebaugh, Helen Rose, and Mary Curry. "Fictive Kin as Social Capital in New Immigrant Communities." *Sociological Perspectives* 43, no 2 (Summer 2000): 189–209.

Eckstein, Susan. *The Immigrant Divide: How Cuban Americans Changed the US and Their Homeland.* New York: Routledge, 2009.

Eisenhower, John D. *So Far from God: The U.S. War with Mexico 1846–1848.* New York: Random House, 1989.

Erdmans, Mary Patrice. "The Poles, the Dutch, and Grand Rapids' Furniture Strike of 1911." *Polish American Studies* 62, no. 2 (Autumn 2005): 5—22.

Erman, Sam. *Almost Citizens: Puerto Rico, the U.S. Constitution, and Empire.* New York: Cambridge University Press, 2019.

Escobedo, Elizabeth Rachel. *From Coveralls to Zoot Suits: The Lives of Mexican American Women on the World War II Home Front.* Chapel Hill: University of North Carolina Press, 2013.

Feimster, Crystal Nicole. *Southern Horrors: Women and the Politics of Rape and Lynching.* Cambridge, MA: Harvard University Press, 2009.

Fernández, Delia. "Becoming Latino: Mexican and Puerto Rican Community Formation in Grand Rapids, Michigan, 1926–1964." *Michigan Historical Review* 39, no. 1 (2013): 71–100.

———. "Rethinking the Urban and Rural Divide in Latino Labor, Recreation, and Activism in West Michigan, 1940s-1970s." *Labor History* 57, no 4. (2016): 482–503.

Fernández, Johanna. *The Young Lords: A Radical History.* Chapel Hill: University of North Carolina Press, 2020.

Fernández, Lilia. *Brown in the Windy City: Mexicans and Puerto Ricans in Postwar Chicago.* Chicago: University of Chicago Press, 2014.

Figueroa, Yomaira. *Decolonizing Diasporas: Radical Mappings of Afro-Atlantic Literature.* Evanston: Northwestern University Press, 2020.

Findlay, Eileen J. Suárez. *We Are Left without a Father Here: Masculinity, Domesticity, and Migration in Postwar Puerto Rico.* Durham, NC: Duke University Press, 2014.

Fine, Sidney. *Expanding the Frontier of Civil Rights: Michigan*. Detroit: Wayne State University Press, 2000.

———. *Violence in the Model City: the Cavanagh Administration, Race Relations, and the Detroit Riot of 1967.* East Lansing: Michigan State University Press, 2007.

Foley, Neil. "Partly Colored or Other White: Mexican Americans and Their Problem with the Color Line." In *Beyond Black and White: Race, Ethnicity, and Gender in the U.S. South and Southwest*, edited by Stephanie Cole and Alison M. Parker, 123–44. College Station: Published for the University of Texas at Arlington by Texas A&M University Press, 2003).

———. *Quest for Equality: The Failed Promise of Black-Brown Solidarity.* Cambridge, MA: Harvard University Press, 2010.

———. *The White Scourge: Mexicans, Blacks, and Poor Whites in Texas Cotton Culture.* Berkeley: University of California Press, 1997.

Foner, Philip S., ed. *The Black Panthers Speak*. Chicago: Haymarket Books, 2014.

Frieden, Bernard J., and Marshall Kaplan. *The Politics of Neglect: Urban Aid from Model Cities to Revenue Sharing*. Cambridge, MA: MIT Press, 1974.

Fuentes, Luis. "The Struggle for Local Political Control." In *The Puerto Rican Struggle: Essays on Survival in the U.S.*, edited by Clara E. Rodriguez, Virginia Sánchez Korrol, and José Oscar Alers, 111–20. New York: Puerto Rican Migration Research Consortium, 1980.

García, Juan Ramon. *Mexicans in the Midwest, 1900–1932*. Tucson: University of Arizona Press, 1996.

García-Colón, Ismael. *Colonial Migrants at the Heart of Empire: Puerto Rican Workers on U.S. Farms*. Oakland: University of California Press, 2020.

Garcilazo, Jeffrey Marcos. *Traqueros: Mexican Railroad Workers in the United States, 1870–1930*. Denton: University of North Texas Press, 2016.

Gardner, Martha. *The Qualities of a Citizen: Women, Immigration, and Citizenship, 1870–1965*. Princeton, NJ: Princeton University Press, 2005.

Gleason, David G. "La Parranda Puertorriqueña: The Music, Symbolism, and Cultural Nationalism of Puerto Rico's Christmas Serenading Tradition." Master's thesis, Tufts University, 2003.

Goldberg, David A. *Black Firefighters and the FDNY: The Struggle for Jobs, Justice, and Equity in New York City*. Chapel Hill: University of North Carolina Press, 2017.

Gómez, Laura E. *Manifest Destinies: The Making of the Mexican American Race*. 2d ed. New York: New York University, 2018.

González, Gilbert. *Chicano Education in the Era of Segregation*. 1st ed. Philadelphia: Balch Institute Press, 1990.

González, Gilbert G., and Raúl Fernández. "Empire and the Origins of Twentieth-Century Migration from Mexico to the United States." *Pacific Historical Review* 71, no. 1 (February 1, 2002): 19–57.

Graff, George P. "Latin Americans: Settlers in Transition." In *The People of Michigan*, 119–23. 2d ed., rev. Lansing: Michigan Department of Education, State Library Services, 1974.

Grossman, James R. *Land of Hope: Chicago, Black Southerners, and the Great Migration*. Chicago: University of Chicago Press, 1991.

Grove, Wayne A. "The Mexican Farm Labor Program, 1942–1964: Government-Administered Labor Market Insurance for Farmers." *Agricultural History* 70, no. 2 (1996): 302–20.

Guardino, Peter. *The Dead March: A History of the Mexican-American War.* Cambridge, MA: Harvard University Press, 2017.

Guerra, Lillian. *Popular Expression and National Identity in Puerto Rico: The Struggle for Self, Community, and Nation.* Gainesville: University Press of Florida, 1998.

Guevarra, Rudy. *Becoming Mexipino: Multiethnic Identities and Communities in San Diego.* New Brunswick, NJ: Rutgers University Press, 2012.

Guglielmo, Thomas A. "Fighting for Caucasian Rights: Mexicans, Mexican Americans, and the Transnational Struggle for Civil Rights in World War II Texas." *Journal of American History* 2 (March 2006): 1212–27.

———. *White on Arrival: Italians, Race, Color, and Power in Chicago, 1890–1945.* New York: Oxford University Press, 2003.

Hahamovitch, Cindy. *The Fruits of Their Labor: Atlantic Coast Farmworkers and the Making of Migrant Poverty, 1870–1945.* Chapel Hill: University of North Carolina Press, 1997.

Hahn, Harlan, and Judson L. Jeffries. *Urban America and Its Police: From the Postcolonial Era through the Turbulent 1960s.* Boulder: University Press of Colorado, 2003.

Haney-López, Ian. *Racism on Trial: The Chicano Fight for Justice.* Cambridge, MA: Harvard University Press, 2003.

Hawkins, Karen M. *Everybody's Problem: The War on Poverty in Eastern North Carolina.* Gainesville: University Press of Florida, 2017.

Heineman, Kenneth J. "Model City: The War on Poverty, Race Relations, and Catholic Social Activism in 1960s Pittsburgh." *Historian (Kingston)* 65, no. 4 (2003): 867–900.

Highsmith, Andrew R. *Demolition Means Progress: Flint, Michigan and the Fate of the American Metropolis.* Chicago: University of Chicago Press, 2015.

Hilliard, David, ed. *The Black Panther Party: Service to the People Programs.* Albuquerque: University of New Mexico Press, 2008.

Hinojosa, Felipe. *Latino Mennonites: Civil Rights, Faith, and Evangelical Culture.* Baltimore: Johns Hopkins University Press, 2014.

Hinojosa, Felipe, Maggie Elmore, and Sergio M. González, eds. *Faith and Power: Latino Religious Politics Since 1945.* New York: New York University Press, 2022.

Hoganson, Kristin. *Fighting for American Manhood: How Gender Politics Provoked the Spanish-American and Philippine-American War.* New Haven, CT: Yale University Press, 1998.

Holden, Vanessa M. *Surviving Southampton: African American Women and Resistance in Nat Turner's Community.* Champaign: University of Illinois Press, 2021.

hooks, bell. *Yearning: Race, Gender, and Cultural Politics.* Boston: South End Press, 1990.

HoSang, Daniel Martínez. "The Changing Valence of White Racial Innocence: Black-Brown Unity in the 1970s Los Angeles School Desegregation Struggles." In *Black and Brown in Los Angeles: Beyond Conflict and Coalition,* edited by Josh Kun and Laura Pulido, 115–42. Berkeley: University of California Press, 2014.

Ignatiev, Noel. *How the Irish Became White.* New York: Routledge, 2015.

Innis-Jiménez, Michael. *Steel Barrio: The Great Mexican Migration to South Chicago, 1915–1940.* New York: New York University Press, 2013).

Jackson, Thomas F. "The State, the Movement, and the Urban Poor: The War on Poverty and Political Mobilization in the 1960s." In *The "Underclass" Debate: Views from History*, edited by Michael B. Katz, 403–39. Princeton, NJ: Princeton University Press, 1993.

Jacobson, Matthew Frye. *Roots Too: White Ethnic Revival in Post–Civil Rights America*. Cambridge, MA: Harvard University Press, 2006.

———. *Whiteness of a Different Color: European Immigrants and the Alchemy of Race*. Cambridge, MA: Harvard University Press, 2002.

Jefferson, Thomas. "Thomas Jefferson to the Governor of Virginia (James Monroe)." Washington, DC. November 24, 1801.

Jelks, Randal Maurice. *African Americans in the Furniture City: The Struggle for Civil Rights in Grand Rapids*. Urbana: University of Illinois Press, 2006.

———. "Making Opportunity: The Struggle against Jim Crow in Grand Rapids, Michigan, 1890–1927." *Michigan Historical Review* 19, no. 2 (1993): 23—48.

Jiménez Román, Miriam, and Juan Flores, eds. *The Afro-Latin@ Reader: History and Culture in the United States*. Durham, NC: Duke University Press, 2010.

Johnson, Benjamin Heber. "The Cosmic Race in Texas: Racial Fusion, White Supremacy, and Civil Rights Politics." *Journal of American History* 98 (September 2011): 401–19.

———. *Revolution in Texas: How a Forgotten Rebellion and Its Bloody Suppression Turned Mexicans into Americans*. New Haven, CT: Yale University Press, 2003.

Jolly, Kenneth S. *By Our Own Strength: William Sherrill, the UNIA, and the Fight for African American Self-Determination in Detroit*. New York: Peter Lang, 2013.

Jones, Martha S. *Birthright Citizens: A History of Race and Rights in Antebellum America*. New York: Cambridge University Press, 2018.

Kanter, Deborah E. *Chicago Católico: Making Catholic Parishes Mexican*. Urbana: University of Illinois Press, 2020.

———. "Faith and Family for Early Mexican Immigrants to Chicago: The Diary of Elidia Barroso." *Diálogo* 16, no. 1 (2013): 21–34.

———. "Making Mexican Parishes: Ethnic Succession in Chicago Churches, 1947–1977." *U.S. Catholic Historian* 30, no. 1 (2012): 35–58.

Katznelson, Ira. *When Affirmative Action Was White: An Untold History of Racial Inequality in Twentieth-Century America*. New York: W. W. Norton, 2006.

Kleiman, Jeffrey D. "The Great Strike: Religion, Labor and Reform in Grand Rapids Michigan, 1890–1916." PhD diss., Michigan State University, 1985.

Knight, Alan. "The Character and Consequences of the Great Depression in Mexico." In *The Great Depression in Latin America*, edited by Paul Drinot and Alan Knight, 213–45. Durham, NC: Duke University Press, 2014.

———. "U.S. Anti-Imperialism and the Mexican Revolution." In *Empire's Twin: U.S. Imperialism from the Founding Era to the Age of Terrorism*, edited by Ian Terrel and Jay Sexton, 97–117. Ithaca, NY: Cornell University Press, 2015.

Kraus, Neil, and Todd Swanstrom. "Minority Mayors and the Hollow-Prize Problem." *PS: Political Science and Politics* 34, no. 1 (2001): 99–105.

Ladson-Billings, Gloria. "Getting to Sesame Street? Fifty Years of Federal Compensatory Education." *RSF: The Russell Sage Foundation Journal of the Social Sciences* 1, no. 3 (2015): 96–111.

Lang, Clarence. *Grassroots at the Gateway: Class Politics and Black Freedom Struggle in St. Louis, 1936–1975.* Ann Arbor: University of Michigan Press, 2009.

Lara, Jesus J. *Latino Placemaking and Planning: Cultural Resilience and Strategies for Re-urbanization.* Tucson: University of Arizona Press, 2018.

Lassiter, Matthew D. *Silent Majority Suburban Politics in the Sunbelt South.* Princeton, NJ: Princeton University Press, 2013.

Lee, Sonia Song-Ha. *Building a Latino Civil Rights Movement: Puerto Ricans, African Americans, and the Pursuit of Racial Justice in New York City.* Chapel Hill: University of North Carolina Press, 2014.

Lemann, Nicholas. *The Promised Land: The Great Black Migration and How It Changed America.* New York: Vintage, 1992.

Lloréns, Hilda. *Imaging the Great Puerto Rican Family: Framing Nation, Race, and Gender during the American Century.* Lanham, MD: Lexington Books, 2014.

López-Rivera, Oscar, and Bernard Headley. "Who Is the Terrorist? The Making of a Puerto Rican Freedom Fighter." *Social Justice* 16, no. 4 (38, 1989): 162–74.

Lucas, Isidro, and Chicago IL Council on Urban Education. *Puerto Rican Dropouts in Chicago: Numbers and Motivation.* N.p.: Distributed by ERIC Clearinghouse, 1971.

Maciel, David, and Erlinda Gonzales-Berry, eds. *The Contested Homeland: A Chicano History of New Mexico.* Albuquerque: University of New Mexico Press, 2000.

Maldonado, A. W. *Teodoro Moscoso and Puerto Rico's Operation Bootstrap.* Gainesville: University Press of Florida, 1997.

Mapes, Kathleen. *Sweet Tyranny: Migrant Labor, Industrial Agriculture, and Imperial Politics.* Urbana: University of Illinois Press, 2009.

Martínez, Elena. "Echoes of Familiar Rhythms: Puerto Rican and Garifuna Drums." *Voices: The Journal of New York Folklore* 42, no. 3/4 (Fall/Winter 2016): 26—30.

Mason, John Dancer. "The Aftermath of the Bracero: A Study of the Economic Impact on the Agricultural Hired Labor Market of Michigan from the Termination of Public Law 78." PhD diss., Michigan State University, 1969.

Matovina, Timothy M. *Latino Catholicism: Transformation in America's Largest Church.* Princeton, NJ: Princeton University Press, 2012.

Matovina, Timothy M., and Gary Riebe-Estrella, eds. *Horizons of the Sacred: Mexican Traditions in U.S. Catholicism.* Ithaca, NY: Cornell University Press, 2002.

May, Elaine Tyler. *Homeward Bound: American Families in the Cold War Era.* New York: Basic Books, 2017.

Mays, Kyle T. *City of Dispossessions: Indigenous Peoples, African Americans, and the Creation of Modern Detroit.* Philadelphia: University of Pennsylvania Press, 2022.

McDuffie, Erik S. "The Diasporic Journeys of Louise Little: Grassroots Garveyism, the Midwest, and Community Feminism." *Women, Gender, and Families of Color* 4, no. 2 (2016): 146–70.

———. "'A New Day Has Dawned for the UNIA': Garveyism, the Diasporic Midwest, and West Africa, 1920–80." *Journal of West African History* 2, no. 1 (2016): 73–114.

Meléndez, Edgardo. *Sponsored Migration: The State and Puerto Rican Postwar Migration to the United States.* Columbus: Ohio State University Press, 2017.

Menefee, Selden Cowles, and Orin Clark Cassmore. *The Pecan Shellers of San Antonio: The Problem of Underpaid and Unemployed Mexican Labor.* Washington, DC: Government Printing Office, 1940.

Meyer, Gerald J. "Pedro Albizu Campos, Gilberto Concepcion de Gracia, and Vito Marcantonio's Collaboration in the Cause of Puerto Rico's Independence." *CENTRO: Journal of the Center for Puerto Rican Studies* 23, no. 1 (March 22, 2011): 86–124.

Meyerowitz, Joanne, ed. *Not June Cleaver: Women and Gender in Postwar America, 1945–1960.* Philadelphia: Temple University Press, 1994.

Mitchell, Pablo, and Haley Pollack. "Making the 'International City Home': Latinos in Twentieth-Century Lorain, Ohio." In *Beyond El Barrio: Everyday Life in Latina/o America*, edited by Gina M. Pérez, Frank A. Guridy, and Adrian Burgos Jr., 149–67. New York: New York University Press, 2010.

Molina, Natalia. *How Race Is Made in America: Immigration, Citizenship, and the Historical Power of Racial Scripts.* Berkeley: University of California Press, 2014.

Mora, G. Cristina. *Making Hispanics: How Activists, Bureaucrats, and Media Constructed a New American.* Chicago, University of Chicago Press, 2014.

Mora, Juan I. "Latino Encounters: Mexicans, *Tejanos*, and Puerto Ricans in Postwar Michigan, 1942–1970." PhD diss., University of Illinois, 2020.

Navarro, Armando. *Mexican American Youth Organization: Avant-Garde of the Chicano Movement in Texas.* Austin: University of Texas Press, 1995.

Oboler, Suzanne. *Ethnic Labels, Latino Lives: Identity and the Politics of (Re)Presentation in the United States.* Minneapolis: University of Minnesota Press, 1995.

Odem, Mary. "Our Lady of Guadalupe in the New South: Latin American Immigrants and the Politics of Integration in the Catholic Church." *Journal of American Ethnic History* 23 (Fall 2004): 26–57.

Olden, Danielle R. *Racial Uncertainties: Mexican Americans, School Desegregation, and the Making of Race in Post–Civil Rights America.* Berkeley: University of California Press, 2022.

Olivas, Michael A. *Colored Men and Hombres Aquí: Hernández v. Texas and the Emergence of Mexican-American Lawyering.* Houston: Arte Público Press, 2014.

Olivas, Michael A., and Ronna Greff Schneider, eds. *Education Law Stories.* New York: Foundation Press, 2008.

Olson, Gordon L. *Grand Rapids: A City Renewed—A History Since World War II.* Grand Rapids, MI: Grand Rapids Historical Commission, 1996.

———. *A Grand Rapids Sampler.* Grand Rapids, MI: Grand Rapids Historical Commission, 1992.

Opie, Frederick Douglass. *Upsetting the Apple Cart: Black-Latino Coalitions in New York City from Protest to Public Office.* New York: Columbia University Press, 2014.

Orleck, Annelise, and Lisa Gayle Hazirjian, eds. *The War on Poverty: A New Grassroots History, 1964–1980.* Athens: University of Georgia Press, 2011.

Oropeza, Lorena. *¡Raza Sí! ¡Guerra No! Chicano Protest and Patriotism during the Viet Nam War Era.* Berkeley: University of California Press, 2005.

Orozco, Cynthia. *No Mexicans, Women, or Dogs Allowed: The Rise of the Mexican American Civil Rights Movement.* Austin: University of Texas Press, 2009.

Orsi, Robert A. *The Madonna of 115th Street: Faith and Community in Italian Harlem, 1880–1950*. New Haven, CT: Yale University Press, 1985.

Padilla, Felix M. *Latino Ethnic Consciousness: The Case of Mexican Americans and Puerto Ricans in Chicago*. Notre Dame, IN: University of Notre Dame Press, 1985.

Pascoe, Peggy. *What Comes Naturally: Miscegenation Law and the Making of Race in America*. New York: Oxford University Press, 2010.

Patiño, Jimmy. *Raza Sí, Migra No: Chicano Movement Struggles for Immigrant Rights in San Diego*. Chapel Hill: University of North Carolina Press, 2017.

Patton, Randall L. *Lockheed, Atlanta, and the Struggle for Racial Integration*. Athens: University of Georgia Press, 2019.

Pérez, Gina M. *The Near Northwest Side Story: Migration, Displacement, and Puerto Rican Families*. Berkeley: University of California Press, 2004.

Pierce, Richard B. *Polite Protest: The Political Economy of Race in Indianapolis, 1920–1970*. Bloomington: Indiana University Press, 2005.

Pitti, Gina Marie. "To 'Hear about God in Spanish': Ethnicity, Church, and Community Activism in the San Francisco Archdiocese's Mexican American Colonias, 1942–1965." PhD diss., Stanford University, 2003.

Poole, Stafford. *Our Lady of Guadalupe: The Origins and Sources of a Mexican National Symbol, 1531–1797*. Tucson: University of Arizona Press, 2017.

Potowski, Kim, and Janine Matts. "MexiRicans: Interethnic Language and Identity." *Journal of Language, Identity and Education* 7, no. 2 (2008): 137–60.

Price, Melanye T. *Dreaming Blackness: Black Nationalism and African American Public Opinion*. New York: New York University Press, 2009.

Proceedings of the Fifth Regional Meeting of American Society of Sugar Beet Technologists— Eastern United States and Canada, Detroit, Michigan. Fort Collins, CO: American Society of Sugar Beet Technologists, 1948.

Ramos, Henry A. J. Foreword to *La Causa: Civil Rights, Social Justice and the Struggle for Equality in the Midwest*, edited by Gilberto Cárdenas. Houston: Arte Público Press, 2004.

Reese, Ellen. *They Say Cut Back, We Say Fight Back! Welfare Activism in an Era of Retrenchment*. New York: Russell Sage Foundation, 2011.

Ribeiro, Alyssa. "'Asking Them and Protesting': Black and Puerto Rican Civic Leadership in Philadelphia Neighborhoods, 1960s-1970s." *Pennsylvania History: A Journal of Mid-Atlantic Studies* 86, no. 3 (Summer 2019): 359–82.

———. "Forgotten Residents Fighting Back: The Ludlow Community Association and Neighborhood Improvement in Philadelphia." In *Civil Rights and Beyond: African American and Latino/a Activism in the Twentieth-Century United States*, edited by Brian D. Behnken, 172–94. Athens: University of Georgia Press, 2016.

Rickford, Russell. *We Are an African People: Independent Education, Black Power, and the Radical Imaginary*. New York: Oxford University Press, 2016.

Ricourt, Milagros, and Ruby Danta. *Hispanas de Queens: Latino Panethnicity in a New York City Neighborhood*. Ithaca, NY: Cornell University Press, 2003.

Robinson, Todd E. *A City within a City: The Black Freedom Struggle in Grand Rapids, Michigan*. Philadelphia: Temple University, 2013.

Rodríguez, Clara E. *Changing Race: Latinos, the Census, and the History of Ethnicity in the United States.* New York: New York University Press, 2000.

Rodríguez, Marc Simon. *Rethinking the Chicano Movement.* New York: Routledge, 2015.

———. *The Tejano Diaspora: Mexican Americanism and Ethnic Politics in Texas and Wisconsin.* Chapel Hill: University of North Carolina Press, 2011.

Rosales, Steven. "'This Street Is Essentially Mexican': An Oral History of the Mexican American Community of Saginaw, Michigan, 1920-1980." *Michigan Historical Review* 40 no. 2 (2014): 33-62.

Rosas, Ana Elizabeth. *Abrazando el Espíritu: Bracero Families Confront the US–Mexico Border.* Oakland: University of California Press, 2014.

Rothstein, Richard. *The Color of Law: A Forgotten History of How Our Government Segregated America.* New York: W. W. Norton, 2017.

Rúa, Mérida M. "Colao Subjectivities: PortoMex and MexiRican Perspectives on Language and Identity." *Centro: Journal of the Center for Puerto Rican Studies* 13, no. 2 (2001): 117-33.

———. *A Grounded Identidad: Making New Lives in Chicago's Puerto Rican Neighborhoods.* New York: Oxford University Press, 2012.

Ruiz, Vicki. *Cannery Women, Cannery Lives: Mexican Women, Unionization and the California Food Processing Industry.* Albuquerque: University of New Mexico Press, 1987.

———. *From Out of the Shadows: Mexican Women in Twentieth-Century America.* New York: Oxford University Press, 1998.

Salas, Nora. "Anti-Colonialism in the Michigan Chicano Movement." PhD diss., Michigan State University, 2015.

———. "'Pablo's Problem': Michigan Chicano Movement Anticolonialism and the Farm Bureau's Peasant Menace, 1962-1972." *Michigan Historical Review* 45, no. 2 (October 1, 2019): 1-38.

Salazar, Ruben. *Border Correspondent: Selected Writings, 1955-1970.* Edited by Mario T. García. Berkeley: University of California Press, 2018.

Sánchez, George J. *Becoming Mexican American: Ethnicity, Culture, and Identity in Chicano Los Angeles, 1900-1945.* New York: Oxford University Press, 1995.

Sánchez Korrol, Virginia. *From Colonia to Community: The History of Puerto Ricans in New York City.* Berkeley: University of California Press, 1994.

Sanders, Crystal R. *A Chance for Change: Head Start and Mississippi's Black Freedom Struggle.* Chapel Hill: University of North Carolina Press, 2016.

San Miguel, Guadalupe, Jr. *Brown, Not White: School Integration and the Chicano Movement in Houston.* College Station: Texas A&M University Press, 2005.

———. *Chicana/o Struggles for Education: Activism in the Community.* College Station: Texas A&M University Press, 2013.

San Miguel, Guadalupe, Jr., and Rubén Donato. "Latino Education in Twentieth-Century America: A Brief History." In *Handbook of Latinos and Education: Theory, Research, and Practice,* edited by Enrique G. Murillo Jr., Sofia A. Villenas, Ruth Trinidad Galván, Juan Sánchez Muñoz, Corinne Martínez, and Margarita Machado-Casas, 27-47. 1st ed. New York: Routledge, 2009.

Self, Robert O. *American Babylon: Race and the Struggle for Postwar Oakland*. Princeton, NJ: Princeton University Press, 2003.

Shaw, Stephen J. *The Catholic Parish as a Way-Station of Ethnicity and Americanization: Chicago's Germans and Italians, 1903–1939*. Brooklyn, NY: Carlson, 1991.

Siegel, Sarah. "'Dominant Decision-Making Authority': Resident Leadership in St. Louis, Missouri, Model Cities Planning." *Journal of Urban History* 45, no. 2 (2019): 333–53.

Sugrue, Thomas J. *The Origins of the Urban Crisis: Race and Inequality in Postwar Detroit*. Princeton, NJ: Princeton University Press, 1996.

Sulzberger, Cyrus Leo. *Sit Down with John L. Lewis*. New York: Random House, 1938.

Summers Sandoval, Tomás. *Latinos at the Golden Gate: Creating Community and Identity in San Francisco*. Chapel Hill: University of North Carolina Press, 2013.

Thomas, Lorrin. *Puerto Rican Citizen: History and Political Identity in Twentieth-Century New York City*. Chicago: University of Chicago Press, 2014.

Thomas, Lorrin, and Aldo A. Lauria-Santiago. *Rethinking the Struggle for Puerto Rican Rights*. New York: Routledge, 2019.

Torres, Andrés, and José E. Velázquez, eds. *The Puerto Rican Movement: Voices from the Diaspora*. Philadelphia: Temple University Press, 1998.

Torres, Maria de los Angeles. *In the Land of Mirrors: Cuban Exile Politics in the United States*. Ann Arbor: University of Michigan Press, 2014.

Valdés, Dennis Nodín. *Al Norte: Agricultural Workers in the Great Lakes Region, 1917–1970*. Austin: University of Texas Press, 1991.

———. *Barrios Norteños: St. Paul and Midwestern Mexican Communities in the Twentieth Century*. Austin: University of Texas Press, 2000.

——— [as Dionicio Valdés]. *Mexicans in Minnesota*. St. Paul: Minnesota Historical Society Press, 2005.

———. *Organized Agriculture and the Labor Movement before the UFW*. Austin: University of Texas Press, 2011.

Valdés, Vanessa K. *Diasporic Blackness: The Life and Times of Arturo Alfonso Schomburg*. Albany: State University of New York Press, 2018.

Valenzuela, Angela. *Subtractive Schooling: U.S.-Mexican Youth and the Politics of Caring*. Albany: State University of New York Press, 1999.

Valerio-Jiménez, Omar S., Santiago R. Vaquera-Vásquez, and Claire F. Fox, eds. *The Latina/o Midwest Reader: Latinos in Chicago and the Midwest*. Urbana: University of Illinois Press, 2017.

Vargas, Zaragosa. *Proletarians of the North: A History of Mexican Industrial Workers in Detroit and the Midwest, 1917–1933*. Berkeley: University of California Press, 1993.

Wall, Wendy. *Inventing the American Way: The Politics of Consensus from the New Deal to the Civil Rights Movement*. New York: Oxford University Press, 2009.

Ward, Thomas J., Jr., and H. J. Geiger. *Out in the Rural: A Mississippi Health Center and Its War on Poverty*. New York: Oxford University Press, 2017.

Weber, Bret A., and Amanda Wallace. "Revealing the Empowerment Revolution: A Literature Review of the Model Cities Program." *Journal of Urban History* 38, no. 1 (2012): 173–92.

Whalen, Carmen Teresa. *From Puerto Rico to Philadelphia: Puerto Rican Workers and Postwar Economies*. Philadelphia, Temple University, 2001.

———. "Radical Contexts: Puerto Rican Politics in the 1960s and 1970s and the Center for Puerto Rican Studies." *CENTRO: Journal of the Center for Puerto Rican Studies* 21, no. 2 (2009): 221–55.

Whalen, Carmen Teresa, and Víctor Vázquez-Hernández, eds. *The Puerto Rican Diaspora: Historical Perspectives*. Philadelphia: Temple University Press, 2005.

Wiggins, Leticia. "Planting the Uprooted Ones: La Raza in the Midwest." PhD diss., Ohio State University, 2016.

———. "'Women Need to Find Their Voice': Latinas Speak Out in the Midwest, 1972." In *Chicana Movidas: New Narratives of Activism and Feminism in the Movement Era*, edited by Dionne Espinoza, María Eugenia Cotera, and Maylei Blackwell, 76–90. Austin: University of Texas Press, 2018.

Wilson, Al. "Grand Rapids Latin American Population Tops 11,000." *Model Neighborhood News* 5, no. 2 (May–June 1972): 6.

Woodsworth, Michael. *Battle for Bed-Stuy: The Long War on Poverty in New York City*. Cambridge, MA: Harvard University Press, 2016.

Zeemering, Eric S. "Grand Rapids: A Lack of Enthusiasm for Change in the Council-Manager Form." In *More than Mayor or Manager: Campaigns to Change Form of Government in America's Large Cities*, edited by James H. Svara and Douglas J. Watson, 163–82. Washington, DC: Georgetown University Press, 2010.

Zentella, Ana Celia. *Growing Up Bilingual: Puerto Rican Children in New York*. Malden, MA: Blackwell, 1997.

Index

Delia Fernández-Jones is an assistant professor of history at Michigan State University.

Latinos in Chicago and the Midwest

Pots of Promise: Mexicans and Pottery at Hull-House, 1920–40
  Edited by Cheryl R. Ganz and Margaret Strobel
Moving Beyond Borders: Julian Samora and the Establishment of Latino Studies
  Edited by Alberto López Pulido, Barbara Driscoll de Alvarado,
  and Carmen Samora
¡Marcha! Latino Chicago and the Immigrant Rights Movement
  Edited by Amalia Pallares and Nilda Flores-González
Bringing Aztlán to Chicago: My Life, My Work, My Art   *José Gamaliel*
  González, edited and with an Introduction by Marc Zimmerman
Latino Urban Ethnography and the Work of Elena Padilla
  Edited by Mérida M. Rúa
Defending Their Own in the Cold: The Cultural Turns of U.S. Puerto Ricans
  Marc Zimmerman
Chicanas of 18th Street: Narratives of a Movement from Latino Chicago
  Leonard G. Ramírez with Yenelli Flores, María Gamboa, Isaura González,
  Victoria Pérez, Magda Ramírez-Castañeda, and Cristina Vital
Compañeros: Latino Activists in the Face of AIDS   *Jesus Ramirez-Valles*
Illegal: Reflections of an Undocumented Immigrant   *José Ángel N.*
Latina Lives in Milwaukee   *Theresa Delgadillo*
The Latina/o Midwest Reader   *Edited by Omar Valerio-Jiménez,*
  Santiago Vaquera-Vásquez, and Claire F. Fox
In Search of Belonging: Latinas, Media, and Citizenship   *Jillian M. Báez*
The Mexican Revolution in Chicago: Immigration Politics from the
  Early Twentieth Century to the Cold War   *John H. Flores*
Ilegal: Reflexiones de un inmigrante indocumentado   *José Ángel N.*
Negotiating Latinidad: Intralatina/o Lives in Chicago   *Frances R. Aparicio*
Chicago Católico: Making Catholic Parishes Mexican   *Deborah E. Kanter*
Puerto Rican Chicago: Schooling the City, 1940–1977   *Mirelsie Velázquez*
Building Sustainable Worlds: Latinx Placemaking in the Midwest
  Edited by Theresa Delgadillo, Claire F. Fox, Ramón Rivera-Servera,
  and Geraldo L. Cadava
Latina/o/x Education in Chicago: Roots, Resistance, and Transformation
  Edited by Isaura Pulido, Angelica Rivera, and Ann M. Aviles
Making the MexiRcan City: Migration, Placemaking, and Activism in
  Grand Rapids, Michigan   *Delia Fernández-Jones*

The University of Illinois Press
is a founding member of the
Association of University Presses.

―――――――――――――――――――――――

University of Illinois Press
1325 South Oak Street
Champaign, IL 61820-6903
www.press.uillinois.edu

Made in the USA
Monee, IL
06 August 2024

63381501R00166